The
Supreme Court
Yearbook
1994 - 1995

Justices assemble in the Supreme Court's conference room for an informal photograph at the start of the 1994–1995 term. From left are Justices Sandra Day O'Connor, Anthony M. Kennedy, and Antonin Scalia; Chief Justice William H. Rehnquist; and Justices David H. Souter, Ruth Bader Ginsburg, Clarence Thomas, Stephen G. Breyer, and John Paul Stevens.

The
Supreme Court
Yearbook
1994 - 1995

Kenneth Jost

Congressional Quarterly Inc.
Washington, D.C.

Photo credits: cover, R. Michael Jenkins; frontispiece, 3, 304, 311, 313, 315, 317, Collection, the Supreme Court Historical Society; 15, Bettman Archive; 28, 44, 47, 51, AP/Wide World Photos; 33, Richard Ellis; 37, Steve Gonzales, *Kansas City Star;* 40, Nathaniel D. Harari; 54, *Columbus Dispatch;* 61, Mike Mills; 276, 279, Helen Davis, *Denver Post.*

Printed in the United States of America

ISBN 0-87187-852-6 (pbk)
ISBN 0-87187-851-8
ISSN 1054-2701

Contents

133645

Preface

Six weeks after the Supreme Court ended its 1994–1995 term, the justices made front-page news in the *Wall Street Journal,* not because of their decisions but because of their summer travel. In a story datelined Salzburg, Austria, reporter Paul Barrett related that five of the justices were traveling in Europe at the expense of law schools that hired them to teach summer courses. The work, Barrett implied, was not too strenuous for the pay (up to $20,000), and the scenery was beautiful besides. As Justice Ruth Bader Ginsburg told him over dinner, the separation was good for the justices' morale. After an often contentious year, Ginsburg remarked, "It's good for us to be apart for a while."

Back in Washington, meanwhile, legal interest groups, law professors, and other Court watchers were studying and debating the Court's most dramatic term in recent years. In its final weeks, the Court appeared to make a significant shift to the right in cases dealing with race and religion. Earlier, however, the Court had dealt a possibly mortal blow to the conservative-backed crusade to impose term limits on members of Congress. The activist decisions were all the more surprising coming from a Court dominated by justices who professed devotion to the principle of judicial restraint.

Now in its sixth year, *The Supreme Court Yearbook* details the Court's decisions during the 1994–1995 term. Chapter 1 analyzes the justices' lineup during the term and examines the likelihood of a continuing shift to the right in coming terms. Experts, not surprisingly, disagree. Chapter 2 gives an overview of the term's decisions and detailed accounts of the most important cases. Chapter 3 contains a comprehensive listing of the Court's decisions from the past term, arranged by subject categories, and excerpts from the major decisions appear in Chapter 4. Chapter 5 previews the 1995–1996 term. The appendix provides a description of how the Court works, a brief biography of each justice, a glossary of legal terms, and the U.S. Constitution.

Again this term, I want to thank the members of the Court's public information office, headed by Toni House, who give prompt and reliable assistance whenever needed. I also want to thank the lawyers, law professors, and others who have shared their analyses of the Court's work and the members of the full-time Supreme Court press corps whose reportage or commentary has helped fill in this account of the past year.

At Congressional Quarterly, my thanks go again to Dave Tarr for inviting me to take over the book three years ago, Shana Wagger for guiding the book in its formative stages, Barbara de Boinville for editing the manuscript, and Kerry Kern for overseeing the production.

As always, the main support in writing this book comes from my best friend, Katie, and our two exceptional children, Nicole and Andrew.

A Dramatic Year

Affirmative action was one of the country's hottest political issues at the start of 1995. The Supreme Court had helped stir the controversy by agreeing in the fall to hear a white contractor's challenge to a federal program aimed at helping minority contractors get government work. It was to be the Court's first look at affirmative action in five years, so the courtroom was packed when the case was argued on January 17. The arguments were spirited. Solicitor General Drew S. Days III, defending the government program, drew some especially critical questions from the Court's conservative members.

The buzz in the Supreme Court building immediately afterward, however, was not about affirmative action. Instead, people were talking in the corridors, in the pressroom, and even in the justices' chambers about the unprecedented addition to Chief Justice William H. Rehnquist's wardrobe. Rehnquist presided over the Court's session that morning wearing a customary black robe but with four most uncustomary golden stripes sewed on the top of each sleeve.

A quick historical check confirmed that the justices had worn unadorned black robes ever since the first chief justice, John Jay, scandalized newly independent Americans by sporting a more ornate black robe with scarlet trim. Rehnquist made no public comment about his new sartorial style. But Toni House, the Court's public information officer, told reporters later that the chief justice had designed the robe himself. She said he modeled it after a robe worn by the Lord Chancellor in a local production the previous summer of the Gilbert and Sullivan operetta "Iolanthe."

Shift to the Right

Rehnquist's theatrical touch, intentionally or not, symbolically foreshadowed the Court's actions over the next six months. As the justices left for their summer recess at the end of June, advocates and observers of all persuasions agreed that the 1994–1995 term was the Court's most dramatic in at least six years and perhaps longer. After several years of quiescence, a conservative majority forcefully asserted itself on a range of legal issues in a way unseen since the Court's 1988–1989 term.

Erwin Chemerinsky, a liberal expert on constitutional law at the University of Southern California Law Center, gave this listing of the dramatic elements of the Court's term:

- For the first time in almost sixty years, the Court overturned a law passed by Congress—a statute prohibiting carrying a gun near a school—on the ground that it exceeded the federal government's power to regulate interstate commerce (*United States v. Lopez*).
- Overturning a precedent only five years old, the Court ruled that federal affirmative action programs must satisfy the most rigorous form of judicial review to be constitutional (*Adarand Constructors, Inc. v. Peña*).
- For the first time ever, the Court not only approved but required direct financial aid from a governmental body to a religious group (*Rosenberger v. Rectors and Visitors of University of Virginia*).
- By upholding random drug testing of high school athletes, the Court approved the biggest exception ever to the Fourth Amendment's requirement that the government have some suspicion of wrongdoing before conducting a search (*Vernonia School District 47J v. Acton*).

"Individually, each of those rulings is very important," Chemerinsky concludes. "Collectively, they mark a real shift to the right."

Conservative activists and experts made a similar assessment of the Court term. Douglas Kmiec, a professor at Notre Dame Law School and a Justice Department official during the Reagan administration, said the term could be summed up with three R's: race, religion, and renewal of federalism.

On race, Kmiec says, the Court moved toward—though not quite to—the idea of a color-blind Constitution on affirmative action and racial redistricting. It also sent a strong signal for federal judges to relinquish school desegregation suits and return school systems to the control of state and local authorities.

On religion, the Court moved close to a new legal principle, according to Kmiec, a longtime advocate of greater government accommodation of religion. "The Court has focused on a new axiom for religion in the public sphere," Kmiec notes. "Religious expression is to be accommodated and not discriminated against in the context of access to generally available public resources and public property."

As for federalism, Kmiec says the Court made clear that the Commerce Clause, the constitutional foundation of the federal government's great expansion of power over economic and social affairs since the New Deal, has some limit. "We don't know exactly what the limit is," Kmiec adds. But the Court indicated that Congress should be wary of extending federal power to areas traditionally left to state and local governments that have only attenuated effects on commerce between the states.

For conservative activists, the Court's burst of energy was welcome, even if slow in coming. "The Court recognized this term that judicial

The justices posed for their annual formal photograph for the Supreme Court's 1994–1995 term. Front row from left are Justices Antonin Scalia and John Paul Stevens; Chief Justice William H. Rehnquist; and Justices Sandra Day O'Connor and Anthony M. Kennedy. Standing from left are Justices Ruth Bader Ginsburg, David H. Souter, Clarence Thomas, and Stephen G. Breyer.

restraint does not mean judicial inaction," said Chip Mellor, president and general counsel of the Institute for Justice, a conservative legal center. "The Court has reclaimed its vital role in curbing excesses of the other branch of government."

Liberal experts agreed that the Court made its mark in the term by taking on other branches of government. By contrast, the Court in earlier conservative periods had often lined up in support of government. Kathleen Sullivan, a professor of constitutional law at Stanford Law School, says the trend was most pronounced in the area of race.

"The Court told all three branches of government to get out of the business of racial remediation," Sullivan observes. "It told the Justice Department to stop creating majority-minority districts for all practical purposes. It told the federal courts to stop quixotically trying to finish the process of integrating the public schools. And it told the Congress to stop promising race preferences in federal jobs and contracts."

Several of the Court's other most important rulings involved challenges to decisions by political branches of government. In its two religion cases, the Court overturned governmental actions that, on grounds of separation of church and state, had denied funding to a religious newspaper at the University of Virginia and tried to bar the Ku Klux Klan from erecting a cross in front of the Ohio State Capitol. In freedom of speech cases, the Court struck down two laws passed by Congress—one regulating beer advertising, the other restricting paid speeches or articles by federal employees—and barred states from enacting bans on anonymous political leaflets.

Erwin Chemerinsky contrasts the contemporary conservatism with the Court's 1988–1989 term. That, too, was a year of conservative rulings, but the decisions were more likely to reflect a deference to governmental power. The Court upheld state restrictions on abortion procedures. It sanctioned capital punishment for teenagers and mentally retarded persons. It permitted drug testing of some railroad employees and law enforcement officers. Today, Chemerinsky says, the Court instead reflects "an activist conservatism" that gives little deference to government in many cases.

The Court's conservative shift was distinctive from previous conservative eras in a second respect. The conservative justices showed no special regard for precedent—traditionally, a cardinal principle of legal conservatism expressed in the Latin phrase *stare decisis* ("the thing is decided"). To be sure, the Court has overturned its own precedents throughout its history, in both conservative and liberal eras. Still, conservatives sharply criticized the liberal Court led by Chief Justice Earl Warren in the 1950s and 1960s for discarding precedent. So the conservative Court of the 1980s and 1990s might have been expected to embrace *stare decisis* and to closely follow rulings from the past.

Instead, under Chief Justice Rehnquist, the Court has been willing, and at times eager, to overturn prior rulings. In a notable decision in 1991, Rehnquist himself declared that the Court need not hesitate to overturn past decisions on individual liberties. He counted at least thirty-three such rulings in the previous twenty years. *(See* Supreme Court Yearbook, 1990–1991, *pp. 35–37.)*

In its rulings in the 1994–1995 term, the Court explicitly overturned three of its own precedents *(see Table 1–1)*. The most important reversal came in the area of affirmative action. By a 5–4 vote, the Court said that federal affirmative action programs can be upheld only if they satisfy the exacting constitutional standard known as "strict scrutiny." The Court had ruled in 1990 that the federal government could adopt minority preference policies under a more lenient "intermediate scrutiny" standard. But in the new decision, the Court's conservatives declared that ruling a mistake and overruled it.

The Court's other two reversals of precedents during the term came in less significant criminal law cases, set aside older rulings, and were less closely divided. Together, the three reversals did not amount to an especially large number. The Court overturned an equal number in its 1992–1993 term and typically reverses at least one of its precedents per term.

Table 1-1 Reversals of Earlier Rulings

The Supreme Court issued three decisions during the 1994–1995 term that explicitly reversed previous rulings by the Court. The rulings brought the total number of such reversals in the Court's history to at least 210.

New Decision	Overruled Decision	New Holding
Hubbard v. United States (1995) [p. 78]	*Bramblett v. United States* (1955)	False statement statute inapplicable to statements in court proceedings
Adarand Constructors v. Peña (1995) [p. 106]	*Metro Broadcasting v. Federal Communications Commission* (1990)	Strict scrutiny for racial classifications in federal programs
United States v. Gaudin (1995) [p. 87]	*Sinclair v. United States* (1929)	Jury decides "materiality" under false statement statute

There were other cases, however, in which the Court so narrowed past rulings as to virtually overrule them. In the most controversial, the Court, by a 5–4 vote, limited the ability of inmates to file constitutional challenges to prison disciplinary actions. Rehnquist, who wrote the opinion, criticized a line of cases going back more than fifteen years but concluded in a footnote that none of them was being "technically" overruled.

In another case, the Court altered a ten-year-old precedent and made it harder to challenge the use of race to disqualify potential jurors in criminal cases. It issued that ruling without even hearing arguments in the case.

Beyond these rulings, the Court's strongest conservatives—Justices Antonin Scalia and Clarence Thomas—continued to signal an even greater willingness to scrap settled legal doctrines. On affirmative action, Scalia and Thomas bluntly declared that any form of racial preference amounts to illegal discrimination. That stance would require overturning precedents going back to the Court's first ruling on affirmative action, its 1978 *Bakke* decision upholding the limited use of racial preferences in university admission policies.

Similarly, when the Court struck down the federal Gun-Free School Zones Act, Thomas declared in a separate opinion that the Court had been too lax in the past sixty years in approving congressional assertions of power under the Commerce Clause. "…[W]e must modify our Commerce Clause jurisprudence," Thomas wrote, while adding that the re-examination would not necessarily require "a wholesale abandonment of our more recent opinions."

Linda Greenhouse, the veteran Supreme Court correspondent for the *New York Times*, encapsulated this precedent-averse philosophy in an end-of-term analysis. The Court, she wrote, was re-examining long-held assumptions about the power of the federal government, the relationship between Washington and the states, and the use of race in public policy. The exercise, she concluded, amounted to "a gaudy show of zero-based jurisprudence."

A Receding Center

The Court's shift to the right surprised some observers. After all, two Republican presidents, Ronald Reagan and George Bush, worked hard to transform the Court, making six appointments in twelve years. Yet in the last year of Bush's presidency, the Court in 1992 rejected the administration's pleas to overturn the *Roe v. Wade* abortion rights ruling and to sanction government-sponsored prayer in public schools. With the election of a Democratic president, the Court seemed even less likely to endorse the agenda of conservative activists. The center had held. Surely, the Court now would steady itself, or even shift toward the left.

With his appointment of two moderately liberal justices, President Bill Clinton appeared to make a conscious effort to strengthen the Court's center. Before their appointments, Ruth Bader Ginsburg and Stephen G. Breyer both served on federal appeals courts where they gained reputations as pragmatic and persuasive consensus-builders. With Ginsburg's nomination in 1993 and again with Breyer's in 1994, observers speculated that the Court's two moderate conservatives—Sandra Day O'Connor and Anthony M. Kennedy—could be pulled toward the center and away from the core conservatives: Rehnquist, Scalia, and Thomas.

That did not happen in the most closely watched and most closely divided decisions of the 1994–1995 term. The justices divided 5–4 in sixteen of the term's eighty-two signed decisions. The most common line-up—seen in six of those rulings—found the five conservatives lined up against the four liberal-leaning justices: John Paul Stevens, David H. Souter, Ginsburg, and Breyer. Together, the rulings—including the decisions on affirmative action, racial redistricting, school desegregation, and the federal gun law—gave the term its marked conservative tone. By picking up Breyer's votes in place of Kennedy's, the conservatives on the Court prevailed in one other end-of-term 5–4 ruling, which upheld a restriction on lawyer advertising.

The ideological center only receded, however. It did not completely disappear. In the controversial area of habeas corpus, for example, the Court three times turned back efforts to make it harder for state prison inmates to challenge their convictions in federal court. O'Connor had been a reliable vote for limiting habeas corpus in the late 1980s and early 1990s. But this term, she sided with the Court's liberal bloc in two 5–4 decisions and a 6–3 ruling that threw out lower court rulings imposing stricter standards for habeas corpus cases.

O'Connor showed centrist tendencies in other areas, too. In the two religion cases, she wrote separate opinions to limit how far she would go in permitting government funding of religious activities or private religious displays on public property. In the affirmative action case, she even went out of her way to qualify her own decision. The new standard of "strict scrutiny" for federal affirmative action, she wrote near the end of the opinion, should not be understood to be "strict in theory" but "fatal in fact."

Kennedy also separated himself from the conservative bloc at several critical junctures. Most notably, he provided the crucial fifth vote in the year's biggest defeat for conservatives—a ruling striking down limits passed by various states on the number of terms their representatives and senators can serve in Congress. In the federal gun law case, he wrote a concurring opinion—joined by O'Connor—that explicitly endorsed use of the Commerce Clause to expand federal power over economic affairs. And he lined up with the liberal bloc in several of the 5–4 rulings—helping form majorities in two cases early in the term and leading the dissenters in the lawyer advertising case near the end.

Voting statistics confirm the picture of a conservative majority that consists of three solid votes (Rehnquist, Scalia, and Thomas) and two swing votes (O'Connor and Kennedy) and a liberal-leaning minority (*see Table 1–2*). Each one of the five conservatives voted with each of the other four conservatives in roughly three-fourths or more of the cases. Each of the four liberals voted with each of the other three liberals in three-fourths or more of the cases.

On the right side of the Court, the core conservatives had the closest alignments. Rehnquist agreed with Scalia and Thomas more than 85 percent of the time. Scalia and Thomas agreed with each other more than 90 percent of the time. "There's a very strong right end of the Court," says Paul Rothstein, a professor at Georgetown University Law Center who follows the Court closely for CNN.

O'Connor and Kennedy distanced themselves from these core conservatives. "Neither O'Connor nor Kennedy likes to be thought of as a conservative or as doctrinaire," comments Dennis Hutchinson, a law professor at the University of Chicago and editor of the *Supreme Court Review.*

O'Connor agreed with Rehnquist, Scalia, and Thomas about 75 percent of the time—somewhat less often than in the past two terms. If one

Table 1–2   Justices' Alignment, 1994–1995 Term

This table shows the percentage of decisions in which each justice agreed with each of the other members of the Court. Of the eighty-two signed decisions for the 1994–1995 term, thirty-four (or 41 percent) were unanimous.

The voting pattern suggests a Court divided into two fairly cohesive blocs. Each of the conservatives—Chief Justice Rehnquist and Justices O'Connor, Scalia, Kennedy, and Thomas—voted with each of the other conservatives in at least 72 percent of the cases. The liberal-leaning justices—Stevens, Souter, Ginsburg, and Breyer—showed a slightly higher degree of cohesiveness. Each of them voted with each of the other liberals at least 77 percent of the time. O'Connor separated herself from the other conservatives somewhat more than in past years. In the 1993–1994 term, she agreed with each of the other four at least 80 percent of the time. In the current term, her alignment with Rehnquist, Scalia, and Thomas fell to 75 percent or below. She agreed with Souter (82 percent) more than she did with Kennedy (78 percent).

Scalia and Thomas again had the closest alignment of any two justices: they voted together 91 percent of the time. Stevens and Thomas had the lowest percentage of agreement. They agreed with each other in only six of forty-eight nonunanimous cases (12.5 percent).

In his first term, Breyer had a moderate-to-liberal voting record. He agreed most often with his fellow Clinton appointee, Ginsburg, but sided with O'Connor and Kennedy more than he did with Stevens.

	Rehnquist	Stevens	O'Connor	Scalia	Kennedy	Souter	Thomas	Ginsburg	Breyer
Rehnquist		27.1 56.8	52.1 72.0	80.9 88.9	75.0 85.4	47.9 69.5	77.1 86.6	46.8 69.1	53.2 71.8
Stevens	27.1 56.8		35.4 61.8	23.4 55.0	47.9 69.1	66.7 80.2	12.5 48.1	76.6 86.2	61.7 76.9
O'Connor	52.1 72.0	35.4 61.8		57.4 75.3	62.5 78.0	68.8 81.7	56.2 74.4	46.8 69.1	66.0 79.5
Scalia	80.9 88.9	23.4 55.0	57.4 75.3		72.3 84.0	44.7 67.9	85.1 91.4	47.8 70.0	50.0 70.1
Kennedy	75.0 85.4	47.9 69.1	62.5 78.0	72.3 84.0		60.4 76.8	64.6 79.3	68.1 81.5	66.0 79.5
Souter	47.9 69.5	66.7 80.2	68.8 81.7	44.7 67.9	60.4 76.8		37.5 63.4	70.2 82.7	76.6 85.9
Thomas	77.1 86.6	12.5 48.1	56.2 74.4	85.1 91.4	64.6 79.3	37.5 63.4		36.2 63.0	42.6 65.4
Ginsburg	46.8 69.1	76.6 86.2	46.8 69.1	47.8 70.0	68.1 81.5	70.2 82.7	36.2 63.0		80.4 88.3
Breyer	53.2 71.8	61.7 76.9	66.0 79.5	50.0 70.1	66.0 79.5	76.6 85.9	42.6 65.4	80.4 88.3	

Note: The first number in each cell represents the percentage of agreement in divided cases. The second number represents the percentage of agreements in all signed opinions.

counts divided decisions only, the disagreements become more evident. O'Connor voted against the three strong conservatives in almost half of the nonunanimous decisions. For his part, Kennedy voted against Thomas in one out of every three divided decisions and against Rehnquist and Scalia in one out of every four.

Tellingly, O'Connor and Kennedy both agreed with individual members of the liberal bloc more often than with some of their conservative colleagues. O'Connor voted with Souter and Breyer more often than with Rehnquist, Scalia, or Thomas. Kennedy agreed with Ginsburg and Breyer more often than with Thomas.

On the left side of the Court, Ginsburg and Breyer had the closest alignment. They voted together in 88 percent of the cases. Both had liberal voting records on most social and constitutional issues. Ginsburg was somewhat more liberal in criminal law cases than was Breyer, while Breyer was somewhat more inclined than she was to support law enforcement.

Souter, Bush's first appointee to the Court, continued to vote with the liberals, to the great and bitter disappointment of conservatives. He lined up with Stevens, Ginsburg, and Breyer each more than 80 percent of the time, while agreeing with conservatives Rehnquist, Scalia, and Thomas in fewer than 70 percent of the cases. "He's off the reservation completely," Paul Capuccio, a conservative Washington lawyer and former law clerk to Justices Scalia and Kennedy, says of Souter. "He's not a conservative. He's not a moderate."

Stevens, who became the Court's senior justice after the 1994 retirement of Justice Harry A. Blackmun, staked out the term's most liberal voting record and the most individualistic. In nonunanimous decisions, Stevens agreed with Rehnquist and Scalia in only one-fourth of the cases and with Thomas in only one out of eight. He took liberal stances not only in closely divided cases but also, frequently, by himself. Stevens dissented alone in eight cases—almost one-tenth of the time. In four of those cases, he sided with criminal defendants against the government. In three others, he backed individuals or small businesses against large companies.

As the term ended, conservatives declared the year's biggest story to be the emergence of Clarence Thomas as the Court's strongest conservative voice. "We were hearing an extremely strong, clear, articulate, eloquent voice from Justice Thomas," noted Theodore Olson, a Washington attorney and assistant attorney general in the Reagan administration. "He was articulating very strong convictions about the Constitution and issues that relate to the Constitution."

Thomas was confirmed to the Court in 1991 by a four-vote margin in the Senate after a former aide, Anita Hill, leveled accusations of sexual harassment against him. The charges, which Thomas categorically and vehemently denied, were aired again in late 1994 with the publication of a new book, *Strange Justice*, written by two reporters who had covered the original hearings on Thomas. The reporters, Jill Abramson and Jane Mayer of the *Wall Street Journal*, brought forth new evidence that Thomas's critics depicted as corroborating Hill's version of events. Thomas's supporters dismissed the evidence, and the authors themselves acknowledged the new information was inconclusive.

Whether coincidentally or not, Thomas began to emerge from a shell as the publication of the book neared. In late October, he met at the Court with an invited group of black journalists and other African-Americans selected by his friend and former aide, Armstrong Williams, a conservative radio talk show host in Washington. Williams told the *Washington Post*'s Joan Biskupic later that he arranged the meeting because the news media had been depicting Thomas as "a monster." "I had an obligation to have him portrayed differently," Williams said.

In the October 26 meeting, according to the account published in Washington's *Afro-American* newspaper and confirmed by Biskupic, Thomas responded defiantly to suggestions that he had turned his back on his roots or that his votes had hurt black people. "I am not an Uncle Tom," Thomas told the group.

The new Clarence Thomas could also be seen in the courtroom. Thomas went through the Court's entire 1993–1994 term without asking a single question from the bench. But this year, he spoke up—only rarely, to be sure, but deliberately and pointedly. In the Ku Klux Klan cross case, for example, Thomas alone cut through the church-state issue to ask whether the cross was not a political rather than religious symbol for the Klan.

In his opinions, Thomas set out a historical interpretation of the Constitution based on the so-called "original understanding" of the document that was, as Kathleen Sullivan remarked, "more original than the originalists." He challenged the broad reading of the Commerce Clause by going back to the Court's earliest rulings interpreting federal power over interstate commerce. He defended the constitutionality of term limits for Congress by poring over the debate at the Constitutional Convention and the first years after ratification. And in the ruling on unsigned political leaflets, he dug out evidence of anonymous pamphleteering in the late 1700s that convinced him the practice was entitled to protection under the First Amendment.

Thomas, who succeeded civil rights pioneer Thurgood Marshall to become the Court's second African-American justice ever, also drew attention for his separate opinions setting forth a black conservative viewpoint on racial issues. In the school desegregation case, he criticized the Court's landmark 1954 ruling *Brown v. Board of Education*, suggesting that it was based on "questionable social science" and an "assumption of black inferiority." (Marshall had argued one of the companion cases to *Brown* as chief counsel for the NAACP Legal Defense and Educational Fund.) Thomas also criticized affirmative action. He called the policies misguided "paternalism" that promoted dependence among blacks and resentment among whites. "Government cannot make us equal," Thomas wrote. "[I]t can only recognize, respect, and protect us as equal before the law."

During the term, Thomas seemed to be enjoying himself on the Court, perhaps for the first time. He had been a sullen figure on the bench in previous terms. But Breyer, who took the seat next to Thomas as the Court's junior justice, got Thomas to smile and even laugh in occasional whispered exchanges on the bench. Friends and supporters confirmed the change in Thomas's mood. "People say that it takes five years to really get onto the job," former Missouri Senator John Danforth, Thomas's main sponsor in the confirmation fight, told *USA Today* reporter Tony Mauro as the term ended. "He's been at it four years now. He seems very confident, very comfortable now."

Liberal advocates and experts acknowledged Thomas's emergence less favorably. "He is speaking out more loudly," Steven Shapiro, national legal director of the American Civil Liberties Union (ACLU), remarked. "I still think he is fundamentally wrong on the vast majority of constitutional issues that the Court has confronted."

Shapiro and other Court watchers, both liberal and moderate, also doubted that Thomas was having much influence on his colleagues. "It's hard to find any evidence of that," Dennis Hutchinson remarked. Except for the term limits dissent, Thomas's other provocative opinions were joined by none of the other justices, not even Scalia.

On its left side, the Court had no strong voice to match the conservatives in eloquence and passion. Stevens was too idiosyncratic, Souter too legalistic, Breyer too new. Ginsburg came closest to taking up the mantle of the recently departed liberal justices: William J. Brennan, Jr., Thurgood Marshall, and Harry A. Blackmun. In her second term, she continued to be an active and pointed questioner from the bench. But she showed new strength and confidence in her written opinions, particularly in her dissents in the three race cases at the end of the term.

On school desegregation, Ginsburg answered the majority's impatience with the federal courts' control of local school systems by contrasting 200 years of legal segregation in Missouri with the thirty years of efforts to dismantle it. She defended racial redistricting by citing the "generations of rank discrimination against African-Americans, as citizens and voters." And she declared that affirmative action policies are still needed to overcome discrimination against black Americans in employment, housing, and other areas. "Bias both conscious and unconscious ... keeps up barriers that must come down," she wrote, "if equal opportunity and nondiscrimination are ever to become this country's law and practice."

President Clinton's other appointee, Breyer, earned good marks for his first term, but his influence remained to be seen. His voting record was generally moderate to liberal, his questions from the bench thoughtful, his opinions lucid. "To the extent that he was allowed, he richly lived up to expectations both in terms of craftsmanship and result," Hutchinson remarked.

Breyer wrote eight majority opinions, but most were relatively minor decisions as is typical for a rookie justice. In his most significant ruling, *O'Neal v. McAninch*, Breyer rejected a tightened standard for inmates to challenge convictions on the basis of constitutional violations at trial. The opinion emphasized the importance of habeas corpus in preventing unjust imprisonment. That was a marked change in tone from other recent rulings in the area, which have imposed limits on habeas corpus in order to promote "finality" in criminal cases.

The new justice's most important opinion, however, came in dissent. Breyer wrote for the minority in the *Lopez* case, defending Congress's power to ban guns near schools. The one-time chief counsel to the Senate Judiciary Committee argued that Congress had authority to try to deter violence in schools because of the connection between education and the country's economic strength.

Akil Ahmar, a Yale law school professor who clerked for Breyer on the federal appeals court, called the opinion "vintage Breyer: clear, pragmatic, empirical, democratic, deferential, and progressive." And, he noted, the opinion was an especially significant one for a first-term justice. "Very rarely does a justice in his or her rookie year get such an important assignment and carry it off so well," Ahmar said.

Breyer, a former Harvard Law School professor who had continued to teach there after joining the Court, showed a professorial style in his work as a justice. During arguments, he adopted the practice of posing long, wrap-up questions to a lawyer near the end of the allotted time. In his written opinions, he methodically parsed complex statutes or laid out issues almost as though he was writing on a classroom blackboard. In the habeas corpus ruling, he began by saying the decision "rests upon three considerations," which he then elaborated— first, second, third—in a crisply written, six-page passage.

Conservative and liberal advocates both found reasons to criticize Breyer's first term. The ACLU's Steven Shapiro said Breyer generally backed civil liberties but faulted him for voting (along with Ginsburg) to uphold random drug testing of high school athletes. From a different perspective, Chip Mellor of the Institute for Justice criticized Breyer as a "lockstep, big government liberal"— citing the *Lopez* dissent as the prime example.

Nevertheless, Court watchers of all persuasions had praise for Breyer's intellect and craftsmanship. "He had a very good, very intelligent rookie year," Kathleen Sullivan remarked. Attorney Paul Capuccio agreed: "He's a great addition to the Court. He's another young energetic justice who likes to mix it up."

Breyer also eliminated one distraction from his duties early in his term by severing his ties to Lloyd's of London, the famous insurance syndicate. Breyer's investment in Lloyd's had been the major sticking point during the Senate confirmation process in July and August 1994. Critics said he had been insensitive to potential conflicts of interest by sitting on some insurance-related cases as an appeals court judge while invested in Lloyd's. To allay the concerns, Breyer promised to recuse himself from any cases that might affect his investment in Lloyd's and also to get out of the Lloyd's syndicate as soon as possible.

In early November, Breyer completed the necessary details. A friend who helped negotiate the arrangement told the *New York Times* that Breyer paid $110,000 for an insurance policy to cover any further liability from his investment in the syndicate. The friend, who asked not to be named, described the cost as a premium necessary to accommodate Breyer's desire to end the investment quickly. Breyer also appeared to follow through on his promise to step out of cases that might pose a conflict of interest. He recused himself in four insurance-related cases that were argued during the term and from a reported 120 cases that were considered for review but rejected.

Liberal advocates took heart from the Ginsburg and Breyer appointments but acknowledged disappointment that the two Clinton justices had failed to stop the Court's shift to the right during the term. "The biggest problem they face is the search for a fifth vote," the ACLU's Steven Shapiro remarked. But the disappointment may have reflected unrealistic expectations about the influence a new justice can have in his or her early terms.

"It takes three to four to five years before a justice reaches his or her stride in doing that sort of thing," attorney Theodore Olson observed. "You have to learn what the Court's docket is all about, what its jurisprudence is all about. And then I think someone can be more muscular in that regard."

An Uncertain Course

For their part, conservatives were pleasantly surprised by the Court's shift to the right. "This was obviously a very interesting term that was not forecast or expected to be so," Notre Dame's Douglas Kmiec remarked. But conservatives knew from experience that one term does not make a legal revolution.

Indeed, the biggest story about the Supreme Court for the previous quarter-century was the conservative counter-revolution that never happened. Richard Nixon, Ronald Reagan, and George Bush all promised during their campaigns to transform the Supreme Court. As president, the three made a total of ten appointments to the Court. Yet the Court never fully embraced the conservative agenda that the three Republican chief executives endorsed and directed the Justice Department to advocate before the justices.

True, after Nixon chose Warren E. Burger as chief justice in 1969, the Court mostly refused to extend greater due process rights to suspects and criminal defendants. But the Burger Court did not overturn the most controversial criminal law rulings from the 1960s, like the *Miranda* decision on police interrogation. On civil rights, Burger himself wrote the opinion in 1971 that rejected the administration's plea to bar court-ordered busing as a remedy in school desegregation cases. And the Burger Court also produced the 1973 *Roe v. Wade* abortion rights ruling as well as the first rulings limiting gender discrimination and permitting affirmative action.

Burger died June 25 at the age of eighty-seven, almost a decade after his retirement in 1986. He was remembered as an able administrator and a strong spokesman for the federal judiciary but a less than successful chief justice, who never achieved intellectual or personal leadership of the Court.

Rehnquist, whom President Reagan chose as Burger's successor, brought to the post the intellectual and personal skills that Burger lacked. He had been a forceful conservative voice since Nixon named him as an associate justice in 1971, but he also was warmly liked by justices on the left and right. In addition, while Burger inherited a Court with a solid liberal core, Rehnquist assumed leadership of a Court already moving toward the right. And Reagan continued to push in that direction by picking Scalia, a well-known conservative law professor, to fill Rehnquist's seat.

In its first few terms, the Rehnquist Court gave signs it might fulfill conservatives' hopes for a sharp turn to the right. Conservatives were disappointed in 1987 when the Senate rejected Reagan's nomination of federal appeals court judge Robert Bork as too conservative. But when Anthony Kennedy emerged as the choice for the vacancy, he seemed likely to give Rehnquist a working conservative majority on many issues. And Kennedy's first full year on the Court—the 1988–1989 term—did produce a flurry of distinctively conservative rulings.

Today, however, conservatives view Kennedy as a disappointment. In 1992, he voted in two critical cases to reaffirm a modified form of *Roe v. Wade* and to bar school-sponsored prayers at commencement ceremonies. Both votes represented reversals of his previous positions. He had voted in 1989 to overturn *Roe v. Wade* and, in a pair of cases involving Christmas displays in government buildings, to ease the rules on separation of church and state.

Conservatives rued Kennedy's rejection of their positions all the more because his vote was so often decisive, as it was in the term limits case this year. In the 1994–1995 term, he was once again the justice with the lowest number of dissenting votes *(see Table 1–3)*. Kennedy dissented in only five of the eighty-two signed decisions and cast a partial dissent in a sixth. That

Pallbearers carry the coffin with the body of retired Chief Justice Warren E. Burger into the Supreme Court building June 28 as current and retired justices watch. Standing from top are Chief Justice William H. Rehnquist, Justices John Paul Stevens, Sandra Day O'Connor, Antonin Scalia, Anthony M. Kennedy, David H. Souter, Clarence Thomas, Ruth Bader Ginsburg, and Stephen G. Breyer, and retired justices Byron R. White, Lewis F. Powell, Jr., and Harry A. Blackmun. Retired justice William J. Brennan, Jr., was unable to stand on the steps, but joined other mourners inside later.

marked the fourth consecutive year Kennedy had the distinction of being most often in the majority. As the *Washington Post* aptly said in a headline on a story about Kennedy's voting record, "When Court Is Split, Kennedy Rules."

Kennedy's votes were not hard to explain, however. He generally sided with law enforcement but parted company with conservatives on issues involving access to the courts and fairness in the courtroom. In the 1993–1994 term, for example, he sided with the Court's liberal bloc in 5–4 decisions that guaranteed criminal defendants a hearing before the government could seize their property and that protected a death row inmate's right to a lawyer to challenge his sentence in federal court. He was also likely to vote with the liberals on constitutional questions, especially First

Table 1–3   Justices in Dissent, 1994–1995 Term

Justice	Division on Court				Total	Percentage
	8–1, 7–1	7–2, 6–2	6–3	5–4		
Rehnquist	—	2	5	6	13	15.9
Stevens	8	6	1	8	23	28.4
O'Connor	1	2	4	5	12	14.6
Scalia	—	3	4	7	14	17.3
Kennedy	—	—	2	3	5	6.1
Souter	—	2	4	10	16	19.5
Thomas	2	4	6	8	20	24.4
Ginsburg	—	4	—	8	12	14.8
Breyer	—	1	1	9	11	14.1

Note: There were eighty-two signed opinions during the 1994–1995 term. Because of recusals, Breyer participated in seventy-eight cases; Stevens, Scalia, and Ginsburg in eighty-one each. The count of dissents includes one decision (*Chandris, Inc. v. Latsis*) where justices were unanimous on the result but divided 6–3 on the legal holding.

Amendment issues. In 1989, he cast a decisive vote in the 5–4 ruling to strike down state laws against flag burning.

O'Connor, the second of the swing justices, had likewise disappointed conservatives with a number of moderate votes since her appointment by Reagan in 1981. She voted to uphold restrictions on abortion procedures but stopped short of overruling *Roe v. Wade.* She voted to narrow affirmative action but stopped short of abolishing it. She voted to relax the restrictions on church-state connections but stopped short of scrapping them. Nina Totenberg, the veteran Supreme Court reporter for National Public Radio, summed up O'Connor as the "yes, but" justice.

Observers explained O'Connor's tentative stands by noting that the one-time Arizona legislator was the only member of the Court ever to have held or run for elective office. "She still seems more of a politician than a jurist," says Georgetown's Paul Rothstein. "She writes broad language that seems to give a little to both sides, that cools down the issue."

O'Connor and Kennedy gave conservatives the edge during the term, but conservatives had no simple explanation why. "The Court was surprising to the extent that the moderate center went in a conservative direction," Kmiec said. "That could not have been predicted by their prior decisions."

Some liberals, however, suggested the justices were being influenced by—or at least were reflecting—larger political trends. "The 1994 midterm elections may have made it seem that the pulse of the country was farther to the right," Stanford's Kathleen Sullivan said. The justices may not be simply following the election returns—as Peter Finley Dunne, the nineteenth century political satirist, wrote in an often-quoted aphorism. But, as Sullivan put it, "they do think that custom, tradition, and public sentiment have some role."

For that reason, the future of the Court's shift to the right may depend on outside events as much as on the justices themselves. By themselves, the core conservatives—Rehnquist, Scalia, and Thomas—cannot take the Court further in that direction. And their influence over their more moderate colleagues is open to doubt. Rehnquist has been a low-key leader, seemingly most concerned with efficient disposition of the Court's work. And neither the uncompromising Scalia or outspoken Thomas seems well suited to taking on the role of forging a stable conservative majority on the Court.

The delicate balance of power on the Court would, of course, be affected by the departure of one of the justices. But there was no immediate prospect of a change in membership. None of the justices has an evident health problem likely to force a retirement soon. Indeed, at the start of the term the justices constituted the second youngest Court in this century, with an average age of just under sixty. (The Court had an average age of fifty-eight in the late 1930s and early 1940s after several appointments by President Franklin D. Roosevelt.)

With a presidential campaign coming up, the odds of a retirement seemed further diminished. In the recent past, justices have tried to avoid having a Supreme Court confirmation in an election year. Potter Stewart and Byron R. White, who both retired in good health, waited until the first year of a new administration, in 1981 and 1993, to leave the Court.

In his end-of-term assessment, Dennis Hutchinson said the Court "was a lot like the Chicago fireworks. It did an enormous amount even if it didn't last very long." Conservatives clearly hope the shift to the right will last longer. But Hutchinson counsels caution in making predictions.

The Court has had two bursts of activism in this century. In the 1920s and 1930s, a conservative Court thwarted progressive legislation in the economic sphere. Then, in the 1950s and 1960s, a liberal Court wrought revolutions in race and criminal justice. With those two exceptions, Hutchinson concludes, the Supreme Court has always been "a set of changing coalitions, responding to changing agendas."

2 | *The 1994–1995 Term*

The Supreme Court dealt civil rights forces two setbacks on affirmative action and school desegregation in mid-June. Now, on the last day of the term, those groups waited anxiously for the decision in a pair of racial redistricting cases that could imperil the recent gains in the number of African-Americans and Hispanics serving in Congress.

The ruling, the second of five decisions announced June 29, went the way the minority lawmakers and their supporters had feared. By a 5–4 vote, the justices declared constitutionally suspect any district lines drawn predominantly on the basis of race. The ruling invited challenges to many of the so-called majority-minority districts in the House of Representatives since race had been openly considered in drawing most of them.

In its other rulings before beginning its three-month summer recess, the Court supported funding for a religious newspaper at the University of Virginia and backed the right of the Ku Klux Klan to erect a cross in front of the Ohio State Capitol. The justices also rejected a plea by business groups to limit enforcement of the Endangered Species Act on private property.

The juxtaposition of the decisions was coincidental, but one member of the Congressional Black Caucus tied them together to sharpen her criticism of the redistricting decision. "The Court that today protected endangered species and the Ku Klux Klan is not likely to protect me," Rep. Eddie Bernice Johnson, a Texas Democrat elected from a district being challenged in a separate case, told reporters.

Johnson's remark was a calculated sound bite, but it held a measure of truth. For more than sixty years, race had been an overriding issue at the Supreme Court, not only in civil rights cases but also in other areas. The Court had ordered increased protections for suspects and criminal defendants to temper the widespread discrimination against blacks in the criminal justice system. It backed the expansion of federal power to overcome official and private resistance to dismantling segregation. It created limits on libel suits in its famous *New York Times v. Sullivan* decision in order to overturn a punishing verdict against the newspaper for publishing a pro–civil rights advertisement.

The trilogy of race cases in the 1994–1995 term, however, appeared to confirm a transformation at the Court. The era of special solicitude for racial minorities was over. The Court validated claims of discrimination brought by white contractors and white voters and told federal judges to rein in their efforts to get white students into predominantly black schools.

"Race in America is to be privatized," Stanford law professor Kathleen Sullivan said of the rulings, "and the federal role is to be diminished."

Liberal advocacy groups heatedly denounced the Court's decisions. "The Supreme Court's historic commitment to racial justice took a severe beating" during the term, the American Civil Liberties Union said. Elaine Jones, director of the NAACP Legal Defense and Educational Fund, likened the redistricting rulings to what she called "the post-Reconstruction purge of African-Americans from elected offices and voting rolls throughout the South."

Conservative organizations, however, hailed the rulings as a vindication rather than a defeat for racial equality. In their view, affirmative action had degenerated into a racial spoils system, voting rights had been perverted into racial gerrymandering, and desegregation had become court-ordered social engineering. "The Court's decisions move us beyond the racial divide and closer to a color-blind Constitution," Clint Bolick, litigation director for the Institute of Justice, claimed.

The Court's formal rulings on affirmative action, racial redistricting, and school desegregation were not the only setbacks for minority groups during the term. The justices also let stand two lower court rulings that limited affirmative action programs. One of the decisions killed a special scholarship program for African-Americans at the University of Maryland. The other ended an affirmative action plan requiring the Birmingham, Alabama, fire department to promote one black for each white promoted. Officially, the Court does not establish a precedent when it declines to review a case. But the actions, announced April 17, sent a signal to federal judges about what kinds of racial remedies the justices would, and would not, vote to uphold.

Against these defeats, traditional civil rights groups could count only the most modest victories. In an important job discrimination case, the Court limited a common defense tactic by employers: the use of evidence of employee misconduct discovered during the course of the litigation. The justices unanimously ruled that this "after-acquired" evidence could not protect an employer from a finding of discrimination, though it could be used to block reinstatement of an employee or limit back pay awards. The decision came in a case filed under the Age Discrimination in Employment Act, but it was likely to be applied to racial bias cases as well.

The only other major civil rights ruling involved the rights of the disabled. The Court limited the ability of municipalities to bar group homes for recovering alcoholics or drug addicts from single-family neighborhoods. Like the job discrimination case, the 6–3 ruling was based on a congressional statute, recently enacted amendments to the Fair Housing Act.

Second only to the race decisions, the Court's rulings in two religion cases also cheered conservatives. Religious advocacy groups made significant gains in their efforts to ease the strictures designed to keep church and state apart. "This was a very good term for us at the Supreme Court," said Jay Alan Sekulow, legal director of the American Center for Law and Justice, the legal center affiliated with television preacher Pat Robertson.

Conservative religious groups contended that the government's professed neutrality toward religion often amounted to discrimination against religion. The two disputes provided good examples. Through a mandatory student activity fee, the University of Virginia funded all sorts of student publications, but not an avowedly evangelical Christian newspaper. In Ohio, a state board refused to let the Ku Klux Klan erect a cross at the same site where a Jewish group had displayed a menorah and the local United Way had put up a chart marking the progress in its annual fundraising drive.

The Court backed the religious groups' position in both cases. Justice Kennedy wrote for the five-justice majority in the student newspaper case, saying the university had violated the First Amendment's Free Speech Clause by singling out a religious publication for disfavored treatment. Justice Scalia, the Court's strongest advocate for greater government accommodation of religion, wrote the main opinion in the Klan cross case. He had four votes for the position that religious groups are entitled to exactly the same access to a public forum that any other group has.

The four dissenters in the student newspaper case argued the Court had breached the rule against establishment of religion by permitting—for the first time, they said—direct government funding of a religious activity. Religious groups gladly accepted their characterization of the ruling. "We've crossed a critical threshold," Sekulow rejoiced.

The victory was tempered only by the emphasis that Kennedy and Justice O'Connor in a separate opinion placed on factual details tending to minimize the connection between the university and the newspaper. Groups advocating separation of church and state cited those passages to argue that the ruling would not provide a precedent for government vouchers for religious schools or for religious groups to distribute Bibles in public schools. "There's plenty of limiting language in the case to indicate that this does not open the door for funding of religious schools," said Barry Lynn, executive director of Americans United for Separation of Church and State.

The ruling in the cross case was more muddled because of the separate concurrence by three justices: O'Connor, Souter, and Breyer. They refused to join Scalia in jettisoning the so-called endorsement test that O'Connor favored in Establishment Clause cases. In O'Connor's view, government goes too far in permitting religious activities if a "reasonable" observer would conclude that the government is endorsing the religious message. The Ku Klux Klan cross would not be seen that way, she said, since it stood in a public forum open to other displays—and even had a disclaimer attached at the bottom. But O'Connor insisted that "careful judicial scrutiny" was still required of any "governmental practices relating to speech on religious topics."

Opposing groups immediately saw the ruling as affecting the perennial litigation over display of Nativity scenes and menorahs on public property. "This is the sensible response to this annual litigation over Christmas displays," said Douglas Laycock, a law professor at the University of Texas who filed a brief supporting the Klan's position in the cross case. "Instead of the government doing it, some association of churches or some other group ought to come in and do it."

Barry Lynn of the separationist group agreed on the impact of the ruling but viewed the prospect with disapproval. "I don't know why we've decided that you can erect your own religious symbol on government property," Lynn complained. "When all of these things start to clutter the space, the government may want to shut the forum down."

On the final day of the term, the Court gave religious conservatives one more piece of good news. It threw out a ruling by the Ninth U.S. Circuit Court of Appeals that had barred a speaker selected by students from offering a prayer at a public high school graduation ceremony. The issue had been simmering since 1992 when the Court barred a school-sponsored prayer at commencement exercises. Religious groups responded by urging the graduates to act on their own, either by having a student offer a prayer or inviting a speaker to do so. Of three federal appeals courts to rule on the issue, only the Ninth Circuit—which covers Western and Pacific Coast states—had rejected the practice.

The Court could have declined to hear the case, leaving the appeals court precedent to stand in the Ninth Circuit. It could have agreed to hear the case and resolve the issue once and for all. But instead, it decided to take jurisdiction over the case long enough to "vacate"—erase—the ruling and dismiss the suit. The rationale: the student who had challenged the prayer had graduated and the case was therefore moot.

Religious groups promptly claimed the action as a victory. Opponents accurately noted that the action left the issue unsettled. "They should have taken the case," Lynn added. "It's ludicrous for this to continue every spring, with no one sure who's right and who's wrong."

The Court heartened conservatives during the term in a third major area: federalism. In a year when the new Republican majority in Congress was calling for shifting power back to the states, the justices too re-examined the allocation of power between Washington and state governments. And in one case, the Court struck down a federal law on grounds that Congress had intruded on states' prerogatives by going beyond its constitutional power to regulate interstate commerce.

Improbably, the dispute arose over efforts to ban guns in or near schools—a goal shared by liberals and conservatives alike. The Gun-Free School Zones Act of 1990 made it a federal crime to possess a firearm anywhere within 1,000 feet of a school. More than forty states had laws on the subject, but Congress had often enacted criminal provisions that over-lapped state statutes.

Congress had based many of these laws on its power—one of the so-called enumerated powers in Article I of the Constitution—to "regulate Commerce with foreign Nations, and among the several States." The Court first upheld this technique of using the Commerce Clause to create what amounted to a federal police power in a 1903 decision that upheld interstate transportation of lottery tickets. The doctrine allowed Congress to expand the federal criminal code to cover everything from unsafe food and prostitution to loan-sharking and racketeering. Over time, the question whether Congress was extending the doctrine too far all but faded away.

The Court revived the issue in its 5–4 decision this term to strike down the gun law. In the majority opinion, Chief Justice Rehnquist acknowledged the Court had given "great deference" to Congress in stretching its Commerce Clause powers in recent years. But the gun law had no direct connection to commerce, he said. The government tried to link the act to interstate commerce by citing the effects of education on the economy, but Rehnquist rejected the argument. "To uphold the Government's contentions here," he wrote, "we would have to pile inference upon inference in a manner that would bid fair to convert congressional authority under the Commerce Clause to a general police power of the sort retained by the States."

The decision touched off immediate speculation that any number of expansive federal laws might be open to challenge on the same ground. The prospect pleased conservatives, while liberals spoke in dire terms of a constitutional revolution. President Clinton himself said in his weekly radio address three days later that he was "terribly disappointed" with the ruling.

After a few days, however, advocates and experts alike offered more modest assessments of the likely impact of the ruling. "There is much less here than meets the eye," Laurence Tribe, a Harvard professor and liberal expert on constitutional law, told the *National Law Journal.* He said the gun law "went over the edge in terms of existing doctrine."

The five justices in the majority were themselves divided on how far the opinion should go. Kennedy, joined by O'Connor, wrote a concurring opinion to reaffirm the Court's precedents that gave Congress a wide berth in regulating economic affairs. Justice Thomas argued in a lone concurrence for re-examining Court doctrine to narrow federal authority. The divisions suggested a tenuous majority that was unlikely to embark on a constitutional sweeping operation for overreaching federal laws. And, in fact, in the next week the Court declined to hear two cases challenging a federal arson law on Commerce Clause grounds. Only Scalia voted to hear the cases.

The Court's second major federalism ruling was a defeat for conservatives and for state power. By a 5–4 vote, the Court rejected measures passed in twenty-three states to limit the terms of their U.S. representatives and senators. Kennedy provided the Court's liberal bloc with the needed fifth vote in the case. The result had been predicted: state term limits seemed to fly in the face of an explicit constitutional provision setting out the qualifications for members of Congress.

Conservatives were nevertheless heartened by the close division in the case and by the strong affirmation of state power in Thomas's opinion for the four dissenters. Thomas said that states had the power to pass term limits in the absence of an explicit prohibition in the Constitution. "Where the Constitution is silent, it raises no bar to action by the States or the people," he wrote. In a footnote, Thomas even noted that as originally drafted, the Preamble to the Constitution was to have read, "We the people of the states of New Hampshire, Massachusetts," and so on.

"The Court is reaching the question at the heart of it all: Did we authorize all this government?" Roger Pilon, a constitutional law expert at the libertarian Cato Institute, told the *New York Times*. "It's absolutely consistent," he added, "with the mood of the country that wants to get Washington off our backs."

For all the sharp rhetoric, the Court's decisions added up to no great shift in power between the federal and state governments. States could claim a few victories in lesser cases. The Court, for example, backed a California law tightening welfare benefits, but it did so only after finding the measure consistent with the federal statute that set up the program. In a different area, however, the Court limited the ability of states to extend their Eleventh Amendment immunity from federal court suits to separate entities. The 5–4 decision allowed a suit by injured railway workers against the Port Authority Trans-Hudson Corporation, a railway established under an interstate compact between New Jersey and New York but financially independent from the two state governments.

The Court invoked the First Amendment several times during the term to strike down actions by both Congress and state governments *(see Table 2–1)*. The Court invalidated two federal laws on free speech grounds: a 1935 statute preventing beer manufacturers from listing alcohol content on product labels and a 1991 ethics law preventing most federal employees from being paid for articles or speeches. Along with the gun law and an act aimed at reviving a handful of federal securities suits already dismissed in court, that brought to four the number of federal statutes declared unconstitutional during the term. In the previous term, no federal law had been ruled unconstitutional.

In another free speech case, the Court invalidated an Ohio law, comparable to laws in virtually every other state, that banned anonymous political campaign materials. The First Amendment's Free Speech Clause was

Table 2–1   Laws Held Unconstitutional

The Supreme Court issued seven decisions that ruled unconstitutional federal laws or state constitutional provisions or statutes.

Decision (in chronological order)	Law Ruled Invalid
Federal Laws	
United States v. National Treasury Employees Union [p. 105]	Ban on honoraria for federal civil servants
Rubin v. Coors Brewing Co. [p. 103]	Ban on listing of alcohol content on beer containers
Plaut v. Spendthrift Farm, Inc. [p. 71]	Act to reinstate certain federal securities fraud suits
United States v. Lopez [p. 79]	Gun Free Schools Zone Act
State Laws	
McIntyre v. Ohio Elections Commission [p. 104]	Ban on anonymous campaign literature
U.S. Term Limits, Inc. v. Thornton [p. 94]	State term limits for members of Congress
Miller v. Johnson [p. 93]	Georgia congressional plan

also the basis for overturning state actions in the two religion cases. And in a final decision expanding First Amendment protections, the Court threw out a ruling by Massachusetts's highest court that required the organizers of Boston's annual St. Patrick's Day parade to permit an organization of Irish-American homosexuals to march in the procession.

The Massachusetts court had ruled that the state's antidiscrimination law required the parade organizers to permit the gay rights group to join. But in a unanimous decision, the Court said that applying the state law in that way would violate the First Amendment. "… [T]he law is not free," Souter wrote, "to interfere with speech for no better reason than promoting an approved message or discouraging a disfavored one, however enlightened either purpose may strike the government."

The Court also extended First Amendment protections in one other case. A New York artist had challenged Amtrak's refusal to permit him to lease a billboard in its Pennsylvania Station in New York City for display of a political advertisement. Amtrak argued that it was an independent corporation not covered by the First Amendment, but the Court, by an 8–1 vote, disagreed. The outcome of the case remained to be decided. The

Court sent the case back to lower courts to rule on the reasonableness of Amtrak's policy of refusing political ads.

Against these First Amendment victories, the Court issued only one decision that rejected a free speech claim. By a 5–4 vote, the Court upheld a regulation of the Florida Bar, an arm of the state's supreme court, that barred lawyers from sending solicitation letters to accident or disaster victims or their families within thirty days after the incident. The ruling went against the Court's recent trend of narrowing regulation of professional advertising and commercial speech generally. But experts questioned whether the decision signaled the start of a new trend or merely the justices' disapproval of an unseemly advertising technique unpopular even within the legal profession.

In contrast to the First Amendment rulings, the Court's most significant civil liberties decision of the term rejected an expansive reading of another Bill of Rights provision, the Fourth Amendment. The 6–3 decision upheld random drug testing for high school athletes. A local school board in Oregon adopted the testing program to curb an outbreak of drug use, but a student and his family challenged the policy as an "unreasonable" search under the Fourth Amendment.

The ACLU represented the family in the challenge and assailed the decision when it came out. National legal director Steven Shapiro called the testing program "an incredibly intrusive Big Brother search." But the ACLU stood alone on the issue. An array of state government groups filed briefs with the Court defending the drug testing policy. The Clinton administration also urged the justices to uphold the policy. No organization joined the case on the ACLU's side.

In criminal law, the Court issued many rulings, but few had dramatic impact. "It was not a year of any earth-shattering developments," said Kent Scheidegger, an attorney with the Criminal Justice Legal Foundation in Sacramento, California, who filed pro-law enforcement briefs in several cases during the term. Shapiro of the ACLU agreed. "It was a pretty slow year in criminal law," he acknowledged.

Overall, law enforcement won about half the signed decisions, but none of the victories could be called major. In one closely watched Fourth Amendment case, the Court refused to bar evidence obtained in a search after a defendant was arrested on the basis of an erroneous computer warrant. The case could have been an important pronouncement about computerized databanks in the criminal justice system. But the Court steered clear of a broad ruling. Instead, Rehnquist limited the decision to the specific facts: a judicial clerk had failed to clear the expired warrant from the computer. Left unsettled was what would happen in a case where the police were responsible for such a mistake.

In another Fourth Amendment case, the Court unanimously ruled that police generally must knock and announce their identity before entering a home with a search warrant. Most states already followed the practice, however. And Thomas's opinion included exceptions that would give police leeway to enter unannounced in many circumstances.

The Court issued three somewhat surprising rulings that backed prison inmates in habeas corpus cases. In recent years, the Court had set a number of procedural hurdles that made it harder for state prisoners to challenge convictions in federal court. But this term the Court stepped back and reversed three lower court rulings that would have further impeded inmates' efforts to win habeas corpus claims.

In the most significant case, the Court said a federal judge should grant a habeas corpus petition if an inmate proves that there was a constitutional error at trial and the judge is in doubt about whether the error affected the outcome. The lower court had placed the burden on the inmate to prove the error might have changed the result. The other two rulings came in death penalty cases. In one case, the inmate had strong new evidence casting doubt on the verdict; the other prisoner presented persuasive evidence of prosecutorial misconduct and ineffective assistance of counsel at trial.

The Court's only direct ruling on capital punishment procedure rejected a bid to set new limits on state laws. By an 8–1 vote, the Court upheld an Alabama law that gave a judge unlimited discretion to impose the death penalty despite a jury recommendation for life imprisonment. The Alabama statute was like other laws the Court had upheld in a prior ruling except that it set no guidelines for the judge to follow in making the decision. O'Connor said the lack of standards did not invalidate the law.

The Court also produced few major rulings in business-related decisions during the term. But business groups said they were generally satisfied with what they got. "It was a pretty good term for us," concluded Robin Conrad, a senior lawyer at the U.S. Chamber of Commerce. "We saw a greater sensitivity in the Court toward business issues."

Overall, business groups could count victories in roughly half the cases where businesses were opposed by workers, consumers, or government regulators. The victories came in decisions that drew little attention among the general public. Conrad cited as one important victory a little-noticed decision easing the way for companies to revise employee health benefit plans. In another important decision, the Court applied the federal Arbitration Act to allow a company to enforce a provision in a consumer contract requiring that disputes be settled by arbitration instead of in court.

The biggest defeat for business groups perhaps came in the Endangered Species Act case. The timber industry brought the challenge to try to narrow federal restrictions on logging on privately owned lands. An array of business groups, including the American Farm Bureau Federation and the U.S. Chamber of Commerce, filed supporting briefs with the Court. But the justices voted 6–3 to uphold the challenged regulation.

Stevens said the regulation was a reasonable interpretation of a statute that Congress intended to be broadly applied.

Affirmative Action

"Strict Scrutiny" for Federal Programs Based on Race

Adarand Constructors, Inc. v. Peña, Secretary of Transportation, decided by a 5–4 vote, June 12, 1995; O'Connor wrote the opinion; Stevens, Souter, Ginsburg, and Breyer dissented. *(See excerpts, p. 162.)*

Randy Pech had a simple explanation for his decision to challenge a federal policy that gave minority contractors an advantage in competing against his own firm for constructing guardrails on federally funded highway projects. "I think it's wrong," the Colorado contractor told reporters. "I think it's wrong to award anything on the basis of race."

Pech's company, Adarand Constructors, based in Colorado Springs, brought a legal challenge to the federal program after losing a $100,000 job to a minority-owned firm in the state. His case led to a Supreme Court ruling that required the federal government to meet the highest level of constitutional review—"strict scrutiny"—to justify any form of racial classification.

Adarand did about $2.5 million in business a year, almost exclusively in guardrails. In 1989, Pech submitted the low bid on a project to build guardrails on a 4.7-mile stretch of highway in the San Juan National Forest in Colorado. But the prime contractor awarded the job instead to a minority-owned firm in the state, Gonzales Construction Co.

Under a Department of Transportation program, the prime contractor, Mountain Gravel & Construction Co., got a $10,000 bonus for awarding the job to a minority-owned firm. The Transportation Department program was established under a 1987 federal highway law, the Surface Transportation and Uniform Relocation Assistance Act. The act required that at least 10 percent of the construction money under the law go to so-called disadvantaged business enterprises or DBEs.

On paper, the "subcontractor compensation clause" did not grant an automatic preference to minority-owned firms or limit the advantage to minority businesses. Instead, the financial incentive was granted for awarding subcontracts to any business owned by "socially or economically disadvantaged" persons. But African-Americans, Hispanics, Asian-Americans, Native Americans, and other minorities were presumed to be disadvantaged. Women were also presumed to qualify. White men, on the other hand, could qualify for the program only if they submitted proof of social or economic disadvantage.

Pech, represented by lawyers from the conservative Mountain States Legal Foundation, filed a federal court suit in Colorado in 1990 challeng-

Randy Pech, owner of Adarand Constructors, Inc., stands beside one of his company trucks in Colorado Springs, Colo., on the day of the Supreme Court's ruling in his challenge to a federal minority contractor preference program. Lower courts had upheld the program, but the justices sent the case back for a new hearing under a stricter standard.

ing the Transportation Department program as a violation of his equal protection rights under the Fifth and Fourteenth amendments. But his suit was rejected by the district court judge and by the Tenth U.S. Circuit Court of Appeals. In its ruling, the appeals court said the program satisfied what it called "the lenient standard, resembling intermediate scrutiny" that the Supreme Court established in a 1980 decision, *Fullilove v. Klutznick*, upholding a federal minority set-aside law.

The political and legal climate surrounding affirmative action changed dramatically after the *Fullilove* decision. Republican presidents Ronald Reagan and George Bush strongly criticized racial preferences and opposed affirmative action plans in court. They also made six appointments to the Court, replacing a tenuous liberal majority with a somewhat stable conservative majority.

The Court had always been ambivalent on affirmative action. In 1978, it voted 5–4 to permit public colleges and universities to consider race as one factor in admissions policies as long as they did not impose rigid quotas (*Regents of University of California v. Bakke*). Over the next decade, the Court ruled that public and private employers could adopt voluntary affirmative action plans, and courts could order quotas to remedy past discrimination as long as more senior white workers were not laid off to make room for minority workers.

In 1989, the Court heard a new case involving minority set-asides. A white contractor challenged a Richmond, Virginia, ordinance that required at least 30 percent of city contracts to go to minority-owned businesses. In a 6–3 decision, *City of Richmond v. J. A. Croson Co.*, the Court invalidated the ordinance. Justice O'Connor, who wrote the opinion, said that state and local set-aside programs could be upheld only if they satisfied "strict scrutiny"—that is, they were necessary to serve a compelling state interest and were narrowly tailored to serve that interest.

One year later, however, the Court voted 5–4 to retain the less exacting standard—"intermediate scrutiny"—for federal minority preference programs. The decision, *Metro Broadcasting, Inc. v. Federal Communications Commission,* upheld two FCC policies favoring minority broadcasters. Two of the justices from the *Croson* majority—Stevens and Byron R. White—provided the critical votes to support the government in the new case.

Justice William J. Brennan, Jr., who wrote the majority opinion in *Metro Broadcasting,* retired later that summer of 1990. His fellow liberal, Thurgood Marshall, retired the next year. With President Bush's appointment of Thomas, a staunch conservative, the Court had a majority generally opposed to most forms of affirmative action. President Clinton named moderate liberals Ginsburg and Breyer to succeed other liberal-leaning justices, leaving the balance on the issue unchanged.

For four years after *Metro Broadcasting,* however, the Court chose not to hear any affirmative action cases. Then, at the start of the 1994–1995 term, the justices agreed to consider the *Adarand* case. When the case came before the Court on January 17, conservative critics of the policies were hopeful, and civil rights groups and other liberal supporters of the programs uneasy.

The arguments turned quickly to the details of the program instead of the broad questions surrounding affirmative action. Under close questioning Adarand's lawyer, William Perry Pendley, made a critical point about the operation of the program: no white contractor had ever qualified as a disadvantaged business enterprise. Later, to Justice Scalia, Pendley said it was "not the real world" to expect a white contractor to take on the burden of contesting the eligibility of a minority-owned concern.

Justices Breyer and Ginsburg pressed Pendley to admit he wanted the Court to overrule *Fullilove.* When Pendley said no, Ginsburg expressed surprise. "How can you say that?" Ginsburg said. "*Fullilove* involved a straight-out set aside, with no flexibility at all. Here, it's as flexible as possible."

Solicitor General Drew S. Days III opened with a broad defense of the program as part of "a national policy" designed "to ensure that federal procurement policies do not compound the effects of well-documented discrimination but rather serve to offset its consequences." But the justices quickly forced him to focus on the specifics of the program. And in the close questioning, he made a telling admission to Scalia that he knew of no case where a minority-owned firm's eligibility for the program had been challenged.

Some observers left the courtroom puzzled. The justices' questions indicated the Court might issue a ruling tightly focused on the specifics of the Transportation Department program or even skirt the issue altogether by ruling that Adarand had not shown a legal injury needed to bring the suit. Meanwhile, the political climate on affirmative action heated up. Republican lawmakers in Congress called for repealing all racial preferences in federal programs, and President Clinton ordered a full-scale review of existing programs.

Against that backdrop, the Court's decision on June 12 produced elation among critics of affirmative action. By a 5–4 vote, the Court held that federal race-based programs were subject to the same strict test as state and local policies. "... [A]ll racial classifications, imposed by whatever federal, state, or local government actor, must be analyzed by a reviewing court under strict scrutiny," O'Connor wrote. "In other words, such classifications are constitutional only if they are narrowly tailored measures that further compelling governmental interests."

In a lengthy review of affirmative action decisions, O'Connor said the Court had generally been skeptical of racial classifications and had imposed identical standards under the Equal Protection Clause on federal, state, or local governments. *Metro Broadcasting*, she explained, had departed from those precedents. For that reason, she said, it was overruled "to the extent that [it] is inconsistent with" the new holding.

O'Connor stopped short of saying that strict scrutiny would prevent the government from ever using racial classifications. "... [W]e wish to dispel the notion that strict scrutiny is 'strict in theory, but fatal in fact,' " she said, quoting a passage from an opinion by Justice Marshall in the *Fullilove* case. "The unhappy persistence of both the practice and lingering effects of racial discrimination against minority groups in this country is an unfortunate reality, and government is not disqualified from acting in response to it."

In conclusion, O'Connor said Adarand's case should be returned to the lower courts since they had used intermediate instead of strict scrutiny to evaluate the Transportation Department program. The courts should look at the mechanics of the program, O'Connor said, as well as two broad questions: whether the government had considered race-neutral means to accomplish its goals and whether the program would last longer than necessary to eliminate the effects of past discrimination.

Chief Justice Rehnquist and Justices Scalia, Kennedy, and Thomas joined the bulk of O'Connor's opinion, but only Kennedy joined all of it. The three other justices did not join a five-page passage justifying the decision to overturn the *Metro Broadcasting* precedent.

In a separate opinion, Scalia wrote that he was flatly opposed to racial classifications. "In my view," Scalia stated, "government can never have a 'compelling interest' in discriminating on the basis of race in order to 'make up for' past racial discrimination in the opposite direction."

In a separate concurrence, Thomas also declared his complete opposition to race-based policies or what he termed "so-called 'benign' discrimination." He said the policies "stamp minorities with a badge of inferiority" while provoking "resentment among those who believe that they have been wronged by the government's use of race."

The four dissenting justices produced three separate opinions. In the longest of the three, Stevens, joined by Ginsburg, complained about what he called the majority's "inability to differentiate between 'invidious' and 'benign' discrimination." The ruling, he said, "would disregard the difference between a 'No Trespassing' sign and a welcome mat. It would treat a Dixiecrat Senator's decision to vote against Thurgood Marshall's confirmation in order to keep African Americans off the Supreme Court as on a par with President Johnson's evaluation of his nominee's race as a positive factor."

Souter wrote a more legalistic dissent, joined by Ginsburg and Breyer. He argued that since Adarand had never asked to overrule *Fullilove,* the Transportation Department program should be evaluated under intermediate scrutiny. And under either standard, he suggested, the program would pass constitutional muster.

In a final dissent, Ginsburg, joined by Breyer, emphasized what she called "the considerable field of agreement" among the justices. "The divisions in this difficult case," she said, "should not obscure the Court's recognition of the persistence of racial inequality and a majority's acknowledgment of Congress' authority to act affirmatively, not only to end discrimination, but also to counteract discrimination's lingering effects."

The Court's ruling cheered opponents of affirmative action. "We see this decision as the beginning of the end of affirmative action as we know it," said Paul Kamenar of the Washington Legal Foundation. Pendley confidently predicted the lower courts would throw out the Transportation Department program. "It's a dead duck," he said.

Minority business leaders voiced disappointment, or even dejection, with the ruling. "I think the decision sounds the death knell for affirmative action and minority set-asides," Robert Johnson, president of the Black Entertainment Television cable network, told the *Washington Post.*

But some civil rights advocates took a more optimistic view, arguing that many affirmative action programs would survive the new test of strict scrutiny. "Federal contracting programs designed to level the playing field for small, disadvantaged businesses were passed by Congress after extensive proof that minority-owned and women-owned businesses had been unfairly excluded—and they still are," Penda Hair, an attorney with the NAACP Legal Defense and Educational Fund, wrote in the *Los Angeles Times*.

On Capitol Hill, lawmakers divided generally along party lines on the issue. Senate Majority Leader Bob Dole, Republican of Kansas, said the ruling was "one more reason for the federal government to get out of the race-preference business." But Rep. Kweisi Mfume, a Maryland Democrat and one-time chairman of the Congressional Black Caucus, glimpsed in the ruling some reason for optimism for his side. He said the Court had "set out the way that you proceed to justify [affirmative action] constitutionally."

At the White House, press secretary Mike McCurry took a wait-and-see attitude on the day of the ruling. "We need to look at it very carefully," he told reporters.

In a longer statement the next day, Clinton tried to have it both ways. "I have always believed that affirmative action is needed to remedy discrimination and to create a more inclusive society that truly provides equal opportunity," the president's statement said. "But I have also said that affirmative action must be carefully justified and must be done the right way. The Court's opinion ... is not inconsistent with that view."

Reapportionment and Redistricting

Race Can't Be "Predominant Factor" for District Lines

Miller v. Johnson, decided by a 5–4 vote, June 29, 1995; Kennedy wrote the opinion; Ginsburg, Stevens, Souter, and Breyer dissented. *(See excerpts, p. 232.)*

When Southern states redrew congressional districts after the 1990 census, the Justice Department pressured them to create additional black-majority districts to comply with the federal Voting Rights Act. While metropolitan areas lent themselves to compact black districts, other so-called majority-minority districts could be created only by stitching together widely dispersed black neighborhoods.

The resulting district maps looked peculiar in some places, but they produced dramatic results. The number of blacks in Congress increased from 26 in 1990 to 39 in 1992, with much of the increase from Southern states. Many white voters were disturbed by the overtly racial line-drawing. Some challenged the redistricting plans as violations of their rights under the Fourteenth Amendment's Equal Protection Clause.

Rep. Cynthia McKinney, Democrat from Georgia, talks with reporters following Supreme Court arguments in a challenge by white voters to the state's congressional redistricting plan. The court threw out the plan, saying that race had improperly been the main consideration in drawing McKinney's district.

The first of those challenges, from North Carolina, reached the Supreme Court in 1993 and produced a controversial 5–4 decision, *Shaw v. Reno,* that allowed white voters to contest "highly irregular" district lines drawn on the basis of race. *(See* Supreme Court Yearbook, 1992–1993, *pp. 20–23.)* Two years later, the Court agreed to hear two similar challenges, these from Georgia and Louisiana. The Louisiana case, *United States v. Hays,* ended anticlimactically, but the Georgia dispute produced a second Court ruling to limit the use of race in drawing voting district lines.

Georgia in 1991 adopted a redistricting plan that called for two of the state's eleven districts to have majority black populations. But the Voting Rights Act required Georgia to obtain "preclearance" from the Justice Department for the plan, and the department refused. A second plan was also rejected before the state agreed on a third plan in 1992 that created three majority-black districts. One of the districts—the Eleventh—stretched from the Atlanta suburbs across the state to pick up black areas in two coastal cities, Augusta and Savannah. Voters in the new district elected a black Democrat, Cynthia McKinney, to the House of Representatives.

Five white voters who were placed in the district filed suit against the plan, claiming that it segregated voters on the basis of race in violation of the Equal Protection Clause. In 1994, a three-judge federal district court agreed. In its 2–1 decision, the panel held that race-based redistricting is subject to strict scrutiny—the most rigorous standard of judicial review—whenever race is "the overriding, predominant force" in drawing the lines. The court said the legislature's racial intent was evident from the shape of the Eleventh Congressional District as well as from the testimony of legislators themselves. And the judges said the state's interest in eradicating past discrimination was not sufficiently compelling to justify the district's design.

The state's governor, Zell Miller, a Democrat, appealed the ruling to the Supreme Court. The Justice Department, which had intervened in the case on the state's side, also appealed, as did a group of black and white voters affected by the ruling. The Court agreed to hear the case, along with a second case challenging a Louisiana redistricting plan that fashioned a black majority district through the state's midsection.

The two cases were argued before the Court on April 19. The Louisiana case went first, but several of the justices questioned the voters' standing to bring the suit because they lived outside the district they were challenging.

Still, conservative justices made clear their leanings in the case. Justice Scalia sharply challenged Louisiana's attorney general, Richard Ieyoub, by asking whether the redistricting plan was based on an assumption that "people vote by race and we must district by race." When Ieyoub said the plan was designed to give blacks "a fair opportunity" to gain office, Scalia shot back: "Do you think this will help society get away from race—eliminate rather than entrench it?"

When Georgia's turn came, its special counsel, David F. Walpert, worked to cast the case as a question of judicial deference to legislative judgment in a highly political area. "I don't think we should be making judgment about what is good and bad in redistricting," Walpert said.

Several of the liberal-leaning justices picked up the point in their questions to Walpert and later to the plaintiffs' attorney, A. Lee Parks of Atlanta. Justice Breyer asked Parks whether courts would have to re-examine every redistricting plan that took race, religion, or nationality into account. "We don't close the door just because it's going to be bothersome," Parks answered.

Solicitor General Drew S. Days III, who argued in defense of both redistricting plans, drew especially critical questions about the Justice Department's role in pressuring the states. "Was it the policy of the Justice Department to insist on maximization [of black districts]?" Justice O'Connor asked. "It certainly appears to be the case."

Days countered with an emphatic denial: "I don't accept the characterization of the Court. I won't dignify it by going into details." Still, even moderate Justice Souter appeared troubled by the department's role. He remarked at one point that the Georgia plan was clearly drawn up solely to comply with Justice Department objections.

The Court announced its rulings in the two cases on the last day of its term, June 29. In the Louisiana case, the Court unanimously ruled that the plaintiffs had no standing to bring the suit and ordered the case dismissed. *(See p. 93.)* But in the Georgia case, the Court ruled the redistricting plan unconstitutional and set a new standard for judging racial line-drawing in all future cases.

Writing for a five-justice majority, Justice Kennedy said the earlier decision in *Shaw* did not limit challenges to plans that created irregularly shaped districts. The shape of the district, he explained, was simply "circumstantial evidence" that race had been "the dominant and controlling rationale" in drawing district lines.

Instead, plaintiffs had to prove that race was "the predominant factor motivating the legislature's decision to place a significant number of voters within or without a particular district," Kennedy said. To make that showing, he continued, plaintiffs had to prove that the legislature "subordinated traditional race-neutral districting principles such as compactness, contiguity, respect for political subdivisions or communities defined by actual shared interests, to racial considerations."

Applying that standard, Kennedy said the lower court had correctly concluded that race had been the predominant factor in drawing Georgia's plan. On that basis, he added, the plan was subject to strict scrutiny and could be sustained only if it served a compelling state interest and was narrowly tailored to meet that purpose. And on that point, Kennedy criticized the Justice Department's reading of the Voting Rights Act, which he said amounted to requiring a maximum number of majority black districts. That interpretation was wrong, he concluded, and thus could not serve as Georgia's justification for the redistricting plan.

Chief Justice Rehnquist and Justices O'Connor, Scalia, and Thomas concurred in the ruling. In a brief concurrence, O'Connor said the decision did not cast doubt on the vast majority of congressional districts in the country even if race had been considered in the redistricting process.

The dissenting justices, however, argued the ruling did throw the redistricting process into uncertainty and turmoil. States may be required to consider race by "statutory mandates and political realities," Justice Ginsburg wrote in the main dissent. The Court's ruling, she said, would invite "searching review" of racial redistricting, leaving lawmakers with no assurance that plans "conscious of race" would be upheld.

Turning to Georgia's plan itself, Ginsburg said it met traditional districting principles since it was not markedly less compact than the state's other districts. The plan, she concluded, "merited this Court's approbation, not its condemnation."

Justices Stevens and Breyer concurred in all of Ginsburg's dissent. Souter joined all but the part discussing the shape of the challenged Eleventh District. Stevens also added a short dissent questioning the standing of the voters to bring the suit at all.

The ruling provoked sharply critical reaction from black lawmakers and civil rights groups. They warned that many of the newly elected black members of Congress could lose their seats. "If we go back and resegregate our political institutions, we're messing up our nation," said Elaine Jones, director of the NAACP Legal Defense and Educational Fund. McKinney, who faced the prospect of seeking re-election in a significantly reshaped district, called the ruling "a setback for democracy."

President Clinton also criticized the decision. In a statement, he called the ruling a "setback in the struggle to ensure that all Americans participate fully in the electoral process."

Conservative interest groups, however, hailed the ruling. "... [T]he Supreme Court has reaffirmed the fundamental principle that people have a right not to be treated according to the color of their skin," said Thomas Jipping, director of the conservative Center for Law and Democracy. The two black Republican members of Congress —Gary Franks of Connecticut and J. C. Watts of Oklahoma—also praised the decision. "We have black districts, red districts, brown districts, yellow districts," Franks told a news conference. "We should have only American districts."

In Georgia, the lead plaintiff, Davida Johnson, said the decision showed that the country has "a color-blind Constitution." Attorney Parks said the ruling would prevent the Justice Department from pressuring states to use race as the basis for redistricting plans. "We've cut off the head of the wicked witch of the Justice Department," Parks told reporters.

Advocates and experts all agreed the Georgia ruling would lead to more challenges to congressional redistricting plans. The justices themselves swiftly provided confirming evidence. Just hours after leaving the bench for the start of the summer recess, the Court announced that it would hear two more racial redistricting cases, from North Carolina and Texas, in its next term. *(See Chapter 5, Preview of 1995–1996 Term.)*

School Desegregation

Judge Told to Reconsider Costly Integration Plan

Missouri v. Jenkins, decided by a 5–4 vote, June 12, 1995; Rehnquist wrote the opinion; Souter, Stevens, Ginsburg, and Breyer dissented. *(See excerpts, p. 183.)*

The federal judge overseeing a school desegregation suit in Kansas City, Missouri, fashioned a bold plan to bring white students from the suburbs back into the predominantly black school system. Beginning in 1985, U.S. District Court Judge Russell Clark ordered a series of far-reaching and costly moves to upgrade Kansas City's schools. Among the changes Clark ordered were 30 percent salary increases for teachers and construction of new "magnet schools" with expensive facilities and equipment.

Clark required the state of Missouri to pay for about half of the overall cost, which reached more than $1.4 billion by 1995. The state fought the plan, arguing that it cost too much and went beyond the need to correct past segregation.

This year, the Supreme Court bluntly told the judge he had gone too far. The decision cleared the way for the state to reduce its payments to Kansas City schools. To federal judges in the 200 other pending desegregation suits, it sent a strong signal that they should move more quickly to restore school systems to local control.

Missouri had taken the Kansas City case, which was originally filed in 1977, to the Court twice before. In 1989, the justices declined to consider the state's request to review Clark's desegregation plan. The Court did agree to look at the state's second appeal, which challenged Clark's order requiring the city to nearly double its local property tax to pay for its share of the desegregation program. But in a 5–4 decision, the Court in 1990

Students at Kansas City's Central High School do warm-up exercises in a physical education class. A federal judge ordered expensive improvements in the school as part of a desegregation plan, but the Supreme Court said he went too far in parts of his ruling.

effectively upheld the judge's order. *(See* Supreme Court Yearbook, 1989–1990, *pp. 20–21.)*

The state filed a third appeal in 1994, asking the Court to consider two issues. The first question was whether the judge had been wrong in refusing to lift his desegregation decrees "solely because" student achievement scores in the district remained below national averages. The state also asked the justices to decide whether the order for salary increases was improper because it did not "directly address and relate to the constitutional violation"— that is, the prior, legally mandated racial segregation.

The arguments before the justices on January 11 were procedurally complex. The state's lawyer, Assistant Attorney General John Munich, faced critical questions on whether the state was improperly making a second request to consider the validity of Clark's overall desegregation plan. Substantively, however, several of the Court's conservatives openly voiced sympathy with Munich's argument that the desegregation plan went too far and had gone on too long.

Justice Scalia, for example, questioned how the substandard achievement scores could be related to past desegregation. "There's nobody in that system below the eighth grade who has been subject to unequal spending," Scalia said. Later, Scalia was even more direct in an exchange with Deputy Solicitor General Paul Bender, who argued for the Clinton administration in support of the judge's ruling. "National norms!" Scalia exclaimed. "Half the country is below national norms."

Theodore M. Shaw, an attorney with the NAACP Legal Defense and Educational Fund who argued for the plaintiffs, countered that Judge Clark had never said that test scores must reach a certain level before court supervision would end. Instead, Shaw said, test scores were "one factor" in determining whether the school district had removed "the vestiges" of past discrimination.

But Kennedy insisted that the judge's plan seemed designed to maintain control over the school system indefinitely. "I see no end to this," he declared.

When Chief Justice Rehnquist opened his opinion for the Court five months later, he also expressed impatience with the length of the litigation. He noted that the case was entering "its 18th year" and later complained that there were "no limits to the duration of the District Court's involvement." And he said the judge had no legal basis for using magnet schools to try to draw white students from the suburbs into the city school systems. The plan amounted to an "interdistrict remedy," Rehnquist said, that would be permissible only if the suburban districts themselves had engaged in racial discrimination.

Rehnquist also said Clark had gone too far in pursuing the goal of "desegregative attractiveness." Pointedly, he noted that the desegregation order had raised expenditures in the Kansas City system to $9,412 per pupil—well above the levels of surrounding districts, which ranged from $2,854 to $5,956 per student. The salary increases were "too far removed" from correcting past discrimination, he concluded. As for the issue of test scores, Rehnquist said they were not "the appropriate test" for determining whether the effects of segregation had been eliminated.

The decision returned the case to the Eighth U.S. Circuit Court of Appeals for further proceedings, presumably including a remand to Judge Clark. Justices O'Connor, Scalia, Kennedy, and Thomas joined in the opinion. O'Connor wrote a concurring opinion to defend the Court's procedures in handling the case, rebutting criticisms made in the dissenting opinion.

Thomas added a strongly written, deeply personal concurring opinion that boldly challenged the use of school desegregation suits to try to remedy racial imbalances. "It never ceases to amaze me," Thomas began, "that the courts are so willing to assume that anything that is predominantly black must be inferior." Racial imbalance did not necessarily harm black youths or violate the Constitution, he wrote. And the courts' efforts to bring about demographic changes had led them into what Thomas called a "usurpation of the traditionally local control over education."

Souter, who wrote the main dissent, sharply attacked the procedures in the case. "The Court's process of orderly adjudication has broken down in this case," he began. The Court agreed to consider only the test score and salary increase issues, he insisted, not the validity of the judge's main desegregation decrees.

On those issues, Souter continued, the Court had no basis for overturning the judge's ruling. The state had not tried to prove that it had eliminated the effects of past discrimination, Souter said, but test scores "will clearly be relevant" if the state did so later. As for the salary increases, they were "an important element in remedying the systemwide reduction in student achievement resulting from segregation" in Kansas City schools.

Justices Stevens, Ginsburg, and Breyer joined Souter's dissent. Ginsburg added a brief dissent. Schools had been racially segregated in Missouri until 1954, she emphasized, and Judge Clark had found that the effects of segregation still lingered thirty years later. "Given the deep, inglorious history of segregation in Missouri," Ginsburg concluded, "to curtail desegregation at this time and in this manner is an action at once too swift and too soon."

In Missouri, the opposing sides in the case continued to clash after the ruling. Attorney General Jay Nixon said the decision would allow the state to "stop the inequity" of providing a disproportionate share of state aid to the Kansas City system. The opinion shows the state must provide "equality of opportunity" but not "equality of result," Nixon said.

But Arthur Benson 2d, the local lawyer for the black school children and parents who brought the case, called the decision "a defeat for school children" that threatened gains made over the past ten years. "We lost," Benson told a meeting of parents three days after the ruling. "It's hard to take it, and we're going to have to pay for it."

One month later, the state and city reached agreement on a schedule for phasing out all state assistance for the desegregation plan by 1999. The agreement did not affect the city's share—about half of the overall cost.

Term Limits

State Measures to Limit Tenure in Congress Thrown Out

U.S. Term Limits, Inc. v. Thornton, decided by a 5–4 vote, May 22, 1995; Stevens wrote the opinion; Thomas, Rehnquist, O'Connor, and Scalia dissented. *(See excerpts, p. 142.)*

Term limits for Congress grew in the space of a few years from a fringe political idea into a powerful national movement. But the Supreme Court dealt the cause a crippling blow by ruling that neither states nor Congress can restrict congressional tenure except by amending the Constitution.

The movement was born from Republican frustration with forty years of Democratic rule on Capitol Hill and fed by an upsurge of antigovernment sentiment. Supporters said term limits would increase public accountability and electoral competition. Polls registered popular support for term limits at 70 percent or higher.

Opponents argued that term limits would limit voter choice, deprive Congress of its ablest members, and cede power to the president and executive branch. Few people were swayed. By November 1994, twenty-one states had adopted term limits by way of ballot initiatives, typically by wide margins; two other states enacted term limits through legislative action: Utah, in 1994, and New Hampshire in early 1995.

The constitutionality of state term limits, however, had been in doubt from the time of the first initiative, in Colorado in 1990. Supporters contended that states derived the authority to fix congressional terms from a provision of the Constitution that gives states power to regulate the "Times, Places, and Manner of holding Elections for Senators and Representatives" (Art. I, Sec. 4).

On that basis, term limit supporters fashioned two kinds of measures to accomplish their goal. The original measures flatly prohibited anyone serving in Congress past the chosen time period—typically, twelve years for senators and six to twelve years for representatives. A modified version, aimed at easing constitutional problems, prohibited a multiterm incumbent from being listed on the ballot but allowed a write-in candidacy.

Opponents maintained that both versions violated the Constitution by adding a qualification to those listed in the document: age, U.S. citizenship,

Paul Jacob, executive director of U.S. Term Limits, Inc., vows to continue the fight for congressional term limits despite the Supreme Court's decision throwing out state laws to restrict congressional tenure. The Court ruled, 5–4, that a constitutional amendment would be needed to set limits on how long representatives or senators can serve.

and residency in the state from which the member was elected (Art. I, Secs. 2 and 3). They said the Court had ruled in a 1969 decision, *Powell v. McCormack*, that Congress itself had no power to add to those qualifications. Neither did the states, they concluded.

The issue reached the Court in a case from Arkansas, where voters had given 2–1 approval in November 1992 to a measure barring senators from the ballot after twelve years in office and House members after six years of service. A state court judge ruled the measure unconstitutional in a suit filed in the name of Bobbie E. Hill, the then-president of the state chapter of the League of Women Voters. The Arkansas Supreme Court upheld the ruling in a 5–2 decision in March 1994.

The national advocacy group U.S. Term Limits, Inc., which had intervened to defend the measure, joined the state in asking the U.S. Supreme Court to settle the issue. Rep. Ray Thornton, a Democratic lawmaker from Little Rock, had the dubious honor of being the first listed respondent in the case. But the League of Women Voters took the lead in urging the Court to affirm the lower court rulings. Over the summer, the Clinton administration joined the case too, telling the Court that state term limit measures for Congress were "inconsistent with the structure of the federal system."

While the case was being argued before the Court on November 29, several dozen pro-term limit demonstrators marched on the sidewalk outside, carrying placards and chanting "Hey, hey, ho, ho, career incumbents have to go." Inside the courtroom, the justices heard arguments in an expanded ninety-minute session from Arkansas Attorney General Winston Bryant and Washington lawyer John G. Kester, who defended term limits, and Washington attorney Louis Cohen and U.S. Solicitor General Drew S. Days III, who opposed them.

Bryant opened by telling the justices that the Framers "envisioned a Congress of citizen-legislators who would not stay in Congress indefinitely." But he and Kester drew skeptical questions from Justices Souter, Ginsburg, and Breyer about the state's authority to prescribe qualifications for Congress or the feasibility of a write-in candidacy for term-limited incumbents. In his turn, Cohen insisted that the Constitution gave voters "the chance to decide every two years who will represent us" in Congress. And Days maintained that the Arkansas measure could not be viewed as a permissible regulation of election mechanics.

Six months later, the Court handed down its decision: a broadly written, 5–4 ruling that invalidated the Arkansas measure and all other state term limits with it. Writing for the majority, Justice Stevens began by stressing that the Court had already reviewed the history of the Constitutional Convention in *Powell* before holding that Congress could not add new qualifications for serving in the House or the Senate. Retracing the debate at the Constitutional Convention, he concluded that the Framers likewise intended the states to have no role in determining the qualifications for serving in Congress.

"Permitting individual States to formulate diverse qualifications for their representatives," Stevens wrote, "would result in a patchwork of state qualifications, undermining the uniformity and the national character that the Framers envisioned and sought to ensure."

Moreover, Stevens said, term limits would also violate one aspect of popular sovereignty: "the right of the people to vote for whom they wish." The option of a write-in candidacy could not save the term limit measure, Stevens added, since the ballot access restriction was aimed at "evading the dictates of the Qualifications Clause." Justices Kennedy, Souter, Ginsburg, and Breyer joined Stevens's opinion.

Kennedy, evidently the swing vote in the case, wrote an eight-page concurring opinion. State term limits would violate "fundamental principles of federalism," he explained. "… [T]here exists a federal right of citizenship, a relationship between the people of the Nation and their National Government with which the States may not interfere."

Thomas wrote an eighty-eight-page dissenting opinion that impressed Court-watchers with its historical breadth and bold vision of state sovereignty. The Constitution is "simply silent" on term limits, Thomas argued.

Under the Tenth Amendment, the states therefore retained the authority to prescribe "eligibility requirements" for candidates for Congress.

Thomas mocked the majority's claimed deference to popular sovereignty. He noted that the ruling invalidated a provision "that won nearly 60 percent of the votes cast in a direct election and that carried every congressional district in the state." Chief Justice Rehnquist and Justices O'Connor and Scalia joined the opinion.

Term limit supporters remained determined despite the ruling. "The American people overwhelmingly want term limits," Paul Jacob, executive director of U.S. Term Limits, told reporters. "Entrenched incumbents in Congress cannot stop it, nor will this Supreme Court decision."

A constitutional amendment seemed unlikely, however, at least in the near term. Many Republicans endorsed term limits in their successful bid to recapture control of the House and the Senate in the November 1994 elections. But when the House voted on the issue March 29, four different constitutional amendments all fell well short of the two-thirds majority required for passage.

To change that result, term limit supporters vowed to try to use the issue in the 1996 campaign against lawmakers who refused to back the amendment. But lawmakers of both parties said they detected waning interest in the issue among voters.

For his part, former House Speaker Thomas Foley, a Washington State Democrat defeated for re-election in 1994 in part because of his opposition to term limits, was ready to write the movement's obituary. "My belief," he told a news conference on the day of the Court's ruling, "is that term limits is dead."

Gun Control

U.S. Ban on Guns Near Schools Held Unconstitutional

United States v. Lopez, decided by a 5–4 vote, April 26, 1995; Rehnquist wrote the opinion; Breyer, Stevens, Souter, and Ginsburg dissented. *(See excerpts, p. 128.)*

When Americans became alarmed about an apparent epidemic of guns in the nation's schools, Congress did the natural thing. It passed a federal law to stem the problem. But five years later, the Supreme Court ruled the law unconstitutional, saying that it went beyond Congress's powers to regulate interstate commerce.

The Gun-Free School Zones Act of 1990 made it a federal crime to possess a firearm anywhere within 1,000 feet of a public, private, or parochial school. The bill passed Congress in 1990 with little opposition. When he signed the bill into law, however, President George Bush did express reser-

A security guard at a high school in Brooklyn, New York, uses a metal detector to check a student before he is allowed to enter the school. Public concern about guns at schools was high, but the Supreme Court threw out a federal law Congress passed to deal with the problem.

vations that it intruded on the law enforcement responsibilities of the states.

Alfonso Lopez, a senior at a San Antonio high school, was charged under the law in March 1992. Lopez, who had not been in trouble with the law before, told officials he was delivering the gun for a friend to another student for use in a gang war. His lawyer, assistant federal defender John Carter, decided to challenge the law on constitutional grounds.

Carter's motion to dismiss the indictment was rejected, and Lopez was convicted and given a six-month prison sentence. But the Fifth U.S. Circuit Court of Appeals ruled that the law could not be applied without proof of some connection to interstate commerce, and it threw out the conviction. The government then took the case to the Supreme Court.

Solicitor General Drew S. Days III argued the case for the Clinton administration on November 8. Days called the appeals court ruling an "extraordinary step." But Days drew sharp questions from several of the justices, who pressed him to specify some limit on Congress's power under the Commerce Clause. "If this is covered, what is left of enumerated powers?" Justice O'Connor asked. "What is left that Congress cannot do?"

Rehnquist picked up the point, but Days again avoided the question. Later, Ginsburg asked again whether there was any limit on what Congress could do. Again, Days ducked. In exasperation, Scalia declared: "Don't give away anything. They might want to do it next year."

In his turn, Carter drew critical questions from some of the Court's liberal justices. Justice Breyer, a former congressional aide, defended Congress's basis for concluding that guns in schools affect interstate commerce. "People will not move to places in this country where children are being killed in schools," Breyer said.

Carter said later he felt confident of victory as he left the courtroom. His confidence was well placed. On April 26, the Court struck the law down by a 5–4 vote.

Rehnquist's opinion for the majority was straightforward and compact—only nineteen pages. The law had nothing to do with commerce or any sort of economic enterprise, he said. Nor was it a part of a larger regulatory scheme. And the law did not require the government to prove a connection to interstate commerce in any individual case.

Upholding the law on that basis, Rehnquist said, "would bid fair to convert congressional authority under the Commerce Clause to a general police power of the sort retained by the States." He conceded that the Court had given "great deference" to Congress in the past. But unless it drew a line this time, he concluded, "there never will be a distinction between what is truly national and what is truly local." Justices O'Connor, Scalia, Kennedy, and Thomas joined the opinion.

In a significant concurrence, Kennedy, joined by O'Connor, depicted the ruling as narrow. Kennedy recalled that the Court had struck down several laws on Commerce Clause grounds in the early twentieth century but had taken a broader view since the New Deal. Now, he said, both the Court and the legal system generally have "an immense stake in the stability of our Commerce Clause jurisprudence." To make the point explicit, Kennedy concluded by saying that Congress was free to regulate "in the commercial sphere" on the assumption that the country has a single national market "and a unified purpose to build a stable national economy."

Thomas, however, took a more provocative tack. He argued in a twenty-one-page concurrence that the Court—"at an appropriate juncture"—should tighten the standards for Congress to exercise its Commerce Clause power. The Court had strayed in the 1930s from "the original understanding" of the Commerce Clause, he said, when it allowed Congress to regulate any activity that "substantially affects" commerce.

In his dissenting opinion, Breyer contended that the gun law "falls well within the scope of the commerce power as this Court has understood that power over the last half-century." The issue, he said, was whether Congress had a rational basis for finding a connection between gun-related school violence and interstate commerce. To prove that it did, Breyer listed in an appendix more than 160 sources—congressional hearings, federal reports, and various books, articles, and news stories—documenting the problems of school violence and the effects of inadequate education on the country's economic strength.

"Congress could therefore have found a substantial educational problem—teachers unable to teach, students unable to learn—and concluded that guns near schools contribute substantially to the size and scope of that problem," Breyer wrote. And that problem, he said, "makes a significant difference to our economic, as well as our social, well-being." Justices Stevens, Souter, and Ginsburg joined in Breyer's dissent.

Souter and Stevens added dissents of their own. Souter argued the ruling amounted to a departure from judicial restraint by second-guessing Congress's judgment about its Commerce Clause power. Stevens answered Thomas's historical point. The market for handguns among school-age children is "substantial" today, Stevens said. "Whether or not the national interest in eliminating that market would have justified federal legislation in 1789," he concluded, "it surely does today."

The ruling provoked strong reaction in many quarters. Sen. Herb Kohl, the Wisconsin Democrat who sponsored the measure, called the decision "legal nitpicking." President Clinton criticized the ruling and asked the Justice Department to come up with a way to get around it. But some conservatives cheered the ruling and said it could start a process of narrowing federal authority in other areas. Notre Dame law professor Douglas Kmiec hailed the decision as the Court's most important case in half a century.

With a little time, however, calmer voices set in, suggesting the ruling was unlikely to have broad impact. "I tend to view this as a shot across Congress's bow," said Barry Friedman, a professor at Vanderbilt Law School who helped write a brief urging the Court to strike the law down. "The Court's saying, 'Why don't you guys pay attention and we won't have to do this?' "

The Court itself helped dampen speculation with a decision five days later in another criminal law case that had Commerce Clause overtones, *United States v. Robertson*. The defendant challenged a federal racketeering conviction on the ground that his operation of an Alaskan gold mine using the proceeds from drug transactions did not affect interstate commerce. The justices rejected his plea unanimously in an unsigned opinion. (*See p. 80.*)

In Congress, Kohl introduced a revised law to ban guns around schools that added some "findings" about the effects of guns in schools and required proof of some connection to interstate commerce for federal jurisdiction. The Clinton administration supported the new measure, but it faced opposition in the Republican-controlled Congress. Many GOP lawmakers favored a strengthened role for the states in the federal system.

Alfonso Lopez celebrated the Court's ruling by getting on with the rest of his life. Lopez had finished high school after his arrest, but he was forced to mark time while the Court pondered his case. Two weeks after the ruling, Lopez shipped out for basic training in the Marines.

James Acton, center, a high school student from Vernonia, Oregon, leaves the Supreme Court with friends and family members following Supreme Court arguments in his challenge to the school's drug-testing program for athletes. From left are Kathy Armstrong of the American Civil Liberties Union, brother Simon, and parents Judy and Wayne Acton. The Court later upheld the drug-testing program.

Drug Testing

Random Drug Tests for School Athletes Upheld

Vernonia School District No. 47J v. Acton, decided by a 6–3 vote, June 26, 1995; Scalia wrote the opinion; O'Connor, Stevens, and Souter dissented. *(See excerpts, p. 202.)*

Vernonia, Oregon, a logging community of about 3,000 people in the northwestern tip of the state, might seem far removed from the problem of teenage drug use. But in the late 1980s, disciplinary problems in the town's high school tripled, and officials became alarmed at what they thought were signs of an epidemic of drug use among students.

The problem seemed to be centered among the school's athletes. So the Vernonia school board in 1989 adopted a targeted antidrug policy: random drug testing for any students who wanted to participate in interscholastic athletics. This year, in a 6–3 ruling, the Supreme Court rejected one family's constitutional challenge to the program, clearing the way for school systems around the country to institute similar drug testing.

Vernonia's drug-testing policy required all student athletes to provide a urine sample at the start of the team's season. Each week thereafter, 10 percent of the team's members were chosen in a blind drawing for a new test. The program appeared to be popular among parents in the community. No one opposed the plan when the school board adopted it in 1989.

But Wayne and Judy Acton refused to give their permission for the drug test when their seventh-grade son, James, wanted to go out for the school's football team. Wayne Acton testified later that he thought the policy "kind of sets a bad tone for citizenship" because it told children "that they have to prove that they're innocent."

The Actons, represented by the Oregon chapter of the American Civil Liberties Union (ACLU), filed suit in federal district court in 1991, contending that the drug testing violated the Fourth Amendment's prohibition against "unreasonable" searches. The Supreme Court in 1989 had upheld mandatory drug testing programs for railroad employees involved in accidents and for federal customs agents, but it had never ruled on the constitutionality of random, suspicionless drug tests.

The trial judge rejected the Actons' suit, but the Ninth U.S. Circuit Court of Appeals in 1994 ruled that the program violated the Fourth Amendment and the comparable provision in the Oregon Constitution. The three-judge panel acknowledged the school district had an interest in deterring drug use and disciplinary problems but said it was outweighed by James Acton's privacy interest.

The ruling conflicted with a decision by the Seventh U.S. Circuit Court of Appeals sustaining a similar program. To resolve the conflict, the Supreme Court agreed in November to hear the Vernonia school board's effort to reinstate the testing.

The arguments in the case on March 28 ranged from the purpose of the Fourth Amendment to the nature of high school locker rooms. Chief Justice Rehnquist questioned whether privacy was really at stake since boys' locker rooms have rows of urinals and "guys walking around naked." But Thomas Christ, the Portland lawyer representing the Actons, insisted that it was "degrading" to be forced by the government to urinate on cue.

In his turn, Timothy Volpert, the Portland attorney representing the school board, argued that the testing was the only effective means for dealing with the increased drug use among students. But Justice O'Connor suggested the board should have first tried a program of testing individual students specifically suspected of drug use. "Isn't individualized suspicion pretty much what the Fourth Amendment was designed to require?" she asked.

The Court's decision two months later was a strong affirmation of the school board's policy. Justice Scalia began by emphasizing that school officials are normally permitted greater control over students than the government could exercise over adults. And the school board had ample justification for its program, both to protect athletes from the risk of injury and to deter drug use among students who viewed athletes as role models.

Against those governmental interests, Scalia said students' privacy interests were "negligible." Athletes have a lowered expectation of privacy, he said, because they "voluntarily" go out for a team and because school athletics have an inherent "element of communal undress." Moreover, he said, the results of the tests were disclosed only to parents and a limited number of school personnel; they were not provided to law enforcement or used for any other school disciplinary function.

The justices' lineup in the case was unusual. The Court's other strong conservatives on law enforcement issues—Rehnquist, Kennedy, and Thomas—joined Scalia's opinion. But so did President Clinton's two appointees, Breyer and Ginsburg, who had taken more moderate stands on most criminal law issues. Ginsburg cautioned in a brief concurrence, however, that the ruling did not necessarily sanction routine drug testing of all students.

More surprisingly, O'Connor broke with her conservative colleagues and wrote a dissenting opinion that severely criticized the drug-testing policy and the Court's rationale for upholding it. Under the ruling, O'Connor wrote, millions of students across the country could be "open to an intrusive bodily search" even though "the overwhelming majority ... have given school officials no reason whatsoever to suspect they use drugs at school." Stevens and Souter joined the opinion.

The Clinton administration, which filed a brief in support of the drug-testing policy, was quick to praise the ruling. Lee Brown, the White House drug policy adviser, called the decision "a victory for kids." But Steven Shapiro, the ACLU's national legal director, criticized the ruling. "It makes students second-class citizens," Shapiro said.

The impact of the ruling remained to be seen. Brown said he expected many school systems to adopt routine drug testing for athletes in middle schools and high schools. Reporters who questioned students found few who complained. But many coaches and school officials said they doubted the need for drug testing in their schools. And some said the costs of the test—about $20 per child to check for street drugs—would discourage widespread testing.

In Oregon, Timothy Volpert was pleased by the breadth of the Court's ruling, which he insisted could be read to support drug testing of all students. Volpert said school systems with serious drug problems "might almost have an obligation to consider" drug testing, but he cautioned that judges would likely scrutinize the justification for any programs that were challenged in court.

For his part, Christ said he and the Actons were disappointed, but they hoped the policy might still be struck down under the Oregon Constitution. That issue remained to be decided. Christ maintained that Oregon courts had applied the state's privacy protections more rigorously than had federal courts. But Volpert said he thought the lower courts would follow the Supreme Court's logic in interpreting the Oregon constitutional provisions.

Church and State

University Told to Fund Student Religious Publication

Rosenberger v. Rector and Visitors of University of Virginia, decided by a 5–4 vote, June 29, 1995; Kennedy wrote the opinion; Souter, Stevens, Ginsburg, and Breyer dissented. *(See excerpts, p. 215.)*

On the front page of its opening issue, the new student newspaper at the University of Virginia in 1990 promised to "challenge Christians to live, in word and deed, according to the faith they proclaim." The newspaper took its name, *Wide Awake,* from St. Paul's exhortation in his letter to the Romans to "awake from your slumber" because the time of salvation was near.

Like many other colleges and universities, the University of Virginia imposed a mandatory activity fee on students. The $14 per year fee went to an activity fund to support student publications and other organizations. After their first issue, the editors of *Wide Awake* sent their printing bill of $5,862 to the board that ran the fund for payment. But the board refused, citing its guidelines against funding "religious activities."

The university's refusal set up a new clash on a 200-year-old Constitutional issue: separation of church and state. And in a narrowly divided decision, the Supreme Court ruled that the university had to fund the newspaper on the same basis as other student publications. The ruling alarmed advocates of separation of church and state but encouraged religious groups, which said it could open the door to government funding for other religious activities.

The founder of the paper, Ronald Rosenberger, and his fellow editors filed a civil rights suit in federal district court, claiming that the refusal to support the paper violated their freedom of speech. The judge ruled that withholding funds from the paper did not violate the students' freedom of speech or freedom of religion.

On appeal, the Fourth U.S. Court of Appeals also rejected the suit but on different grounds. The three-judge panel agreed that the university's action violated the students' free speech rights but ruled it was necessary nonetheless to avoid an unconstitutional establishment of religion. Rosenberger asked the Court to review the ruling.

Ronald Rosenberger, right, cofounder of the religious newspaper *Wide Awake,* holds a copy outside the Supreme Court after arguments in his effort to force the University of Virginia to subsidize the publication through a student activity fund. The justices later ruled that the action violated Rosenberger's freedom of speech. At left is cofounder Robert Prince.

When the case was argued before the justices March 1, Rosenberger's lawyer, University of Chicago law professor Michael McConnell, opened by strongly insisting the university's refusal to fund the newspaper was simple discrimination against religion. "If my clients were the SDS [Students for a Democratic Society], if they were vegetarians, if they were black separatists, or whatever, there would be no need to be here today," said McConnell, a leading academic advocate of greater governmental "accommodation" of religion.

The university also turned to a law school professor, John C. Jeffries, Jr., to argue its case. Jeffries tried to bolster the school's position by shifting his argument away from the religion issue. "This case is not specifically about religion," Jeffries said. "It's about funding." The university, he said, was free to decide not to fund specific types of student activities as long as it did not censor particular viewpoints.

Both lawyers encountered critical questioning. Justice Ginsburg asked McConnell whether the Court had ever sanctioned direct financial support to a religious organization. McConnell cited a 1981 ruling that allowed a seminary student to receive aid from a scholarship program for the blind, but he acknowledged the case was not exactly the same. "I don't know of a case," Ginsburg concluded, sharply.

But Jeffries met a skeptical response when he acknowledged that the university guidelines permitted funding for a political advocacy organization such as the liberal Americans for Democratic Action. "Why is that different from a group that is trying to convert people to a particular religious belief?" Justice Scalia asked.

The Court's ruling, on the final day of its term June 29, gave religious advocates a nearly complete victory. Writing for a five-member majority, Justice Kennedy said the university was violating the First Amendment's Free Speech Clause because it "selects for disfavored treatment those student journalistic efforts with religious editorial viewpoints."

Funding the newspaper would not violate the Establishment Clause, however, Kennedy continued. He stressed that the student activity fund was not set up to advance religion and that organizations receiving funds had to disclaim any official sponsorship by the university. In addition, the money was not given directly to the newspaper but was used to pay its bills.

Chief Justice Rehnquist and Justices O'Connor, Scalia, and Thomas joined Kennedy's opinion. But O'Connor added a concurrence that took away slightly from the religious groups' victory. She stressed that she approved the funding because of the particular provisions of the program, including the requirement for disclaimers, the disbursement of funds to third-party vendors, and "the vigorous nature" of the university forum. The ruling, she added, should not be read to signal "the demise of the funding prohibition in Establishment Clause jurisprudence."

In his dissenting opinion, Justice Souter maintained that the ruling did cross a line that had never been crossed before. "The Court today, for the first time, approves direct funding of core religious activities by an arm of the state," Souter began. He stressed the evangelical nature of the newspaper, describing its articles as "straightforward exhortation" and "nothing other than the preaching of the word." Souter discounted the distinctions relied on by the majority to avoid finding an Establishment Clause violation. He said there was no constitutional difference between paying the bills for the newspaper and giving it money directly. The case did differ from a 1993 decision guaranteeing religious groups after-hours access to public school facilities on the same basis as other organizations, Souter said, because that case did not involve direct expenditure of public funds.

Justices Stevens, Ginsburg, and Breyer joined the opinion, which also traced the history of the Establishment Clause. Souter portrayed the clause as aimed at prohibiting any direct government support of religion. Justice

Thomas challenged that interpretation in a concurring opinion, insisting that the clause was never aimed at preventing incidental benefits to religious activities from neutral government programs.

Rosenberger, who had left the university while the case was pending, cheered the ruling. "No longer will universities be allowed to treat religious students as second-class students and religious speech as second-class speech," Rosenberger told reporters the day of the ruling.

Jay Alan Sekulow, legal director of the American Center for Law and Justice, an organization affiliated with television evangelist Pat Robertson, declared the Court had crossed "a critical threshold" in guaranteeing religious groups equal access to government programs. Groups that advocated strict separation of church and state agreed the ruling had crossed a significant barrier. "This is a sad day for religious liberty," said J. Brent Walker, general counsel for the Joint Baptist Committee on Public Affairs, which filed a brief in support of the university in the case.

Religious advocates immediately looked on the ruling as authority for upholding government vouchers for church-affiliated schools, but some experts cautioned that the ruling might not go that far. "The opinion does not announce a bright-line rule," said Douglas Laycock, a professor at the University of Texas Law School who filed a brief on Rosenberger's side in the case. "There are a lot of hedges and limitations to it."

"Both sides were either hoping or fearing that this would be a precedent for school vouchers," Laycock added. But the decision "left that issue open."

Church and State

State Cannot Bar Klan Cross from Capitol Plaza

Capitol Square Review and Advisory Board v. Pinette, decided by a 7–2 vote, June 29, 1995; Scalia wrote the main opinion; Stevens and Ginsburg dissented. *(See excerpts, p. 248.)*

A dispute over the right of the Ku Klux Klan to erect a cross next to the Ohio state capitol produced a Supreme Court ruling that could resolve the perennial fight over Christmas and Hanukkah displays on government property.

The Klan has used the burning cross as a rallying symbol and an instrument of intimidation since the nineteenth century. But in late November 1993, the Ohio chapter of the Klan sought permission to erect a nonincendiary Latin cross in front of the Ohio State Capitol. The purpose, Klan officer Donnie Carr stated in the application, was to express "respect for the holiday season" and "to assert the right of all religious views to be expressed on an equal basis on public property."

Ku Klux Klan members and protesters struggle over a cross the Klan erected in front of the Ohio state capitol in Columbus in 1993. Ohio officials tried to block the display, but the Supreme Court ruled that such action violated the First Amendment.

The Capitol Square Review and Advisory Board, which manages the Capitol Square area, had tried earlier in the month to head off the issue. The board voted on November 18 to bar all unattended displays from the area. But the action provoked a public protest since it also would have barred the Christmas tree and menorah traditionally displayed on the Capitol grounds every December. So, under pressure from the governor, the board nullified the action five days later.

The reversal cleared the way for the board to approve the Christmas tree and menorah, as usual, but left it in a bind on the Klan's application. After stalling for a few days, the board in early December turned the Klan down in what it called "a good faith attempt to comply with the Ohio and United States Constitutions, as they have been interpreted in relevant decisions by the Federal and State Courts."

The Klan promptly wrapped itself around the First Amendment in a federal civil rights suit brought in the name of its "grand titan," Vincent Pinette, and filed by an attorney from the Ohio chapter of the American Civil Liberties Union, Benson Wolman. A federal district court judge issued an injunction barring the state from blocking the cross. He agreed with the Klan that the Capitol Square was a traditional public forum, that the Klan's cross was private speech entitled to constitutional protection, and that permitting the display would not amount to an unconstitutional endorsement of religion by the state.

With its legal victory, the Klan proceeded to erect the ten-foot-high wooden cross. A cardboard sign attached at the base specified that the cross was "erected by private individuals without government support." Vandals tore the cross down within a day. Church leaders in Columbus then responded by erecting a dozen or so crosses on the site where the Klan cross had stood.

After the Christmas season ended, the state filed an appeal, insisting that it had to bar the Klan cross to avoid violating the First Amendment's ban against establishment of religion. But the Sixth U.S. Circuit Court of Appeals in July 1994 rejected the plea. Ohio then asked the Supreme Court to review the ruling, and the justices agreed.

Michael Renner, chief counsel in the Ohio attorney general's office, encountered rough going as soon as the arguments began before the justices April 26. Under critical questions from several of the justices, Renner tried to argue that the location of a cross "at the very seat of state government" would appear to the "reasonable observer" to be an endorsement of religion. But Justice Scalia forced him to acknowledge that if the state permitted posters by the Libertarian Party or the Nazi Party, the public probably would not regard them as supported by the government.

For his part, attorney Benson Wolman, a member of the Ohio and national ACLU boards, walked a delicate line. He defended the Klan's right to erect a cross but argued that religious displays could be barred if they would be seen as government-endorsed. Some restrictions, he said, "might be appropriate if there were [an] overwhelming appearance of endorsement."

Court watchers felt sure the justices would rule against the state, so many wondered why the case was still pending when the Court met on the last day of its term, June 29. The reason, it turned out, was a division among the justices on the legal rationale for the decision. Seven justices agreed the state had violated the Klan's free speech rights by seeking to bar the cross. But they split into two groups on the reason.

Scalia led a plurality of four justices in taking a maximum position to accommodate religious expression on public property. As long as a public forum was open to all on a nondiscriminatory basis, private religious expression had to be allowed, Scalia said. As for "the so-called endorsement test," Scalia said it had "no basis in our Establishment Clause jurisprudence." Chief Justice Rehnquist and Justices Kennedy and Thomas concurred.

The critical votes for the ruling, however, came from Justices O'Connor, Souter, and Breyer. The three said that the Klan cross would not be viewed as a government-sponsored display but insisted that the endorsement test was the proper standard for deciding the case. "I see no necessity to carve out ... an exception to the endorsement test for the public forum context," O'Connor wrote in an opinion joined by the other two.

Souter wrote a second concurring opinion, arguing the state should have taken steps short of prohibiting the cross such as requiring a more prominent disclaimer or even barring all unattended displays in the area. O'Connor and Breyer joined his opinion, too.

Stevens was the only justice to side with the state's position that private religious displays could be prohibited at the Capitol altogether. Free-standing structures "in front of buildings plainly identified with the state" imply state approval, he said. For that reason, the state should have "considerable leeway" in approving such displays.

Ginsburg dissented more narrowly. She said that the judge's injunction violated the Establishment Clause because it did not mandate a disclaimer. With a sturdy, explicit disclaimer on the cross, the case would have presented a "more difficult" question, Ginsburg said—a question better left "for another day and case."

The Klan case ruling was somewhat obscured in the rush of last-day decisions, which included a second religion decision barring public universities from discriminating against student religious publications. *(See p. 50.)* Later, however, advocates and experts on both sides of the issue agreed the ruling on the Klan cross would encourage private groups to put up more Christmas and Hanukkah displays on government property.

"Clearly, private Nativity scenes can be displayed in public forums," said Jay Alan Sekulow of the American Center for Law and Justice. "That should end that dispute."

Barry Lynn, executive director of Americans United for Separation of Church and State, agreed, but he viewed the development less favorably. "There will be more symbols this December than there were last December," Lynn said, "but I'm quite sure that the spiritual nature of Americans will not be elevated by their presence."

Freedom of Speech

State's Ban on Anonymous Leafleting Is Struck Down

McIntyre v. Ohio Elections Commission, decided by a 7–2 vote, April 19, 1995; Stevens wrote the opinion; Scalia and Rehnquist dissented. *(See excerpts, p. 119.)*

Margaret McIntyre thought of herself as a concerned citizen and tax-payer when she passed out leaflets in 1988 opposing a proposed school tax levy in the Westerville, Ohio, school district. But an official of the suburban district along Columbus's northeast side viewed her as a lawbreaker. And after she was fined $100 for violating a state law banning unsigned campaign literature, she initiated a First Amendment challenge that produced a Supreme Court ruling affirming freedom of speech for anonymous political agitators.

"Waste of taxpayers' dollars must be stopped," McIntyre warned her fellow residents in a one-page flyer distributed at a meeting at one of the Westerville schools in April 1988. "Our children's education and welfare must come first. WASTE CAN NO LONGER BE TOLERATED."

Noting that the flyer was unsigned, an assistant school superintendent warned McIntyre that she was violating an Ohio law—comparable to provisions in virtually every other state—that required campaign literature to include the name and address of the author or campaign organization. McIntyre, undeterred, returned to a later meeting to pass out more leaflets.

The school levy failed at the next two elections but finally passed in November 1988. McIntyre's tactics still rankled school officials, however. So in April 1989 the assistant superintendent who had originally warned her filed a complaint charging McIntyre with violating the election law. The Ohio Elections Commission agreed and fined her $100.

A lower court judge in Columbus threw out the citation and fine, saying the law was unconstitutional as applied to McIntyre because she "did not mislead the public nor act in a surreptitious manner." But the Ohio Supreme Court upheld the law and fine. In a divided decision, the state high court said the law served important state interests by providing voters information to judge the validity of campaign literature and identifying anyone engaged in "fraud, libel, or false advertising." The court added that the law imposed only a "minor burden" on political activists.

McIntyre died after the Ohio court ruling, but her husband, Joseph McIntyre, continued the case, represented by David Goldberger, a lawyer with the Ohio American Civil Liberties Union and director of the clinical program at the Ohio State University College of Law. In a petition to the Supreme Court, Goldberger contended the state law violated the First Amendment's protection for freedom of speech. The justices agreed to review the case and scheduled it for argument in the first month of the 1994–1995 term.

Andrew Sutter, the assistant attorney general defending the law, drew especially rough questioning from the justices when the case was argued October 12. Sutter reiterated that the state had an interest in informing the electorate about the authorship of campaign literature and preventing fraud. But Justice O'Connor was unconvinced.

Margaret McIntyre circulated an unsigned leaflet that asked voters in the Westerville, Ohio, school district to reject a proposed property tax levy. McIntyre was fined $100 for violating a state law against anonymous campaign materials, but the Supreme Court ruled the measure was unconstitutional.

VOTE NO

ISSUE 19 SCHOOL TAX LEVY

Last election Westerville Schools asked us to vote yes for new buildings and expansions programs. We gave them what they asked. We knew there was crowded conditions and new growth in the district.

Now we find out there is a 4 million dollar deficit - WHY?

We are told the 3 middle schools must be split because of over-crowding, and yet we are told 3 schools are being closed - WHY?

A magnet school is not a full operating school, but a specials school.

Residents were asked to work on a 20 member commission to help formulate the new boundaries. For 4 weeks they worked long and hard and came up with a very workable plan. Their plan was totally disregarded - WHY?

WASTE of tax payers dollars must be stopped. Our children's education and welfare must come first. WASTE CAN NO LONGER BE TOLERATED.

PLEASE VOTE NO

ISSUE 19

THANK YOU.

CONCERNED PARENTS
AND
TAX PAYERS

"I would have thought that if the First Amendment stood for anything, it would stand for the right to pass out a leaflet about a local school board election without disclosing my name," O'Connor said. "What does the First Amendment protect if not that core political speech?"

But Goldberger also faced difficult questions as justices probed the implications of McIntyre's case for other campaign disclosure laws. O'Connor asked whether spending disclosure requirements are constitutional. After hesitating, Goldberger said yes. What about requiring identification on a television commercial? O'Connor continued. Broadcasting is different from a political leaflet, Goldberger said.

Ginsburg joined the questioning, asking whether the state could require disclosure of spending by corporations. That also would be all right, Goldberger said. But he concluded by insisting that a state cannot impose disclosure requirements "at the expense of individuals who are engaged in pure speech who wish to remain anonymous."

The Court's 7–2 decision April 19 settled the main issue by striking down Ohio's law while skirting the secondary questions. In his opinion for six justices, Stevens first extolled the tradition of anonymity in literature and in politics and then dismissed the state's justifications for seeking to ban anonymity in political campaigns.

Stevens noted that authors such as Mark Twain and O'Henry had used pseudonyms for their writings. In politics, he continued, the tradition of anonymity was "most famously embodied" in the *Federalist Papers,* which played a critical part in the ratification of the Constitution and were written under pseudonyms by John Adams, Alexander Hamilton, and James Madison. On that basis, Stevens concluded, "an author's decision to remain anonymous ... is an aspect of the freedom of speech protected by the First Amendment."

As for the state's justifications, Stevens found them insubstantial. The desire to provide voters additional information was "plainly insufficient" to require a writer to disclose her identity if she did not want to, he said. And the state had other means to deal with misleading or libelous campaign materials. "... [A] state's enforcement interest might justify a more limited identification requirement," Stevens concluded, "but Ohio has shown scant cause for inhibiting the leafletting at issue here."

Justices O'Connor, Kennedy, Souter, Ginsburg, and Breyer joined the opinion. In a brief concurrence, Ginsburg stressed the limited nature of the ruling. The decision did not mean, she wrote, that a state could not require a speaker to "disclose its interest by disclosing its identity" in "other, larger circumstances."

In a separate concurrence, Justice Thomas agreed the law was unconstitutional but not for the reasons Stevens gave. Thomas, an advocate of interpreting the Constitution according to the "original understanding" of the Framers, said the real issue was whether a right of anonymous political leafleting was recognized when the First Amendment was ratified in 1791. After extensive research, Thomas concluded that it was.

Thomas's stance put him at odds with his normal ally, Justice Scalia, who wrote the dissenting opinion in the case. Scalia, who also favors an original understanding approach to constitutional adjudication, said he was unpersuaded by Thomas's historical argument or by the majority's embrace of what he called "a hitherto unknown right-to-be-unknown while engaging in electoral politics."

Instead, Scalia cited "the widespread and longstanding traditions" of state laws requiring authors of campaign materials to disclose their identity. Campaign disclosure laws had been enacted by Congress and by forty-eight other states besides Ohio, he said. Striking them down, Scalia continued, was likely to lead to an increase in "mudslinging" and "dirty tricks" in campaigns. Chief Justice Rehnquist joined the opinion.

In Ohio, attorney Buck Baile, who represented McIntyre in the state court cases, said the McIntyre family was "elated" with the decision. "They felt it justified what their mother had done and she would have been pleased with the ruling," he said.

Ohio election officials moved to amend the state law to comply with the decision. But the amendments retained disclosure requirements for candidates, campaign organizations, political action committees, and any individuals or groups that spent at least $100 in local races, $250 in a state legislative race, or $500 in a gubernatorial campaign. Mark Weaver, an assistant attorney general, said the revision was aimed at protecting "grassroots neighborhood activity" while limiting the ability of political action committees "to come in and try to abuse the loophole."

Goldberger voiced doubts, however, that the amended law would comply with the Court's ruling. "The state is treating this as though the only issue before the Court was the lone person standing on a street corner," Goldberger said. "I think the decision was broader than that."

Endangered Species

Government's Power to Protect Wildlife Habitat Backed

Babbitt, Secretary of the Interior v. Sweet Home Chapter of Communities for a Great Oregon, decided by a 6–3 vote, June 29, 1995; Stevens wrote the opinion; Scalia, Rehnquist, and Thomas dissented. *(See excerpts, p. 260.)*

When Congress passed the Endangered Species Act in 1973, the public joined the environmentalist movement in cheering. The law was billed as a way of saving revered symbols of American wildlife like the bald eagle and the grizzly bear from possible extinction.

THERE ARE 26 FAMILYS THAT LIVE ON THIS ROAD WE ALL DEPEND ON AND DO SUPPORT THE TIMBER INDUSTRY

Timber industry workers plead for public support in their fight against federal environmental regulations to limit logging in some areas. The Supreme Court rejected a legal effort to prevent the government from using the Endangered Species Act to restrict logging on private property.

Over the next two decades, however, the law became a target of controversy and derision from business interests, conservatives, and much of the public. Critics said the federal government had turned to protecting all sorts of rare animal and plant species at the expense of normal economic activities on public and private lands. But the critics were disappointed this year when the Supreme Court rejected a business-backed challenge to endangered species enforcement against private property owners.

Admittedly, the Endangered Species Act had been used for purposes not recognized at the time of its adoption. In the 1970s, environmentalists used a tiny fish called the "snail darter" to block the Tennessee Valley Authority from finishing the multimillion-dollar Tellico Dam in eastern Tennessee. The Supreme Court upheld the challenge in a unanimous ruling: *TVA v. Hill* (1977). But Congress later passed a law allowing the dam to be completed. Supporters said few government projects were seriously affected by compliance with the law anyway.

Then, in the 1980s and 1990s, the Interior Department, under pressure from environmentalist organizations, began enforcing the act to limit activities such as grazing and logging on public lands and also on private property. The government worked on plans to limit logging in order to protect habitat in the Pacific Northwest for the northern spotted owl, listed as a threatened species, and for the endangered red-cockaded woodpecker in the Southeast. The timber industry—companies and workers—rose in protest.

The fight ranged for several years across the federal bureaucracy, the White House, Congress, and the courts. In 1991, timber interests filed a broad legal challenge in federal court in Washington, D.C., attacking any use of the law to limit activities on private property.

The suit, filed in the name of an Oregon citizens' group in the tiny logging community of Sweet Home but financed by the timber industry, focused on an Interior Department regulation dating to 1975. The act itself made it illegal to "take" an endangered species. Within the act, "take" was broadly defined to mean "to harass, harm, pursue, hunt, shoot, wound, kill, trap, capture, or collect, or to attempt to engage in any such conduct." The regulation then defined "harm" to include "any significant habitat modification or degradation where it actually kills or injures wildlife by significantly impairing essential behavioral patterns, including breeding, feeding, or sheltering."

The plaintiffs contended that the regulation went beyond the law as enacted. They said the word "take" applied only to direct harm to individual animals, not to indirect harm to wildlife habitat. A federal district court judge disagreed. Initially, a three-judge panel of the U.S. Court of Appeals for the District of Columbia also rejected the suit, in a split decision. But on rehearing, one of the appeals court judges reversed himself and agreed with the timber groups that the definition of harm was not authorized by Congress nor a reasonable administrative interpretation of the statute.

The argument of the case before the Supreme Court on April 17 featured spirited exchanges between the lawyers and justices with differing points of view. Justice Scalia bluntly called the government's interpretation of the act "weird." "To 'take' an animal applies to hunting," he told Deputy Solicitor General Edwin S. Kneedler. Instead, he said, the government was saying, "You 'take' an animal when you plow the land."

Several other justices, however, indicated approval of the broad interpretation of the law. "If you know that the destruction of the habitat is going to harm the species, that's enough," Justice Souter told Washington attorney John Macleod, who represented the plaintiffs.

The Court's ruling, issued on the last day of the term, backed the government. Writing for the majority, Justice Stevens called the definition of harm a "reasonable" interpretation of the law given Congress's broad purpose of protecting rare wildlife. Justices O'Connor, Kennedy, Souter, Ginsburg, and Breyer joined the opinion. But O'Connor also wrote a concurring opinion that suggested the law should not be applied to activities on land that have unforeseen impact on wildlife habitat.

In an acerbic dissent, Scalia said the ruling allowed the government to shift the cost of protecting endangered species to private individuals. The decision, he wrote, "imposes unfairness to the point of financial ruin—not just upon the rich, but upon the simplest farmer who finds his land conscripted to national zoological use." Chief Justice Rehnquist and Justice Thomas joined the dissent.

The Clinton administration said it was pleased with the ruling. But George Frampton, assistant secretary of the Interior for fish and wildlife, also said the administration wanted to enforce the act "in partnership with state and local governments and private individuals."

Environmentalist groups also voiced satisfaction with the decision. "It reaffirms one of the basic principles of the Endangered Species Act—that you can only save species by saving habitat," said John Kostyack, a lawyer with the National Wildlife Federation in Washington.

For their part, lawyers representing business interests in the case noted that both Stevens and O'Connor left the door open for landowners to challenge enforcement of the act in specific cases. And they said Congress was likely to re-examine the issue while working on a reauthorization of the act. "There's a very strong likelihood that Congress will overrule the secretary on this regulation," said Steven Quarles, co-counsel for the plaintiffs in the case.

On Capitol Hill, Republican lawmakers agreed. "Congress needs to establish policy and clarify the intent of the law, or the court system and the bureaucracy will do it for us," said Rep. Richard Pombo, a California Republican who headed the House Endangered Species Task Force. But environmentalists predicted they would prevail. "Opponents of the act are still moving forward with their plans to gut its basic protections," Kostyack warned, "but I believe the American people are awakening to the threat."

3 | *Case Summaries*

When the Supreme Court's schedule for the term's final two-week session of arguments was released, some long-time reporters at the Court felt a touch of nostalgia. The seventeen cases to be argued from April 17 through April 26 included several emotionally charged issues, such as racial redistricting, free speech, church and state, and the Endangered Species Act. These were cases certain to generate front-page news when the decisions came out.

By contrast, the Court had been making less news over the past several years as it heard fewer and fewer cases, many of them on issues of limited interest to most Americans. But the April schedule was the busiest session of the term, and the issues were understandable and relevant for the public. "This is like the old days," one reporter remarked.

The Court did make plenty of news as its term ended in June. Nonetheless, final statistics showed that its output of signed opinions had declined once again. The Court issued signed decisions in eighty-two cases. That was slightly lower than the number for the previous term (84) and almost one-fourth lower than the number for the 1992–1993 term (107). It represented a sharp decline from the average number of signed opinions during the 1970s (131) or 1980s (139). In fact, it was the lowest number since the 1955–1956 term, when the Court also issued eighty-two signed opinions.

The declining output continued despite a continuing increase in the number of cases brought to the Court. The total docket for the term reached a new record of 8,100 cases. That amounted to a 4 percent increase over the previous term's figure of 7,786 cases *(see Figure 3–1)*.

Reporters whose visibility depends on the Court's output of headline-making decisions were not the only people concerned about the low number of decisions. The lawyers who regularly appear before the Court had reason to be troubled too. "We're getting to the point that they're taking just 1 percent of the cases," Theodore Olson, a Washington attorney, remarked. "So it all depends on what they take."

The justices do not announce their reasons for declining to hear a case, but the continuing drop in the number of decisions indicated the Court was acting deliberately to lower its profile. The justices have almost complete freedom to determine their workload under a 1988 judicial reform act that eliminated requirements to hear certain types of cases.

Court-watchers posited some plausible explanations for the reduced caseload. The conservative majority's devotion to federalism naturally results in greater deference to state courts, it was thought. In addition, the

Figure 3–1 Supreme Court Caseload, 1960 Term–1994 Term

Total cases on docket

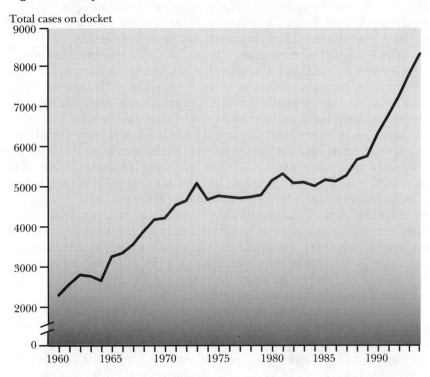

Number of signed opinions of the Court

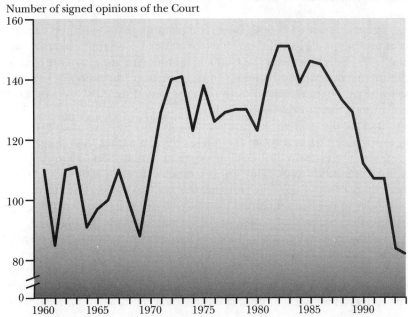

Court may have less cause to rein in federal judges since the federal bench has come to be dominated by like-minded conservatives appointed by Presidents Ronald Reagan and George Bush. But the explanations were necessarily speculative and, in any event, seemed incomplete.

The Court did a bit more work during the term than the number of signed opinions indicated. It disposed of an additional three cases after argument by *per curiam*—that is, unsigned—opinions. In one of those cases, the Court sidestepped a constitutional challenge to a California law setting lower welfare benefits for new arrivals to the state than for long-time residents (*Anderson v. Green*). The law, it turned out, had been invalidated in a separate case after the justices agreed to hear the dispute. The Court also issued *per curiam* opinions in cases upholding a federal racketeering conviction (*United States v. Robertson*) and reviving a damage suit by a federal inmate against Justice Department officials (*Kimberlin v. Quinlan*).

In addition, the Court issued *per curiam* decisions in three criminal law cases without hearing arguments. These summary decisions are normally unanimous and noncontroversial. The procedure is used to correct lower court rulings so evidently erroneous that argument is deemed unnecessary. But two of the summary decisions this term drew dissents that attacked the rulings as well as the truncated procedure.

In one of the decisions, the Court made it harder for criminal defendants to prove that a prosecutor was improperly excluding potential jurors on account of their race (*Purkett v. Elem*). The other decision strictly applied the requirement that a prison inmate cannot raise a constitutional claim in a federal habeas corpus proceeding unless the issue was first raised in state courts (*Duncan v. Henry*).

Stevens dissented in both cases, complaining that the rulings departed from precedent and should not have been decided without hearing arguments. "... [I]t is unwise for the Court to announce a law-changing decision without first ordering full briefing and argument on the merits of the case," he wrote in the jury-selection case. Breyer joined the dissent in that case; in the other, Stevens dissented alone.

Overall, the justices were unanimous in thirty-four of eighty-two rulings—or about 41 percent of the time. That was higher than the previous term, when 36 percent of the rulings were unanimous, but about the same as the 1992–1993 term. The justices divided 5–4 in sixteen cases—or about 20 percent of the time, roughly the same as the past two terms. The remainder of the cases included eleven decisions with one dissenting vote, twelve with two dissenting votes, and nine with three dissenting votes.

Following are the case summaries for the eighty-two signed opinions and six *per curiam* opinions issued during the 1994–1995 term. They are organized by subject matter: business law, courts and procedure, criminal law and procedure, election law, environmental law, federal government, First Amendment, immigration law, individual rights, labor law, and states.

Business Law

Aviation Law

American Airlines, Inc. v. Wollens, decided by a 6–2 vote, January 18, 1995; Ginsburg wrote the opinion; O'Connor and Thomas dissented; Scalia did not participate in the case.

Airline passengers can bring breach-of-contract suits in state courts to enforce provisions of airlines' frequent-flyer programs.

The ruling allowed a group of American Airlines customers to proceed with part of a suit contesting newly added restrictions to the airline's frequent-flyer program. The airline claimed the state court suits were blocked by the federal Airline Deregulation Act, which supersedes state laws relating to airlines' "rates, routes, or services."

Writing for the Court, Ginsburg said the federal law does permit state court jurisdiction over contract disputes. "A remedy confined to a contract's terms simply holds parties to their agreements — in this instance, to business judgments an airline made public about its rates and services," she wrote.

Ginsburg said, however, that the federal law did preempt part of the consumers' suit brought under the Illinois consumer fraud statute. Stevens dissented on that point, saying he would allow both claims to proceed.

In the main dissent, O'Connor, joined by Thomas, said both claims were preempted. She said the decision conflicted with the Court's 1992 ruling, *Morale v. Trans World Airlines, Inc.*, which barred state regulation of airlines' advertising.

Banking

NationsBank of North Carolina, N.A. v. Variable Annuity Life Insurance Co., decided by a 9–0 vote, January 18, 1995; Ginsburg wrote the opinion.

The Court upheld the power of national banks to sell annuities, rejecting efforts by the insurance industry to stifle competition in the growing market for long-term investment instruments.

The unanimous ruling upheld a decision by the Comptroller of the Currency permitting the North Carolina-based NationsBank to sell annuities as a service "incidental" to the "business of banking." An insurance company specializing in variable annuities challenged the action, arguing that federal law prohibits banks in most cities from selling insurance.

Writing for the Court, Ginsburg said the comptroller was entitled to deference in his conclusion that the sale of annuities is "incidental" to banking. "Modern annuities, though more sophisticated than the standard savings bank deposits of old, answer essentially the same need," she wrote.

Ginsburg also said the comptroller had acted reasonably in concluding that because of their investment features, annuities were not insurance. On that basis, she did not resolve the issue whether federal law does bar banks from the insurance business.

Bankruptcy

Celotex Corp. v. Edwards, decided by a 7–2 vote, April 19, 1995; Rehnquist wrote the opinion; Stevens and Ginsburg dissented.

The Court made it more difficult for people to collect money they have won in lawsuits from companies that later seek bankruptcy-law protection from creditors.

The decision, significant though highly technical, blocked an effort by Bennie Edwards, a former insulation installer in Texas, to collect an appeal bond posted by Celotex Corp. after he won a $281,000 award for asbestos-related injuries. After Celotex filed for bankruptcy reorganization in federal court in Tampa, Florida, the bankruptcy court judge issued an injunction preventing Celotex's insurance company from paying off the bond. But a federal judge in Texas and the federal appeals court in New Orleans ruled that Edwards could collect the bond.

In a 7–2 ruling, the Court said the bankruptcy injunction had to be obeyed. Rehnquist said the bankruptcy court had jurisdiction because Edwards's effort to collect the award "related to" Celotex's reorganization. Edwards could have challenged the injunction in the bankruptcy court, Rehnquist added, but any other procedure would seriously undercut "the orderly process of law."

Celotex faced $70 million in asbestos-related judgments at the time it filed for bankruptcy protection. The dissenting justices said the bankruptcy court had no power to issue an injunction preventing collection on bonds issued by a third-party insurance company instead of the debtor company.

Maritime Law

Jerome B. Grubart, Inc. v. Great Lakes Dredge & Dock Co., decided by a 7–0 vote, February 22, 1995; Souter wrote the opinion; Stevens and Breyer did not participate in the case.

Federal courts have maritime law jurisdiction over suits arising from the Great Chicago Flood of 1992, a costly disaster caused by damage to a freight tunnel under the Chicago River.

The unanimous decision—with two justices recusing themselves—was a victory for the Great Lakes Dredge & Dock Co., which the city of Chicago and owners of flooded downtown buildings blamed for the accident. They said the company damaged the tunnel while using a crane on a barge to repair piers. Under maritime law, the company's liability would be limited to the value of the "vessel"—the barge—involved in the accident.

Writing for a five-justice majority, Souter said the accident met the traditional tests for admiralty jurisdiction because it occurred on a navigable waterway and involved a vessel. He continued by saying it met two additional tests established in a 1990 ruling, *Sisson v. Ruby*: the accident had "a potentially disruptive impact on maritime commerce," and the repair work had a "substantial relationship to traditional maritime activity."

In a separate concurrence, Thomas, joined by Scalia, argued for discarding the *Sisson* factors and returning to a simpler "bright-line test" that looked only to the location and use of a vessel to determine admiralty jurisdiction.

The ruling returned the case to lower federal courts for further proceedings. O'Connor, who joined the majority opinion, wrote a brief concurrence. The federal judges, she said, could still decide that some claims arising from the accident should be tried in state court.

City of Milwaukee v. Cement Division, National Gypsum Co., decided by an 8–0 vote, June 12, 1995; Stevens wrote the opinion; Breyer did not participate in the case.

Prejudgment interest should be awarded in an admiralty collision case even if there is a dispute over who is to blame and both sides are ultimately determined to be at fault.

The ruling favored the owner of a ship that sank in Milwaukee harbor in 1979 after breaking loose from a city-owned wharf. The city agreed to pay $1.5 million in damages after an appeals court found the company two-thirds at fault and the city one-third at fault. But a federal judge refused to award an additional $5.3 million for interest from the time of the accident, saying the company was mostly to blame for the mishap.

In a unanimous decision, the Court said that the judge was wrong to depart from the normal rule favoring prejudgment interest in maritime cases. "... [N]either a good-faith dispute over liability nor the existence of mutual fault justifies the denial of prejudgment interest in an admiralty collision case," Stevens wrote.

Vimar Seguros y Reaseguros, S.A. v. M/V Sky Reefer, decided by a 7–1 vote, June 19, 1995; Kennedy wrote the opinion; Stevens dissented; Breyer did not participate in the case.

The Court upheld the enforceability of foreign arbitration clauses in maritime contracts, rejecting arguments that they lessen ship owners' liability in violation of a federal law aimed at protecting shippers.

The ruling cleared the way for an arbitration in Tokyo of a dispute over a $1 million shipment of Moroccan oranges and lemons damaged in transit aboard a ship owned by a Panamanian company and chartered to a

Japanese concern. The U.S. fruit distributor and its maritime insurer sued the ship and its owner for damages in federal court despite a clause in the bill of lading requiring that disputes be arbitrated before a maritime law forum in Tokyo. They argued foreign arbitration would violate provisions of a 1936 law — the Carriage of Goods by Sea Act (COGSA) — that prohibits ship owners from lessening their liability for negligence.

By a nearly unanimous vote, the Court allowed the arbitration to proceed. Kennedy rejected arguments that the foreign arbitration clause lessened a shipper's liability under COGSA by increasing the transaction costs of obtaining relief. He also rejected as premature the argument that the arbitrator in Tokyo would not apply the federal law.

The decision effectively overruled a widely followed 1967 ruling by the federal appeals court in New York that foreign forum selection clauses were invalid under COGSA. O'Connor concurred in the result in the case but said she disagreed with overruling the 1967 decision.

Stevens, the lone dissenter, called the decision "an excellent example of overzealous formalism" that "drained [COGSA] of much of [its] potency."

Patents

Asgrow Seed Co. v. Winterboer dba DeeBees, decided by an 8–1 vote, January 18, 1995; Scalia wrote the opinion; Stevens dissented.

Seed companies won a victory in their effort to use a federal law giving patent-like protection to the development of new seeds against farmers engaged in unauthorized sale of the seeds.

The Court ruled that an Iowa farm family, Dennis and Becky Winterboer, violated the federal Plant Variety Protection Act by selling soybean seed saved from crops grown after using new seeds developed by Asgrow Seed Co. The Winterboers made substantial income from so-called "brown-bag" sales of extra seed to other farmers. They said the law permitted such sales, but Scalia said the law allowed a farmer to sell seed only if it was "saved for the purpose of replanting his own acreage."

Stevens was the lone dissenter. The ruling had limited significance because Congress in 1994 amended the law to eliminate farmers' right to resell novel seed varieties for use as seed.

Securities Law

Gustafson v. Alloyd Co., Inc., decided by a 5–4 vote, February 28, 1995; Kennedy wrote the opinion; Thomas, Scalia, Ginsburg, and Breyer dissented.

A powerful securities law remedy for investors who have been misled about the value of stock applies only to initial public offerings, not to the purchase of stock in subsequent "secondary" trading.

The closely divided decision narrowed the scope of a securities law provision— section 12(2) of the Securities Act of 1933— that allows investors to rescind a stock sale if they were given misleading information "by means of a prospectus or oral communication." Investors who purchased a privately held company invoked the section to try to cancel the transaction on grounds the value of the company had been inflated.

The Court ruled, however, that the section applies only to initial stock offerings. Kennedy reasoned that a "prospectus" refers only to the formal financial disclosure required for an initial public offering, not to the more informal exchange of information in a private stock sale. A different reading, he warned, would result in "extensive liability for every casual communication between buyer and seller in the secondary market."

The dissenting justices argued that securities law defined "prospectus" more broadly than the majority acknowledged. And they said that Congress, not the Court, should decide whether broad application of the section would have undesirable consequences.

The division in the case crossed normal ideological lines, with conservatives Scalia and Thomas joining the liberal-leaning Ginsburg and Breyer in dissent. Observers said Kennedy's opinion appeared to have been written originally as a dissent, suggesting that he gained a fifth vote for his position only at a late stage of the justices' deliberations.

Plaut v. Spendthrift Farm, Inc., decided by a 7–2 vote, April 18, 1995; Scalia wrote the opinion; Stevens and Ginsburg dissented.

The Court struck down, on separation-of-powers grounds, a law passed by Congress reinstating a group of securities fraud suits that had been dismissed because of an earlier ruling by the Court.

The decision nullified Congress's effort to resolve an issue created by the Court's June 1991 decision *Lampf, Pleva, Lipkind, Prupis & Petigrow v. Gilbertson*, which shortened the time for bringing federal securities fraud suits. The law, signed in December 1991, provided that the new statute of limitations would not apply to pending cases and that cases dismissed because of the ruling could be reinstated.

In a 7–2 ruling, the Court said Congress "exceeded its authority" by requiring federal courts to "reopen final judgments entered before [the law's] enactment." Scalia said the Constitution gave the courts "the power, not merely to rule on cases, but to *decide* them.... By retroactively commanding the federal courts to reopen final judgments, Congress has violated this fundamental principle."

Breyer did not join Scalia's opinion. He wrote separately that Congress in some circumstances might have power to legislatively rescind a final court judgment.

In a dissent, Stevens, joined by Ginsburg, said the law "reflects constructive legislative cooperation rather than a usurpation of judicial prerogatives."

Taxation

Commissioner of Internal Revenue v. Schleier, decided by a 6–3 vote, June 14, 1995; Stevens wrote the opinion; O'Connor, Souter, and Thomas dissented.

Any money recovered for back pay or damages in a federal age discrimination suit is subject to federal income taxation.

The decision overturned a Tax Court ruling in favor of a former United Airlines pilot who sought to avoid tax on a $145,629 settlement of an age discrimination suit against the airline. The Tax Court cited an Internal Revenue Code provision that exempts "damages received ... on account of personal injuries or sickness."

In a 6–3 ruling, the Court held that any recovery for back pay or damages under the age discrimination act is subject to taxation. Stevens said age discrimination awards or settlements are not based on personal injury or sickness as the statute requires. In addition, he said that an Internal Revenue Service regulation exempts damage awards only if they are based on a "tort or tort type" suits, such as an automobile accident case.

Scalia agreed with the result but did not join Stevens's opinion or write a separate opinion to explain his views.

O'Connor opened her dissenting opinion with a blunt disagreement on the interpretation of the statutory provision. "Age discrimination inflicts a personal injury," she wrote. She also said the ruling contradicted prior Court decisions on taxability of damage awards. Thomas joined the entire dissent; Souter joined only the part dealing with prior rulings.

United States v. Williams, decided by a 6–3 vote, April 25, 1995; Ginsburg wrote the opinion; Rehnquist, Kennedy, and Thomas dissented.

The Court created a limited exception to the general rule against allowing tax refund suits by someone other than the person who was assessed the tax.

The decision rejected an effort by the Internal Revenue Service to bar a refund suit brought by a California woman after she paid her former husband's $41,000 federal tax bill. Lori Williams said she paid the past due tax in order to clear a tax lien on the couple's former home before selling it.

In a 6–3 decision, Ginsburg said Williams "had no realistic alternative to payment of a tax she did not owe, and we do not believe Congress intended to leave parties in [Williams's] position without a remedy." But Ginsburg stressed that the ruling was limited and did not necessarily allow a refund suit by someone who "volunteers" to pay someone else's tax.

Writing for the dissenters, Rehnquist said the ruling violated the "bedrock principle" requiring strict construction of statutory provisions authorizing suits against the government.

Trademarks

Qualitex Co. v. Jacobson Products Co., Inc., decided by a 9–0 vote, March 28, 1995; Breyer wrote the opinion.

A color can be registered as a trademark under federal law and provide the basis for a trademark infringement claim.

The unanimous decision reinstated a trademark infringement claim won by Qualitex Co., which manufactures distinctively green-and-gold-colored dry cleaning press pads, against a competitor that began making pads using a similar color in 1989.

Writing for the Court, Breyer said the broadly worded federal trademark law — the Lanham Act — permits "the registration of a trademark that consists, purely and simply, of a color." Breyer noted that the U.S. Patent and Trademark Office had previously permitted the registration of a particular shape (the Coca-Cola bottle), a particular sound (the NBC chimes), and a particular odor (a scented thread). "If a shape, a sound, and a fragrance can act as symbols," Breyer said, "why, one might ask, can a color not do the same?" Breyer rejected arguments that courts would be unable to resolve trademark disputes over colors.

Federal appeals courts had split on the issue. The U.S. Patent and Trademark Office urged the Court to permit color trademarks.

Courts and Procedure

Appeals

Swint v. Chambers County Commission, decided by a 9–0 vote, March 1, 1995; Ginsburg wrote the opinion.

The Court cleared the way for trial of a civil rights suit against an Alabama county and the county sheriff after ruling that a federal appeals court had no power to grant the county's plea for favorable ruling without trial.

The ruling stemmed from a suit against the Chambers County (Alabama) Commission and County Sheriff James C. Morgan concerning drug raids on a nightclub in the small town of Wadley. The Court agreed to hear the case to review a federal appeals court's decision that the county could not be held liable because Morgan was not a "policymaking official" for the county.

The Court did not decide the legal question, however, because it concluded the appeals court had no jurisdiction over the county's appeal. Under previous rulings, Ginsburg explained, the appeals court had power to review the sheriff's effort to avoid trial based on official immunity. But she said the county's motion for summary judgment was not the kind of issue that could be reviewed on appeal prior to trial.

Arbitration

Allied-Bruce Terminix Cos., Inc. v. Dobson, decided by a 7–2 vote, January 18, 1995; Breyer wrote the opinion; Thomas and Scalia dissented.

States must enforce mandatory arbitration clauses in consumer contracts for any transactions that involve interstate commerce.

The ruling ordered a dispute between an Alabama family and a termite inspection company to be arbitrated instead of being tried in state court. The Federal Arbitration Act, passed in 1925, provides that courts must enforce arbitration agreements in any "contract evidencing a transaction involving commerce." The Alabama Supreme Court refused to enforce the arbitration agreement in the termite inspection contract, however, on grounds that the family did not intend for the transaction to be involved in interstate commerce.

In a 7–2 decision, the Court held that the act applies even if the parties to a contract "did not contemplate" a transaction in interstate commerce. " ... [W]e conclude that the word 'involving' ... signals an intent to exercise Congress's commerce power to the full." Breyer wrote.

In a dissent, Thomas, joined by Scalia, called for overturning the Court's 1984 ruling that the arbitration law applies to state as well as to federal courts. O'Connor, who dissented from the 1984 ruling, wrote a brief concurrence to say she would not vote to overrule the decision. "It remains now for Congress to correct this interpretation if it wishes to preserve state autonomy in state courts," she wrote.

First Options of Chicago, Inc. v. Kaplan, decided by a 9–0 vote, May 22, 1995; Breyer wrote the opinion.

Courts can independently determine whether a dispute is subject to arbitration unless the parties have clearly agreed that the issue of arbitrability is itself to be decided by arbitration.

The ruling clarified an important issue in commercial arbitration disputes. The issue arose in a case involving a Philadelphia couple, Manuel and Carol Kaplan, and a so-called "clearing firm," First Options of Chicago, which cleared stock trades for them on the Philadelphia Stock Exchange.

When a dispute arose over a plan for the Kaplans to pay off debts resulting from stock losses, First Options submitted the disagreement to the stock exchange's arbitration unit. An arbitrator ruled in the firm's favor, but the Kaplans contested the ruling in federal court, saying they had not agreed to arbitration in their contract with the firm.

In a unanimous decision, the Court agreed with the Kaplans. "Courts should not assume that the parties agreed to arbitrate arbitrability unless there is 'clear and unmistakable' evidence that they did so," Breyer wrote. If there is such an agreement, however, Breyer said courts should defer to an arbitrator's decision on the issue.

Mastrobuono v. Shearson Lehman Hutton, Inc., decided by an 8–1 vote, March 6, 1995; Stevens wrote the opinion; Thomas dissented.

The Court reinstated a punitive damage award imposed by an arbitrator against a securities brokerage firm, saying the firm's contract with customers did not clearly bar punitive damages in arbitration.

The arbitrator had awarded an Illinois couple, Antonio and Diana Mastrobuono, $159,327 in compensatory damages and $40,000 in punitive damages after finding Shearson Lehman Hutton had mishandled their investments. The Shearson firm challenged the punitive damages on grounds that the customer contract called for arbitration to be governed by New York law, which does not permit arbitrators to award punitive damages. Two lower federal courts agreed.

In a nearly unanimous ruling, the Court said the contract provision was not "an unequivocal exclusion of punitive damages claims." Noting that the contract never mentioned punitive damages, Stevens said it was "unlikely" that the Mastrobuonos understood they might be giving up "an important substantive right."

Thomas, the lone dissenter, said the contract term was clear and should be enforced under federal law designed to encourage arbitration. But he stressed the ruling was "limited and narrow." Securities industry officials agreed, saying that customer agreements could be rewritten to preclude punitive damage awards.

Attorneys

Heintz v. Jenkins, decided by a 9–0 vote, April 18, 1995; Breyer wrote the opinion.

Attorneys who regularly engage in consumer debt-collection litigation are subject to the federal Fair Debt Collection Practices Act.

The ruling rejected an argument by an Indiana lawyer that the law, aimed at controlling abusive debt-collection practices, does not apply to attorneys' handling of court cases.

Writing for a unanimous Court, Breyer said lawyers regularly engaged in debt-collection litigation met the act's definition of a debt collector. He noted that a broad exemption for lawyers included in the original law in 1977 had been repealed and not replaced in 1986.

Declaratory Judgments

Wilton v. Seven Falls Co., decided by an 8–0 vote, June 12, 1995; O'Connor wrote the opinion; Breyer did not participate in the case.

Federal courts have broad discretion to hold up proceedings in a declaratory judgment action while a state court considers the same issues in a parallel case.

The decision came in an insurance coverage dispute between London Underwriters and a group of investors called the Hill Group, which had been ordered to pay $100 million in litigation involving some Texas oil and gas properties. The underwriters denied coverage of the claim and filed an action for declaratory judgment in federal court. But the federal judge stayed proceedings in the action after the Hill Group filed a state court suit to interpret the policies.

In a unanimous ruling, the Court reinforced a 1942 precedent that courts may hold off ruling in a declaratory judgment action to await a state court decision on the issue. O'Connor said the lower court "acted within its bounds in staying this action for declaratory relief where parallel proceedings, presenting opportunity for ventilation of the same state law issues, were underway in state court."

Judgments

U.S. Bancorp Mortgage Co. v. Bonner Mall Partnership, decided by a 9–0 vote, November 8, 1994; Scalia wrote the opinion.

Lower courts cannot routinely vacate — or wipe out — rulings in civil cases if the parties reach a settlement while the case is on appeal.

The unanimous decision stemmed from the common practice — called "vacatur" — whereby defendants agree to settle a civil case after an unfavorable ruling in exchange for an agreement from the plaintiffs to have the court vacate the decision. Supporters said the practice encouraged settlements. Critics said it allowed insurance companies and other deep-pocket defendants to skew the development of the law by erasing unfavorable precedents.

Writing for the Court, Scalia said that a settlement does not justify the use of vacatur because court rulings are not "the private property of litigants." He rejected arguments that the practice promoted settlements, saying the effect was impossible to know.

The ruling came in a bankruptcy dispute between an Idaho shopping mall developer and a mortgage company. The dispute had been settled after the Court agreed to review the case. The effect was to leave on the books the federal appeals court's favorable decision for creditors in the case.

Statutes of Limitations

Reynoldsville Casket Co. v. Hyde, decided by a 9–0 vote, May 15, 1995; Breyer wrote the opinion.

An Ohio woman failed to get around an earlier ruling by the Court that invalidated a state law giving Ohio plaintiffs extra time to file suit against out-of-state residents.

Carol Hyde filed a personal injury suit against Reynoldsville Casket Co. three years after she was involved in a traffic accident with a truck owned by the Pennsylvania firm. At the time, Ohio law gave state residents unlimited time to file a suit against an out-of-state company but only two years to bring an action against an in-state company.

The Court in 1988 invalidated the law as an unconstitutional discrimination against interstate commerce. But the Ohio Supreme Court allowed Hyde to proceed with her suit, saying the Court's decision did not apply retroactively.

In a unanimous decision, the Court said that its earlier ruling did apply to cases pending at the time. Breyer also rejected Hyde's arguments that her suit should not be thrown out because she had relied on the unlimited time period in effect when the suit was filed.

In a separate opinion, Kennedy, joined by O'Connor, said that in some circumstances the Court might have the authority to limit the retroactive effect of a ruling "in light of disruption of important reliance interests or the unfairness caused by unexpected judicial decisions."

Criminal Law and Procedure

Capital Punishment

Harris v. Alabama, decided by an 8–1 vote, February 22, 1995; O'Connor wrote the opinion; Stevens dissented.

States may give judges the power to sentence a capital defendant to death even if the jury votes not to impose the death penalty.

The decision upheld the Alabama death penalty law, which allows judges to override a capital jury's recommendation. The law requires the judge to "consider" the verdict but does not specify what weight the jury's recommendation should be given.

An Alabama woman who was convicted of the contract-murder of her husband in order to collect his insurance challenged the law after a judge sentenced her to death in the face of a 7–5 jury recommendation for life imprisonment.

Writing for the nearly unanimous Court, O'Connor said the Alabama law did not violate the Eighth Amendment's Cruel and Unusual Punishment Clause. She acknowledged that the Court had previously upheld a Florida law requiring judges to give "great weight" to a jury recommendation in capital cases. But she said that mandating such a limitation would amount to "micromanagement" of issues that "properly rest within the State's discretion."

Stevens, the lone dissenter, argued that the Alabama law gave judges "unbridled discretion" in capital sentencing and complained that "political pressures" make judges more likely than juries to impose the death penalty. He noted that in Alabama judges had overridden jury recommendations to impose the death penalty in forty-seven cases but had vetoed recommended death sentences only five times.

Criminal Offenses

Hubbard v. United States, decided by a 6–3 vote, May 15, 1995; Stevens wrote the opinion; Rehnquist, O'Connor, and Souter dissented.

Overturning a forty-year-old precedent, the Court held that the federal law against making false statements to a "department or agency" of the government does not apply to statements made to a federal court.

The decision overturned the conviction of a Michigan man for making two false statements in an unsworn filing in a bankruptcy proceeding. Prosecutors charged him under a 1934 law that makes it a crime to make a false statement or conceal a material fact "in any matter within the jurisdiction of any department or agency of the United States."

In a 1955 decision, *Bramblett v. United States,* the Court had upheld the use of the statute to prosecute a member of Congress for falsifying payroll information. Since then, lower federal courts had limited the law by carving out a "judicial function" exception for statements made in court. But the law had also been applied broadly in other settings — most notably, in connection with false testimony before congressional committees in the Iran-contra investigation in 1986.

In a 6–3 decision, the Court said the previous decision was wrong and should be overruled. "In ordinary parlance, federal courts are not described as 'departments' or 'agencies' of the Government," Stevens wrote. He added that the history of the New Deal era statute indicated that it was aimed at penalizing those who make false statements to executive branch agencies.

The six justices in the majority offered different reasons for departing from the principle of *stare decisis*— respect for precedent. Stevens, joined by Ginsburg and Breyer, said the lower courts' recognition of a "judicial function" exception amounted to "a competing legal doctrine that can lay a legitimate claim to respect as a settled body of law." Scalia, joined by Kennedy, said use of the false statements statute in judicial proceedings could "deter vigorous representation in adversarial litigation." Thomas, the sixth justice in the majority, did not specify his reasons for overturning the precedent.

The dissenting justices argued that the ruling violated the traditional rule for giving precedent especially strong respect in cases of statutory interpretation. "... [I]f the rule of [the prior case] is to be overturned," Rehnquist wrote, "it should be at the hands of Congress, and not of this Court."

In his dissent, Rehnquist said the ruling would also bar use of the statute for false statements made in legislative proceedings. But Stevens said other federal laws—including perjury, obstruction of justice, and false claims statutes—could be used for prosecuting false statements made to courts or to Congress.

United States v. Aguilar, decided by votes of 8–1 and 6–3, June 21, 1995; Rehnquist wrote the opinion; Stevens dissented in part; Scalia, Kennedy, and Thomas dissented in part.

The Court reinstated the conviction of a federal judge for disclosing a court-ordered wiretap but agreed with a federal appeals court in striking down his conviction for obstruction of justice.

Robert Aguilar, a federal district judge in San Jose, had been found guilty of telling an acquaintance about a government wiretap in a racketeering investigation and obstructing a grand jury investigation by lying to FBI agents about the matter. The Ninth U.S. Circuit Court of Appeals reversed both convictions. It struck down the wiretap count because the court order had already expired, even though Aguilar was unaware of the fact. And it reversed the obstruction count by concluding that Aguilar had not actively attempted to impede the grand jury investigation.

The Court closely examined the statutory language on both charges in reinstating the wiretap conviction, by an 8–1 vote, and rejecting the conviction for obstruction, on a 6–3 vote.

On the wiretap charge, Rehnquist said that Aguilar's actions fell within the statutory prohibition against disclosing a wiretap "in order to obstruct, impede, or prevent such interception." Stevens dissented alone on this part of the decision. He said the ruling had the effect of "criminalizing nothing more than an evil intent accompanied by a harmless act."

Rehnquist said that Aguilar's interview with the FBI agents did not violate the obstruction statute because it did not have "the natural and probable effect" of impeding the grand jury probe. Scalia, joined by Kennedy and Thomas, dissented. They said the ruling added a requirement that had "no basis in the words Congress enacted."

The decision returned the case to the appeals court to consider Aguilar's challenge to jury instructions used at trial. Aguilar, who received concurrent six-month sentences on the two counts, remained on the bench pending his appeal, but he was limited to trying civil cases.

United States v. Lopez, decided by a 5–4 vote, April 26, 1995; Rehnquist wrote the opinion; Breyer, Stevens, Souter, and Ginsburg dissented.

The Court overturned a popular federal criminal law banning possession of a firearm in or near a school on grounds it went beyond Congress's power to regulate interstate commerce.

The narrowly divided decision invalidated the 1990 Gun-Free School Zones Act, which made it a federal crime to possess a firearm within 1,000 feet of a school. The government asked the Court to uphold the act after the Fifth U.S. Circuit Court of Appeals overturned the conviction of a San Antonio teenager charged under the law.

Writing for the Court, Rehnquist said the law exceeded Congress's power under the Constitution's Commerce Clause. "The possession of a gun in a local school zone is in no sense an economic activity that might, through repetition elsewhere, substantially affect any sort of interstate commerce," Rehnquist wrote. Upholding the law, he warned, "would bid fair to convert congressional authority under the Commerce Clause to a general police power of the sort retained by the States."

Two of the justices in the majority wrote additional opinions from different perspectives. Kennedy, joined by O'Connor, depicted the decision as narrow and cautioned against any wholesale re-examination of laws passed by Congress under the Commerce Clause. But Thomas called for adopting a stricter view of Congress's power. He said the Court had been too lax in determining whether a regulated activity had a "substantial effect" on interstate commerce to support federal jurisdiction.

Writing for the four dissenters, Breyer said the ruling would thwart Congress's power "to enact criminal laws aimed at criminal behavior that ... seriously threatens the economic as well as the social well-being of Americans." In an additional dissent, Souter complained that the decision did not show sufficient respect for "the institutional competence of Congress on a subject expressly assigned to it by the Constitution." Stevens also wrote a brief separate dissent, calling the ruling "an extraordinary decision" and its legal holding "radical." *(See entry, p. 43; excerpts, p. 128.)*

United States v. Robertson, decided by a 9–0 vote, May 1, 1995; *per curiam* (unsigned) opinion.

The Court reinstated the federal racketeering conviction of a former prosecutor-turned-narcotics-trafficker for using proceeds of drug transactions to operate an Alaska gold mine.

The unanimous ruling overturned a decision by the Ninth U.S. Circuit Court of Appeals that federal law did not apply because the gold mine was strictly an intrastate operation. In a brief, unsigned opinion, the Court noted that the defendant, Juan Paul Robertson, had bought supplies and hired workers from out of state and had taken about $30,000 worth of gold with him out of Alaska. On that basis, the Court said, the gold mine was "engaged ... in interstate or foreign commerce" for purposes of invoking the federal racketeering law.

The ruling came less than a week after the Court's decision in *United States v. Lopez,* striking down the federal Gun-Free School Zones Act on grounds Congress had exceeded its power under the Commerce Clause.

(See above.) The justices had raised similar questions about congressional jurisdiction during arguments in Robertson's case, but the three-page opinion made no reference to broad constitutional issues.

United States v. Shabani, decided by a 9–0 vote, November 1, 1994; O'Connor wrote the opinion.

A defendant can be convicted under the federal drug conspiracy statute even if the government fails to prove any "overt act" he committed to carry out the conspiracy.

The ruling reinstated the conviction of an Alaska man charged with conspiring to smuggle drugs from California. The Ninth U.S. Circuit Court of Appeals overturned the conviction because the indictment failed to allege any action in furtherance of the conspiracy. The government argued that the drug conspiracy statute did not require such proof.

In a brief and unanimous opinion, the Court agreed. O'Connor noted that the drug conspiracy statute, enacted in 1970, followed the general federal conspiracy statute in omitting any need to prove an overt act. "Congress appears to have made the choice quite deliberately," O'Connor wrote.

United States v. X-Citement Video, Inc., decided by a 7–2 vote, November 29, 1994; Rehnquist wrote the opinion; Scalia and Thomas dissented.

The Court saved the federal child pornography statute from constitutional attack by construing the law to require prosecutors to prove the defendant knew that minors were depicted in the material.

The 1977 child pornography law makes it a criminal offense to "knowingly" transport or ship in interstate commerce "any visual depiction" if the production "involves the use of a minor engaging in sexually explicit conduct." A Los Angeles company convicted of distributing pornographic videotapes argued on appeal that the law improperly failed to require proof the defendant knew of the underage performers. The Ninth U.S. Circuit Court of Appeals agreed, reversing the conviction and declaring the law unconstitutional.

In a 7–2 decision, the Court rejected what it called the appeals court's "natural grammatical reading" of the law. Rehnquist said the word "knowingly" should instead be interpreted to modify all the elements of the statute to avoid constitutional doubts. "... [W]e do not impute to Congress an intent to pass legislation that is inconsistent with the Constitution," the chief justice wrote.

In a dissent, Scalia, joined by Thomas, said the majority had interpreted the law "in a manner that its language simply will not bear." He argued the law should be struck down because it did not require proof that the defendant knew of the pornographic content of the material in question.

Under Scalia's approach, however, Congress could rewrite the law and still omit any requirement to prove the defendant knew that underage children were depicted.

Double Jeopardy

Witte v. United States, decided by an 8–1 vote, June 14, 1995; O'Connor wrote the opinion; Stevens dissented.

Double jeopardy principles do not prevent the government from prosecuting a defendant for conduct that was previously used to increase the defendant's sentence for a separate conviction.

The Court softened the impact of the decision, however, by ruling that the sentence for a second conviction in such cases ordinarily should run concurrently with the remainder of the term for the first offense.

The ruling cleared the way for a second federal drug prosecution of a defendant, Steven Kurt Witte, who was charged with several co-conspirators in 1990 with importing large amounts of marijuana and cocaine from Mexico and Guatemala. Witte pleaded guilty in 1991 to a reduced marijuana charge. But the judge considered all the charged offenses as "relevant conduct" in imposing a final prison term of 144 months (12 years).

The government then indicted Witte in 1992 for conspiring to import cocaine. Witte claimed the second prosecution amounted to double jeopardy because he had already been punished for the cocaine offense. The federal district court judge agreed, but the Fifth U.S. Circuit Court of Appeals ruled that the prosecution could go forward.

In a near unanimous decision, the Court agreed that the second prosecution did not violate the constitutional protection against double jeopardy. " ... [U]se of evidence of related criminal conduct to enhance a defendant's sentence for a separate crime within the authorized statutory limits does not constitute punishment for that conduct within the meaning of the Double Jeopardy Clause," O'Connor wrote.

Five justices joined in that part of O'Connor's opinion: Rehnquist, Kennedy, Souter, Ginsburg, and Breyer. In a separate concurrence, Scalia, joined by Thomas, repeated his view that the Double Jeopardy Clause does not apply to sentencing issues at all.

In a lone dissent, Stevens said the constitutional ruling "weakens the fundamental protections the Double Jeopardy Clause was intended to provide." He noted that the use of the uncharged offenses raised Witte's maximum term under the Federal Sentencing Guidelines from a range of 78 to 97 months to a range of 292 to 365 months.

Stevens did join O'Connor and three other justices—Souter, Ginsburg, and Breyer—in saying that the guidelines generally would prevent a second sentence from being added on to a previous term in such cases. Rehnquist and Kennedy did not join that part of O'Connor's opinion and did not write separately to state their views on the question; Scalia and Thomas also did not address the issue.

Evidence

Tome v. United States, decided by a 5–4 vote, January 10, 1995; Kennedy wrote the opinion; Breyer, Rehnquist, O'Connor, and Thomas dissented.

The Court strictly construed an evidentiary rule limiting the introduction of out-of-court statements made by a witness to try to support the credibility of her in-court testimony.

The ruling overturned the 1992 child abuse conviction of a New Mexico man who had fought a court battle with his former wife for custody of their young daughter. At trial, the prosecution introduced the girl's testimony as well as testimony from six witnesses who said she made similar charges before trial. The court said it allowed the use of the hearsay evidence to rebut the defense theory that the girl made up the accusations because she wanted to live with her mother instead of with her father.

Reversing the conviction, the Court said the trial judge misinterpreted the hearsay rule exception contained in the Federal Rules of Evidence. Kennedy said the prior statements could be used to rebut a charge of "recent fabrication" only if they were made before a motive for lying arose.

Writing for the dissenters, Breyer said a judge should be allowed to permit the use of what he called "postmotive statements" if they were "significantly probative."

United States v. Mezzanatto, decided by a 7–2 vote, January 18, 1995; Thomas wrote the opinion; Souter and Stevens dissented.

The Court cleared the way for federal prosecutors to enforce agreements permitting them to use statements made by a defendant during plea bargaining to cross-examine the defendant at trial.

The Federal Rules of Evidence and Federal Rules of Criminal Procedure both provide that, with limited exceptions, a defendant's statements during plea negotiations cannot be used against the defendant later. But in a 7–2 decision, the Court upheld a growing practice among federal prosecutors to have defendants waive that right as a condition of entering into plea discussions.

Writing for the Court, Thomas said that most legal rights are subject to voluntary waiver and that defense arguments for refusing to honor the waiver were not persuasive. He said the practice would not discourage—and might encourage—plea bargaining. In addition, he said, permitting use of the defendant's statements "will result in more accurate verdicts."

In a dissenting opinion, Souter, joined by Stevens, said that the Court's interpretation was contrary to Congress's intent in enacting the rules and would discourage plea bargaining. He also said that the ruling invited prosecutors to use a defendant's statements during plea bargaining not only for impeachment purposes but also as part of the government's main case. However, three of the justices in the majority—Ginsburg, O'Connor, and Breyer—wrote in a concurring opinion that that issue had not been decided.

The decision reinstated the drug conviction of a California man whose trial testimony conflicted with statements made during plea negotiations. The ruling directly applied only to federal cases, but it also indicated that the Court would not prohibit the same practice in state courts.

Habeas Corpus

Duncan, Warden v. Henry, decided by an 8–1 vote, January 23, 1995; *per curiam* (unsigned) opinion; Stevens dissented.

The Court tightened the requirements for prison inmates to raise constitutional issues in state courts before using the same claims to challenge convictions through federal habeas corpus proceedings.

The decision reinstated the child molestation conviction of a former rector of a church day school in California. In appealing the conviction, he contended the use of testimony by another child who claimed to have been molested twenty years earlier amounted to "miscarriage of justice." State courts upheld the conviction, but two federal courts found a due process violation in use of the testimony and ordered a new trial.

Reversing the federal courts without hearing arguments in the case, the Court said the defendant had failed to raise the due process issue in his state appeal. "If a habeas petitioner wishes to claim that an evidentiary ruling at a state court trial denied him the due process of law guaranteed by the Fourteenth Amendment," the Court said in an unsigned opinion, "he must say so, not only in federal court, but in state court."

Stevens, the lone dissenter, called the ruling "hypertechnical" and "a substantial departure from our precedents." He also criticized the decision to rule on the case summarily without arguments.

Garlotte v. Fordice, Governor of Mississippi, decided by a 7–2 vote, May 30, 1995; Ginsburg wrote the opinion; Thomas and Rehnquist dissented.

A state prison inmate serving consecutive sentences for separate offenses can use federal habeas corpus law to challenge a conviction even if he has completed the sentence for that offense.

The ruling allowed a Mississippi inmate who was serving concurrent life prison sentences for murder convictions to challenge a marijuana conviction even though he had completed the three-year term for that case. The inmate argued that his parole date would be advanced if the expired marijuana conviction were invalidated. But a federal appeals court barred the petition because the inmate was no longer "in custody" under the marijuana conviction.

In a 7–2 decision, the Court held that the inmate was "in custody" for purposes of the federal habeas corpus law. Ginsburg said the inmate's challenge "implicates the core purpose of the habeas review" because it would "shorten his term of incarceration if he proves unconstitutionality."

The dissenting justices argued that the Court was wrong to extend a previous ruling that allowed a habeas corpus challenge to a prison sentence that had not yet begun.

Goeke, Superintendent, Renz Correctional Center v. Branch, decided by a 9–0 vote, March 20, 1995; *per curiam* (unsigned) opinion.

The Court summarily wiped out a federal appeals court ruling that would have limited the power of state courts to dismiss appeals by defendants who become fugitives while their appeals are pending.

The Eighth U.S. Circuit Court of Appeals granted habeas corpus relief to a Missouri prison inmate whose original appeal had been dismissed in state courts. The Eighth Circuit panel said the dismissal violated the inmate's constitutional rights because her "pre-appeal flight" had "no adverse effect" on the state appellate process.

In an unsigned opinion issued without oral argument, the Court said the appeals court ruling amounted to a new rule of law that could not be retroactively applied in a habeas corpus case. The Court acknowledged that it had adopted a similar limit on the power of courts to dismiss appeals by fugitive defendants in 1993 but said that ruling applied only in federal, not state, courts.

Kyles v. Whitley, Warden, decided by a 5–4 vote, April 19, 1995; Souter wrote the opinion; Scalia, Rehnquist, Kennedy, and Thomas dissented.

The Court ordered a new trial for a Louisiana death row inmate because the prosecution failed to disclose material evidence it found that might have produced a different result at trial. The narrowly divided ruling produced a sharp dissent over the Court's decision to review the case at all.

The decision granted habeas corpus relief to a Louisiana man, Curtis Lee Kyles, who had been convicted of murder in the 1984 robbery-shooting of an elderly woman in a New Orleans grocery store parking lot. Kyles's first trial ended with a hung jury; he was convicted in a second trial largely on the strength of identification testimony by four eyewitnesses.

Kyle challenged the conviction in state and federal habeas corpus petitions on grounds the prosecutors failed to disclose potentially favorable evidence, including interviews with the eyewitnesses and with the informant who first implicated Kyles. The Fifth U.S. Circuit Court of Appeals rejected the plea in a 2–1 decision, but the dissenting judge said he had "serious reservations about whether the State has sentenced to death the right man."

Writing for a five-justice majority, Souter said the failure to disclose the evidence required a new trial under previous Court rulings because it "would have made a different result reasonably probable." The detailed, thirty-seven-page opinion dealt mostly with the facts of the case, but it said the appeals court made a legal mistake by treating the withholding of the evidence as a "harmless error."

In his dissent, Scalia said the prosecution produced "a massive core of evidence" of Kyles's guilt and said the effect of the withheld evidence would have been "immaterial." Scalia also criticized the decision to review what he called "an intensely fact-specific case," saying responsibility for correcting factual mistakes rests with lower courts. Stevens, joined by Ginsburg and Breyer, responded by saying the Court's need to carefully review evidence in some cases was "especially important" because of "the current popularity of capital punishment."

O'Neal v. McAninch, Warden, decided by a 6–3 vote, February 21, 1995; Breyer wrote the opinion; Thomas, Rehnquist, and Scalia dissented.

A federal judge should grant a state prison inmate's habeas corpus petition if the prisoner proves a constitutional error at trial and the judge is in doubt whether the error might have affected the outcome.

The decision reversed a ruling by the Sixth U.S. Circuit Court of Appeals requiring that inmates challenging their state court convictions had the burden of showing prejudice from a constitutional violation at trial. The Court in 1993 ruled that an error should be considered harmless unless it had a substantial effect on the trial but left unresolved whether the state or the inmate had the burden of proof on the question.

Writing for the majority in the new case, Breyer said precedent and the "basic purpose" of habeas corpus required a judge in grave doubt about the effect of a trial error to grant the inmate's petition and order a new trial. The opposite rule, he wrote, "would virtually guarantee that many [inmates], *in fact,* will be held in unlawful custody."

The dissenting justices argued that the federal habeas corpus statute requires inmates to prove prejudicial error. Thomas also said the ruling undermined the states' interest in finality in criminal cases.

Thomas, Rehnquist, and Scalia had been in the majority in the 5–4 decision in the 1993 case. But the other two justices from the majority— Stevens and O'Connor—changed sides and voted to ease the rules for inmates in the new case.

Schlup v. Delo, Superintendent, Potosi Correctional Center, decided by a 5–4 vote, January 23, 1995; Stevens wrote the opinion; Rehnquist, Scalia, Kennedy, and Thomas dissented.

The Court made it somewhat easier for a state death row inmate who claims to be innocent to win a federal court hearing on alleged constitutional errors at his trial.

The decision relaxed the standard for permitting a death row inmate to avoid the normal rule against consideration of successive habeas corpus petitions in federal courts. The Court held that an inmate is entitled to a hearing on his claim if he shows that a constitutional violation "probably resulted" in the conviction of one who is actually innocent.

The ruling came in the case of a Missouri death row inmate, Lloyd E. Schlup, Jr., who had been convicted of murder in the 1984 stabbing death of a fellow prisoner. In his second federal habeas corpus petition, Schlup cited newly discovered evidence to support his claim that he was innocent and that the verdict had been tainted by ineffective assistance from his trial counsel and by the prosecution's withholding of exculpatory evidence.

A federal district court judge and the Eighth U.S. Circuit Court of Appeals both refused to grant Schlup a hearing on the claim. In its decision, the appeals court denied relief on the basis of a 1992 Supreme Court decision, *Sawyer v. Whitley*. That ruling bars repeat habeas corpus petitions unless an inmate shows by clear and convincing evidence that no reasonable juror would have convicted him but for a constitutional defect at trial.

In a densely technical, thirty-four-page opinion, Stevens said the "clear-and-convincing" standard was too "stringent" for a death row inmate with claims of actual innocence and constitutional error. The "overriding importance" of avoiding the execution of an innocent person, Stevens said, requires what he called "a less exacting standard" adapted from an earlier case, *Murray v. Carrier* (1986). The ruling returned the case to federal district court to decide whether Schlup should get a hearing under the new standard.

In the main dissent, Rehnquist, joined by Kennedy and Thomas, said the ruling "waters down" the Court's standard for successive habeas corpus petitions and would "inevitably create confusion" in lower courts. In a separate dissent, Scalia argued that the federal habeas corpus statute gives federal judges broad discretion to refuse to entertain an inmate's second habeas corpus petition. Thomas also joined Scalia's dissent.

Juries

United States v. Gaudin, decided by a 9–0 vote, June 19, 1995; Scalia wrote the opinion.

A trial judge violated the jury trial rights of a defendant charged under the federal false statement statute by refusing to allow jurors to decide whether the statements were "material" as required for a conviction.

The ruling rejected the government's plea to reinstate the conviction of a Montana man who was charged with making various false statements on Federal Housing Administration (FHA) loan documents in a scheme to defraud the agency. The false statement statute — section 1001 of Title 18 — makes it a crime to falsify or conceal "a material fact" in "any matter" before a federal department or agency. The judge in the case ruled that the issue of materiality was a matter of law for him to decide. The Ninth U.S. Circuit Court of Appeals ruled that the question should have been presented to the jury.

In a unanimous decision, the Court agreed. Scalia said "materiality" was an element of the offense under the law and was the sort of mixed question of law and fact historically given to juries to decide. "The Constitution gives a criminal defendant the right to have a jury determine, beyond a reasonable doubt, his guilt of every element of which he is charged," Scalia concluded.

The decision overruled a 1929 ruling by the Court in *Sinclair v. United States,* which upheld a defendant's conviction for contempt of Congress for refusing to answer a question "pertinent to" a congressional inquiry. In that case, the Court ruled "pertinency" was for the judge, not the jury, to decide.

Jury Selection

Purkett, Superintendent, Farmington Corrections Center v. Elem, decided by a 7–2 vote, May 15, 1995; *per curiam* (unsigned) opinion; Stevens and Breyer dissented.

The Court eased the burden on prosecutors to refute charges of improperly using peremptory challenges to exclude potential jurors because of their race. The justification must be race-neutral but not necessarily rational, the Court said.

The ruling overturned a federal appeals court's decision to order a new trial for a Missouri prison inmate who had questioned the prosecutor's decision to exclude two black men from the jury panel. The prosecutor said he objected to the two men because they had mustaches and beards, but the appeals court said that was not a "legitimate race-neutral" reason as required by the Supreme Court's ruling in a 1986 case, *Batson v. Kentucky.*

In an unsigned opinion issued without hearing arguments in the case, the Court said the appellate panel misinterpreted the prior ruling. "What it means by a 'legitimate reason' is not a reason that makes sense, but a reason that does not deny equal protection," the Court said.

In a dissent, Stevens, joined by Breyer, said the ruling amounted to overturning a portion of the earlier decision. "It is not too much to ask that a prosecutor's explanation for his strikes be race neutral, reasonably specific, *and* trial related," Stevens wrote. He also complained that the Court should not have decided the case without hearing arguments.

Parole

California Department of Corrections v. Morales, decided by a 7–2 vote, April 25, 1995; Thomas wrote the opinion; Stevens and Souter dissented.

States may retroactively reduce the frequency of parole hearings for convicted murderers without violating the Constitution's Ex Post Facto Clause.

The 7–2 decision upheld a California law passed in 1981 that generally required multiple murderers to wait three years after an initial hearing for a subsequent opportunity to gain parole. Previously, inmates were entitled to annual parole hearings.

Jose Morales, an inmate serving a fifteen-year sentence for a 1980 murder committed after completing a term for a previous offense, argued that the new provision retroactively increased his sentence in violation of the Ex Post Facto Clause. California courts upheld the law, but the Ninth U.S. Circuit Court of Appeals sustained Morales's claim and ordered a new parole hearing.

Writing for the Court, Thomas said the new law does not violate the Ex Post Facto Clause because it "simply alters the method to be followed in fixing a parole release date." He said the amendment "creates only the most speculative and attenuated possibility" of increasing Morales's sentence.

Dissenting justices argued that the law improperly changed "the consequences of past conduct." Stevens noted that broader laws delaying parole hearings for all or most prisoners had been struck down by a number of state and federal courts.

Prisons and Jails

Sandin, Unit Team Manager, Halawa Correctional Facility v. Conner, decided by a 5–4 vote, June 19, 1995; Rehnquist wrote the opinion; Breyer, Stevens, Souter, and Ginsburg dissented.

Inmates must show that they are being subjected to unusual and significant hardship in order to bring a due process challenge to their treatment by prison management.

The narrowly divided decision raised the standard for a common type of inmate suit by repudiating a line of Court decisions since 1979. The ruling involved a Hawaii prison inmate, DeMont Conner, who was placed in disciplinary segregation for thirty days after obscenely objecting to a strip search by a prison guard. Conner, serving a thirty-year to life sentence for murder, kidnapping, and robbery, essentially admitted the accusations but was denied the chance to present witnesses.

Prison officials later reversed the finding and expunged the inmate's record, but Conner filed a federal civil rights suit seeking damages. A federal district court judge ruled for prison officials, but the Ninth U.S. Circuit Court of Appeals reinstated the suit.

The Court's 5–4 ruling killed Conner's suit by holding that he had no "liberty interest" that would require procedural rights under the Due Process Clause. Rehnquist said the Court had gone astray in several decisions since 1979 by ruling that mandatory prison regulations gave prisoners rights enforceable in court. Those cases "led to the involvement of federal courts in the day-to-day management of federal prisons," the chief justice ruled.

Under the new standard, inmates raising due process claims must show that their treatment "imposes atypical and significant hardship ... in relation to the ordinary incidents of prison life," Rehnquist said. Applying that standard, he said Conner's 30-day isolation did not present "a dramatic departure from the basic conditions" of his sentence.

The dissenting justices divided into two groups. Breyer, joined by Souter, questioned the need to revise the Court's precedents and contended Conner had suffered a "significant" deprivation under any definition. Ginsburg, joined by Stevens, argued that inmates' rights should be decided by looking to the Due Process Clause instead of to the individual state's prison regulations. All four dissenters said, however, that Conner had not been denied any procedural right in his hearing and would have lost his suit if the case had been remanded.

Search and Seizure

Arizona v. Evans, decided by a 7–2 vote, March 1, 1995; Rehnquist wrote the opinion; Ginsburg and Stevens dissented.

The Court refused to bar the use of evidence obtained from a defendant after he was arrested on the basis of an erroneous computer warrant. But it limited the ruling to mistakes made by court employees, not law enforcement officials.

The decision reinstated the marijuana conviction of an Arizona man, Isaac Evans, who was stopped for a traffic violation and then arrested when a computer check showed an outstanding misdemeanor warrant against him. The arrest warrant had actually been thrown out seventeen days earlier. On that basis, Evans claimed the arrest was unlawful and the marijuana found in his car should be excluded. The Arizona Supreme Court agreed.

Writing for the Court, Rehnquist said the exclusionary rule should not be applied because it would not help deter "clerical mistakes" by court employees. "There is no basis for believing that application of the exclusionary rule ... will have a significant effect on court employees responsible for informing the police that a warrant has been quashed," he wrote.

Rehnquist carefully limited the scope of his opinion. And in a concurring opinion, O'Connor, joined by Souter and Breyer, stressed that the decision did not apply to mistakes made by police.

Ginsburg dissented without discussing the merits of the issue. She said the Court should have treated the Arizona court's decision as based on state law grounds and refrained from deciding the issue. Stevens joined Ginsburg's opinion but wrote in his own dissent that the ruling would have a "serious impact" on privacy protections for "innocent" citizens.

Wilson v. Arkansas, decided by a 9–0 vote, May 22, 1995; Thomas wrote the opinion.

Police should ordinarily knock and announce their identity before entering a home with a search warrant. But an unannounced entry may be reasonable if police fear physical violence or destruction of evidence.

The ruling reversed a decision by the Arkansas Supreme Court affirming the conviction of Sharlene Wilson on drug charges resulting from evidence found after an unannounced entry of her home. The state court ruled that the Fourth Amendment did not require a "knock and announce" rule.

In a unanimous decision, the Court held that the "knock and announce" rule was part of the Fourth Amendment because it had been established in English and American common law. As authority, Thomas cited an English case decided in 1603 but said the requirement might date back as far as the thirteenth century.

"Given the longstanding common-law endorsement of the practice of announcement," Thomas wrote, "we have little doubt that the Framers of the Fourth Amendment thought that the method of an officer's entry into a dwelling was among the factors to be considered in assessing the reasonableness of a search or seizure."

Thomas stressed, however, that police could show that an unannounced entry was reasonable under some circumstances. As some examples, Thomas listed the threat of physical harm to officers, pursuit of an escaped prisoner, and fear of destruction of evidence. The decision returned the case to Arkansas courts to decide whether the police had sufficient justification for an unannounced entry in Wilson's case.

Sentencing

Reno, Attorney General v. Koray, decided by an 8–1 vote, June 5, 1995; Rehnquist wrote the opinion; Stevens dissented.

Federal prisoners are not entitled to credit for time served in private community treatment centers or halfway houses prior to sentencing.

The nearly unanimous ruling rejected an effort by a defendant convicted of money laundering to get credit against his 46-month sentence for 150 days served in a community treatment center before sentencing. Most federal appeals courts had refused to give sentencing credit in such cases, but the Third U.S. Circuit Court of Appeals in Philadelphia ruled that the defendant would get credit if he could show that he had been confined in "jail-like conditions."

Reversing the appellate ruling, the Court held that time spent in a private treatment center or halfway house does not amount to "official detention" for purposes of federal sentencing law. Rehnquist cited several factors for the restrictive interpretation, including the context and history of the law and the Bureau of Prisons' internal guideline denying sentence credit for time in treatment centers. In a short concurring opinion, Ginsburg suggested that defendants should be told they will not get sentencing credit before they agree to being released to a halfway house.

Stevens, the lone dissenter, noted that the defendant had been confined to the center twenty-four hours a day, given limited access to visitors, and subjected to random breath and urine tests. "In my opinion, [the defendant's] confinement was unquestionably both 'official' and 'detention,' within the meaning of [the sentencing law]," Stevens wrote.

Election Law

Federal Election Commission

Federal Election Commission v. NRA Political Victory Fund, decided by a 7–1 vote, December 6, 1994; Rehnquist wrote the opinion; Stevens dissented; Ginsburg did not participate in the case.

The Federal Election Commission (FEC) has no independent statutory authority to represent itself in cases before the Supreme Court.

The procedural ruling turned aside the FEC's effort to overturn a federal appeals court decision that it had been illegally constituted for many years because two congressional representatives served as nonvoting members. A political arm of the National Rifle Association challenged the arrangement after it was fined $40,000 for a campaign finance violation.

Without reaching the separation of powers issue, the Court said that the law establishing the FEC gives it no authority to pursue cases beyond the appeals court level. The solicitor general's office, which normally represents the federal government before the Court, tried to skirt the issue by authorizing the agency's appeal. But Rehnquist said the move came after the filing deadline.

Stevens, the lone dissenter, said the decision misread the statute and ignored the importance of giving the FEC legal authority independent of the executive branch.

The ruling nullified the fine against the NRA fund and kept a legal cloud over about two dozen other enforcement actions by the FEC. The congressional representatives were dropped from the commission after the appeals court ruling in 1993.

Reapportionment and Redistricting

Miller v. Johnson, decided by a 5–4 vote, June 29, 1995; Kennedy wrote the opinion; Ginsburg, Stevens, Souter, and Breyer dissented.

The use of race as "the predominant factor" in drawing voting district lines is presumptively unconstitutional.

The closely divided ruling required the state of Georgia to revise a plan that created three congressional districts with majority black populations. The plan, drawn under pressure from the U.S. Justice Department, included one district that joined black populations in areas separated by about 260 miles. A three-judge federal court upheld a challenge by white voters to the plan, saying that race had been "the predominant and overriding factor" in drawing the district.

The Court agreed in a decision expanding its 1993 ruling, *Shaw v. Reno,* that barred "bizarrely shaped" district lines based on race. Writing for the majority, Kennedy said that voters can challenge a districting plan whenever race is the predominant factor. The government "may not separate its citizens into different voting districts on the basis of race," Kennedy wrote.

Kennedy said that a race-based plan can be upheld only if it satisfies "strict scrutiny"—that is, it serves a compelling government interest and is narrowly tailored to serve that interest. And Kennedy said that Georgia's plan did not serve a compelling interest because the Justice Department had misinterpreted the federal Voting Rights Act to require a plan with the maximum number of majority black districts.

In a concurring opinion, O'Connor said the ruling would apply only to "extreme instances of gerrymandering" and would not invalidate "the vast majority" of the nation's 435 congressional districts.

Writing for the dissenters, Ginsburg said the ruling allowed an "unwarranted" enlargement of the judicial role in reviewing district lines. Stevens wrote a briefer dissent, arguing that the white voters had failed to show how they were injured by the plan. *(See entry, p. 32; excerpts, p. 232.)*

United States v. Hays, decided by a 9–0 vote, June 29, 1995; O'Connor wrote the opinion.

The Court sidestepped a decision on a racial redistricting plan for congressional seats in Louisiana on grounds that the voters contesting the plan did not live in the district being challenged.

Louisiana drew a congressional redistricting plan that created two districts with majority black populations, one of which zigzagged across half the state. A three-judge court ruled the plan invalid in a challenge filed by a group of white voters placed in the new district. In a new plan, the state legislature created a more compact district with a majority black population in the central part of the state. The voters challenging the plan were no longer included in the new district.

In a unanimous decision, the Court held that the voters lacked standing to challenge the plan. "[The voters] do not live in the district that is the primary focus of their racial gerrymandering claim, and they have not otherwise demonstrated that they, personally, have been subjected to a racial classification," O'Connor wrote. The ruling came on the same day that the Court adopted a stricter standard for judging racial redistricting plans in a Georgia case, *Miller v. Johnson. (See above.)*

Four justices distanced themselves from O'Connor's opinion, which reaffirmed that white voters living within a racially drawn district can bring legal challenges. Souter, joined by Breyer, said he agreed only with the part of the opinion dealing with nonresidents. Stevens, concurring in the judgment, argued for limiting the ability of white voters to challenge such plans. And Ginsburg concurred in the judgment without filing a separate opinion.

Term Limits

U.S. Term Limits, Inc. v. Thornton, decided by a 5–4 vote, May 22, 1995; Stevens wrote the opinion; Thomas, Rehnquist, O'Connor, and Scalia dissented.

Neither Congress nor the states can directly limit the number of terms for members of Congress or try to accomplish the same goal by handicapping incumbents' access to the ballot.

In a closely divided ruling, the Court held that congressional term limit measures adopted in nearly half the states were unconstitutional because they attempted to impose qualifications for serving in Congress beyond those listed in the Constitution. "Allowing individual States to adopt their own qualifications for congressional service would be inconsistent with the Framers' vision of a uniform National Legislature representing the people of the United States," Stevens wrote.

The ruling came in a voter challenge to a term limits initiative adopted by Arkansas voters in 1992. The measure barred House incumbents with six years' service and senators with twelve years' service from the ballot but allowed them to run as write-in candidates.

Stevens rejected supporters' arguments that the measure was a valid regulation of state ballot procedures. "... [A]n amendment with the avowed purpose and obvious effect of evading the Qualifications Clause by handicapping a class of candidates cannot stand," he wrote.

Writing for the four dissenters, Thomas argued that the states retained the power under the Tenth Amendment to add to the qualifications listed in the Constitution. "Nothing in the Constitution deprives the people of each State of the power to prescribe eligibility requirements for the candidates who seek to represent them in Congress," Thomas wrote.

In a concurring opinion, Kennedy said the two opposing opinions showed "the intricacy of the question" whether the qualifications listed in the Constitution were exclusive. But he concluded that the term limit measures amounted to an improper "state interference with the most basic relation between the National Government and its citizens, the selection of legislative representatives." *(See entry, p. 40; excerpts, p. 142.)*

Environmental Law

Endangered Species Act

Babbitt, Secretary of the Interior v. Sweet Home Chapter of Communities for a Great Oregon, decided by a 6–3 vote, June 29, 1995; Stevens wrote the opinion; Scalia, Rehnquist, and Thomas dissented.

The Endangered Species Act gives the federal government authority to regulate the use of private land in order to protect habitat for rare wildlife species.

The ruling turned back a challenge backed by the timber industry to an Interior Department regulation that extended the landmark 1973 law to cover "significant habitat modification" for endangered species on private lands. The law made it illegal to "take" a species and then defined "take" to include, among other things, "harm." The groups challenging the regulation contended that the statute applied only to deliberate harm to wildlife. The federal appeals court in Washington, D.C., agreed.

In a 6–3 decision, the Court reinstated the regulation. "Given Congress' clear expression of the ESA's broad purpose to protect endangered and threatened wildlife, the Secretary's definition of 'harm' is reasonable," Stevens wrote.

In a concurring opinion, O'Connor suggested that the law might not apply to uses of land that have unforeseeable impacts on animal life. Both Stevens and O'Connor stressed that the ruling still allowed individual landowners to challenge enforcement of the law in specific cases.

Writing for the dissenters, Scalia said the regulation went beyond the language of the law. *(See entry, p. 60; excerpts, p. 260.)*

Federal Government

Federal Employees

Gutierrez de Martinez v. Lamagno, decided by a 5–4 vote, June 14, 1995; Ginsburg wrote the opinion; Souter, Rehnquist, Scalia, and Thomas dissented.

Federal courts can review a Justice Department determination that a federal employee named in a civil suit was acting within the scope of employment and should be dismissed from the suit.

The ruling resolved an issue involving a 1988 law called the Westfall Act that, as the Court explained, only rarely affects a plaintiff's chances of recovery. Under the law, once a federal employee is dismissed from a suit, the United States is substituted as a defendant, and the case can proceed under the Federal Tort Claims Act.

The law had the effect of killing a suit by two Colombian citizens involved in a 1991 automobile accident with a Drug Enforcement Administration (DEA) agent in Colombia. The law had this effect because the Federal Tort Claims Act bars recovery for actions overseas. To keep their suit alive, the Colombians asked a federal court to review the certification that the agent, who was driving in his car shortly before midnight with an unidentified woman passenger, was acting within the scope of his employment at the time. But the Fourth U.S. Circuit Court of Appeals ruled the certification was not reviewable in court.

In a 5–4 decision, the Court disagreed. Ginsburg acknowledged that the statute was ambiguous but said the normal rule favors court review of executive action. "No persuasive reason for restricting access to judicial review is discernible in the statutory fog we confront here," she wrote.

The Clinton administration itself urged the Court to permit courts to review Justice Department findings in such cases—an unusual position that forced the justices to appoint an outside lawyer to defend the appeals court ruling. But the dissenting justices insisted the statute clearly prohibited judicial review.

Federal Regulation

Anderson, Director, California Department of Social Services v. Edwards, decided by a 9–0 vote, March 22, 1995; Thomas wrote the opinion.

States can count all children living in a home as a single family unit, whether or not they are siblings, in setting payments under the Aid to Families With Dependent Children (AFDC) program.

The decision reinstated a California rule adopted in 1991 that treated a household with nonsibling children as a single "assistance unit." The effect was to lower the benefits per child just as they would be scaled back for a household consisting only of sibling children.

A woman who cared for a granddaughter and two grandnieces challenged the regulation as a violation of federal law. Under the rule, she received $207 per month less than she would have if the grandnieces had not been treated as a single family unit.

Two lower federal courts invalidated the rule, but the Court unanimously held that it did not violate federal regulations governing the AFDC program. Thomas said the rule "sensibly and equitably" provides that "equally sized and equally needy households will receive equal AFDC assistance." He stressed that the states have "great latitude" in administering the AFDC program.

About half the states had similar rules, according to briefs filed by state attorneys general supporting the California rule. The Clinton administration also urged the Court to uphold the regulation.

Anderson, Director, California Department of Social Services v. Green, decided by a 9–0 vote, February 22, 1995; *per curiam* (unsigned) opinion.

The Court dismissed a case testing the constitutionality of a California law limiting welfare benefits for new arrivals to the state.

The California law limited payments to new residents under the Aid to Families With Dependent Children program to the level of benefits paid in their former state. A federal appeals court ruled the law violated the constitutional right to travel. After the Court agreed to review the case, however, California lost a separate case challenging the federal waiver it had needed to put the law into effect.

In a brief, unsigned opinion, the Court dismissed the case and vacated the appeals court decision to "clear the path for future relitigation" of the issue.

Freightliner Corp. v. Myrick, decided by a 9–0 vote, April 18, 1995; Thomas wrote the opinion.

Two truck manufacturers failed in their effort to bar product liability suits in state courts because of a suspended federal safety standard. But the ruling included a passage that could help similar federal preemption claims in other product liability suits.

The unanimous decision reinstated separate suits filed in Georgia state courts blaming the manufacturers for traffic accidents because their trucks lacked antilock braking systems and were prone to "jack-knifing" in a sudden stop. The companies claimed the state suits were preempted because a federal court in 1978 had blocked a regulation issued by the National Highway Traffic Safety Administration in 1971 effectively requiring antilock braking systems.

The Court said, however, that the suspended standard did not override state law governing product defect suits. "The absence of a federal standard cannot implicitly extinguish state common law," Thomas wrote.

But Thomas added that some federal courts had too strictly interpreted the Court's 1992 ruling disallowing a similar preemption claim in a suit against a cigarette manufacturer. Contrary to those lower court rulings, Thomas said, a federal statute may impliedly preempt state law on some issues even if the act specifies that it does not preempt state law on other issues.

Scalia did not join Thomas's opinion but did not write separately to explain his views.

Interstate Commerce Commission v. Transcon Lines, decided by a 9–0 vote, January 10, 1995; Kennedy wrote the opinion.

Motor carriers can be blocked from collecting normal charges from shippers under previous rate regulations if they failed to comply with federal credit-disclosure regulations.

The unanimous ruling upheld an effort by the Interstate Commerce Commission (ICC) to prevent the trustee for a bankrupt motor carrier from collecting unpaid charges from several shippers. The ICC said the company did not follow procedures required by its credit regulations. But two federal courts barred the enforcement action because of the so-called "filed rate doctrine," which generally requires carriers and shippers to follow the rates posted with the ICC.

Writing for the Court, Kennedy said the ICC had power to seek an injunction in the case, calling it "both necessary and appropriate" to enforcement of the credit regulations. He said the filed rate doctrine was inapplicable because the agency's enforcement action did not create the risk of price discrimination the rule was aimed at preventing.

New York State Conference of Blue Cross & Blue Shield Plans v. Travelers Insurance Co., decided by a 9–0 vote, April 26, 1995; Souter wrote the opinion.

States may require health insurers and health maintenance organizations (HMOs) to pay surcharges to hospitals to cover the costs of uninsured patients without violating the federal law regulating employee health benefit plans.

The decision upheld a New York law similar to provisions in about half the states. Under the law, hospital reimbursement rates for private insurers included two surcharges totaling 24 percent and a 9 percent surcharge for HMOs that failed to enroll a certain number of Medicaid-eligible people. Private insurers and HMOs argued the New York law was preempted by the federal Employee Retirement Income Security Act (ERISA), which generally supersedes any state law that relates to employee benefit plans.

In a unanimous opinion, Souter said the New York law was not preempted because it had only an indirect effect on employee benefit plans. The decision, reversing lower federal court rulings in the case, backed away from broad language in previous Court decisions on the question of ERISA preemption of state health laws.

Shalala, Secretary of Health and Human Services v. Guernsey Memorial Hospital, decided by a 5–4 vote, March 6, 1995; Kennedy wrote the opinion; O'Connor, Scalia, Souter, and Thomas dissented.

The secretary of Health and Human Services (HHS) does not have to follow general accounting principles in determining reimbursements under the Medicare program for hospitals or other health care providers.

The ruling upheld a decision to stretch out reimbursement to a hospital for an accounting loss of $672,000 resulting from a refinancing of bonds. The hospital argued standard accounting rules—so-called Generally Accepted Accounting Principles or GAAP—called for the loss to be recognized in the year of the financing. The department cited informal guidelines in ruling that the loss should be amortized over the life of the original bonds.

In a closely divided decision, the Court said HHS had authority to depart from general accounting principles on the issue. Kennedy said GAAP did not provide definitive answers to all accounting questions, and the department was not required to go through formal rulemaking if it followed a different rule. The dissenting justices argued that HHS did have to follow formal procedures to depart from general accounting principles.

Shalala, Secretary of Health and Human Services v. Whitecotton, decided by a 9–0 vote, April 18, 1995; Souter wrote the opinion.

A person claiming compensation under the federal law for vaccine-related injuries must show that the first symptoms of the injury occurred after the vaccination.

The unanimous ruling somewhat strictly construed burden-of-proof provisions of the National Childhood Vaccine Injury Act, which Congress passed to simplify compensation for vaccine-related injuries. The act permits compensation without proof of causation if a child or infant suffers any of a number of specified conditions after receiving a vaccination and "the first symptom" of the condition was manifested after the vaccination.

The parents of Margaret Whitecotton filed a claim under the act after their four-month-old infant experienced seizures following a vaccination for diphtheria, pertussis, and tetanus (DPT). But an administrative law judge barred the claim because the infant had a medical condition—an abnormally small head—that is a symptom of the condition that caused the seizures.

The Court ruled that the Whitecottons did not meet the statutory requirements for their claim because the evidence "fails to indicate that [the child] had no symptoms of injury before the vaccination." The decision remanded the case for further proceedings. In a concurring opinion, O'Connor, joined by Breyer, noted that the Whitecottons might still be entitled to compensation if they proved that the vaccination aggravated a pre-existing condition.

Government Corporations

Lebron v. National Railroad Passenger Corporation (Amtrak), decided by an 8–1 vote, February 21, 1995; Scalia wrote the opinion; O'Connor dissented.

Amtrak, the government-created rail passenger corporation, is to be treated as a government agency for purposes of the First Amendment.

The ruling allowed artist Michael Lebron to pursue a free speech claim against Amtrak for refusing to permit him to display a political advertisement on a giant billboard in Pennsylvania Station in New York City. Amtrak, citing language in its authorizing congressional statute, argued that it was not subject to the First Amendment because it is not "an agency or establishment of the United States."

In a nearly unanimous ruling, the Court held that Amtrak is "part of the Government for First Amendment purposes." Scalia noted that Amtrak was created "for the very purpose of pursuing federal governmental objectives" and that the government retained permanent authority to appoint a majority of its board of directors. A different ruling, he said, would allow state or federal governments "to evade the most solemn obligations imposed in the Constitution by simply resorting to the corporate form."

O'Connor, the lone dissenter, refused to consider whether Amtrak should be treated as a government agency because Lebron had not made that argument in lower courts. Instead, she said that Amtrak should be treated as a private entity, and its decision to bar political advertising should be upheld as "a matter of private business judgment."

The decision returned the case to lower federal courts to determine whether Amtrak's policy of refusing all political advertising violated the First Amendment.

Military

Ryder v. United States, decided by a 9–0 vote, June 12, 1995; Rehnquist wrote the opinion.

The Court refused to let the military justice system get around a ruling that appellate panels in a handful of cases had been illegally constituted.

The decision overturned a ruling by the Court of Military Appeals affirming the court-martial conviction of a Coast Guard enlistee on drug offenses. The defendant claimed that two of the three members of the appellate panel that reviewed his case had been improperly appointed. The Court of Military Appeals agreed but upheld the conviction anyway. It relied on the so-called *de facto* officer doctrine, which allows courts to validate governmental actions even if the official who took the action is not properly qualified.

In a unanimous ruling, the Court said the military court had misapplied the doctrine in rejecting the defendant's plea. "Any other ruling would create a disincentive to raise Appointments Clause challenges with respect to questionable judicial appointments," Rehnquist wrote. He noted that the government and the defendant had agreed that the issue would affect only seven to ten cases.

Veterans

Brown, Secretary of Veterans Affairs v. Gardner, decided by a 9–0 vote, December 12, 1994; Souter wrote the opinion.

Veterans may recover damages for injuries received during medical treatment at facilities of the Department of Veterans Affairs (VA) without proving that the injury was caused by medical negligence.

The Court unanimously ruled that a sixty-year-old regulation requiring proof of fault went beyond the 1924 statute authorizing compensation for veterans' medical injuries. Souter said the statute did not contain "so much as a word about fault" and rejected as "implausible" the government's effort to read a fault requirement into the act.

The decision upheld a ruling by the U.S. Court of Appeals for the Federal Circuit in favor of a Korean War veteran, Fred Gardner, who said he suffered nerve damage following back surgery at a VA facility in Texas. The government said that striking down the fault requirement could cost $1 billion over five years.

First Amendment

Church and State

Capitol Square Review and Advisory Board v. Pinette, decided by a 7–2 vote, June 29, 1995; Scalia wrote the main opinion; Stevens and Ginsburg dissented.

A private group can place a religious display on government property traditionally used as a public forum if there is no appearance of government endorsement of the religious message.

The 7–2 ruling upheld the right of the Ku Klux Klan to erect a ten-foot cross on a plaza adjacent to the Ohio state capitol. State officials had sought to bar the display because of its "sectarian" message. But the Sixth U.S. Circuit Court of Appeals ruled that the display would not violate the ban on establishment of religion.

Writing for a plurality of four justices, Scalia said that purely private religious expression cannot violate the Establishment Clause if it "occurs in a traditional or designated public forum, publicly announced and open to all on equal terms." Rehnquist, Kennedy, and Thomas joined the opinion.

The three other justices in the majority—O'Connor, Souter, and Breyer—concurred on narrower grounds. O'Connor and Souter each wrote opinions that were joined by the other two justices.

In her opinion, O'Connor applied what she called "the endorsement test," saying that no reasonable observer would conclude that the government had endorsed the religious message. Souter said the state's effort to bar the display was not "narrowly tailored" because it could have required a clear disclaimer or set aside a specific area on the plaza for unattended, private displays.

Stevens argued in dissent that no religious displays should be allowed at "the seat of government." Ginsburg took a narrower position, saying that the display should not have been allowed without a "plainly visible sign" dissociating it from the government. *(See entry, p. 53; excerpts, p. 260.)*

Rosenberger v. Rector and Visitors of University of Virginia, decided by a 5–4 vote, June 29, 1995; Kennedy wrote the opinion; Souter, Stevens, Ginsburg, and Breyer dissented.

A state university that funds student publications from a mandatory student activity fee cannot deny funding to a religious magazine solely because of its religious content.

The ruling required the University of Virginia to reimburse expenses for a student newspaper *Wide Awake,* which had an avowed "Christian perspective." University officials said that guidelines for the student activity fund barred subsidies for a "religious organization." The student editors of the newspaper filed a federal court challenge to require payment. But the Fourth U.S. Circuit Court of Appeals rejected the suit. It ruled that subsidizing the newspaper would amount to an establishment of religion in violation of the First Amendment.

In a closely divided decision, the Court held instead that the refusal to subsidize the newspaper on grounds of its religious content constituted improper "viewpoint discrimination" in violation of the First Amendment's Free Speech Clause. Kennedy also said the university would not violate the Establishment Clause by subsidizing the publication. "There is no Establishment Clause violation in the University's honoring its duties under the Free Speech Clause," he wrote.

O'Connor and Thomas wrote additional concurring opinions. O'Connor stressed that the rules for student publications minimized the danger of what she called an "impermissible" use of public funds to endorse the newspaper's religious message. Thomas answered the dissenters by saying that the Establishment Clause does not prevent the government from allowing religious organizations to receive funds from "evenhanded government programs."

Writing for the dissenters, however, Souter said university funding for the publication would be "a flat violation of the Establishment Clause." *(See entry, p. 50; excerpts, p. 215.)*

Commercial Speech

Florida Bar v. Went For It, Inc., decided by a 5–4 vote, June 21, 1995; O'Connor wrote the opinion; Kennedy, Stevens, Souter, and Ginsburg dissented.

States may temporarily ban lawyers from direct mail solicitation of accident victims or their families in order to protect the victims' privacy and enhance the public image of the legal profession.

The narrowly divided ruling reversed the Court's trend of striking down regulation of lawyer advertising and other forms of commercial speech. The decision upheld a rule by the Florida Bar, an arm of the state's supreme court, that prohibited lawyers from sending targeted mailings to accident or disaster victims or their families until thirty days after the incident.

The rule was challenged by a Tampa lawyer, G. Stewart McHenry, who operated a private lawyer referral service called Went For It, Inc., that routinely used the solicitation technique. McHenry challenged the rule as a violation of the First Amendment, citing the line of Court decisions from 1977 upholding lawyers' right to advertising. McHenry was later disbarred, but the case continued in the name of his company and another lawyer.

In a 5–4 decision, the Court held that the state bar had presented sufficient justification to uphold the regulation. O'Connor, a longtime critic of lawyer advertising, applied a three-part test that requires regulation of commercial speech to be based on a substantial governmental interest, to directly advance that interest, and to be narrowly tailored.

O'Connor said the regulation served valid purposes by "protecting injured Floridians from invasive conduct by lawyers" and "preventing the erosion of confidence in the profession that such repeated invasions have engendered." She said the thirty-day ban was narrowly tailored and emphasized that accident victims had "ample alternative channels" to find out about legal services, such as telephone directories, newspaper and broadcast advertising, and bar association referral services.

Writing for the four dissenters, Kennedy called the regulation "censorship pure and simple" that denied accident victims information they need to protect their legal rights. "When an accident results in death or injury, it is often urgent at once to investigate the occurrence, identify witnesses, and preserve evidence," Kennedy wrote. He noted that the ban did not require attorneys for potential defendants to wait before contacting victims or their families to gather evidence or offer settlements.

Rubin, Secretary of the Treasury v. Coors Brewing Co., decided by a 9–0 vote, April 19, 1995; Thomas wrote the opinion.

The Court struck down a sixty-year-old law that prohibited brewers from listing the alcohol content of their products on labels, saying the measure violated the First Amendment protections for commercial speech.

Two lower federal courts had struck down the 1935 law in a challenge brought by the Colorado-based Coors Brewing Co. The government defended the 1935 law by claiming that it prevented brewers from engaging in so-called "strength wars"—competing for customers on the basis of a higher alcohol content.

Writing for the Court, Thomas accepted the government's interest as legitimate but said the law did not directly advance that interest because of "the overall irrationality of the Government's regulatory scheme." He noted that federal regulations permit brewers to include alcohol content in advertising and also allow — and for some products require — the listing of alcohol content on wines and spirits.

Stevens, concurring separately, said he saw "no basis" for prohibiting "the dissemination of truthful, nonmisleading information about an alcoholic beverage merely because the message is propounded in a commercial context."

Freedom of Speech

Hurley v. Irish-American Gay, Lesbian and Bisexual Group of Boston, decided by a 9–0 vote, June 19, 1995; Souter wrote the opinion.

The Court overturned rulings by Massachusetts courts requiring the private organizers of the St. Patrick's Day parade in Boston to allow a group of Irish-American homosexuals to march in the event.

Massachusetts courts ruled that the South Boston Allied War Veterans Council violated the state's antidiscrimination law by refusing to allow the Irish-American Gay, Lesbian and Bisexual Group — known by the acronym GLIB — to march as a unit in the parade. Massachusetts law prohibits discrimination in public accommodations on the basis of sexual orientation.

The council, a predominantly Irish-American organization, said it excluded the group because the parade was designed to celebrate "traditional religious and social values." It argued that the state courts' rulings violated its freedom of speech under the First Amendment.

In a unanimous decision, the Court agreed. "Parades are a form of expression," Souter wrote. The selection of who can and cannot participate in a parade, he said, is entitled to protection from government control, even for the "enlightened" purpose of combating discrimination.

"... [T]he Council clearly decided to exclude a message it did not like from the communication it chose to make, and that is enough to invoke its right as a private speaker to shape its expression by speaking on one subject while remaining silent on another," Souter concluded.

Souter noted that the city ran the parade until 1947 when it gave the responsibility to the private group. In state courts, GLIB had contended that the city was still involved in running the parade, and the council's rejection therefore amounted to "state action" subject to constitutional limits. But the state courts rejected that argument, and GLIB did not press the issue before the Court.

McIntyre v. Ohio Elections Commission, decided by a 7–2 vote, April 19, 1995; Stevens wrote the opinion; Scalia and Rehnquist dissented.

The First Amendment protects an individual's right to distribute anonymous campaign literature.

The ruling overturned a $100 fine imposed on an Ohio woman, Margaret McIntyre, for passing out unsigned leaflets during a 1988 campaign over a proposed school tax increase in the small city of Westerville. Ohio law required campaign literature to include the name and address of the author or a campaign official. The Ohio Supreme Court upheld the law in a split decision. McIntyre died while the case was pending, but her husband continued the legal challenge after her death.

In a 7–2 decision, the Court ruled that the law abridged freedom of speech in violation of the First Amendment. "Under our Constitution, anonymous pamphleteering is not a pernicious, fraudulent practice, but an honorable tradition of advocacy and of dissent," Stevens wrote.

Stevens rejected the state's efforts to justify the law on grounds of providing information to voters or of preventing fraud or libels during political campaigns. But he left the door open to some campaign disclosure regulations.

Thomas voted to strike down the law but did not join Stevens's opinion. After a lengthy examination of revolutionary-era history, Thomas concluded that anonymous political leafleting was protected by the First Amendment "as originally understood."

In a dissent, Scalia, joined by Rehnquist, complained that the decision was based on "a hitherto unknown right-to-be-unknown while engaging in electoral politics." *(See entry, p. 57; excerpts, p. 119.)*

United States v. National Treasury Employees Union, decided by 6–3 and 5–4 votes, February 22, 1995; Stevens wrote the opinion; O'Connor dissented in part; Rehnquist, Scalia, and Thomas dissented.

The Court struck down on free speech grounds a federal law banning most federal civil servants from being paid for outside speeches, articles, or appearances.

Extending a ban on so-called honoraria for its members, Congress in 1991 barred payments to executive branch employees for outside speeches and writings even if they had no connection to the employee's official duties. In a challenge brought by a federal employee union and a number of individual employees, two federal courts struck the law down as a violation of the First Amendment.

In a 6–3 decision, the Court agreed. Stevens said the government had failed to show any "evidence of misconduct related to honoraria in the vast rank and file of federal employees...."

Stevens rejected the government's plea to rewrite the law to retain a ban on receiving honoraria for work-related speeches, appearances, or articles. O'Connor concurred in the Court's main ruling but said she would keep the ban on work-related honoraria in place.

Writing for the three dissenters, Rehnquist said the decision "understates the weight which should be accorded to the governmental justifications for the honoraria ban and overstates the amount of speech which actually will be deterred."

Immigration Law

Immigration Procedure

Stone v. Immigration and Naturalization Service, decided by a 6–3 vote, April 19, 1995; Kennedy wrote the opinion; Breyer, O'Connor, and Souter dissented.

Filing a motion for reconsideration of a deportation order issued by the Board of Immigration Appeals (BIA) does not extend the ninety-day time limit for seeking review of the order by a federal court of appeals.

The highly technical decision endorsed a stand taken by the Immigration and Naturalization Service to reduce an alien's opportunities to use review procedures to delay deportation. The issue involved the interaction of two separate provisions of immigration law. One permits an alien to ask the BIA to reconsider a deportation order; the other establishes a ninety-day time limit for seeking judicial review of a "final" deportation order.

Writing for the Court, Kennedy said that a reconsideration motion does not "toll the running of the ninety-day period." He cited a provision in a 1990 immigration act that consolidates a reconsideration motion with judicial review of a deportation order. That provision, Kennedy said, reflected "an intent on the part of Congress that deportation orders are to be reviewed in a timely fashion after issuance, irrespective of the later filing of a motion to reopen or reconsider."

Dissenting justices argued that the ruling departed from normal rules for reviewing administrative agency decisions and created "a serious risk of unfair loss of a right to appeal."

Individual Rights

Affirmative Action

Adarand Constructors, Inc. v. Peña, Secretary of Transportation, decided by a 5–4 vote, June 12, 1995; O'Connor wrote the opinion; Stevens, Souter, Ginsburg, and Breyer dissented.

In a sharp setback for advocates of affirmative action, the Court raised the standard for reviewing racial classifications in federal programs to the same high level applied to state and local programs six years earlier.

By a 5–4 vote, the Court held that federal minority contracting provisions or other affirmative action policies are subject to "strict scrutiny" in court and can be upheld only if they serve a compelling governmental interest and are narrowly tailored to achieve that goal.

The decision returned to lower courts a challenge by a white contractor in Colorado to a Department of Transportation program that gave contractors a financial incentive to award subcontracts to minority-owned concerns. Adarand Constructors, a guardrail construction company, filed the challenge after it lost a bid on a federal highway project to an Hispanic-owned company. Federal courts upheld the program, applying an intermediate level of review used by the Supreme Court in prior challenges to federal minority preference programs.

Writing for the majority, O'Connor said that the same strict standard should apply to racial classifications in federal, state, or local programs. " ... [A]ll governmental action based on race ... should be subjected to detailed judicial inquiry to ensure that the *personal* right to equal protection of the laws has not been infringed," she wrote.

The decision expressly overruled the 1990 ruling, *Metro Broadcasting v. Federal Communications Commission*, which permitted a lower standard for federal policies. Four justices—Rehnquist, Scalia, Kennedy, and Thomas—joined the bulk of O'Connor's opinion.

Scalia and Thomas both wrote concurring opinions to say that they would never permit the use of racial classifications to make up for past discrimination. Along with Rehnquist, the two also did not join the passage of O'Connor's opinion that explained justifications for overruling the 1990 precedent.

Stevens, Souter, and Ginsburg each wrote dissents. In the longest of these three opinions, Stevens, joined by Ginsburg, criticized the majority for ignoring what he called "a critical difference between state action that imposes burdens on a disfavored few and state action that benefits the few 'in spite of' its adverse effects on the many." Souter's shorter dissent, joined by Ginsburg and Breyer, was based primarily on procedural grounds. Ginsburg also wrote a short opinion, joined by Breyer, stressing that a majority of the Court still recognized Congress's power to enact some forms of affirmative action. *(See story, p. 27; excerpts, p. 162.)*

Damage Suits

Johnson v. Jones, decided by a 9–0 vote, June 12, 1995; Breyer wrote the opinion.

Public officials cannot appeal a pretrial ruling that rejects the factual basis for raising a qualified immunity defense in a damage suit charging them with violating an individual's constitutional rights.

The ruling cleared the way for trial of a federal civil rights suit by an

Illinois man, Houston Jones. The suit charged five police officers with using excessive force in arresting him and beating him at the police station. Three of the officers moved for summary judgment, claiming that Jones had no evidence they took part in the alleged beating.

The lower court judge denied the motion, and a federal appeals court refused to consider the officers' appeal of the ruling. They pointed to a previous Court ruling that allowed public officials to make an immediate appeal of a ruling on a qualified immunity defense in order to shield officials from the time and expense of unwarranted litigation.

In a unanimous decision, the Court said the appellate court had properly dismissed the appeal. Breyer explained that the previous ruling permitted immediate appeals of purely legal issues but not of factual disputes.

Kimberlin v. Quinlan, decided by a 9–0 vote, June 12, 1995; *per curiam* (unsigned) opinion.

The Court revived a damage suit by a former federal prison inmate who claimed officials improperly prevented him from airing allegations that he once sold marijuana to former vice president Dan Quayle.

The unsigned decision ordered a lower court to reconsider its ruling dismissing the suit brought by Brett Kimberlin against the director of the federal Bureau of Prisons, Michael Quinlan, and a former Justice Department spokesman. Kimberlin claimed that Quinlan blocked him from holding a news conference just before the 1988 election and ordered him placed in special detention. Quayle, a candidate for vice president at the time, denied the allegation.

In a one-sentence ruling, the Court directed the federal appeals court to re-examine Kimberlin's suit in the light of a decision in an unrelated case released the same day, *Johnson v. Jones (see above).* That ruling made it harder for public officials to avoid trials in so-called constitutional tort suits.

Disability Rights

City of Edmonds v. Oxford House, Inc., decided by a 6–3 vote, May 15, 1995; Ginsburg wrote the opinion; Thomas, Scalia, and Kennedy dissented.

Municipalities cannot use single-family zoning laws to completely exclude group homes for disabled persons, including recovering alcoholics and drug addicts.

The ruling came in a dispute between Oxford House, a national organization that operates more than 500 group homes for recovering alcoholics and drug addicts, and the city of Edmonds, Washington, a small coastal suburb outside Seattle. The city sought to bar Oxford House from operating a facility for eight to twelve individuals in an area zoned for single-family residences. A local ordinance limited the number of unrelated adults living in a single dwelling to five or fewer.

Oxford House argued the ordinance violated the federal Fair Housing Act, which prohibits discrimination in housing against people with handicaps. The law defines discrimination to include "a refusal to make reasonable accommodations" in rules or policies if necessary to give handicapped persons an "equal opportunity to use and enjoy a dwelling." The federal law also exempts from coverage any "reasonable ... restriction regarding the maximum number of occupants permitted to occupy a dwelling."

In a 6–3 decision, the Court held that the city's limit on the number of unrelated persons living together was a family composition rule, covered by the fair housing law, instead of a maximum occupancy restriction that would be exempt. "Family living, not living space per occupant, is what [the ordinance] describes," Ginsburg wrote. The ruling returned the case to lower courts to determine whether the city was required to allow the group home as a "reasonable accommodation" under the fair housing law.

Dissenting justices argued the city's ordinance was covered by the exemption for maximum-occupancy restrictions. "... [T]he Court's conclusion fails to give effect to the plain language of the statute," Thomas wrote.

Drug Testing

Vernonia School District No. 47J v. Acton, decided by a 6–3 vote, June 26, 1995; Scalia wrote the opinion; O'Connor, Stevens, and Souter dissented.

Public schools can require athletes to submit to random drug testing even if there is no basis for suspecting the individual of using drugs.

The 6–3 ruling rejected a federal constitutional challenge to a drug testing policy adopted in 1989 by the school system in Vernonia, Oregon, a small logging community. The policy required urinalyses for all school athletes at any grade level at the beginning of the season and random testing of 10 percent of a school's athletes each week thereafter. The parents of seventh-grader James Acton challenged the policy as a violation of the Fourth Amendment and the comparable provision of the Oregon constitution. A federal district court judge upheld the policy, but the Ninth U.S. Circuit Court of Appeals ruled the policy violated both the federal and state constitutions.

Writing for the Court, Scalia said the policy was "reasonable and hence constitutional" because it served the "important" purpose of deterring drug use by school children while resulting in only "negligible" intrusion on personal privacy. Scalia was joined in the opinion by three of the Court's conservatives—Rehnquist, Kennedy, and Thomas—and by both of President Bill Clinton's appointees, Ginsburg and Breyer.

In a dissent, O'Connor, joined by Stevens and Souter, said the ruling contradicted the Fourth Amendment's normal requirement for "individualized suspicion" to justify a search. "For most of our constitutional history," she wrote, "mass, suspicionless searches have been generally considered *per se* unreasonable under the Fourth Amendment."

In a brief concurrence, Ginsburg stressed that the ruling did not determine whether school districts could require drug testing of all students. The Court's decision also did not resolve the state constitutional issue but returned the case to the appeals court "for further proceedings consistent with this opinion." *(See entry, p. 47; excerpts, p. 202.)*

Job Discrimination

McKennon v. Nashville Banner Publishing Co., decided by a 9–0 vote, January 23, 1995; Kennedy wrote the opinion.

An employee in a job discrimination suit does not lose her right to any relief if the employer discovers evidence of wrongdoing that would have justified her dismissal if known earlier.

The ruling reinstated a federal age discrimination suit brought by Catherine McKennon, a former bookkeeper, after she was fired from her job with the *Nashville Banner* newspaper. McKennon admitted during pretrial discovery that she had made photocopies of confidential financial documents before her dismissal. The newspaper moved to dismiss the suit, saying the misconduct would have been grounds for terminating McKennon. Two federal courts agreed.

In a unanimous opinion, Kennedy said that barring an employee's suit because of so-called "after-acquired evidence" would undermine "the objective of forcing employers to consider and examine their motivations, and of penalizing them for employment decisions that spring from age discrimination." But he said lower courts could consider an employee's misconduct in refusing to order reinstatement and in limiting back pay.

Although the decision involved the Age Discrimination in Employment Act, civil rights experts expected it to apply also to job discrimination suits brought under the broader Title VII of the Civil Rights Act of 1964.

School Desegregation

Missouri v. Jenkins, decided by a 5–4 vote, June 12, 1995; Rehnquist wrote the opinion; Souter, Stevens, Ginsburg, and Breyer dissented.

The federal judge overseeing the Kansas City school desegregation case exceeded his authority by ordering salary increases and creation of magnet schools to attract white students from neighboring districts.

The decision required lower courts to reconsider parts of a showcase plan aimed at increasing what the judge called the "desegregative attractiveness" and "suburban comparability" of the predominantly black school district. Specifically, the state attacked two orders requiring salary increases for virtually all of the school district's 5,000 employees and converting all high schools and middle schools and half of the district's elementary schools into magnet schools.

By a 5–4 vote, the Court held that the orders went beyond federal courts' power to remedy the "vestiges" of previous legal segregation. Rehnquist said the effort to attract white students from adjoining suburban districts amounted to an impermissible "interdistrict remedy." He criticized the judge's use of below-normal achievement scores to justify continued supervision over the school system. "Insistence upon academic goals unrelated to the effects of legal segregation unwarrantably postpones the day when the [Kansas City district] will be able to operate on its own," he wrote.

In a strongly worded concurring opinion, Thomas sharply questioned some of the fundamental principles of school desegregation cases going back to the landmark ruling, *Brown v. Board of Education* (1954). He complained that the Court's decisions had allowed lower courts "to exercise virtually unlimited equitable powers" in trying to eliminate racially identifiable schools. O'Connor also wrote a concurring opinion, answering some of the points made by the dissenting justices.

Writing for the four dissenters, Souter complained that the majority had not followed proper procedure in reviewing the judge's remedy. On the merits, he contended that the lower courts had properly concluded that past segregation had contributed to white flight and that the desegregation decree could include steps to draw them back to the Kansas City system. Ginsburg added a brief dissent to emphasize the long history of school segregation in Missouri. *(See entry, p. 36; excerpts, p. 183.)*

Labor Law

Layoffs and Plant Closings

North Star Steel Co. v. Thomas, decided by a 9–0 vote, May 30, 1995; Souter wrote the opinion.

State law determines the time period for employees to sue their employer for violating a federal law requiring at least sixty-days' advance notice before a plant closing or mass layoff.

The unanimous ruling interpreting the Worker Adjustment and Retraining Notice Act backed labor unions' argument for a longer statute of limitations than would have been provided under federal law. The 1988 law allowed workers to sue to enforce the law in federal court but did not specify a statute of limitations. Federal courts in Pennsylvania differed on whether to apply a six-months' time period under federal labor law or any of several longer statutes of limitations—ranging from two years to six years—under state labor law.

Writing for the Court, Souter said state law generally determines the time period for bringing suits in cases where Congress fails to specify one unless the state statute of limitations would frustrate the enforcement of the federal law. Use of the longer time period under the layoff notice law would have no "frustrating consequences," he concluded. Scalia concurred in the judgment but did not join Souter's opinion.

Pensions and Benefits

Curtiss-Wright Corp. v. Schoonejongen, decided by a 9–0 vote, March 6, 1995; O'Connor wrote the opinion.

The Court eased the legal requirements for companies to amend employee health benefit plans.

In a unanimous ruling, the Court held that a standard provision reserving a company's right "to amend or modify" an employee health plan satisfies a provision of the Employee Retirement Income Security Act that requires plans to specify the "procedure" for changes. "Certainly, a plan that says it may be amended only by a unilateral company decision adequately sets forth a particular way of making an amendment," O'Connor wrote.

The decision overturned a ruling by the Third U.S. Circuit Court of Appeals in a suit brought by former employees of the Curtiss-Wright Corp. The aircraft manufacturer terminated the employees' postretirement health benefits after closing the plant where they had worked. The Court returned the case to lower courts to determine whether the company followed its own corporate procedures in adopting the change.

Milwaukee Brewery Workers' Pension Plan v. Jos. Schlitz Brewing Co., decided by a 9–0 vote, February 21, 1995; Breyer wrote the opinion.

The Court slightly eased a company's cost of withdrawing from an underfunded industry pension plan by reducing the interest on the contributions required under federal law.

The unanimous decision agreed with business groups' interpretation of a provision of the Multiemployer Pension Plan Amendments Act, a 1980 law aimed at shoring up financially troubled industrywide pension plans. The law imposes a withdrawal charge, to be paid in annual installments with interest, on companies that pull out of multiemployer plans.

Two federal appeals courts interpreting the law disagreed on whether interest began with the year of the company's withdrawal from the plan or the subsequent year. In an intricate piece of statutory construction, Breyer said interest "begins accruing on the first day of the plan year following withdrawal."

The ruling reduced by nearly $2.6 million the amount the Jos. Schlitz Brewing Co.—later acquired by Stroh Brewing Co.—had to pay to withdraw from the brewery workers' plan. The Clinton administration sided with labor unions in urging the Court to calculate interest from the earlier date.

Workers' Compensation

Chandris, Inc. v. Latsis, decided by 9–0 and 6–3 votes, June 14, 1995; O'Connor wrote the opinion; Stevens, Thomas, and Breyer concurred in the result but dissented from the legal ruling.

A maritime worker must have a substantial connection to a ship in navigation to qualify as a "seaman" under the federal law allowing damage suits for on-the-job injuries.

The ruling was aimed at clarifying the dividing line between two categories of maritime workers: seamen and longshore workers. A 1920 law called the Jones Act allows a seaman to file a damage suit for job-related injuries. The Longshore and Harbor Workers' Compensation Act limits longshore workers to scheduled payments under an administrative workers' compensation system.

The Court decided to settle a longstanding conflict among lower federal courts on the issue in a case brought by a superintendent engineer employed by a cruise line company. The engineer, Antonios Latsis, worked both on shore and onboard ships. While on a cruise, he complained of an eye problem but was not treated and ended up losing 75 percent of his vision in one eye. At trial, the jury concluded Latsis was not a seaman, but a federal appeals court ruled the judge's instructions were erroneous.

In her opinion for the Court, O'Connor rejected Lastis's argument that any maritime worker on board a ship at sea qualifies as a seaman under the Jones Act. Instead, she said, the worker must also have "a connection to a vessel in navigation ... that is substantial both in terms of its duration and its nature." As a "rule of thumb," O'Connor said a worker normally should spend 30 percent of his time serving on a vessel to qualify.

The ruling upheld the appeals court decision setting aside the jury verdict. In a concurring opinion, Stevens, joined by Thomas and Breyer, agreed the jury verdict should be set aside, but disagreed with the Court's holding. "In my judgment," Stevens wrote, "an employee of the ship who is injured at sea in the course of his employment is always a 'seaman.' "

Director, Office of Workers' Compensation Programs, Department of Labor v. Newport News Shipbuilding & Dry Dock Co., decided by a 9–0 vote, March 21, 1995; Scalia wrote the opinion.

The Court barred the Labor Department office responsible for two federal workers' compensation programs from appealing decisions by the agency's benefits review board on claims brought by longshore workers.

The case involved a longshore worker who was awarded partial instead of total disability for a period of unemployment following an injury.

Although the worker did not challenge the decision, the director of the Office of Workers' Compensation Programs (OWCP) asked a federal appeals court to overturn it. She said she had standing to file the appeal because of her role in "ensuring adequate compensation to claimants."

In a unanimous decision, the Court held that the OWCP has no statutory authority to appeal administrative decisions on individual claims by longshore workers. Scalia said that "an agency acting in its governmental capacity" is not an "aggrieved party" for purposes of bringing an appeal unless a statute specifically says so.

Ginsburg, in a separate concurring opinion, noted that the OWCP also administers the black lung benefits program for coal miners and the director has authority under that statute to appeal individual decisions. She said Congress could amend the longshore workers' statute if it wanted to reconcile the two programs.

Metropolitan Stevedore Co. v. Rambo, decided by an 8–1 vote, June 12, 1995; Kennedy wrote the opinion; Stevens dissented.

Federal disability benefits to injured longshore workers can be modified when there is a change in the employee's wage-earning capacity even without a change in the employee's physical condition.

The ruling rejected an effort by longshore worker John Rambo to reinstate benefits awarded for an on-the-job injury in 1980. An administrative law judge terminated the benefits because Rambo had gotten a new job as a crane operator that paid three times as much as his previous position. But a federal appeals court ruled that the provision of the Longshore and Harbor Workers' Compensation Act permitting modification of benefits after a "change of conditions" applied only to changes in medical conditions.

Writing for the Court, Kennedy said that benefits could also be modified because of a change in an employee's wage-earning capacity. Under the act, Kennedy said, disability "is in essence an economic, not a medical concept."

Stevens, the lone dissenter, argued that the ruling contradicted "over 60 years of otherwise consistent precedent" except for one federal appeals court ruling in 1985. But Kennedy characterized the earlier rulings as "an accumulation of more than 50 years of dicta."

States

Immunity

Hess v. Port Authority Trans-Hudson Corporation, decided by a 5–4 vote, November 14, 1994; Ginsburg wrote the opinion; O'Connor, Rehnquist, Scalia, and Thomas dissented.

The Court somewhat narrowed the constitutional protection for interstate agencies from being sued in federal court.

The closely divided decision cleared the way for two federal court suits on behalf of injured workers of a bistate railway, the Port Authority Trans-Hudson Corporation (PATH). The workers brought the suit under the Federal Employers' Liability Act, a 1907 law providing federal court jurisdiction over railway workers' suits. But PATH, a subsidiary of the Port Authority of New York and New Jersey, said the federal court suit was barred by the Eleventh Amendment, which gives state governments immunity from federal court suit. The federal appeals court in Philadelphia upheld the immunity claim, but earlier the federal appeals court in New York had rejected a similar argument.

Resolving the conflict, the Court ruled that the railway was not entitled to protection from federal court suit because it was financially independent from its parent states, New Jersey and New York. Ginsburg said that allowing the workers' suit "does not touch the concerns—the state's solvency and dignity—that underpin the 11th Amendment."

Writing for the dissenting justices, O'Connor said the railway should be immune from federal court suit because the two states retained control over its operations.

Taxation

National Private Truck Council, Inc. v. Oklahoma Tax Commission, decided by a 9–0 vote, June 19, 1995; Thomas wrote the opinion.

A taxpayer cannot use federal civil rights law in state tax cases to block enforcement of a state levy or seek attorneys' fees as long as the state provides other procedures for contesting a tax.

The ruling denied an effort by a trucking trade association to broaden its legal victory in a successful challenge to an Oklahoma truck tax. The Oklahoma Supreme Court ruled the tax invalid as an impermissible burden on interstate commerce, and it awarded refunds. But it refused the group's effort to use the federal civil rights law known as section 1983 of Title 42 to get an injunction blocking enforcement of the tax or a declaratory judgment that the tax was invalid. The court also refused to award attorneys' fees, which are allowed in section 1983 cases.

In a unanimous decision, the Court upheld the Oklahoma court's ruling. Thomas noted that Congress has generally limited the power of federal courts to interfere with administration of state taxes. "We simply do not read §1983 to provide for injunctive or declaratory relief against a state tax, either in federal or state court, when an adequate legal remedy exists," he said. Since the taxpayer could not bring a §1983 suit, no attorneys' fees could be awarded either, Thomas concluded.

Nebraska Dept. of Revenue v. Loewenstein, decided by a 9–0 vote, December 12, 1994; Thomas wrote the opinion.

States may tax income from mutual funds that invest in federal securities through so-called repurchase agreements, or "repos."

The ruling resolved the tax status of a financial instrument in which an investor transfers federal securities to a mutual fund and agrees to "repurchase" it later at a premium. A Nebraska man sought to exclude his proceeds from a repo mutual fund on the basis of federal law that exempts interest on federal securities from state taxation.

The Court unanimously held that the income actually amounted to taxable interest on a loan. Thomas explained that the securities served as collateral for the loan and noted that the interest was tied to prevailing rates instead of U.S. Treasury yields.

The Nebraska Supreme Court, alone among the state courts to address the issue, had barred state taxation of repos. More than twenty states urged the Court to reverse the ruling.

Oklahoma Tax Commission v. Chickasaw Nation, decided by 9–0 and 5–4 votes, June 14, 1995; Ginsburg wrote the opinion; Breyer, Stevens, O'Connor, and Souter dissented in part.

The Court barred Oklahoma from enforcing a gasoline excise tax on retail outlets owned by members of the Chickasaw tribe and operated on tribal lands. But it allowed the state to collect income taxes from tribal members who are employed by the tribe but live outside the Chickasaw reservation.

The Chickasaws contended that both taxes violated general principles limiting state taxation of Indian tribes and the provisions of an 1837 treaty between the United States and the Chickasaws. The treaty promised that no "State shall ever have a right to pass laws for the government" of the Chickasaw nation. Two lower federal courts agreed and blocked both taxes.

The Court unanimously agreed that the gasoline tax could not be enforced against tribal retailers, but it left the door open for the state to revise the tax to fall directly on consumers instead. On the income tax issue, however, the justices divided 5–4 in ruling for the state.

Writing for the majority, Ginsburg pointed to what she called the "well-established principle" that a jurisdiction "may tax *all* the income of its residents, even income earned outside the taxing jurisdiction." In the dissenting opinion, Breyer said the treaty provision—"read broadly and in light of its purpose"—barred taxation of tribal members working for the tribe whether or not they lived within Indian country.

Oklahoma Tax Commission v. Jefferson Lines, Inc., decided by a 7–2 vote, April 3, 1995; Souter wrote the opinion; Breyer and O'Connor dissented.

A state may impose a sales tax on the sale of bus tickets for interstate travel without dividing the proceeds with other states.

The 7–2 decision upheld an Oklahoma levy that three federal courts had struck down as an improper state tax on interstate commerce. Souter said the tax met a four-part test adopted by the Court in a 1977 case: the tax was applied to an activity with a "substantial nexus" to the state, was fairly apportioned, did not discriminate against interstate commerce, and was fairly related to services provided by the state.

The dissenting justices said the tax was "for all relevant purposes identical" to a New York gross receipts tax on interstate bus travel that the Court struck down in a 1948 ruling. Souter said the two taxes were different because the New York tax was levied against the bus company, which might be subject to double taxation by other states, while Oklahoma's sales tax "falls on the buyer of the services."

Reich v. Collins, Revenue Commissioner of Georgia, decided by a 9–0 vote, December 6, 1994; O'Connor wrote the opinion.

The Court overturned efforts by the state of Georgia to avoid paying refunds to federal retirees for state income taxes paid under a scheme that had been struck down in earlier Court decisions.

In a unanimous decision, the Court said that the state had, in effect, changed the rules for obtaining refunds in the midst of the dispute. The ruling favored a military retiree who sought refunds under the Court's 1989 decision overturning state laws that granted tax exemptions to state pensioners but not to federal pensioners.

Georgia law provided for refunds of taxes that were "erroneously or illegally assessed," but state tax officials denied the refunds because the retiree had not protested the tax before paying it. O'Connor acknowledged that a state could permit taxpayers to contest taxes either before or after payment. "But what a State may *not* do," she continued, "is to reconfigure its scheme, unfairly, in *mid-course*—to 'bait and switch,' as some have described it."

The decision was viewed as likely to affect similar cases in four other states: Kentucky, New York, North Carolina, and Virginia.

Water Rights

Kansas v. Colorado, decided by a 9-0 vote, May 15, 1995; Rehnquist wrote the opinion.

Colorado violated an interstate compact with Kansas on dividing the waters of the Arkansas River by allowing well-pumping to increase above the amount set when the agreement was reached in 1949.

The Court rejected two other complaints, however, that Kansas made when it brought the case in 1985. It ruled that Kansas had failed to prove

Colorado "depleted" the river flow by the operation of a winter water storage program or by storage in the Trinidad Reservoir in Colorado.

Colorado argued that Kansas had waited too long—twenty-nine years—to bring the complaint, but the Court said Kansas did not have enough information until 1985 to back up its claim. The ruling returned the case to the Court-appointed "special master" for further proceedings.

Nebraska v. Wyoming, decided by an 8–1 vote, May 30, 1995; Souter wrote the opinion; Thomas dissented in part.

The Court allowed both Nebraska and Wyoming to add new claims to a long-running dispute over water rights.

The dispute concerned the North Platte River, which originates in Wyoming and flows through Colorado and Nebraska before joining the Platte River. The Court in 1945 issued a decree dividing the water among the three states. Nebraska returned to the Court in 1986 claiming that Wyoming was taking more than its share of water under the decree.

The Court settled some of the issues in a ruling in 1993. Both states then sought to raise new issues. Most notably, Nebraska sought to add a claim that Wyoming's violations of the decree were harming wildlife in the state, while Wyoming contended that the United States was reducing its water allocations by improper management of federal reservoirs in the state.

In a near-unanimous ruling, the Court said the "special master" appointed to hear the case had acted properly in allowing most of the new claims. Thomas dissented on one point. He argued that Wyoming's attack on the management of federal reservoirs was not related to the 1945 decree and should be raised in separate litigation in lower federal courts. But Souter, writing for the majority, said it "makes sense" to consider the claim in the broader litigation.

4 | *Opinion Excerpts*

Following are excerpts from some of the most important rulings of the Supreme Court's 1994–1995 term. They appear in the order in which they were announced. Footnotes and legal citations are omitted.

No. 93–986

Joseph McIntyre, executor of estate of Margaret McIntyre, deceased, Petitioner v. Ohio Elections Commission

On writ of certiorari to the Supreme Court of Ohio

[April 19, 1995]

JUSTICE STEVENS delivered the opinion of the Court.

The question presented is whether an Ohio statute that prohibits the distribution of anonymous campaign literature is a "law … abridging the freedom of speech" within the meaning of the First Amendment.

I

On April 27, 1988, Margaret McIntyre distributed leaflets to persons attending a public meeting at the Blendon Middle School in Westerville, Ohio. At this meeting, the superintendent of schools planned to discuss an imminent referendum on a proposed school tax levy. The leaflets expressed Mrs. McIntyre's opposition to the levy. There is no suggestion that the text of her message was false, misleading, or libelous. She had composed and printed it on her home computer and had paid a professional printer to make additional copies. Some of the handbills identified her as the author; others merely purported to express the views of "CONCERNED PARENTS AND TAX PAYERS." Except for the help provided by her son and a friend, who placed some of the leaflets on car windshields in the school parking lot, Mrs. McIntyre acted independently.

While Mrs. McIntyre distributed her handbills, an official of the school district, who supported the tax proposal, advised her that the unsigned leaflets did not conform to the Ohio election laws. Undeterred, Mrs. McIntyre appeared at another meeting on the next evening and handed out more of the handbills.

The proposed school levy was defeated at the next two elections, but it finally passed on its third try in November 1988. Five months later, the same school official filed a complaint with the Ohio Elections Commission charging that Mrs. McIntyre's distribution of unsigned leaflets violated §3599.09(A) of the Ohio Code. The Commission agreed and imposed a fine of $100.

The Franklin County Court of Common Pleas reversed. Finding that Mrs. McIntyre did not "mislead the public nor act in a surreptitious manner," the court concluded that the statute was unconstitutional as applied to her conduct. The

Ohio Court of Appeals, by a divided vote, reinstated the fine. Notwithstanding doubts about the continuing validity of a 1922 decision of the Ohio Supreme Court upholding the statutory predecessor of §3599.09(A), the majority considered itself bound by that precedent. The dissenting judge thought that our intervening decision in *Talley* v. *California*, (1960), in which we invalidated a city ordinance prohibiting all anonymous leafletting, compelled the Ohio court to adopt a narrowing construction of the statute to save its constitutionality.

The Ohio Supreme Court affirmed by a divided vote....

Mrs. McIntyre passed away during the pendency of this litigation. Even though the amount in controversy is only $100, petitioner, as the executor of her estate, has pursued her claim in this Court. Our grant of certiorari (1994) reflects our agreement with his appraisal of the importance of the question presented.

II

Ohio maintains that the statute under review is a reasonable regulation of the electoral process. The State does not suggest that all anonymous publications are pernicious or that a statute totally excluding them from the marketplace of ideas would be valid. This is a wise (albeit implicit) concession, for the anonymity of an author is not ordinarily a sufficient reason to exclude her work product from the protections of the First Amendment.

"Anonymous pamphlets, leaflets, brochures and even books have played an important role in the progress of mankind." *Talley* v. *California* (1960). Great works of literature have frequently been produced by authors writing under assumed names. Despite readers' curiosity and the public's interest in identifying the creator of a work of art, an author generally is free to decide whether or not to disclose her true identity. The decision in favor of anonymity may be motivated by fear of economic or official retaliation, by concern about social ostracism, or merely by a desire to preserve as much of one's privacy as possible. Whatever the motivation may be, at least in the field of literary endeavor, the interest in having anonymous works enter the marketplace of ideas unquestionably outweighs any public interest in requiring disclosure as a condition of entry. Accordingly, an author's decision to remain anonymous, like other decisions concerning omissions or additions to the content of a publication, is an aspect of the freedom of speech protected by the First Amendment.

The freedom to publish anonymously extends beyond the literary realm. In *Talley*, the Court held that the First Amendment protects the distribution of unsigned handbills urging readers to boycott certain Los Angeles merchants who were allegedly engaging in discriminatory employment practices.... The specific holding in *Talley* related to advocacy of an economic boycott, but the Court's reasoning embraced a respected tradition of anonymity in the advocacy of political causes. This tradition is perhaps best exemplified by the secret ballot, the hard-won right to vote one's conscience without fear of retaliation.

III

California had defended the Los Angeles ordinance at issue in *Talley* as a law "aimed at providing a way to identify those responsible for fraud, false advertising and libel." We rejected that argument because nothing in the text or legislative history of the ordinance limited its application to those evils. We then made clear that we did "not pass on the validity of an ordinance limited to prevent these or any other supposed evils." The Ohio statute likewise contains no language limiting its application to fraudulent, false, or libelous statements; to the extent, therefore, that Ohio seeks to justify §3599.09(A) as a means to prevent the dissemination of untruths, its defense must fail for the same reason given in *Talley*. As the facts of this case demonstrate, the ordinance plainly applies even when there is no hint of falsity or libel.

Ohio's statute does, however, contain a different limitation: It applies only to unsigned documents designed to influence voters in an election. In contrast, the Los Angeles ordinance prohibited all anonymous handbilling "in any place under any circumstances." For that reason, Ohio correctly argues that *Talley* does not necessarily control the disposition of this case. We must, therefore, decide whether and to what extent the First Amendment's protection of anonymity encompasses documents intended to influence the electoral process.

Ohio places its principal reliance on cases such as *Anderson* v. *Celebrezze* (1983); *Storer* v. *Brown* (1974); and *Burdick* v. *Takushi* (1992), in which we reviewed election code provisions governing the voting process itself. See *Anderson* (filing deadlines); *Storer* (ballot access); *Burdick* (write-in voting); see also *Tashjian* v. *Republican Party of Connecticut* (1986) (eligibility of independent voters to vote in party primaries). In those cases ... we pursued an analytical process comparable to that used by courts "in ordinary litigation": we considered the relative interests of the State and the injured voters, and we evaluated the extent to which the State's interests necessitated the contested restrictions. Applying similar reasoning in this case, the Ohio Supreme Court upheld §3599.09(A) as a "reasonable" and "nondiscriminatory" burden on the rights of voters.

The "ordinary litigation" test does not apply here. Unlike the statutory provisions challenged in *Storer* and *Anderson* §3599.09(A) of the Ohio Code does not control the mechanics of the electoral process. It is a regulation of pure speech. Moreover, even though this provision applies evenhandedly to advocates of differing viewpoints, it is a direct regulation of the content of speech. Every written document covered by the statute must contain "the name and residence or business address of the chairman, treasurer, or secretary of the organization issuing the same, or the person who issues, makes, or is responsible therefor." Furthermore, the category of covered documents is defined by their content—only those publications containing speech designed to influence the voters in an election need bear the required markings. Consequently, we are not faced with an ordinary election restriction; this case "involves a limitation on political expression subject to exacting scrutiny."

Indeed, as we have explained on many prior occasions, the category of speech regulated by the Ohio statute occupies the core of the protection afforded by the First Amendment....

Of course, core political speech need not center on a candidate for office.... Indeed, the speech in which Mrs. McIntyre engaged—handing out leaflets in the advocacy of a politically controversial viewpoint—is the essence of First Amendment expression. That this advocacy occurred in the heat of a controversial referendum vote only strengthens the protection afforded to Mrs.

McIntyre's expression: urgent, important, and effective speech can be no less protected than impotent speech, lest the right to speak be relegated to those instances when it is least needed. No form of speech is entitled to greater constitutional protection than Mrs. McIntyre's.

When a law burdens core political speech, we apply "exacting scrutiny," and we uphold the restriction only if it is narrowly tailored to serve an overriding state interest. Our precedents thus make abundantly clear that the Ohio Supreme Court applied a significantly more lenient standard than is appropriate in a case of this kind.

IV

Nevertheless, the State argues that even under the strictest standard of review, the disclosure requirement in §3599.09(A) is justified by two important and legitimate state interests. Ohio judges its interest in preventing fraudulent and libelous statements and its interest in providing the electorate with relevant information to be sufficiently compelling to justify the anonymous speech ban....

Insofar as the interest in informing the electorate means nothing more than the provision of additional information that may either buttress or undermine the argument in a document, we think the identity of the speaker is no different from other components of the document's content that the author is free to include or exclude.... The simple interest in providing voters with additional relevant information does not justify a state requirement that a writer make statements or disclosures she would otherwise omit. Moreover, in the case of a handbill written by a private citizen who is not known to the recipient, the name and address of the author adds little, if anything, to the reader's ability to evaluate the document's message. Thus, Ohio's informational interest is plainly insufficient to support the constitutionality of its disclosure requirement.

The state interest in preventing fraud and libel stands on a different footing. We agree with Ohio's submission that this interest carries special weight during election campaigns when false statements, if credited, may have serious adverse consequences for the public at large. Ohio does not, however, rely solely on §3599.09(A) to protect that interest. Its Election Code includes detailed and specific prohibitions against making or disseminating false statements during political campaigns. These regulations apply both to candidate elections and to issue-driven ballot measures. Thus, Ohio's prohibition of anonymous leaflets plainly is not its principal weapon against fraud. Rather, it serves as an aid to enforcement of the specific prohibitions and as a deterrent to the making of false statements by unscrupulous prevaricators. Although these ancillary benefits are assuredly legitimate, we are not persuaded that they justify §3599.09(A)'s extremely broad prohibition.

As this case demonstrates, the prohibition encompasses documents that are not even arguably false or misleading. It applies not only to the activities of candidates and their organized supporters, but also to individuals acting independently and using only their own modest resources. It applies not only to elections of public officers, but also to ballot issues that present neither a substantial risk of libel nor any potential appearance of corrupt advantage. It applies not only to leaflets distributed on the eve of an election, when the opportunity for reply is limited, but also to those distributed months in advance. It applies no matter what the character or strength of the author's interest in anonymity. Moreover, as this case also demonstrates, the absence of the author's name on a document does not necessarily protect either that person or a distributor of a forbidden document from being held responsible for compliance with the election code. Nor has the State explained why it can more easily enforce the direct bans on disseminating false documents against anonymous authors and distributors than against wrongdoers who might use false names and addresses in an attempt to avoid detection. We recognize that a State's enforcement interest might justify a more limited identification requirement, but Ohio has shown scant cause for inhibiting the leafletting at issue here.

V

Finally, Ohio vigorously argues that our opinions in *First Nat. Bank of Boston v. Bellotti* (1978) and *Buckley* v. *Valeo* (1976) amply support the constitutionality of its disclosure requirement. Neither case is controlling: the former concerned the scope of First Amendment protection afforded to corporations; the relevant portion of the latter concerned mandatory disclosure of campaign-related expenditures. Neither case involved a prohibition of anonymous campaign literature....

VI

Under our Constitution, anonymous pamphleteering is not a pernicious, fraudulent practice, but an honorable tradition of advocacy and of dissent. Anonymity is a shield from the tyranny of the majority. It thus exemplifies the purpose behind the Bill of Rights, and of the First Amendment in particular: to protect unpopular individuals from retaliation—and their ideas from suppression—at the hand of an intolerant society. The right to remain anonymous may be abused when it shields fraudulent conduct. But political speech by its nature will sometimes have unpalatable consequences, and, in general, our society accords greater weight to the value of free speech than to the dangers of its misuse. Ohio has not shown that its interest in preventing the misuse of anonymous election-related speech justifies a prohibition of all uses of that speech. The State may, and does, punish fraud directly. But it cannot seek to punish fraud indirectly by indiscriminately outlawing a category of speech, based on its content, with no necessary relationship to the danger sought to be prevented. One would be hard pressed to think of a better example of the pitfalls of Ohio's blunderbuss approach than the facts of the case before us.

The judgment of the Ohio Supreme Court is reversed.

It is so ordered.

JUSTICE GINSBURG, concurring.

... The Court's decision finds unnecessary, overintrusive, and inconsistent with American ideals the State's imposition of a fine on an individual leafleteer who, within her local community, spoke her mind, but sometimes not her name. We do not thereby hold that the State may not in other, larger circumstances, require the speaker to disclose its interest by disclosing its identity. Appropriately leaving open matters not presented by McIntyre's handbills, the Court recognizes that a State's interest in protecting an election process "might justify a more limited identification requirement." But the Court has convincingly explained why Ohio lacks cause for inhibiting the leafletting at issue here."

JUSTICE THOMAS, concurring in the judgment.

I agree with the majority's conclusion that Ohio's election law, Ohio Rev. Code Ann. §3599.09(A), is inconsistent with the First Amendment. I would apply, however, a different methodology to this case. Instead of asking whether "an honorable tradition" of anonymous speech has existed throughout American history, or what the "value" of anonymous speech might be, we should determine whether the phrase "freedom of speech, or of the press," as originally understood, protected anonymous political leafletting. I believe that it did....

JUSTICE SCALIA, with whom THE CHIEF JUSTICE joins, dissenting.

At a time when both political branches of Government and both political parties reflect a popular desire to leave more decisionmaking authority to the States, today's decision moves in the opposite direction, adding to the legacy of inflexible central mandates (irrevocable even by Congress) imposed by this Court's constitutional jurisprudence. In an opinion which reads as though it is addressing some peculiar law like the Los Angeles municipal ordinance at issue in *Talley* v. *California*, the Court invalidates a species of protection for the election process that exists, in a variety of forms, in every State except California, and that has a pedigree dating back to the end of the 19th century. Preferring the views of the English utilitarian philosopher John Stuart Mill, to the considered judgment of the American people's elected representatives from coast to coast, the Court discovers a hitherto unknown right-to-be-unknown while engaging in electoral politics. I dissent from this imposition of free speech imperatives that are demonstrably not those of the American people today, and that there is inadequate reason to believe were those of the society that begat the First Amendment or the Fourteenth.

I

... Anonymous electioneering was not prohibited by law in 1791 or in 1868. In fact, it was widely practiced at the earlier date, an understandable legacy of the revolutionary era in which political dissent could produce governmental reprisal.... The practice of anonymous electioneering may have been less general in 1868, when the Fourteenth Amendment was adopted, but at least as late as 1837 it was respectable enough to be engaged in by Abraham Lincoln.

But to prove that anonymous electioneering was used frequently is not to establish that it is a constitutional right....

Evidence that anonymous electioneering was regarded as a constitutional right is sparse, and as far as I am aware evidence that it was *generally* regarded as such is nonexistent. The concurrence points to "freedom of the press" objections that were made against the refusal of some Federalist newspapers to publish unsigned essays opposing the proposed constitution (on the ground that they might be the work of foreign agents). But of course if every partisan cry of "freedom of the press" were accepted as valid, our Constitution would be unrecognizable....

The concurrence recounts other pre- and post-Revolution examples of defense of anonymity in the name of "freedom of the press," but not a single one involves the context of restrictions imposed in connection with a free, democratic election, which is all that is at issue here. For many of them, moreover, ... the issue of anonymity was incidental to the (unquestionably free-speech) issue of whether criticism of the government could be *punished* by the state.

Thus, the sum total of the historical evidence marshalled by the concurrence for the principle of *constitutional entitlement* to anonymous electioneering is partisan claims in the debate on ratification (which was *almost* like an election) that a viewpoint-based restriction on anonymity by newspaper editors violates freedom of speech. This absence of historical testimony concerning the point before us is hardly remarkable. The issue of a governmental prohibition upon anonymous electioneering in particular (as opposed to a government prohibition upon anonymous publication in general) simply never arose. Indeed, there probably never arose even the abstract question of whether electoral openness and regularity was worth such a governmental restriction upon the normal right to anonymous speech. The idea of close government regulation of the electoral process is a more modern phenomenon, arriving in this country in the late 1800's.

What we have, then, is the most difficult case for determining the meaning of the Constitution. No accepted existence of governmental restrictions of the sort at issue here demonstrates their constitutionality, but neither can their nonexistence clearly be attributed to constitutional objections. In such a case, constitutional adjudication necessarily involves not just history but judgment: judgment as to whether the government action under challenge is consonant with the concept of the protected freedom (in this case, the freedom of speech and of the press) that existed when the constitutional protection was accorded. In the present case, *absent other indication* I would be inclined to agree with the concurrence that a society which used anonymous political debate so regularly would not regard as constitutional even moderate restrictions made to improve the election process....

But there *is* other indication, of the most weighty sort: the widespread and longstanding traditions of our people. Principles of liberty fundamental enough to have been embodied within constitutional guarantees are not readily erased from the Nation's consciousness. A governmental practice that has become general throughout the United States, and particularly one that has the validation of long, accepted usage, bears a strong presumption of constitutionality. And that is what we have before us here. Section §3599.09(A) was enacted by the General Assembly of the State of Ohio almost 80 years ago. Even at the time of its adoption, there was nothing unique or extraordinary about it. The earliest statute of this sort was adopted by Massachusetts in 1890, little more than 20 years after the Fourteenth Amendment was ratified. No less than 24 States had similar laws by the end of World War I, and today every State of the Union except California has one, as does the District of Columbia, and as does the Federal Government where advertising relating to candidates for federal office is concerned. Such a universal and long established American legislative practice must be given precedence, I think, over historical and academic speculation regarding a restriction that assuredly does not go to the heart of free speech....

II

The foregoing analysis suffices to decide this case for me. Where the meaning of a constitutional text (such as "the freedom of speech") is unclear, the widespread and long-accepted practices of the American people are the best indication of what fundamental beliefs it was intended to enshrine. Even if I were to close my eyes to practice, however, and were to be guided exclusively by deductive analysis from our case law, I would reach the same result.

Three basic questions must be answered to decide this case. Two of them are readily answered by our precedents; the third is readily answered by common sense and by a decent regard for the practical judgment of those more familiar with elections than we are. The first question is whether protection of the election process justifies limitations upon speech that cannot constitutionally be imposed generally.... Our cases plainly answer that question in the affirmative—indeed, they suggest that no justification for regulation is more compelling than protection of the electoral process....

The second question relevant to our decision is whether a "right to anonymity" is such a prominent value in our constitutional system that even protection of the electoral process cannot be purchased at its expense. The answer, again, is clear: no. Several of our cases have held that *in peculiar circumstances* the compelled disclosure of a person's identity would unconstitutionally deter the exercise of First Amendment associational rights. But those cases did not acknowledge any general right to anonymity, or even any right on the part of all citizens to ignore the particular laws under challenge. Rather, they recognized a right to an exemption from otherwise valid disclosure requirements on the part of someone who could show a "reasonable probability" that the compelled disclosure would result in "threats, harassment, or reprisals from either Government officials or private parties." This last quotation is from *Buckley* v. *Valeo* (1976) (*per curiam*), which prescribed the safety-valve of a similar exemption in upholding the disclosure requirements of the Federal Election Campaign Act.... The record in this case contains not even a hint that Mrs. McIntyre feared "threats, harassment, or reprisals"; indeed, she placed her name on some of her fliers and meant to place it on all of them....

The Court's unprecedented protection for anonymous speech does not even have the virtue of establishing a clear (albeit erroneous) rule of law. For after having announced that this statute, because it "burdens core political speech," requires "exacting scrutiny" and must be "narrowly tailored to serve an overriding state interest," (ordinarily the kiss of death), the opinion goes on to proclaim soothingly (and unhelpfully) that "a State's enforcement interest might justify a more limited identification requirement."... Perhaps, then, not *all* the State statutes I have alluded to are invalid, but just *some* of them; or indeed maybe *all* of them remain valid in "larger circumstances"! It may take decades to work out the shape of this newly expanded right-to-speak-incognito, even in the elections field....

The third and last question relevant to our decision is whether the prohibition of anonymous campaigning is effective in protecting and enhancing democratic elections. In answering this question no, the Justices of the majority set their own views—on a practical matter that bears closely upon the real-life experience of elected politicians and not upon that of unelected judges—up against the views of 49 ... state legislatures and the federal Congress....

The Court says that the State has not explained "why it can more easily enforce the direct bans on disseminating false documents against anonymous authors and distributors than against wrongdoers who might use false names and addresses in an attempt to avoid detection."...

But the usefulness of a signing requirement lies not only in promoting observance of the law against campaign falsehoods (though that alone is enough to sustain it). It lies also in promoting a civil and dignified level of campaign debate—which the State has no power to command, but ample power to encourage by such undemanding measures as a signature requirement. Observers of the past few national elections have expressed concern about the increase of character assassination—"mudslinging" is the colloquial term—engaged in by political candidates and their supporters to the detriment of the democratic process. Not all of this, in fact not much of it, consists of actionable untruth; most is innuendo, or demeaning characterization, or mere disclosure of items of personal life that have no bearing upon suitability for office. Imagine how much all of this would increase if it could be done anonymously. The principal impediment against it is the reluctance of most individuals and organizations to be publicly associated with uncharitable and uncivil expression. Consider, moreover, the increased potential for "dirty tricks." It is not unheard-of for campaign operatives to circulate material over the name of their opponents or their opponents' supporters (a violation of election laws) in order to attract or alienate certain interest groups.... How much easier—and sanction-free!—it would be to circulate anonymous material (for example, a *really* tasteless, though not actionably false, attack upon one's own candidate) with the hope and expectation that it will be attributed to, and held against, the other side....

I do not know where the Court derives its perception that "anonymous pamphleteering is not a pernicious, fraudulent practice, but an honorable tradition of advocacy and of dissent." I can imagine no reason why an anonymous leaflet is any more honorable, as a general matter, than an anonymous phone call or an anonymous letter. It facilitates wrong by eliminating accountability, which is ordinarily the very purpose of the anonymity. There are of course exceptions, and where anonymity is needed to avoid "threats, harassment, or reprisals" the First Amendment will require an exemption from the Ohio law. But to strike down the Ohio law in its general application—and similar laws of 48 other States and the Federal Government—on the ground that all anonymous communication is in our society traditionally sacrosanct, seems to me a distortion of the past that will lead to a coarsening of the future.

I respectfully dissent.

□ □ □

No. 93–1260

United States, Petitioner v. Alfonso Lopez, Jr.

On writ of certiorari to the United States Court of Appeals for the Fifth Circuit

[April 26, 1995]

CHIEF JUSTICE REHNQUIST delivered the opinion of the Court.

In the Gun-Free School Zones Act of 1990, Congress made it a federal offense "for any individual knowingly to possess a firearm at a place that the individual knows, or has reasonable cause to believe, is a school zone." 18 U.S.C. §922 (q)(1)(A). The Act neither regulates a commercial activity nor contains a requirement that the possession be connected in any way to interstate commerce. We hold that the Act exceeds the authority of Congress "[t]o regulate Commerce ... among the several States.... " U.S. Const., Art. I, §8, cl. 3.

On March 10, 1992, respondent, who was then a 12th-grade student, arrived at Edison High School in San Antonio, Texas, carrying a concealed .38 caliber handgun and five bullets. Acting upon an anonymous tip, school authorities confronted respondent, who admitted that he was carrying the weapon. He was arrested and charged under Texas law with firearm possession on school premises. The next day, the state charges were dismissed after federal agents charged respondent by complaint with violating the Gun-Free School Zones Act of 1990.

A federal grand jury indicted respondent on one count of knowing possession of a firearm at a school zone, in violation of §922(q). Respondent moved to dismiss his federal indictment on the ground that §922(q) "is unconstitutional as it is beyond the power of Congress to legislate control over our public schools." The District Court denied the motion, concluding that §922(q) "is a constitutional exercise of Congress' well-defined power to regulate activities in and affecting commerce, and the 'business' of elementary, middle and high schools ... affects interstate commerce." Respondent waived his right to a jury trial. The District Court conducted a bench trial, found him guilty of violating §922(q), and sentenced him to six months' imprisonment and two years' supervised release.

On appeal, respondent challenged his conviction based on his claim that §922(q) exceeded Congress' power to legislate under the Commerce Clause. The Court of Appeals for the Fifth Circuit agreed and reversed respondent's conviction. It held that, in light of what it characterized as insufficient congressional findings and legislative history, "section 922(q), in the full reach of its terms, is invalid as beyond the power of Congress under the Commerce Clause." Because of the importance of the issue, we granted certiorari (1994), and we now affirm.

We start with first principles. The Constitution creates a Federal Government of enumerated powers. See U.S. Const., Art. I, §8. As James Madison wrote, "the powers delegated by the proposed Constitution to the federal government are few and defined. Those which are to remain in the State governments are numerous and indefinite." The Federalist No. 45. This constitutionally mandated division of authority "was adopted by the Framers to ensure protection of our fundamental liberties." *Gregory* v. *Ashcroft* (1991). "Just as the separation and independence of the coordinate branches of the Federal Government serves to prevent the accumulation of excessive power in any one branch, a healthy balance of power between the States and the Federal Government will reduce the risk of tyranny and abuse from either front."

The Constitution delegates to Congress the power "[t]o regulate Commerce with foreign Nations, and among the several States, and with the Indian Tribes." The Court, through Chief Justice Marshall, first defined the nature of Congress' commerce power in *Gibbons* v. *Ogden* (1824):

> "Commerce, undoubtedly, is traffic, but it is something more: it is intercourse. It describes the commercial intercourse between nations, and parts of nations, in all its branches, and is regulated by prescribing rules for carrying on that intercourse."

The commerce power "is the power to regulate; that is, to prescribe the rule by which commerce is to be governed. This power, like all others vested in Congress, is complete in itself, may be exercised to its utmost extent, and acknowledges no limitations, other than are prescribed in the constitution." The *Gibbons* Court, however, acknowledged that limitations on the commerce power are inherent in the very language of the Commerce Clause.

> "It is not intended to say that these words comprehend that commerce, which is completely internal, which is carried on between man and man in a State, or between different parts of the same State, and which does not extend to or affect other States. Such a power would be inconvenient, and is certainly unnecessary."...

For nearly a century thereafter, the Court's Commerce Clause decisions dealt but rarely with the extent of Congress' power, and almost entirely with the Commerce Clause as a limit on state legislation that discriminated against interstate commerce.... Under this line of precedent, the Court held that certain categories of activity such as "production," "manufacturing," and "mining" were within the province of state governments, and thus were beyond the power of Congress under the Commerce Clause.

In 1887, Congress enacted the Interstate Commerce Act, and in 1890, Congress enacted the Sherman Antitrust Act. These laws ushered in a new era of federal regulation under the commerce power. When cases involving these laws first reached this Court, we imported from our negative Commerce Clause cases the approach that Congress could not regulate activities such as "production," "manufacturing," and "mining."... Simultaneously, however, the Court held that, where the interstate and intrastate aspects of commerce were so mingled together that full regulation of interstate commerce required incidental regulation of intrastate commerce, the Commerce Clause authorized such regulation.

In *A. L. A. Schechter Poultry Corp.* v. *United States* (1935), the Court struck down regulations that fixed the hours and wages of individuals employed by an intrastate business because the activity being regulated related to interstate commerce only indirectly. In doing so, the Court characterized the distinction between direct and indirect effects of intrastate transactions upon interstate commerce as "a fundamental one, essential to the maintenance of our constitutional system." Activities that affected interstate commerce directly were within Congress' power; activities that affected interstate commerce indirectly were beyond Congress' reach. The justification for this formal distinction was rooted in the fear that otherwise "there would be virtually no limit to the federal power and for all practical purposes we should have a completely centralized government."

Two years later, in the watershed case of *NLRB* v. *Jones & Laughlin Steel Corp.* (1937), the Court upheld the National Labor Relations Act against a Commerce Clause challenge, and in the process, departed from the distinction between "direct" and "indirect" effects on interstate commerce.... The Court held that intrastate activities that "have such a close and substantial relation to interstate commerce that their control is essential or appropriate to protect that commerce from burdens and obstructions" are within Congress' power to regulate.

In *United States* v. *Darby* (1941), the Court upheld the Fair Labor Standards Act, stating:

> "The power of Congress over interstate commerce is not confined to the regulation of commerce among the states. It extends to those activities intrastate which so affect interstate commerce or the exercise of the power of Congress over it as to make regulation of them appropriate means to the attainment of a legitimate end, the exercise of the granted power of Congress to regulate interstate commerce."...

In *Wickard* v. *Filburn* [1942], the Court upheld the application of amendments to the Agricultural Adjustment Act of 1938 to the production and consumption of home-grown wheat. The *Wickard* Court explicitly rejected earlier distinctions between direct and indirect effects on interstate commerce, stating:

> "[E]ven if appellee's activity be local and though it may not be regarded as commerce, it may still, whatever its nature, be reached by Congress if it exerts a substantial economic effect on interstate commerce, and this irrespective of whether such effect is what might at some earlier time have been defined as 'direct' or 'indirect.' "

The *Wickard* Court emphasized that although Filburn's own contribution to the demand for wheat may have been trivial by itself, that was not "enough to remove him from the scope of federal regulation where, as here, his contribution, taken together with that of many others similarly situated, is far from trivial."

Jones & Laughlin Steel, Darby, and *Wickard* ushered in an era of Commerce Clause jurisprudence that greatly expanded the previously defined authority of Congress under that Clause. In part, this was a recognition of the great changes that had occurred in the way business was carried on in this country. Enterprises that had once been local or at most regional in nature had become national in scope. But the doctrinal change also reflected a view that earlier Commerce Clause cases artificially had constrained the authority of Congress to regulate interstate commerce.

But even these modern-era precedents which have expanded congressional power under the Commerce Clause confirm that this power is subject to outer limits....

Consistent with this structure, we have identified three broad categories of activity that Congress may regulate under its commerce power. First, Congress may regulate the use of the channels of interstate commerce.... Second, Congress is empowered to regulate and protect the instrumentalities of interstate commerce, or persons or things in interstate commerce, even though the threat may come only from intrastate activities.... Finally, Congress' commerce authority includes the power to regulate those activities having a substantial relation to interstate commerce, *i.e.*, those activities that substantially affect interstate commerce.

Within this final category, admittedly, our case law has not been clear whether an activity must "affect" or "substantially affect" interstate commerce in order to be within Congress' power to regulate it under the Commerce Clause.... We conclude, consistent with the great weight of our case law, that the proper test requires an analysis of whether the regulated activity "substantially affects" interstate commerce.

We now turn to consider the power of Congress, in the light of this framework, to enact §922(q). The first two categories of authority may be quickly disposed of: §922(q) is not a regulation of the use of the channels of interstate commerce, nor is it an attempt to prohibit the interstate transportation of a commodity through the channels of commerce; nor can §922(q) be justified as a regulation by which Congress has sought to protect an instrumentality of interstate commerce or a thing in interstate commerce. Thus, if §922(q) is to be sustained, it must be under the third category as a regulation of an activity that substantially affects interstate commerce.

First, we have upheld a wide variety of congressional Acts regulating intrastate economic activity where we have concluded that the activity substantially affected interstate commerce....

Section 922(q) is a criminal statute that by its terms has nothing to do with "commerce" or any sort of economic enterprise, however broadly one might define those terms. Section 922(q) is not an essential part of a larger regulation of economic activity, in which the regulatory scheme could be undercut unless the intrastate activity were regulated. It cannot, therefore, be sustained under our cases upholding regulations of activities that arise out of or are connected with a commercial transaction, which viewed in the aggregate, substantially affects interstate commerce.

Second, §922(q) contains no jurisdictional element which would ensure, through case-by-case inquiry, that the firearm possession in question affects interstate commerce. For example, in *United States* v. *Bass* (1971), the Court interpreted former 18 U.S.C. §1202(a), which made it a crime for a felon to "receive, possess, or transport in commerce or affecting commerce ... any firearm." The Court interpreted the possession component of §1202(a) to require an additional nexus to interstate commerce.... Unlike the statute in *Bass*, §922(q) has no express jurisdictional element which might limit its reach to a discrete set of firearm possessions that additionally have an explicit connection with or effect on interstate commerce.

Although as part of our independent evaluation of constitutionality under the Commerce Clause we of course consider legislative findings, and indeed even congressional committee findings, regarding effect on interstate commerce, the Government concedes that "[n]either the statute nor its legislative history contain[s] express congressional findings regarding the effects upon interstate commerce of gun possession in a school zone." We agree with the Government that Congress normally is not required to make formal findings as to the substantial burdens that an activity has on interstate commerce.... But to the extent that congressional findings would enable us to evaluate the legislative judgment that the activity in question substantially affected interstate commerce, even though no such substantial effect was visible to the naked eye, they are lacking here.

The Government argues that Congress has accumulated institutional expertise regarding the regulation of firearms through previous enactments. We agree, however, with the Fifth Circuit that importation of previous findings to justify §922(q) is especially inappropriate here because the "prior federal enactments or Congressional findings [do not] speak to the subject matter of section 922(q) or its relationship to interstate commerce. Indeed, section 922(q) plows thoroughly new ground and represents a sharp break with the long-standing pattern of federal firearms legislation."

The Government's essential contention, *in fine,* is that we may determine here that §922(q) is valid because possession of a firearm in a local school zone does indeed substantially affect interstate commerce. The Government argues that possession of a firearm in a school zone may result in violent crime and that violent crime can be expected to affect the functioning of the national economy in two ways. First, the costs of violent crime are substantial, and, through the mechanism of insurance, those costs are spread throughout the population. Second, violent crime reduces the willingness of individuals to travel to areas within the country that are perceived to be unsafe. The Government also argues that the presence of guns in schools poses a substantial threat to the educational process by threatening the learning environment. A handicapped educational process, in turn, will result in a less productive citizenry. That, in turn, would have an adverse effect on the Nation's economic well-being. As a result, the Government argues that Congress could rationally have concluded that §922(q) substantially affects interstate commerce.

We pause to consider the implications of the Government's arguments. The Government admits, under its "costs of crime" reasoning, that Congress could regulate not only all violent crime, but all activities that might lead to violent crime, regardless of how tenuously they relate to interstate commerce. Similarly, under the Government's "national productivity" reasoning, Congress could regulate any activity that it found was related to the economic productivity of individual citizens: family law (including marriage, divorce, and child custody), for example. Under the theories that the Government presents in support of §922(q), it is difficult to perceive any limitation on federal power, even in areas such as criminal law enforcement or education where States historically have been sovereign. Thus, if we were to accept the Government's arguments, we are hard-pressed to posit any activity by an individual that Congress is without power to regulate.

Although JUSTICE BREYER argues that acceptance of the Government's rationales would not authorize a general federal police power, he is unable to identify any activity that the States may regulate but Congress may not. JUSTICE BREYER posits that there might be some limitations on Congress' commerce power such as family law or certain aspects of education. These suggested limitations, when viewed in light of the dissent's expansive analysis, are devoid of substance.

JUSTICE BREYER focuses, for the most part, on the threat that firearm possession in and near schools poses to the educational process and the potential economic consequences flowing from that threat. Specifically, the dissent reasons that (1) gun-related violence is a serious problem; (2) that problem, in turn, has an adverse effect on classroom learning; and (3) that adverse effect on classroom learning, in turn, represents a substantial threat to trade and commerce. This analysis would be equally applicable, if not more so, to subjects such as family law and direct regulation of education.

For instance, if Congress can, pursuant to its Commerce Clause power, regulate activities that adversely affect the learning environment, then, *a fortiori*, it also can regulate the educational process directly. Congress could determine that a school's curriculum has a "significant" effect on the extent of classroom learning. As a result, Congress could mandate a federal curriculum for local elementary and secondary schools because what is taught in local schools has a significant "effect on classroom learning" and that, in turn, has a substantial effect on interstate commerce.

JUSTICE BREYER rejects our reading of precedent and argues that "Congress ... could rationally conclude that schools fall on the commercial side of the line." Again, JUSTICE BREYER's rationale lacks any real limits because, depending on the level of generality, any activity can be looked upon as commercial. Under the dissent's rationale, Congress could just as easily look at child rearing as "fall[ing] on the commercial side of the line" because it provides a "valuable service — namely, to equip [children] with the skills they need to survive in life and, more specifically, in the workplace." We do not doubt that Congress has authority under the Commerce Clause to regulate numerous commercial activities that substantially affect interstate commerce and also affect the educational process. That authority, though broad, does not include the authority to regulate each and every aspect of local schools.

Admittedly, a determination whether an intrastate activity is commercial or noncommercial may in some cases result in legal uncertainty. But, so long as Congress' authority is limited to those powers enumerated in the Constitution, and so long as those enumerated powers are interpreted as having judicially enforceable outer limits, congressional legislation under the Commerce Clause always will engender "legal uncertainty.".... The Constitution mandates this uncertainty by withholding from Congress a plenary police power that would authorize enactment of every type of legislation. Any possible benefit from eliminating this "legal uncertainty" would be at the expense of the Constitution's system of enumerated powers.

In *Jones & Laughlin Steel*, we held that the question of congressional power under the Commerce Clause "is necessarily one of degree." To the same effect is the concurring opinion of Justice Cardozo in *Schechter Poultry*:

> "There is a view of causation that would obliterate the distinction of what is national and what is local in the activities of commerce. Motion at the outer rim is communicated perceptibly, though minutely, to recording instruments at the center. A society such as ours 'is an elastic medium

which transmits all tremors throughout its territory; the only question is of their size.' "

These are not precise formulations, and in the nature of things they cannot be. But we think they point the way to a correct decision of this case. The possession of a gun in a local school zone is in no sense an economic activity that might, through repetition elsewhere, substantially affect any sort of interstate commerce. Respondent was a local student at a local school; there is no indication that he had recently moved in interstate commerce, and there is no requirement that his possession of the firearm have any concrete tie to interstate commerce.

To uphold the Government's contentions here, we would have to pile inference upon inference in a manner that would bid fair to convert congressional authority under the Commerce Clause to a general police power of the sort retained by the States. Admittedly, some of our prior cases have taken long steps down that road, giving great deference to congressional action. The broad language in these opinions has suggested the possibility of additional expansion, but we decline here to proceed any further. To do so would require us to conclude that the Constitution's enumeration of powers does not presuppose something not enumerated and that there never will be a distinction between what is truly national and what is truly local. This we are unwilling to do.

For the foregoing reasons the judgment of the Court of Appeals is

Affirmed.

JUSTICE KENNEDY, with whom JUSTICE O'CONNOR joins, concurring.

The history of the judicial struggle to interpret the Commerce Clause during the transition from the economic system the Founders knew to the single, national market still emergent in our own era counsels great restraint before the Court determines that the Clause is insufficient to support an exercise of the national power. That history gives me some pause about today's decision, but I join the Court's opinion with these observations on what I conceive to be its necessary though limited holding....

The history of our Commerce Clause decisions contains at least two lessons of relevance to this case. The first, as stated at the outset, is the imprecision of content-based boundaries used without more to define the limits of the Commerce Clause. The second, related to the first but of even greater consequence, is that the Court as an institution and the legal system as a whole have an immense stake in the stability of our Commerce Clause jurisprudence as it has evolved to this point. *Stare decisis* operates with great force in counseling us not to call in question the essential principles now in place respecting the congressional power to regulate transactions of a commercial nature. That fundamental restraint on our power forecloses us from reverting to an understanding of commerce that would serve only an 18th-century economy, dependent then upon production and trading practices that had changed but little over the preceding centuries; it also mandates against returning to the time when congressional authority to regulate undoubted commercial activities was limited by a judicial determination that those matters had an insufficient connection to an interstate system. Congress can regulate in the commercial sphere on the assumption that we have a single market and a unified purpose to build a stable national economy....

The statute before us upsets the federal balance to a degree that renders it an unconstitutional assertion of the commerce power, and our intervention is required. As the CHIEF JUSTICE explains, unlike the earlier cases to come before the Court here neither the actors nor their conduct have a commercial character, and neither the purposes nor the design of the statute have an evident commercial nexus. The statute makes the simple possession of a gun within 1,000 feet of the grounds of the school a criminal offense. In a sense any conduct in this interdependent world of ours has an ultimate commercial origin or consequence, but we have not yet said the commerce power may reach so far. If Congress attempts that extension, then at the least we must inquire whether the exercise of national power seeks to intrude upon an area of traditional state concern.

An interference of these dimensions occurs here, for it is well established that education is a traditional concern of the States. The proximity to schools, including of course schools owned and operated by the States or their subdivisions, is the very premise for making the conduct criminal. In these circumstances, we have a particular duty to insure that the federal-state balance is not destroyed....

While it is doubtful that any State, or indeed any reasonable person, would argue that it is wise policy to allow students to carry guns on school premises, considerable disagreement exists about how best to accomplish that goal. In this circumstance, the theory and utility of our federalism are revealed, for the States may perform their role as laboratories for experimentation to devise various solutions where the best solution is far from clear.

If a State or municipality determines that harsh criminal sanctions are necessary and wise to deter students from carrying guns on school premises, the reserved powers of the States are sufficient to enact those measures. Indeed, over 40 States already have criminal laws outlawing the possession of firearms on or near school grounds.

Other, more practicable means to rid the schools of guns may be thought by the citizens of some States to be preferable for the safety and welfare of the schools those States are charged with maintaining.... These might include inducements to inform on violators where the information leads to arrests or confiscation of the guns, programs to encourage the voluntary surrender of guns with some provision for amnesty, penalties imposed on parents or guardians for failure to supervise the child, laws providing for suspension or expulsion of gun-toting students, or programs for expulsion with assignment to special facilities.

The statute now before us forecloses the States from experimenting and exercising their own judgment in an area to which States lay claim by right of history and expertise, and it does so by regulating an activity beyond the realm of commerce in the ordinary and usual sense of that term. The tendency of this statute to displace state regulation in areas of traditional state concern is evident from its territorial operation. There are over 100,000 elementary and secondary schools in the United States. Each of these now has an invisible federal zone extending 1,000 feet beyond the (often irregular) boundaries of the school property. In some communities no doubt it would be difficult to navigate without infringing on those zones. Yet throughout these areas, school officials would find their own programs for the prohibition of guns in danger of displacement by the federal authority unless the State chooses to enact a parallel rule....

For these reasons, I join in the opinion and judgment of the Court.

JUSTICE THOMAS, concurring.

The Court today properly concludes that the Commerce Clause does not grant Congress the authority to prohibit gun possession within 1,000 feet of a school, as it attempted to do in the Gun-Free School Zones Act of 1990. Although I join the majority, I write separately to observe that our case law has drifted far from the original understanding of the Commerce Clause. In a future case, we ought to temper our Commerce Clause jurisprudence in a manner that both makes sense of our more recent case law and is more faithful to the original understanding of that Clause.

We have said that Congress may regulate not only "Commerce ... among the several states," but also anything that has a "substantial effect" on such commerce. This test, if taken to its logical extreme, would give Congress a "police power" over all aspects of American life. Unfortunately, we have never come to grips with this implication of our substantial effects formula. Although we have supposedly applied the substantial effects test for the past 60 years, we *always* have rejected readings of the Commerce Clause and the scope of federal power that would permit Congress to exercise a police power; our cases are quite clear that there are real limits to federal power....

While the principal dissent concedes that there are limits to federal power, the sweeping nature of our current test enables the dissent to argue that Congress can regulate gun possession. But it seems to me that the power to regulate "commerce" can by no means encompass authority over mere gun possession, any more than it empowers the Federal Government to regulate marriage, littering, or cruelty to animals, throughout the 50 States. Our Constitution quite properly leaves such matters to the individual States, notwithstanding these activities' effects on interstate commerce. Any interpretation of the Commerce Clause that even suggests that Congress could regulate such matters is in need of reexamination.

In an appropriate case, I believe that we must further reconsider our "substantial effects" test with an eye toward constructing a standard that reflects the text and history of the Commerce Clause without totally rejecting our more recent Commerce Clause jurisprudence....

JUSTICE STEVENS, dissenting.

The welfare of our future "Commerce with foreign Nations, and among the several States" is vitally dependent on the character of the education of our children. I therefore agree entirely with JUSTICE BREYER's explanation of why Congress has ample power to prohibit the possession of firearms in or near schools—just as it may protect the school environment from harms posed by controlled substances such as asbestos or alcohol. I also agree with JUSTICE SOUTER's exposition of the radical character of the Court's holding and its kinship with the discredited, pre-Depression version of substantive due process. I believe, however, that the Court's extraordinary decision merits this additional comment.

Guns are both articles of commerce and articles that can be used to restrain commerce. Their possession is the consequence, either directly or indirectly, of commercial activity. In my judgment, Congress' power to regulate commerce in firearms includes the power to prohibit possession of guns at any location because of their potentially harmful use; it necessarily follows that Congress may also prohibit their possession in particular markets. The market for the possession of handguns by school-age children is, distressingly, substantial. Whether or not the national interest in eliminating that market would have justified federal legislation in 1789, it surely does today.

JUSTICE SOUTER, dissenting.

In reviewing congressional legislation under the Commerce Clause, we defer to what is often a merely implicit congressional judgment that its regulation addresses a subject substantially affecting interstate commerce "if there is any rational basis for such a finding." If that congressional determination is within the realm of reason, "the only remaining question for judicial inquiry is whether 'the means chosen by Congress [are] reasonably adapted to the end permitted by the Constitution.' "

The practice of deferring to rationally based legislative judgments "is a paradigm of judicial restraint." In judicial review under the Commerce Clause, it reflects our respect for the institutional competence of the Congress on a subject expressly assigned to it by the Constitution and our appreciation of the legitimacy that comes from Congress's political accountability in dealing with matters open to a wide range of possible choices.

It was not ever thus, however, as even a brief overview of Commerce Clause history during the past century reminds us. The modern respect for the competence and primacy of Congress in matters affecting commerce developed only after one of this Court's most chastening experiences, when it perforce repudiated an earlier and untenably expansive conception of judicial review in derogation of congressional commerce power.... [T]oday's decision tugs the Court off course, leading it to suggest opportunities for further developments that would be at odds with the rule of restraint to which the Court still wisely states adherence....

JUSTICE BREYER, with whom JUSTICE STEVENS, JUSTICE SOUTER, and JUSTICE GINSBURG join, dissenting.

The issue in this case is whether the Commerce Clause authorizes Congress to enact a statute that makes it a crime to possess a gun in, or near, a school. 18 U.S.C. §922(q)(1)(A). In my view, the statute falls well within the scope of the commerce power as this Court has understood that power over the last half-century.

I

In reaching this conclusion, I apply three basic principles of Commerce Clause interpretation. First, the power to "regulate Commerce ... among the several States," U.S. Const., Art. I, §8, cl. 3, encompasses the power to regulate local activities insofar as they significantly affect interstate commerce.... I use the word "significant" because the word "substantial" implies a somewhat narrower power than recent precedent suggests. But, to speak of "substantial effect" rather than "significant effect" would make no difference in this case.

Second, in determining whether a local activity will likely have a significant effect upon interstate commerce, a court must consider, not the effect of an individual act (a single instance of gun possession), but rather the cumulative effect of all similar instances (*i.e.*, the effect of all guns possessed in or near schools)....

Third, the Constitution requires us to judge the connection between a regulated activity and interstate commerce, not directly, but at one remove. Courts must give Congress a degree of leeway in determining the existence of a significant factual connection between the regulated activity and interstate commerce—both because the Constitution delegates the commerce power directly to Congress and because the determination requires an empirical judgment of a kind that a legislature is more likely than a court to make with accuracy. The traditional words "rational basis" capture this leeway. Thus, the specific question before us, as the Court recognizes, is not whether the "regulated activity sufficiently affected interstate commerce," but, rather, whether Congress could have had *"a rational basis"* for so concluding (emphasis added).

I recognize that we must judge this matter independently.... And, I also recognize that Congress did not write specific "interstate commerce" findings into the law under which Lopez was convicted. Nonetheless, as I have already noted, the matter that we review independently (*i.e.*, whether there is a "rational basis") already has considerable leeway built into it. And, the absence of findings, at most, deprives a statute of the benefit of some *extra* leeway. This extra deference, in principle, might change the result in a close case, though, in practice, it has not made a critical legal difference.... And, it would seem particularly unfortunate to make the validity of the statute at hand turn on the presence or absence of findings. Because Congress did make findings (though not until after Lopez was prosecuted), doing so would appear to elevate form over substance.

In addition, despite the Court of Appeals' suggestion to the contrary, there is no special need here for a clear indication of Congress' rationale. The statute does not interfere with the exercise of state or local authority.... Moreover, any clear statement rule would apply only to determine Congress' intended result, *not* to clarify the source of its authority or measure the level of consideration that went into its decision, and here there is no doubt as to which activities Congress intended to regulate....

II

Applying these principles to the case at hand, we must ask whether Congress could have had a *rational basis* for finding a significant (or substantial) connection between gun-related school violence and interstate commerce. Or, to put the question in the language of the explicit finding that Congress made when it amended this law in 1994: Could Congress rationally have found that "violent crime in school zones," through its effect on the "quality of education," significantly (or substantially) affects "interstate" or "foreign commerce"? As long as one views the commerce connection, not as a "technical legal conception," but as "a practical one," the answer to this question must be yes. Numerous reports and studies—generated both inside and outside government—make clear that Congress could reasonably have found the empirical connection that its law, implicitly or explicitly, asserts. (See Appendix for a sample of the documentation....) [omitted]

For one thing, reports, hearings, and other readily available literature make clear that the problem of guns in and around schools is widespread and extremely serious. These materials report, for example, that four percent of American high school students (and six percent of inner-city high school students) carry a gun to school at least occasionally; that 12 percent of urban high school students have had guns fired at them; that 20 percent of those students have been threatened with guns; and that, in any 6-month period, several hundred thousand schoolchildren are victims of violent crimes in or near their schools. And, they report that this widespread violence in schools throughout the Nation significantly interferes with the quality of education in those schools.... Based on reports such as these, Congress obviously could have thought that guns and learning are mutually exclusive. And, Congress could therefore have found a substantial educational problem—teachers unable to teach, students unable to learn—and concluded that guns near schools contribute substantially to the size and scope of that problem.

Having found that guns in schools significantly undermine the quality of education in our Nation's classrooms, Congress could also have found, given the effect of education upon interstate and foreign commerce, that gun-related violence in and around schools is a commercial, as well as a human, problem. Education, although far more than a matter of economics, has long been inextricably intertwined with the Nation's economy. When this Nation began, most workers received their education in the workplace, typically (like Benjamin Franklin) as apprentices. As late as the 1920's, many workers still received general education directly from their employers—from large corporations, such as General Electric, Ford, and Goodyear, which created schools within their firms to help both the worker and the firm. (Throughout most of the 19th century fewer than one percent of all Americans received secondary education through attending a high school.) As public school enrollment grew in the early 20th century, the need for industry to teach basic educational skills diminished. But, the direct economic link between basic education and industrial productivity remained. Scholars estimate that nearly a quarter of America's economic growth in the early years of this century is traceable directly to increased schooling; that investment in "human capital" (through spending on education) exceeded investment in "physical capital" by a ratio of almost two to one; and that the economic returns to this investment in education exceeded the returns to conventional capital investment.

In recent years the link between secondary education and business has strengthened, becoming both more direct and more important. Scholars on the subject report that technological changes and innovations in management techniques have altered the nature of the workplace so that more jobs now demand greater educational skills....

Increasing global competition also has made primary and secondary education economically more important....

Finally, there is evidence that, today more than ever, many firms base their location decisions upon the presence, or absence, of a work force with a basic education.... In light of this increased importance of education to individual firms, it is no surprise that half of the Nation's manufacturers have become involved with setting standards and shaping curricula for local schools, that 88 percent think this kind of involvement is important, that more than 20 States have recently passed educational reforms to attract new business, and that business magazines have begun to rank cities according to the quality of their schools.

The economic links I have just sketched seem fairly obvious. Why then is it not equally obvious, in light of those links, that a widespread, serious, and substantial physical threat to teaching and learning *also* substantially threatens the commerce to which that teaching and learning is inextricably tied? That is to say, guns in the hands of six percent of inner-city high school students and gun-related violence throughout a city's schools must threaten the trade and commerce that those schools support. The only question, then, is whether the latter threat is (to use the majority's terminology) "substantial." And, the evidence of (1) the *extent* of the gun-related violence problem, (2) the *extent* of the resulting negative effect on classroom learning, and (3) the *extent* of the consequent negative commercial effects, when taken together, indicate a threat to trade and commerce that is "substantial." At the very least, Congress could rationally have concluded that the links are "substantial."

Specifically, Congress could have found that gun-related violence near the classroom poses a serious economic threat (1) to consequently inadequately educated workers who must endure low-paying jobs, and (2) to communities and businesses that might (in today's "information society") otherwise gain, from a well-educated work force, an important commercial advantage. ... Congress might also have found these threats to be no different in kind from other threats that this Court has found within the commerce power, such as the threat that loan sharking poses to the "funds" of "numerous localities," *Perez* v. *United States* [1971], and that unfair labor practices pose to instrumentalities of commerce, see *Consolidated Edison Co.* v. *NLRB* (1938). As I have pointed out, Congress has written that "the occurrence of violent crime in school zones" has brought about a "decline in the quality of education" that "has an adverse impact on interstate commerce and the foreign commerce of the United States." 18 U.S.C.A. §§922 (q)(1)(F), (G) (Nov. 1994 Supp.). The violence-related facts, the educational facts, and the economic facts, taken together, make this conclusion rational. And, because under our case law, the sufficiency of the constitutionally necessary Commerce Clause link between a crime of violence and interstate commerce turns simply upon size or degree, those same facts make the statute constitutional.

To hold this statute constitutional is not to "obliterate" the "distinction of what is national and what is local"; nor is it to hold that the Commerce Clause permits the Federal Government to "regulate any activity that it found was related to the economic productivity of individual citizens," to regulate "marriage, divorce, and child custody," or to regulate any and all aspects of education. For one thing, this statute is aimed at curbing a particularly acute threat to the educational process—the possession (and use) of life-threatening firearms in, or near, the classroom. The empirical evidence that I have discussed above unmistakably documents the special way in which guns and education are incompatible. This Court has previously recognized the singularly disruptive potential on interstate commerce that acts of violence may have. For another thing, the immediacy of the connection between education and the national economic well-being is documented by scholars and accepted by society at large in a way and to a degree that may not hold true for other social institutions. It must surely be the rare case, then, that a statute strikes at conduct that (when considered in the abstract) seems so removed from commerce, but which (practically speaking) has so significant an impact upon commerce.

In sum, a holding that the particular statute before us falls within the commerce power would not expand the scope of that Clause. Rather, it simply would apply pre-existing law to changing economic circumstances. It would recognize that, in today's economic world, gun-related violence near the classroom makes a significant difference to our economic, as well as our social, well-being....

III

The majority's holding—that §922 falls outside the scope of the Commerce Clause—creates three serious legal problems. First, the majority's holding runs contrary to modern Supreme Court cases that have upheld congressional actions despite connections to interstate or foreign commerce that are less significant than the effect of school violence....

The second legal problem the Court creates comes from its apparent belief that it can reconcile its holding with earlier cases by making a critical distinction between "commercial" and noncommercial "transactions." That is to say, the Court believes the Constitution would distinguish between two local activities, each of which has an identical effect upon interstate commerce, if one, but not the other, is "commercial" in nature. As a general matter, this approach fails to heed this Court's earlier warning not to turn "questions of the power of Congress" upon "formula[s]" that would give

> "controlling force to nomenclature such as 'production' and 'indirect' and foreclose consideration of the actual effects of the activity in question upon interstate commerce." *Wickard* [v. *Filburn* (1942)].

... Moreover, the majority's test is not consistent with what the Court saw as the point of the cases that the majority now characterizes.... In fact, the *Wickard* Court expressly held that Wickard's consumption of home grown wheat, *"though it may not be regarded as commerce,"* could nevertheless be regulated— *"whatever its nature"*— so long as "it exerts a substantial economic effect on interstate commerce." (emphasis added).

The third legal problem created by the Court's holding is that it threatens legal uncertainty in an area of law that, until this case, seemed reasonably well settled. Congress has enacted many statutes (more than 100 sections of the United States Code), including criminal statutes (at least 25 sections), that use the words "affecting commerce" to define their scope, see, *e.g.*, 18 U.S.C. §844(i) (destruction of buildings used in activity affecting interstate commerce), and other statutes that contain no jurisdictional language at all, see, *e.g.*, 18 U.S.C. §922(o)(1) (possession of machine guns). Do these, or similar, statutes regulate noncommercial activities? If so, would that alter the meaning of "affecting commerce" in a jurisdictional element? ... More importantly, in the absence of a jurisdictional element, are the courts nevertheless to take *Wickard* (and later similar cases) as inapplicable, and to judge the effect of a single noncommercial activity on interstate commerce without considering similar instances of the forbidden conduct? However these questions are eventually resolved, the legal uncertainty now created will restrict Congress' ability to enact criminal laws aimed at criminal behavior that, considered problem by problem rather than instance by instance, seriously threatens the economic, as well as social, well-being of Americans.

IV

In sum, to find this legislation within the scope of the Commerce Clause would permit "Congress ... to act in terms of economic ... realities." It would interpret the Clause as this Court has traditionally interpreted it.... Upholding this legislation would do no more than simply recognize that Congress had a "rational basis" for finding a significant connection between guns in or near schools and (through their effect on education) the interstate and foreign commerce they threaten. For these reasons, I would reverse the judgment of the Court of Appeals. Respectfully, I dissent. [Appendix omitted.]

□ □ □

Nos. 93-1456 and 93-1828

U.S. Term Limits, Inc., et al., Petitioners v. Ray Thornton et al.

Winston Bryant, Attorney General of Arkansas, Petitioner v. Bobbie E. Hill et al.

On writs of certiorari to the Supreme Court of Arkansas

[May 22, 1995]

JUSTICE STEVENS delivered the opinion of the Court.

The Constitution sets forth qualifications for membership in the Congress of the United States. Article I, §2, cl. 2, which applies to the House of Representatives, provides:

> "No Person shall be a Representative who shall not have attained to the Age of twenty five Years, and been seven Years a Citizen of the United States, and who shall not, when elected, be an Inhabitant of that State in which he shall be chosen."

Article I, §3, cl. 3, which applies to the Senate, similarly provides:

> "No Person shall be a Senator who shall not have attained to the Age of thirty Years, and been nine Years a Citizen of the United States, and who

shall not, when elected, be an Inhabitant of that State for which he shall be chosen."

Today's cases present a challenge to an amendment to the Arkansas State Constitution that prohibits the name of an otherwise-eligible candidate for Congress from appearing on the general election ballot if that candidate has already served three terms in the House of Representatives or two terms in the Senate. The Arkansas Supreme Court held that the amendment violates the Federal Constitution. We agree with that holding. Such a state-imposed restriction is contrary to the "fundamental principle of our representative democracy," embodied in the Constitution, that "the people should choose whom they please to govern them." *Powell* v. *McCormack* (1969). Allowing individual States to adopt their own qualifications for congressional service would be inconsistent with the Framers' vision of a uniform National Legislature representing the people of the United States. If the qualifications set forth in the text of the Constitution are to be changed, that text must be amended.

I

At the general election on November 3, 1992, the voters of Arkansas adopted Amendment 73 to their State Constitution. Proposed as a "Term Limitation Amendment," its preamble stated:

> "The people of Arkansas find and declare that elected officials who remain in office too long become preoccupied with reelection and ignore their duties as representatives of the people. Entrenched incumbency has reduced voter participation and has led to an electoral system that is less free, less competitive, and less representative than the system established by the Founding Fathers. Therefore, the people of Arkansas, exercising their reserved powers, herein limit the terms of the elected officials."

The limitations in Amendment 73 apply to three categories of elected officials.... Section 3, the provision at issue in these cases, applies to the Arkansas Congressional Delegation. It provides:

> "(a) Any person having been elected to three or more terms as a member of the United States House of Representatives from Arkansas shall not be certified as a candidate and shall not be eligible to have his/her name placed on the ballot for election to the United States House of Representatives from Arkansas.

> "(b) Any person having been elected to two or more terms as a member of the United States Senate from Arkansas shall not be certified as a candidate and shall not be eligible to have his/her name placed on the ballot for election to the United States Senate from Arkansas."

Amendment 73 states that it is self-executing and shall apply to all persons seeking election after January 1, 1993.

On November 13, 1992, respondent Bobbie Hill, on behalf of herself, similarly situated Arkansas "citizens, residents, taxpayers and registered voters," and the League of Women Voters of Arkansas, filed a complaint in the Circuit Court for Pulaski County, Arkansas, seeking a declaratory judgment that §3 of

Amendment 73 is "unconstitutional and void." Her complaint named as defendants then-Governor Clinton, other state officers, the Republican Party of Arkansas, and the Democratic Party of Arkansas. The State of Arkansas, through its Attorney General, petitioner Winston Bryant, intervened as a party defendant in support of the amendment. Several proponents of the amendment also intervened, including petitioner U.S. Term Limits, Inc.

On cross-motions for summary judgment, the Circuit Court held that §3 of Amendment 73 violated Article I of the Federal Constitution.

With respect to that holding, in a 5-to-2 decision, the Arkansas Supreme Court affirmed. *U.S. Term Limits, Inc. v. Hill* (1994). Writing for a plurality of three justices, Justice Robert L. Brown concluded that the congressional restrictions in Amendment 73 are unconstitutional because the States have no authority "to change, add to, or diminish" the requirements for congressional service enumerated in the Qualifications Clauses....

Justice Brown's plurality opinion also rejected the argument that Amendment 73 is "merely a ballot access amendment," concluding that "[t]he intent and the effect of Amendment 73 are to disqualify congressional incumbents from further service."... In separate opinions, Justice Dudley and Justice Gerald P. Brown agreed that Amendment 73 violates the Federal Constitution.

Two Justices dissented from the federal constitutional holding....

The State of Arkansas, by its Attorney General, and the intervenors petitioned for writs of certiorari. Because of the importance of the issues, we granted both petitions and consolidated the cases for argument. We now affirm.

II

As the opinions of the Arkansas Supreme Court suggest, the constitutionality of Amendment 73 depends critically on the resolution of two distinct issues. The first is whether the Constitution forbids States from adding to or altering the qualifications specifically enumerated in the Constitution. The second is, if the Constitution does so forbid, whether the fact that Amendment 73 is formulated as a ballot access restriction rather than as an outright disqualification is of constitutional significance. Our resolution of these issues draws upon our prior resolution of a related but distinct issue: whether Congress has the power to add to or alter the qualifications of its Members.

Twenty-six years ago, in *Powell v. McCormack* (1969), we reviewed the history and text of the Qualifications Clauses in a case involving an attempted exclusion of a duly elected Member of Congress. The principal issue was whether the power granted to each House in Art. I, §5, to judge the "Qualifications of its own Members" includes the power to impose qualifications other than those set forth in the text of the Constitution. In an opinion by Chief Justice Warren for eight Members of the Court, we held that it does not. Because of the obvious importance of the issue, the Court's review of the history and meaning of the relevant constitutional text was especially thorough.

[Stevens discussed the Court's ruling in *Powell* at length. He said the Court conducted a "detailed and persuasive" historical analysis before concluding that, with respect to Congress, the Framers intended the Constitution to establish "fixed qualifications" for serving in Congress. He said that *Powell* relied on two "democratic principles." The first was "the egalitarian concept that the opportunity to be elected was open to all." The second, Stevens continued, was "the critical postulate that sovereignty is vested in the people, and that sovereignty confers on the people the right to choose freely their representatives to the National Government."]

In sum, after examining *Powell*'s historical analysis and its articulation of the "basic principles of our democratic system," we reaffirm that the qualifications for service in Congress set forth in the text of the Constitution are "fixed," at least in the sense that they may not be supplemented by Congress.

III

Our reaffirmation of *Powell* does not necessarily resolve the specific questions presented in these cases. For petitioners argue that whatever the constitutionality of additional qualifications for membership imposed by Congress, the historical and textual materials discussed in *Powell* do not support the conclusion that the Constitution prohibits additional qualifications imposed by States. In the absence of such a constitutional prohibition, petitioners argue, the Tenth Amendment and the principle of reserved powers require that States be allowed to add such qualifications.

Before addressing these arguments, we find it appropriate to take note of the striking unanimity among the courts that have considered the issue. None of the overwhelming array of briefs submitted by the parties and amici has called to our attention even a single case in which a state court or federal court has approved of a State's addition of qualifications for a member of Congress. To the contrary, an impressive number of courts have determined that States lack the authority to add qualifications. [Citations omitted.] This impressive and uniform body of judicial decisions and learned commentary indicates that the obstacles confronting petitioners are formidable indeed.

Petitioners argue that the Constitution contains no express prohibition against state-added qualifications, and that Amendment 73 is therefore an appropriate exercise of a State's reserved power to place additional restrictions on the choices that its own voters may make. We disagree for two independent reasons. First, we conclude that the power to add qualifications is not within the "original powers" of the States, and thus is not reserved to the States by the Tenth Amendment. Second, even if States possessed some original power in this area, we conclude that the Framers intended the Constitution to be the exclusive source of qualifications for members of Congress, and that the Framers thereby "divested" States of any power to add qualifications....

As we have frequently noted, "[t]he States unquestionably do retain a significant measure of sovereign authority. They do so, however, *only to the extent that the Constitution has not divested them of their original powers and* transferred those powers to the Federal Government." *Garcia* v. *San Antonio Metropolitan Transit Authority* (1985) (emphasis added).

Source of the Power

Contrary to petitioners' assertions, the power to add qualifications is not part of the original powers of sovereignty that the Tenth Amendment reserved to the States. Petitioners' Tenth Amendment argument misconceives the nature of the right at issue because that Amendment could only "reserve" that which existed before....

With respect to setting qualifications for service in Congress, no such right existed before the Constitution was ratified. The contrary argument overlooks the revolutionary character of the government that the Framers conceived. Prior to the adoption of the Constitution, the States had joined together under the Articles of Confederation. In that system, "the States retained most of their sovereignty, like independent nations bound together only by treaties." *Wesberry* v. *Sanders* (1964). After the Constitutional Convention convened, the Framers were presented with, and eventually adopted a variation of, "a plan not merely to amend the Articles of Confederation but to create an entirely new National Government with a National Executive, National Judiciary, and a National Legislature." In adopting that plan, the Framers envisioned a uniform national system, rejecting the notion that the Nation was a collection of States, and instead creating a direct link between the National Government and the people of the United States.... In that National Government, representatives owe primary allegiance not to the people of a State, but to the people of the Nation. As Justice Story observed, each Member of Congress is "an officer of the union, deriving his powers and qualifications from the constitution, and neither created by, dependent upon, nor controllable by, the states."...

We believe that the Constitution reflects the Framers' general agreement with the approach later articulated by Justice Story. For example, Art. I, §5, cl. 1 provides: "Each House shall be the Judge of the Elections, Returns and Qualifications of its own Members." The text of the Constitution thus gives the representatives of all the people the final say in judging the qualifications of the representatives of any one State. For this reason, the dissent falters when it states that "the people of Georgia have no say over whom the people of Massachusetts select to represent them in Congress."

Two other sections of the Constitution further support our view of the Framers' vision. First, consistent with Story's view, the Constitution provides that the salaries of representatives should "be ascertained by Law, and paid out of the Treasury of the United States," Art. I, §6, rather than by individual States. The salary provisions reflect the view that representatives owe their allegiance to the people, and not to States. Second, the provisions governing elections reveal the Framers' understanding that powers over the election of federal officers had to be delegated to, rather than reserved by, the States. It is surely no coincidence that the context of federal elections provides one of the few areas in which the Constitution expressly requires action by the States, namely that "[t]he Times, Places and Manner of holding Elections for Senators and Representatives, shall be prescribed in each State by the legislature thereof." This duty parallels the duty under Article II that "Each State shall appoint, in such Manner as the Legislature thereof may direct, a Number of Electors." Art II., §1, cl. 2. These Clauses are express delegations of power to the States to act with respect to federal elections....

In short, as the Framers recognized, electing representatives to the National Legislature was a new right, arising from the Constitution itself. The Tenth Amendment thus provides no basis for concluding that the States possess reserved power to add qualifications to those that are fixed in the Constitution.

Instead, any state power to set the qualifications for membership in Congress must derive not from the reserved powers of state sovereignty, but rather from the delegated powers of national sovereignty. In the absence of any constitutional delegation to the States of power to add qualifications to those enumerated in the Constitution, such a power does not exist.

The Preclusion of State Power

Even if we believed that States possessed as part of their original powers some control over congressional qualifications, the text and structure of the Constitution, the relevant historical materials, and, most importantly, the "basic principles of our democratic system" all demonstrate that the Qualifications Clauses were intended to preclude the States from exercising any such power and to fix as exclusive the qualifications in the Constitution.

Much of the historical analysis was undertaken by the Court in *Powell.* There is, however, additional historical evidence that pertains directly to the power of States. That evidence, though perhaps not as extensive as that reviewed in *Powell,* leads unavoidably to the conclusion that the States lack the power to add qualifications.

The Convention and Ratification Debates

The available affirmative evidence indicates the Framers' intent that States have no role in the setting of qualifications. In Federalist Paper No. 52, dealing with the House of Representatives, Madison addressed the "qualifications of the electors and the elected." The Federalist No. 52 at 325. Madison first noted the difficulty in achieving uniformity in the qualifications for electors, which resulted in the Framers' decision to require only that the qualifications for federal electors be the same as those for state electors.... Madison then explicitly contrasted the state control over the qualifications of electors with the lack of state control over the qualifications of the elected:

> "The qualifications of the elected, being less carefully and properly defined by the State constitutions, and being at the same time more susceptible of uniformity, have been very properly considered and regulated by the convention. A representative of the United States must be of the age of twenty-five years; must have been seven years a citizen of the United States; must, at the time of his election be an inhabitant of the State he is to represent; and, during the time of his service must be in no office under the United States. Under these reasonable limitations, the door of this part of the federal government is open to merit of every description, whether native or adoptive, whether young or old, and without regard to poverty or wealth, or to any particular profession of religious faith."...

The provisions in the Constitution governing federal elections confirm the Framers' intent that States lack power to add qualifications. The Framers feared that the diverse interests of the States would undermine the National Legislature, and thus they adopted provisions intended to minimize the possibility of state interference with federal elections. For example, to prevent discrimination against federal electors, the Framers required in Art. I, §2, cl. 1, that the qualifications for federal electors be the same as those for state electors.... Similarly, in Art. I, §4, cl. 1, though giving the States the freedom to regulate the "Times, Places and Manner of holding Elections," the Framers created a safeguard against state abuse by giving Congress the power to "by Law make or alter such Regulations." The Convention debates make clear that the Framers' overriding concern was the potential for States' abuse of the power to set the "Times, Places and Manner" of elections....

The dissent nevertheless contends that the Framers' distrust of the States with respect to elections does not preclude the people of the States from adopting eligibility requirements to help narrow their own choices. As the dissent concedes, however, the Framers were unquestionably concerned that the States would simply not hold elections for federal officers, and therefore the Framers gave Congress the power to "make or alter" state election regulations. Yet under the dissent's approach, the States could achieve exactly the same result by simply setting qualifications for federal office sufficiently high that no one could meet those qualifications. In our view, it is inconceivable that the Framers would provide a specific constitutional provision to ensure that federal elections would be held while at the same time allowing States to render those elections meaningless by simply ensuring that no candidate could be qualified for office. Given the Framers' wariness over the potential for state abuse, we must conclude that the specification of fixed qualifications in the constitutional text was intended to prescribe uniform rules that would preclude modification by either Congress or the States.

We find further evidence of the Framers' intent in Art. 1, §5, cl. 1, which provides: "Each House shall be the Judge of the Elections, Returns and Qualifications of its own Members." That Art. I, §5 vests a federal tribunal with ultimate authority to judge a Member's qualifications is fully consistent with the understanding that those qualifications are fixed in the Federal Constitution, but not with the understanding that they can be altered by the States. If the States had the right to prescribe additional qualifications — such as property, educational, or professional qualifications — for their own representatives, state law would provide the standard for judging a Member's eligibility....

We also find compelling the complete absence in the ratification debates of any assertion that States had the power to add qualifications. In those debates, the question whether to require term limits, or "rotation," was a major source of controversy....

Regardless of which side has the better of the debate over rotation, it is most striking that nowhere in the extensive ratification debates have we found any statement by either a proponent or an opponent of rotation that the draft constitution would permit States to require rotation for the representatives of their own citizens.... The absence in an otherwise freewheeling debate of any suggestion that States had the power to impose additional qualifications unquestionably reflects the Framers' common understanding that States lacked that power....

Congressional Experience

Congress' subsequent experience with state-imposed qualifications provides further evidence of the general consensus on the lack of state power in this area. In *Powell*, we examined that experience and noted that during the first

100 years of its existence, "Congress strictly limited its power to judge the qualifications of its members to those enumerated in the Constitution." Congress first confronted the issue in 1807 when it faced a challenge to the qualifications of William McCreery, a Representative from Maryland who allegedly did not satisfy a residency requirement imposed by that State. In recommending that McCreery be seated, the Report of the House Committee on Elections noted:

> " 'The committee proceeded to examine the Constitution, with relation to the case submitted to them, and find that *qualifications of members are therein determined, without reserving any authority to the State Legislatures to change, add to, or diminish those qualifications...*' " (emphasis added).

... As we noted in *Powell*, the congressional debate over the Committee's recommendation tended to focus on the "narrow issue of the power of the States to add to the standing qualifications set forth in the Constitution." The whole House, however, did not vote on the Committee's report, and instead voted only on a simple resolution: "*Resolved*, That William McCreery is entitled to his seat in this House." That resolution passed by a vote of 89 to 18.

Though the House Debate may be inconclusive, commentators at the time apparently viewed the seating of McCreery as confirmation of the States' lack of power to add qualifications....

Similarly, for over 150 years prior to *Powell*, commentators viewed the seating of McCreery as an expression of the view of the House that States could not add to the qualifications established in the Constitution.... Finally, it is clear that in *Powell* we viewed the seating of McCreery as the House's acknowledgment that the qualifications in the Constitution were fixed.

The Senate experience with state-imposed qualifications further supports our conclusions. In 1887, for example, the Senate seated Charles Faulkner of West Virginia, despite the fact that a provision of the West Virginia Constitution purported to render him ineligible to serve. The Senate Committee on Privileges and Elections unanimously concluded that "no State can prescribe any qualification to the office of United States Senator in addition to those declared in the Constitution of the United States." The Senate Committee on Rules and Administration reached the same conclusion in 1964 when faced with a challenge to Pierre Salinger, who had been appointed to serve as Senator from California....

We recognize, as we did in *Powell*, that "congressional practice has been erratic" and that the precedential value of congressional exclusion cases is "quite limited." Nevertheless, those incidents lend support to the result we reach today.

Democratic Principles

Our conclusion that States lack the power to impose qualifications vindicates the same "fundamental principle of our representative democracy" that we recognized in *Powell*, namely that "the people should choose whom they please to govern them."

As we noted earlier, the *Powell* Court recognized that an egalitarian ideal—that election to the National Legislature should be open to all people of merit—provided a critical foundation for the Constitutional structure. This egalitarian theme echoes throughout the constitutional debates. In The Federalist No. 57, for example, Madison wrote:

"Who are to be the objects of popular choice? Every citizen whose merit may recommend him to the esteem and confidence of his country. No qualification of wealth, of birth, of religious faith, or of civil profession is permitted to fetter the judgment or disappoint the inclination of the people."

... Additional qualifications pose the same obstacle to open elections whatever their source. The egalitarian ideal, so valued by the Framers, is thus compromised to the same degree by additional qualifications imposed by States as by those imposed by Congress.

Similarly, we believe that state-imposed qualifications, as much as congressionally imposed qualifications, would undermine the second critical idea recognized in *Powell*: that an aspect of sovereignty is the right of the people to vote for whom they wish. Again, the source of the qualification is of little moment in assessing the qualification's restrictive impact.

Finally, state-imposed restrictions, unlike the congressionally imposed restrictions at issue in *Powell*, violate a third idea central to this basic principle: that the right to choose representatives belongs not to the States, but to the people. From the start, the Framers recognized that the "great and radical vice" of the Articles of Confederation was "the principle of LEGISLATION for STATES or GOVERNMENTS, in their CORPORATE or COLLECTIVE CAPACITIES, and as contradistinguished from the INDIVIDUALS of whom they consist." The Federalist No. 15, (Hamilton). Thus the Framers, in perhaps their most important contribution, conceived of a Federal Government directly responsible to the people, possessed of direct power over the people, and chosen directly, not by States, but by the people....

Consistent with these views, the constitutional structure provides for a uniform salary to be paid from the national treasury, allows the States but a limited role in federal elections, and maintains strict checks on state interference with the federal election process. The Constitution also provides that the qualifications of the representatives of each State will be judged by the representatives of the entire Nation. The Constitution thus creates a uniform national body representing the interests of a single people.

Permitting individual States to formulate diverse qualifications for their representatives would result in a patchwork of state qualifications, undermining the uniformity and the national character that the Framers envisioned and sought to ensure.... Such a patchwork would also sever the direct link that the Framers found so critical between the National Government and the people of the United States.

State Practice

Petitioners attempt to overcome this formidable array of evidence against the States' power to impose qualifications by arguing that the practice of the States immediately after the adoption of the Constitution demonstrates their understanding that they possessed such power. One may properly question the extent to which the States' own practice is a reliable indicator of the contours of restrictions that the Constitution imposed on States, especially when no court has ever upheld a state-imposed qualification of any sort. But petitioners' argument is unpersuasive even on its own terms. At the time of the Convention, "[a]lmost all the State Constitutions required members of their Legislatures to possess considerable property." Despite this near uniformity, only one State, Virginia, placed similar restrictions on members of Congress, requiring that a representative be, *inter alia*, a "freeholder." Just 15 years after imposing a property qualification, Virginia replaced that requirement with a provision requiring that representatives be only "qualified according to the constitution of the United States." Moreover, several States, including New Hampshire, Georgia, Delaware, and South Carolina, revised their Constitutions at around the time of the Federal Constitution. In the revised Constitutions, each State retained property qualifications for its own state elected officials yet placed no property qualification on its congressional representatives.

The contemporaneous state practice with respect to term limits is similar. At the time of the Convention, States widely supported term limits in at least some circumstances. The Articles of Confederation contained a provision for term limits. As we have noted, some members of the Convention had sought to impose term limits for Members of Congress. In addition, many States imposed term limits on state officers, four placed limits on delegates to the Continental Congress, and several States voiced support for term limits for Members of Congress. Despite this widespread support, no State sought to impose any term limits on its own federal representatives. Thus, a proper assessment of contemporaneous state practice provides further persuasive evidence of a general understanding that the qualifications in the Constitution were unalterable by the States.

In sum, the available historical and textual evidence, read in light of the basic principles of democracy underlying the Constitution and recognized by this Court in *Powell*, reveal the Framers' intent that neither Congress nor the States should possess the power to supplement the exclusive qualifications set forth in the text of the Constitution.

IV

Petitioners argue that, even if States may not add qualifications, Amendment 73 is constitutional because it is not such a qualification, and because Amendment 73 is a permissible exercise of state power to regulate the "Times, Places and Manner of Holding Elections." We reject these contentions.

Unlike §§1 and 2 of Amendment 73, which create absolute bars to service for long-term incumbents running for state office, §3 merely provides that certain Senators and Representatives shall not be certified as candidates and shall not have their names appear on the ballot. They may run as write-in candidates and, if elected, they may serve. Petitioners contend that only a legal bar to service creates an impermissible qualification, and that Amendment 73 is therefore consistent with the Constitution.

Petitioners support their restrictive definition of qualifications with language from *Storer* v. *Brown* (1974), in which we faced a constitutional challenge to provisions of the California Elections Code that regulated the procedures by which both independent candidates and candidates affiliated with qualified political parties could obtain ballot position in general elections. The Code required candidates affiliated with a qualified party to win a primary election, and required independents to make timely filing of nomination papers signed by at least 5% of the entire vote cast in the last general election. The Code also denied ballot position to independents who had voted in the most recent primary election or who had registered their affiliation with a qualified party during the previous year.

In *Storer*, we rejected the argument that the challenged procedures created additional qualifications as "wholly without merit.".... We concluded that the California Code "no more establishes an additional requirement for the office of Representative than the requirement that the candidate win the primary to secure a place on the general ballot or otherwise demonstrate substantial community support." Petitioners maintain that, under *Storer*, Amendment 73 is not a qualification.

We need not decide whether petitioners' narrow understanding of qualifications is correct because, even if it is, Amendment 73 may not stand....

In our view, Amendment 73 is an indirect attempt to accomplish what the Constitution prohibits Arkansas from accomplishing directly. As the plurality opinion of the Arkansas Supreme Court recognized, Amendment 73 is an "effort to dress eligibility to stand for Congress in ballot access clothing," because the "intent and the effect of Amendment 73 are to disqualify congressional incumbents from further service." We must, of course, accept the State Court's view of the purpose of its own law: we are thus authoritatively informed that the sole purpose of §3 of Amendment 73 was to attempt to achieve a result that is forbidden by the Federal Constitution. Indeed, it cannot be seriously contended that the intent behind Amendment 73 is other than to prevent the election of incumbents. The preamble of Amendment 73 states explicitly: "[T]he people of Arkansas ... herein limit the terms of elected officials." Sections 1 and 2 create absolute limits on the number of terms that may be served. There is no hint that §3 was intended to have any other purpose.

Petitioners do, however, contest the Arkansas Supreme Court's conclusion that the Amendment has the same practical effect as an absolute bar. They argue that the possibility of a write-in campaign creates a real possibility for victory, especially for an entrenched incumbent. One may reasonably question the merits of that contention. Indeed, we are advised by the state court that there is nothing more than a faint glimmer of possibility that the excluded candidate will win. Our prior cases, too, have suggested that write-in candidates have only a slight chance of victory. But even if petitioners are correct that incumbents may occasionally win reelection as write-in candidates, there is no denying that the ballot restrictions will make it significantly more difficult for the barred candidate to win the election. In our view, an amendment with the avowed purpose and obvious effect of evading the requirements of the Qualifications Clauses by handicapping a class of candidates cannot stand....

Petitioners make the related argument that Amendment 73 merely regulates the "Manner" of elections, and that the Amendment is therefore a permissible exercise of state power under Article I, §4, cl. 1 (the Elections Clause) to regulate the "Times, Places and Manner" of elections. We cannot agree.

A necessary consequence of petitioners' argument is that Congress itself would have the power to "make or alter" a measure such as Amendment 73. That the Framers would have approved of such a result is unfathomable. As our decision in *Powell* and our discussion above make clear, the Framers were particularly concerned that a grant to Congress of the authority to set its own qualifications would lead inevitably to congressional self-aggrandizement and the upsetting of the delicate constitutional balance. Petitioners would have us believe, however, that even as the Framers carefully circumscribed congressional power to set qualifications, they intended to allow Congress to achieve the same result by simply formulating the regulation as a ballot access restriction under the Elections Clause. We refuse to adopt an interpretation of the Elections Clause that would so cavalierly disregard what the Framers intended to be a fundamental constitutional safeguard.

Moreover, petitioners' broad construction of the Elections Clause is fundamentally inconsistent with the Framers' view of that Clause. The Framers intended the Elections Clause to grant States authority to create procedural regulations, not to provide States with license to exclude classes of candidates from federal office....

We do not understand the dissent to contest our primary thesis, namely that if the qualifications for Congress are fixed in the Constitution, then a State-passed measure with the avowed purpose of imposing indirectly such an additional qualification violates the Constitution. The dissent, instead, raises two objections, challenging the assertion that the Arkansas amendment has the likely effect of creating a qualification, and suggesting that the true intent of Amendment 73 was not to evade the Qualifications Clause but rather to simply "level the playing field." Neither of these objections has merit.

As to the first, it is simply irrelevant to our holding today.... [O]ur prior cases strongly suggest that write-in candidates will have only a slim chance of success, and the Arkansas plurality agreed. However, we expressly do not rest on this Court's prior observations regarding write-in candidates. Instead, we hold that a state amendment is unconstitutional when it has the likely effect of handicapping a class of candidates and has the sole purpose of creating additional qualifications indirectly. Thus, the dissent's discussion of the evidence concerning the possibility that a popular incumbent will win a write-in election is simply beside the point.

As to the second argument, we find wholly unpersuasive the dissent's suggestion that Amendment 73 was designed merely to "level the playing field."... [I]t is obvious that the sole purpose of Amendment 73 was to limit the terms of elected officials, both State and federal, and that Amendment 73, therefore, may not stand.

V

The merits of term limits, or "rotation," have been the subject of debate since the formation of our Constitution, when the Framers unanimously rejected a proposal to add such limits to the Constitution. The cogent arguments on both sides of the question that were articulated during the process of ratification largely retain their force today. Over half the States have adopted measures that impose such limits on some offices either directly or indirectly, and the

Nation as a whole, notably by constitutional amendment, has imposed a limit on the number of terms that the President may serve. Term limits, like any other qualification for office, unquestionably restrict the ability of voters to vote for whom they wish. On the other hand, such limits may provide for the infusion of fresh ideas and new perspectives, and may decrease the likelihood that representatives will lose touch with their constituents. It is not our province to resolve this longstanding debate.

We are, however, firmly convinced that allowing the several States to adopt term limits for congressional service would effect a fundamental change in the constitutional framework. Any such change must come not by legislation adopted either by Congress or by an individual State, but rather—as have other important changes in the electoral process— through the Amendment procedures set forth in Article V. The Framers decided that the qualifications for service in the Congress of the United States be fixed in the Constitution and be uniform throughout the Nation. That decision reflects the Framers' understanding that Members of Congress are chosen by separate constituencies, but that they become, when elected, servants of the people of the United States. They are not merely delegates appointed by separate, sovereign States; they occupy offices that are integral and essential components of a single National Government. In the absence of a properly passed constitutional amendment, allowing individual States to craft their own qualifications for Congress would thus erode the structure envisioned by the Framers, a structure that was designed, in the words of the Preamble to our Constitution, to form a "more perfect Union."

The judgment is affirmed.

It is so ordered.

JUSTICE KENNEDY, concurring.

I join the opinion of the Court.

The majority and dissenting opinions demonstrate the intricacy of the question whether or not the Qualifications Clauses are exclusive. In my view, however, it is well settled that the whole people of the United States asserted their political identity and unity of purpose when they created the federal system. The dissent's course of reasoning suggesting otherwise might be construed to disparage the republican character of the National Government, and it seems appropriate to add these few remarks to explain why that course of argumentation runs counter to fundamental principles of federalism.

Federalism was our Nation's own discovery. The Framers split the atom of sovereignty. It was the genius of their idea that our citizens would have two political capacities, one state and one federal, each protected from incursion by the other. The resulting Constitution created a legal system unprecedented in form and design, establishing two orders of government, each with its own direct relationship, its own privity, its own set of mutual rights and obligations to the people who sustain it and are governed by it....

In one sense it is true that "the people of each State retained their separate political identities," for the Constitution takes care both to preserve the States and to make use of their identities and structures at various points in organizing the federal union. It does not at all follow from this that the sole political identity of an American is with the State of his or her residence. It denies the dual character of the Federal Government which is its very foundation to assert that the people of the United States do not have a political identity as well, one independent of, though consistent with, their identity as citizens of the State of their residence....

It is maintained by our dissenting colleagues that the State of Arkansas seeks nothing more than to grant its people surer control over the National Government, a control, it is said, that will be enhanced by the law at issue here. The arguments for term limitations (or ballot restrictions having the same effect) are not lacking in force; but the issue, as all of us must acknowledge, is not the efficacy of those measures but whether they have a legitimate source, given their origin in the enactments of a single State. There can be no doubt, if we are to respect the republican origins of the Nation and preserve its federal character, that there exists a federal right of citizenship, a relationship between the people of the Nation and their National Government, with which the States may not interfere. Because the Arkansas enactment intrudes upon this federal domain, it exceeds the boundaries of the Constitution.

JUSTICE THOMAS, with whom THE CHIEF JUSTICE, JUSTICE O'CONNOR, and JUSTICE SCALIA join, dissenting.

It is ironic that the Court bases today's decision on the right of the people to "choose whom they please to govern them." Under our Constitution, there is only one State whose people have the right to "choose whom they please" to represent Arkansas in Congress. The Court holds, however, that neither the elected legislature of that State nor the people themselves (acting by ballot initiative) may prescribe any qualifications for those representatives. The majority therefore defends the right of the people of Arkansas to "choose whom they please to govern them" by invalidating a provision that won nearly 60% of the votes cast in a direct election and that carried every congressional district in the State.

I dissent. Nothing in the Constitution deprives the people of each State of the power to prescribe eligibility requirements for the candidates who seek to represent them in Congress. The Constitution is simply silent on this question. And where the Constitution is silent, it raises no bar to action by the States or the people.

I

Because the majority fundamentally misunderstands the notion of "reserved" powers, I start with some first principles. Contrary to the majority's suggestion, the people of the States need not point to any affirmative grant of power in the Constitution in order to prescribe qualifications for their representatives in Congress, or to authorize their elected state legislators to do so.

A

Our system of government rests on one overriding principle: all power stems from the consent of the people. To phrase the principle in this way, however, is to be imprecise about something important to the notion of "reserved" powers. The ultimate source of the Constitution's authority is the consent of the people of each individual State, not the consent of the undifferentiated people of the Nation as a whole....

When they adopted the Federal Constitution, of course, the people of each State surrendered some of their authority to the United States (and hence to entities accountable to the people of other States as well as to themselves).... Because the people of the several States are the only true source of power, however, the Federal Government enjoys no authority beyond what the Constitution confers: the Federal Government's powers are limited and enumerated....

In each State, the remainder of the people's powers—"[t]he powers not delegated to the United States by the Constitution, nor prohibited by it to the States," Amdt. 10—are either delegated to the state government or retained by the people. The Federal Constitution does not specify which of these two possibilities obtains; it is up to the various state constitutions to declare which powers the people of each State have delegated to their state government. As far as the Federal Constitution is concerned, then, the States can exercise all powers that the Constitution does not withhold from them....

These basic principles are enshrined in the Tenth Amendment, which declares that all powers neither delegated to the Federal Government nor prohibited to the States "are reserved to the States respectively, or to the people."...

To be sure, when the Tenth Amendment uses the phrase "the people," it does not specify whether it is referring to the people of each State or the people of the Nation as a whole. But the latter interpretation would make the Amendment pointless: there would have been no reason to provide that where the Constitution is silent about whether a particular power resides at the state level, it might or might not do so....

Any ambiguity in the Tenth Amendment's use of the phrase "the people" is cleared up by the body of the Constitution itself. Article I begins by providing that the Congress of the United States enjoys "all legislative Powers herein granted," §1, and goes on to give a careful enumeration of Congress' powers, §8. It then concludes by enumerating certain powers that are *prohibited* to the States. The import of this structure is the same as the import of the Tenth Amendment: if we are to invalidate Arkansas' Amendment 73, we must point to something in the Federal Constitution that deprives the people of Arkansas of the power to enact such measures.

B

The majority disagrees that it bears this burden. But its arguments are unpersuasive.

1

The majority begins by announcing an enormous and untenable limitation on the principle expressed by the Tenth Amendment....

The majority's essential logic is that the state governments could not "reserve" any powers that they did not control at the time the Constitution was drafted. But it was not the state governments that were doing the reserving. The Constitution derives its authority instead from the consent of *the people* of the States. Given the fundamental principle that all governmental powers stem from the people of the States, it would simply be incoherent to assert that the people of the States could not reserve any powers that they had not previously controlled....

2

The majority also sketches out what may be an alternative (and narrower) argument.... [The] majority suggests that it would be inconsistent with the notion of "national sovereignty" for the States or the people of the States to have any reserved powers over the selection of Members of Congress....

Political scientists can debate about who commands the primary allegiance of Members of Congress once they reach Washington. From the framing to the present, however, the *selection* of the Representatives and Senators from each State has been left entirely to the people of that State or to their state legislature.... The very name "congress" suggests a coming together of representatives from distinct entities. In keeping with the complexity of our federal system, once the representatives chosen by the people of each State assemble in Congress, they form a national body and are beyond the control of the individual States until the next election. But the selection of representatives in Congress is indisputably an act of the people of each State, not some abstract people of the Nation as a whole.

The concurring opinion suggests that this cannot be so, because it is the Federal Constitution that guarantees the right of the people of each State (so long as they are qualified electors under state law) to take part in choosing the Members of Congress from that State. But the presence of a federally guaranteed right hardly means that the selection of those representatives constitutes "the exercise of federal authority." When the people of Georgia pick their representatives in Congress, they are acting as the people of Georgia, not as the corporate agents for the undifferentiated people of the Nation as a whole.... The concurring opinion protests that the exercise of "reserved" powers in the area of congressional elections would constitute "state interference with the most basic relation between the National Government and its citizens, the selection of legislative representatives." But when one strips away its abstractions, the concurring opinion is simply saying that the people of Arkansas cannot be permitted to inject themselves into the process by which they themselves select Arkansas' representatives in Congress....

3

In a final effort to deny that the people of the States enjoy "reserved" powers over the selection of their representatives in Congress, the majority suggests that the Constitution expressly delegates to the States certain powers over congressional elections. Such delegations of power, the majority argues, would be superfluous if the people of the States enjoyed reserved powers in this area.

Only one constitutional provision—the Times, Places and Manner Clause of Article I, §4—even arguably supports the majority's suggestion....

Contrary to the majority's assumption, however, this Clause does not delegate any authority to the States. Instead, it simply imposes a duty upon them. The majority gets it exactly right: by specifying that the state legislatures "shall" prescribe the details necessary to hold congressional elections, the Clause "expressly requires action by the States."...

Of course, the second part of the Times, Places and Manner Clause does grant a power rather than impose a duty. As its contrasting uses of the words "shall" and "may" confirm, however, the Clause grants power exclusively to Congress, not to the States. If the Clause did not exist at all, the States would still be able to prescribe the times, places, and manner of holding congressional elections; the deletion of the provision would simply deprive Congress of the power to override these state regulations.…

II

I take it to be established, then, that the people of Arkansas do enjoy "reserved" powers over the selection of their representatives in Congress. Purporting to exercise those reserved powers, they have agreed among themselves that the candidates covered by §3 of Amendment 73—those whom they have already elected to three or more terms in the House of Representatives or to two or more terms in the Senate—should not be eligible to appear on the ballot for reelection, but should nonetheless be returned to Congress if enough voters are   sufficiently enthusiastic about their candidacy to write in their names. Whatever one might think of the wisdom of this arrangement, we may not override the decision of the people of Arkansas unless something in the Federal Constitution deprives them of the power to enact such measures.

The majority settles on "the Qualifications Clauses" as the constitutional provisions that Amendment 73 violates. Because I do not read those provisions to impose any unstated prohibitions on the States, it is unnecessary for me to decide whether the majority is correct to identify Arkansas' ballot-access restriction with laws fixing true term limits or otherwise prescribing "qualifications" for congressional office. As I discuss in Part A below, the Qualifications Clauses are merely straightforward recitations of the minimum eligibility requirements that the Framers thought it essential for every Member of Congress to meet. They restrict state power only in that they prevent the States from *abolishing* all eligibility requirements for membership in Congress.

Because the text of the Qualifications Clauses does not support its position, the majority turns instead to its vision of the democratic principles that animated the Framers. But the majority's analysis goes to a question that is not before us: whether Congress has the power to prescribe qualifications for its own members. As I discuss in Part B, the democratic principles that contributed to the Framers' decision to withhold this power from Congress do not prove that the Framers also deprived the people of the States of their reserved authority to set eligibility requirements for their own representatives.

In Part C, I review the majority's more specific historical evidence.… [T]he records of the Philadelphia Convention affirmatively support my unwillingness to find hidden meaning in the Qualifications Clauses, while the surviving records from the ratification debates help neither side. As for the postratification period, five States supplemented the constitutional disqualifications in their very first election laws. The historical evidence thus refutes any notion that the Qualifications Clauses were generally understood to be exclusive. Yet the majority must establish just such an understanding in order to justify its position that the Clauses impose unstated prohibitions on the States and the people. In my view, the historical evidence is simply inadequate to warrant the majority's conclusion that the Qualifications Clauses mean anything more than what they say. [Remainder of section omitted.]

III

It is radical enough for the majority to hold that the Constitution implicitly precludes the people of the States from prescribing any eligibility requirements for the congressional candidates who seek their votes. This holding, after all, does not stop with negating the term limits that many States have seen fit to impose on their Senators and Representatives. Today's decision also means that no State may disqualify congressional candidates whom a court has found to be mentally incompetent, who are currently in prison, or who have past vote-fraud convictions. Likewise, after today's decision, the people of each State must leave open the possibility that they will trust someone with their vote in Congress even though they do not trust him with *a* vote in the election for Congress.

In order to invalidate §3 of Amendment 73, however, the majority must go farther. The bulk of the majority's analysis—like Part II of my dissent— addresses the issues that would be raised if Arkansas had prescribed "genuine, unadulterated, undiluted term limits." But as the parties have agreed, Amendment 73 does not actually create this kind of disqualification. It does not say that covered candidates may not serve any more terms in Congress if reelected, and it does not indirectly achieve the same result by barring those candidates from seeking reelection. It says only that if they are to win reelection, they must do so by write-in votes.

One might think that this is a distinction without a difference. As the majority notes, "[t]he uncontested data submitted to the Arkansas Supreme Court" show that write-in candidates have won only six congressional elections in this century. But while the data's accuracy is indeed "uncontested," petitioners filed an equally uncontested affidavit challenging the data's relevance. As political science professor James S. Fay swore to the Arkansas Supreme Court, "[m]ost write-in candidacies in the past have been waged by fringe candidates, with little public support and extremely low name identification." To the best of Professor Fay's knowledge, in modern times only two incumbent Congressmen have ever sought reelection as write-in candidates. One of them was Dale Alford of Arkansas, who had first entered the House of Representatives by winning 51% of the vote as a write-in candidate in 1958; Alford then waged a write-in campaign for reelection in 1960, winning a landslide 83% of the vote against an opponent who enjoyed a place on the ballot. The other incumbent write-in candidate was Philip J. Philbin of Massachusetts, who — despite losing his party primary and thus his spot on the ballot—won 27% of the vote in his unsuccessful write-in candidacy. According to Professor Fay, these results ... "demonstrate that when a write-in candidate is well-known and well-funded, it is quite possible for him or her to win an election."

The majority responds that whether "the Arkansas amendment has the likely effect of creating a qualification" is "simply irrelevant to our holding today." But the majority ... never adequately explains how it can take this position and still reach its conclusion.

One possible explanation for why the actual effect of the Arkansas amendment might be irrelevant is that the Arkansas Supreme Court has already issued a binding determination of fact on this point. Thus, the majority notes that "the state court" has advised us "that there is nothing more than a faint glimmer of possibility that the excluded candidate will win." But the majority is referring to a mere plurality opinion, signed by only three of the seven Justices who decided the case below....

... Accordingly, the majority explicitly disclaims any reliance on the state court's purported finding about the effect of Amendment 73.

Instead, the majority emphasizes another purported conclusion of the Arkansas Supreme Court. As the majority notes, the plurality below asserted that "[t]he intent" of Amendment 73 was "to disqualify congressional incumbents from further service."...

I am not sure why the intent behind a law should affect our analysis under the Qualifications Clauses.... But in any event, the majority is wrong about what "the State Court" has told us. Even the plurality below did not flatly assert that the desire to "disqualify" congressional incumbents was the sole purpose behind §3 of Amendment 73. More important, neither of the Justices who concurred in the plurality's holding said anything at all about the intent behind Amendment 73. As a result, we cannot attribute any findings on this issue to the Arkansas Supreme Court.

The majority suggests that this does not matter, because Amendment 73 itself says that it has the purpose of "evading the requirements of the Qualifications Clauses." The majority bases this assertion on the Amendment's preamble, which speaks of "limiting the terms of elected officials." But this statement may be referring only to §§1 and 2 of Amendment 73, which impose true term limits on state officeholders. Even if the statement refers to §3 as well, it may simply reflect the limiting effects that the drafters of the preamble expected to flow from what they perceived as the restoration of electoral competition to congressional races. In any event, inquiries into legislative intent are even more difficult than usual when the legislative body whose unified intent must be determined consists of 825,162 Arkansas voters.

The majority nonetheless thinks it clear that the goal of §3 is "to prevent the election of incumbents." In reaching this conclusion at the summary-judgment stage, however, the majority has given short shrift to petitioners' contrary claim. Petitioners do not deny that §3 of Amendment 73 intentionally handicaps a class of candidates, in the sense that it decreases their pre-existing electoral chances. But petitioners do deny that §3 is intended to (or will in fact) "prevent" the covered candidates from winning reelection, or "disqualify" them from further service. One of petitioners' central arguments is that congressionally conferred advantages have artificially inflated the pre-existing electoral chances of the covered candidates, and that Amendment 73 is merely designed to level the playing field on which challengers compete with them.

To understand this argument requires some background. Current federal law (enacted, of course, by congressional incumbents) confers numerous advantages on incumbents, and these advantages are widely thought to make it "significantly more difficult" for challengers to defeat them. For instance, federal law gives incumbents enormous advantages in building name recognition and good will in their home districts.... At the same time that incumbent Members of Congress enjoy these in-kind benefits, Congress imposes spending and contribution limits in congressional campaigns that "can prevent challengers from spending more ... to overcome their disadvantage in name recognition." Many observers believe that the campaign-finance laws also give incumbents an "enormous fund-raising edge" over their challengers by giving a large financing role to entities with incentives to curry favor with incumbents. In addition, the internal rules of Congress put a substantial premium on seniority, with the result that each Member's already plentiful opportunities to distribute benefits to his constituents increase with the length of his tenure. In this manner, Congress effectively "fines" the electorate for voting against incumbents....

At the same time that incumbents enjoy the electoral advantages that they have conferred upon themselves, they also enjoy astonishingly high reelection rates....

The voters of Arkansas evidently believe that incumbents would not enjoy such overwhelming success if electoral contests were truly fair—that is, if the government did not put its thumb on either side of the scale. The majority offers no reason to question the accuracy of this belief. Given this context, petitioners portray §3 of Amendment 73 as an effort at the state level to offset the electoral advantages that congressional incumbents have conferred upon themselves at the federal level.

To be sure, the offset is only rough and approximate; no one knows exactly how large an electoral benefit comes with having been a long-term Member of Congress, and no one knows exactly how large an electoral disadvantage comes from forcing a well-funded candidate with high name recognition to run a write-in campaign. But the majority does not base its holding on the premise that Arkansas has struck the wrong balance. Instead, the majority holds that the Qualifications Clauses preclude Arkansas from trying to strike any balance at all; the majority simply says that "an amendment with the avowed purpose and obvious effect of evading the requirements of the Qualifications Clauses by handicapping a class of candidates cannot stand." Thus, the majority apparently would reach the same result even if one could demonstrate at trial that the electoral advantage conferred by Amendment 73 upon challengers precisely counterbalances the electoral advantages conferred by federal law upon long-term Members of Congress.

For me, this suggests only two possibilities. Either the majority's holding is wrong and Amendment 73 does not violate the Qualifications Clauses, or (assuming the accuracy of petitioners' factual claims) the electoral system that exists without Amendment 73 is no less unconstitutional than the electoral system that exists with Amendment 73.

I do not mean to suggest that States have unbridled power to handicap particular classes of candidates, even when those candidates enjoy federally conferred advantages that may threaten to skew the electoral process. But laws that allegedly have the purpose and effect of handicapping a particular class of candidates traditionally are reviewed under the First and Fourteenth Amendments rather than the Qualifications Clauses.... Term-limit measures have tended to survive such review without difficulty. See, e.g., *Moore v. McCartney* (1976) (dismissing an appeal on the ground that limits on the terms of state officeholders do not even raise a substantial federal question under the First and Fourteenth Amendments).

To analyze such laws under the Qualifications Clauses may open up whole new vistas for courts. If it is true that "the current congressional campaign finance system ... has created an electoral system so stacked against challengers that in many elections voters have no real choices," are the Federal Election Campaign Act Amendments of 1974 unconstitutional under (of all things) the Qualifications Clauses? ... If it can be shown that nonminorities are at a significant disadvantage when they seek election in districts dominated by minority voters, would the intentional creation of "majority-minority districts" violate the Qualifications Clauses even if it were to survive scrutiny under the Fourteenth Amendment? ... More generally, if "[d]istrict lines are rarely neutral phenomena" and if "districting inevitably has and is intended to have substantial political consequences," will plausible Qualifications Clause challenges greet virtually every redistricting decision? ...

The majority's opinion may not go so far, although it does not itself suggest any principled stopping point. No matter how narrowly construed, however, today's decision reads the Qualifications Clauses to impose substantial implicit prohibitions on the States and the people of the States. I would not draw such an expansive negative inference from the fact that the Constitution requires Members of Congress to be a certain age, to be inhabitants of the States that they represent, and to have been United States citizens for a specified period. Rather, I would read the Qualifications Clauses to do no more than what they say. I respectfully dissent.

No. 93–1841

Adarand Constructors, Inc., Petitioner v. Federico Peña, Secretary of Transportation, et al.

On writ of certiorari to the United States Court of Appeals for the Tenth Circuit

[June 12, 1995]

JUSTICE O'CONNOR announced the judgment of the Court and delivered an opinion with respect to Parts I, II, III-A, III-B, III-D, and IV, which is for the Court except insofar as it might be inconsistent with the views expressed in JUSTICE SCALIA's concurrence, and an opinion with respect to Part III-C in which JUSTICE KENNEDY joins.

Petitioner Adarand Constructors, Inc., claims that the Federal Government's practice of giving general contractors on government projects a financial incentive to hire subcontractors controlled by "socially and economically disadvantaged individuals," and in particular, the Government's use of race-based presumptions in identifying such individuals, violates the equal protection component of the Fifth Amendment's Due Process Clause. The Court of Appeals rejected Adarand's claim. We conclude, however, that courts should analyze cases of this kind under a different standard of review than the one the Court of Appeals applied. We therefore vacate the Court of Appeals' judgment and remand the case for further proceedings.

I

In 1989, the Central Federal Lands Highway Division (CFLHD), which is part of the United States Department of Transportation (DOT), awarded the prime contract for a highway construction project in Colorado to Mountain Gravel & Construction Company. Mountain Gravel then solicited bids from subcontractors for the guardrail portion of the contract. Adarand, a Colorado-based highway construction company specializing in guardrail work, submitted the low bid. Gonzales Construction Company also submitted a bid.

The prime contract's terms provide that Mountain Gravel would receive additional compensation if it hired subcontractors certified as small businesses controlled by "socially and economically disadvantaged individuals." Gonzales is certified as such a business; Adarand is not. Mountain Gravel awarded the subcontract to Gonzales, despite Adarand's low bid, and Mountain Gravel's Chief Estimator has submitted an affidavit stating that Mountain Gravel would have accepted Adarand's bid, had it not been for the additional payment it received by hiring Gonzales instead. Federal law requires that a subcontracting clause similar to the one used here must appear in most federal agency contracts, and it also requires the clause to state that "the contractor shall presume that socially and economically disadvantaged individuals include Black Americans, Hispanic Americans, Native Americans, Asian Pacific Americans, and other minorities, or any other individual found to be disadvantaged by the [Small Business] Administration pursuant to section 8(a) of the Small Business Act." Adarand claims that the presumption set forth in that statute discriminates on the basis of race in violation of the Federal Government's Fifth Amendment obligation not to deny anyone equal protection of the laws.

These fairly straightforward facts implicate a complex scheme of federal statutes and regulations.... The Small Business Act, as amended, 15 U.S.C. §631 *et seq.* (Act), declares it to be "the policy of the United States that small business concerns, [and] small business concerns owned and controlled by socially and economically disadvantaged individuals, ... shall have the maximum practicable opportunity to participate in the performance of contracts let by any Federal agency." §8(d)(1). The Act defines "socially disadvantaged individuals" as "those who have been subjected to racial or ethnic prejudice or cultural bias because of their identity as a member of a group without regard to their individual qualities," and it defines "economically disadvantaged individuals" as "those socially disadvantaged individuals whose ability to compete in the free enterprise system has been impaired due to diminished capital and credit opportunities as compared to others in the same business area who are not socially disadvantaged."

In furtherance of the policy stated in §8(d)(1), the Act establishes "[t]he Government-wide goal for participation by small business concerns owned and controlled by socially and economically disadvantaged individuals" at "not less than 5 percent of the total value of all prime contract and subcontract awards for each fiscal year." It also requires the head of each Federal agency to set agency-specific goals for participation by businesses controlled by socially and economically disadvantaged individuals.

The Small Business Administration (SBA) has implemented these statutory directives in a variety of ways, two of which are relevant here. One is the "8(a) program," which is available to small businesses controlled by socially and economically disadvantaged individuals as the SBA has defined those terms. The 8(a) program confers a wide range of benefits on participating businesses.... To participate in the 8(a) program, a business must be "small," and it must be 51% owned by individuals who qualify as "socially and economically disadvantaged." The SBA presumes that Black, Hispanic, Asian Pacific, Subcontinent Asian, and Native Americans, as well as "members of other groups designated from time to time by SBA," are "socially disadvantaged." It also allows any individual not a member of a listed group to prove social disadvantage "on the basis of clear and convincing evidence." Social disadvantage is not enough to establish eligibility, however; SBA also requires each 8(a) program participant to prove "economic disadvantage."...

The other SBA program relevant to this case is the "8(d) subcontracting program," which unlike the 8(a) program is limited to eligibility for subcontracting provisions like the one at issue here. In determining eligibility, the SBA presumes social disadvantage based on membership in certain minority groups, just as in the 8(a) program, and again appears to require an individualized, although "less restrictive," showing of economic disadvantage. A different set of regulations, however, says that members of minority groups wishing to participate in the 8(d) subcontracting program are entitled to a race-based presumption of social *and* economic disadvantage. We are left with some uncertainty as to whether participation in the 8(d) subcontracting program requires an individualized showing of economic disadvantage. In any event, in both the 8(a) and the 8(d) programs, the presumptions of disadvantage are rebuttable if a third party comes forward with evidence suggesting that the participant is not, in fact, either economically or socially disadvantaged.

The contract giving rise to the dispute in this case came about as a result of the Surface Transportation and Uniform Relocation Assistance Act of 1987 (STURAA), a DOT appropriations measure. Section 106(c)(1) of STURAA provides that "not less than 10 percent" of the appropriated funds "shall be expended with small business concerns owned and controlled by socially and economically disadvantaged individuals." STURAA adopts the Small Business Act's definition of "socially and economically disadvantaged individual," including the applicable race-based presumptions, and adds that "women shall be presumed to be socially and economically disadvantaged individuals for purposes of this subsection." STURAA also requires the Secretary of Transportation to establish "minimum uniform criteria for State governments to use in certifying whether a concern qualifies for purposes of this subsection."... Those regulations say that the certifying authority should presume both social and economic disadvantage (*i. e.*, eligibility to participate) if the applicant belongs to certain racial groups, or is a woman. As with the SBA programs, third parties may come forward with evidence in an effort to rebut the presumption of disadvantage for a particular business.

[The Court quoted the operative clause of the contract in the case. It provides "monetary compensation" to a contractor that awards a subcontract to a "Disadvantaged Business Enterprise (DBE)" in the amount of 10 percent of the subcontract, not to exceed 1.5 percent of the original contract.] To benefit from this clause, Mountain Gravel had to hire a subcontractor who had been certified as a small disadvantaged business by the SBA, a state highway agency, or some other certifying authority acceptable to the Contracting Officer....

After losing the guardrail subcontract to Gonzales, Adarand filed suit against various federal officials in the United States District Court for the District of Colorado, claiming that the race-based presumptions involved in the use of subcontracting compensation clauses violate Adarand's right to equal protection. The District Court granted the Government's motion for summary judgment. The Court of Appeals for the Tenth Circuit affirmed. It understood our decision in *Fullilove* v. *Klutznick* (1980) to have adopted "a lenient standard, resembling intermediate scrutiny, in assessing" the constitutionality of federal race-based action. Applying that "lenient standard," as further developed in *Metro Broadcasting Inc.* v. *FCC* (1990), the Court of Appeals upheld the use of subcontractor compensation clauses. We granted certiorari. (1994).

[II omitted]

III

The Government urges that "the Subcontracting Compensation Clause program is ... a program based on *disadvantage*, not on race," and thus that it is subject only to "the most relaxed judicial scrutiny." To the extent that the statutes and regulations involved in this case are race neutral, we agree. The Government concedes, however, that "the race-based rebuttable presumption used in some certification determinations under the Subcontracting Compensation Clause" is subject to some heightened level of scrutiny. The parties disagree as to what that level should be....

Adarand's claim arises under the Fifth Amendment to the Constitution, which provides that "No person shall ... be deprived of life, liberty, or property, without due process of law." Although this Court has always understood that Clause to provide some measure of protection against *arbitrary* treatment by the Federal Government, it is not as explicit a guarantee of *equal* treatment as the Fourteenth Amendment, which provides that "No *State* shall ... deny to any person within its jurisdiction the equal protection of the laws" (emphasis added). Our cases have accorded varying degrees of significance to the difference in the language of those two Clauses. We think it necessary to revisit the issue here.

A

Through the 1940s, this Court had routinely taken the view in non-race-related cases that, "unlike the Fourteenth Amendment, the Fifth contains no equal protection clause and it provides no guaranty against discriminatory legislation by Congress." *Detroit Bank* v. *United States* (1943) ... When the Court first faced a Fifth Amendment equal protection challenge to a federal racial classification, it adopted a similar approach, with most unfortunate results. [The Court summarized the two World War II decisions, *Hirabayashi* v. *United States*

(1943), and *Korematsu* v. *United States* (1944), that rejected equal protection challenges to the curfew and wartime relocation of Japanese-Americans.]

In *Bolling* v. *Sharpe* (1954), the Court for the first time explicitly questioned the existence of any difference between the obligations of the Federal Government and the States to avoid racial classifications. *Bolling* did note that "[t]he 'equal protection of the laws' is a more explicit safeguard of prohibited unfairness than 'due process of law.' " But *Bolling* then concluded that, "[i]n view of [the] decision that the Constitution prohibits the states from maintaining racially segregated public schools, it would be unthinkable that the same Constitution would impose a lesser duty on the Federal Government."

Bolling's facts concerned school desegregation, but its reasoning was not so limited.... Later cases in contexts other than school desegregation did not distinguish between the duties of the States and the Federal Government to avoid racial classifications. [The Court noted that its opinion in *McLaughlin* v. *Florida*, a 1964 case that struck down a race-based state law, cited passages from *Bolling, Korematsu*, and *Hirabayashi* to show that racial classifications are "constitutionally suspect."] *McLaughlin*'s reliance on cases involving federal action for the standards applicable to a case involving state legislation suggests that the Court understood the standards for federal and state racial classifications to be the same.

Cases decided after *McLaughlin* continued to treat the equal protection obligations imposed by the Fifth and the Fourteenth Amendments as indistinguishable. *Loving* v. *Virginia* [1967], which struck down a race-based state law [prohibiting interracial marriage], cited *Korematsu* for the proposition that "the Equal Protection Clause demands that racial classifications ... be subjected to the 'most rigid scrutiny.' " The various opinions in *Frontiero* v. *Richardson*, (1973), which concerned sex discrimination by the Federal Government, took their equal protection standard of review from *Reed* v. *Reed*, (1971), a case that invalidated sex discrimination by a State, without mentioning any possibility of a difference between the standards applicable to state and federal action. Thus, in 1975, the Court stated explicitly that "[t]his Court's approach to Fifth Amendment equal protection claims has always been precisely the same as to equal protection claims under the Fourteenth Amendment." *Weinberger* v. *Wiesenfeld* (1975)....

B

Most of the cases discussed above involved classifications burdening groups that have suffered discrimination in our society. In 1978, the Court confronted the question whether race-based governmental action designed to *benefit* such groups should also be subject to "the most rigid scrutiny." *Regents of Univ. of California* v. *Bakke* involved an equal protection challenge to a state-run medical school's practice of reserving a number of spaces in its entering class for minority students. The petitioners argued that "strict scrutiny" should apply only to "classifications that disadvantage 'discrete and insular minorities.' " *Bakke* did not produce an opinion for the Court, but Justice Powell's opinion announcing the Court's judgment rejected the argument. In a passage joined by Justice White, Justice Powell wrote that "[t]he guarantee of equal protection cannot mean one thing when applied to one individual and something else when applied to a person of another color." He concluded that "[r]acial and ethnic distinctions of any sort are inherently suspect and thus call for the most exacting judicial examination."...

Two years after *Bakke*, the Court faced another challenge to remedial race-based action, this time involving action undertaken by the Federal Government. In *Fullilove* v. *Klutznick* (1980), the Court upheld Congress' inclusion of a 10% set-aside for minority-owned businesses in the Public Works Employment Act of 1977. As in *Bakke*, there was no opinion for the Court. Chief Justice Burger, in an opinion joined by Justices White and Powell, observed that "[a]ny preference based on racial or ethnic criteria must necessarily receive a most searching examination to make sure that it does not conflict with constitutional guarantees." That opinion, however, "d[id] not adopt, either expressly or implicitly, the formulas of analysis articulated in such cases as [*Bakke*]." It employed instead a two-part test which asked, first, "whether the *objectives* of th[e] legislation are within the power of Congress," and second, "whether the limited use of racial and ethnic criteria, in the context presented, is a constitutionally permissible *means* for achieving the congressional objectives." It then upheld the program under that test.... Justice Powell wrote separately to express his view that the plurality opinion had essentially applied "strict scrutiny" as described in his *Bakke* opinion ... and had done so correctly. Justice Stewart (joined by then-JUSTICE REHNQUIST) dissented, arguing that the Constitution required the Federal Government to meet the same strict standard as the States when enacting racial classifications, and that the program before the Court failed that standard. JUSTICE STEVENS also dissented, arguing that "[r]acial classifications are simply too pernicious to permit any but the most exact connection between justification and classification," and that the program before the Court could not be characterized "as a 'narrowly tailored' remedial measure." Justice Marshall (joined by Justices Brennan and Blackmun) concurred in the judgment, reiterating the view of four Justices in *Bakke* that any race-based governmental action designed to "remed[y] the present effects of past racial discrimination" should be upheld if it was "substantially related" to the achievement of an "important governmental objective"—*i.e.*, such action should be subjected only to what we now call "intermediate scrutiny."

In *Wygant* v. *Jackson Board of Ed.* (1986), the Court considered a Fourteenth Amendment challenge to another form of remedial racial classification. The issue in *Wygant* was whether a school board could adopt race-based preferences in determining which teachers to lay off. Justice Powell's plurality opinion observed that "the level of scrutiny does not change merely because the challenged classification operates against a group that historically has not been subject to governmental discrimination" and stated the two-part inquiry as "whether the layoff provision is supported by a compelling state purpose and whether the means chosen to accomplish that purpose are narrowly tailored." ... The plurality then concluded that the school board's interest in "providing minority role models for its minority students, as an attempt to alleviate the effects of societal discrimination," was not a compelling interest that could justify the use of a racial classification. It added that "[s]ocietal discrimination, without more, is too amorphous a basis for imposing a racially classified remedy," and insisted instead that "a public employer ... must ensure that, before it embarks on an affirmative-action program, it has convincing evidence that remedial action is warranted. That is, it must have sufficient evidence to justify the conclusion that there has been prior discrimination." Justice White concurred only in the judgment, although he agreed that the school board's asserted interests could not, "singly or together, justify this racially discriminatory layoff policy."...

The Court's failure to produce a majority opinion in *Bakke, Fullilove,* and *Wygant* left unresolved the proper analysis for remedial race-based governmental action....

The Court resolved the issue, at least in part, in 1989. *Richmond* v. *J. A. Croson Co.* concerned a city's determination that 30% of its contracting work should go to minority-owned businesses. A majority of the Court in *Croson* held that "the standard of review under the Equal Protection Clause is not dependent on the race of those burdened or benefited by a particular classification," and that the single standard of review for racial classifications should be "strict scrutiny." (opinion of O'CONNOR, J., joined by REHNQUIST, C.J., WHITE, J., and KENNEDY, J.); (SCALIA, J., concurring in judgment) ("I agree ... with JUSTICE O'CONNOR's conclusion that strict scrutiny must be applied to all governmental classification by race"). As to the classification before the Court, the plurality agreed that "a state or local subdivision ... has the authority to eradicate the effects of private discrimination within its own legislative jurisdiction," but the Court thought that the city had not acted with "a 'strong basis in evidence for its conclusion that remedial action was necessary.'" The Court also thought it "obvious that [the] program is not narrowly tailored to remedy the effects of prior discrimination."

With *Croson,* the Court finally agreed that the Fourteenth Amendment requires strict scrutiny of all race-based action by state and local governments. But *Croson* of course had no occasion to declare what standard of review the Fifth Amendment requires for such action taken by the Federal Government.... On the other hand, the Court subsequently indicated that *Croson* had at least some bearing on federal race-based action when it vacated a decision upholding such action and remanded for further consideration in light of *Croson. H. K. Porter Co.* v. *Metropolitan Dade County* (1989)....

Despite lingering uncertainty in the details, however, the Court's cases through *Croson* had established three general propositions with respect to governmental racial classifications. First, skepticism: "'[a]ny preference based on racial or ethnic criteria must necessarily receive a most searching examination.'" [Citations omitted.] Second, consistency: "the standard of review under the Equal Protection Clause is not dependent on the race of those burdened or benefited by a particular classification," [citing *Croson* and *Bakke*] i.e., all racial classifications reviewable under the Equal Protection Clause must be strictly scrutinized. And third, congruence: "[e]qual protection analysis in the Fifth Amendment area is the same as that under the Fourteenth Amendment" [citations omitted].Taken together, these three propositions lead to the conclusion that any person, of whatever race, has the right to demand that any governmental actor subject to the Constitution justify any racial classification subjecting that person to unequal treatment under the strictest judicial scrutiny....

A year later, however, the Court took a surprising turn. *Metro Broadcasting, Inc.* v. *FCC* (1990) involved a Fifth Amendment challenge to two race-based policies of the Federal Communications Commission. In *Metro Broadcasting,* the Court repudiated the long-held notion that "it would be unthinkable that the same Constitution would impose a lesser duty on the Federal Government" than it does on a State to afford equal protection of the laws. It did so by holding that "benign" federal racial classifications need only satisfy intermediate scrutiny, even though *Croson* had recently concluded that such classifications enacted by a State must satisfy strict scrutiny. "[B]enign" federal racial classifications, the Court said, "—even if those measures are not 'remedial' in the sense of being designed to compensate victims of past governmental or societal discrimination—are constitutionally permissible to the extent that they serve *important* governmental objectives within the power of Congress and are *substantially related* to achievement of those objectives." (Emphasis added.) The Court did not explain how to tell whether a racial classification should be deemed "benign," other than to express "confiden[ce] that an 'examination of the legislative scheme and its history' will separate benign measures from other types of racial classifications."

Applying this test, the Court first noted that the FCC policies at issue did not serve as a remedy for past discrimination. Proceeding on the assumption that the policies were nonetheless "benign," it concluded that they served the "important governmental objective" of "enhancing broadcast diversity" and that they were "substantially related" to that objective. It therefore upheld the policies.

By adopting intermediate scrutiny as the standard of review for congressionally mandated "benign" racial classifications, *Metro Broadcasting* departed from prior cases in two significant respects. First, it turned its back on *Croson's* explanation of why strict scrutiny of all governmental racial classifications is essential:

> "Absent searching judicial inquiry into the justification for such race-based measures, there is simply no way of determining what classifications are 'benign' or 'remedial' and what classifications are in fact motivated by illegitimate notions of racial inferiority or simple racial politics...." *Croson* (plurality opinion of O'CONNOR, J.).

We adhere to that view today, despite the surface appeal of holding "benign" racial classifications to a lower standard, because "it may not always be clear that a so-called preference is in fact benign." *Bakke* (opinion of Powell, J.)....

Second, *Metro Broadcasting* squarely rejected one of the three propositions established by the Court's earlier equal protection cases, namely, congruence between the standards applicable to federal and state racial classifications, and in so doing also undermined the other two—skepticism of all racial classifications, and consistency of treatment irrespective of the race of the burdened or benefited group. Under *Metro Broadcasting,* certain racial classifications ("benign" ones enacted by the Federal Government) should be treated less skeptically than others; and the race of the benefited group is critical to the determination of which standard of review to apply. *Metro Broadcasting* was thus a significant departure from much of what had come before it.

The three propositions undermined by *Metro Broadcasting* all derive from the basic principle that the Fifth and Fourteenth Amendments to the Constitution protect *persons,* not *groups.* It follows from that principle that all governmental action based on race ... should be subjected to detailed judicial inquiry to ensure that the *personal* right to equal protection of the laws has not been infringed. These ideas have long been central to this Court's understanding of equal protection, and holding "benign" state and federal racial classifications to different standards does not square with them.... Accordingly, we hold today that all racial classifications, imposed by whatever federal, state, or local governmental actor, must be analyzed by a reviewing court under strict scrutiny. In other words, such classifications are constitutional only if they are narrowly tailored measures that further compelling governmental interests. To the extent that *Metro Broadcasting* is inconsistent with that holding, it is overruled.

In dissent, JUSTICE STEVENS criticizes us for "delivering a disconcerting lecture about the evils of governmental racial classifications." With respect, we believe his criticisms reflect a serious misunderstanding of our opinion.

JUSTICE STEVENS concurs in our view that courts should take a skeptical view of all governmental racial classifications. He also allows that "nothing is inherently wrong with applying a single standard to fundamentally different situations, as long as that standard takes relevant differences into account." What he fails to recognize is that strict scrutiny *does* take "relevant differences" into account—indeed, that is its fundamental purpose. The point of carefully examining the interest asserted by the government in support of a racial classification, and the evidence offered to show that the classification is needed, is precisely to distinguish legitimate from illegitimate uses of race in governmental decisionmaking. And JUSTICE STEVENS concedes that "some cases may be difficult to classify," all the more reason, in our view, to examine all racial classifications carefully. Strict scrutiny does not "trea[t] dissimilar race-based decisions as though they were equally objectionable"; to the contrary, it evaluates carefully all governmental race-based decisions *in order to decide* which are constitutionally objectionable and which are not....

JUSTICE STEVENS chides us for our "supposed inability to differentiate between 'invidious' and 'benign' discrimination," because it is in his view sufficient that "people understand the difference between good intentions and bad." But, as we have just explained, the point of strict scrutiny is to "differentiate between" permissible and impermissible governmental use of race....

Perhaps it is not the standard of strict scrutiny itself, but our use of the concepts of "consistency" and "congruence" in conjunction with it, that leads JUSTICE STEVENS to dissent. According to JUSTICE STEVENS, our view of consistency "equates remedial preferences with invidious discrimination" and ignores the difference between "an engine of oppression" and an effort "to foster equality in society," or, more colorfully, "between a 'No Trespassing' sign and a welcome mat." It does nothing of the kind. The principle of consistency simply means that whenever the government treats any person unequally because of his or her race, that person has suffered an injury that falls squarely within the language and spirit of the Constitution's guarantee of equal protection. It says nothing about the ultimate validity of any particular law; that determination is the job of the court applying strict scrutiny. The principle of consistency explains the circumstances in which the injury requiring strict scrutiny occurs. The application of strict scrutiny, in turn, determines whether a compelling governmental interest justifies the infliction of that injury.

Consistency *does* recognize that any individual suffers an injury when he or she is disadvantaged by the government because of his or her race, whatever that race may be. This Court clearly stated that principle in *Croson*. JUSTICE STEVENS does not explain how his views square with *Croson*, or with the long line of cases understanding equal protection as a personal right.

JUSTICE STEVENS also claims that we have ignored any difference between federal and state legislatures. But requiring that Congress, like the States, enact racial classifications only when doing so is necessary to further a "compelling interest" does not contravene any principle of appropriate respect for a co-equal Branch of the Government. It is true that various Members of this Court have taken different views of the authority §5 of the Fourteenth Amendment confers upon Congress to deal with the problem of racial discrimination, and the extent to which courts should defer to Congress' exercise of that authority. We need not, and do not, address these differences today. For now, it is enough to observe that JUSTICE STEVENS' suggestion that any Member of this Court has repudiated in this case his or her previously expressed views on the subject is incorrect.

C

"Although adherence to precedent is not rigidly required in constitutional cases, any departure from the doctrine of *stare decisis* demands special justification." *Arizona* v. *Rumsey* (1984). In deciding whether this case presents such justification, we recall Justice Frankfurter's admonition that "*stare decisis* is a principle of policy and not a mechanical formula of adherence to the latest decision, however recent and questionable, when such adherence involves collision with a prior doctrine more embracing in its scope, intrinsically sounder, and verified by experience." *Helvering* v. *Hallock* (1940). Remaining true to an "intrinsically sounder" doctrine established in prior cases better serves the values of *stare decisis* than would following a more recently decided case inconsistent with the decisions that came before it; the latter course would simply compound the recent error and would likely make the unjustified break from previously established doctrine complete. In such a situation, "special justification" exists to depart from the recently decided case.

As we have explained, *Metro Broadcasting* undermined important principles of this Court's equal protection jurisprudence, established in a line of cases stretching back over fifty years.... This case therefore presents precisely the situation described by Justice Frankfurter in *Helvering*: we cannot adhere to our most recent decision without colliding with an accepted and established doctrine. We also note that *Metro Broadcasting*'s application of different standards of review to federal and state racial classifications has been consistently criticized by commentators....

JUSTICE STEVENS takes us to task for what he perceives to be an erroneous application of the doctrine of *stare decisis*. But again, he misunderstands our position. We have acknowledged that, after *Croson*, "some uncertainty persisted with respect to the standard of review for federal racial classifications," and we therefore do not say that we "merely restore the *status quo ante*" today. But as we have described, we think that well-settled legal principles pointed toward a conclusion different from that reached in *Metro Broadcasting*, and we therefore disagree with JUSTICE STEVENS that "the law at the time of that decision was entirely open to the result the Court reached."...

"The real problem," Justice Frankfurter explained, "is whether a principle shall prevail over its later misapplications." *Metro Broadcasting*'s untenable distinction between state and federal racial classifications lacks support in our precedent, and undermines the fundamental principle of equal protection as a personal right. In this case, as between that principle and "its later misapplications," the principle must prevail.

D

Our action today makes explicit what Justice Powell thought implicit in the *Fullilove* lead opinion: federal racial classifications, like those of a State, must serve a compelling governmental interest, and must be narrowly tailored to further that interest.... Of course, it follows that to the extent (if any) that *Fullilove* held federal racial classifications to be subject to a less rigorous standard, it is no longer controlling. But we need not decide today whether the program upheld in *Fullilove* would survive strict scrutiny as our more recent cases have defined it.

Some have questioned the importance of debating the proper standard of review of race-based legislation.... We think that requiring strict scrutiny is the best way to ensure that courts will consistently give racial classifications that kind of detailed examination, both as to ends and as to means. *Korematsu* demonstrates vividly that even "the most rigid scrutiny" can sometimes fail to detect an illegitimate racial classification.... Any retreat from the most searching judicial inquiry can only increase the risk of another such error occurring in the future.

Finally, we wish to dispel the notion that strict scrutiny is "strict in theory, but fatal in fact." *Fullilove* (Marshall, J., concurring in judgment). The unhappy persistence of both the practice and the lingering effects of racial discrimination against minority groups in this country is an unfortunate reality, and government is not disqualified from acting in response to it. As recently as 1987, for example, every Justice of this Court agreed that the Alabama Department of Public Safety's "pervasive, systematic, and obstinate discriminatory conduct" justified a narrowly tailored race-based remedy. See *United States* v. *Paradise*. When race-based action is necessary to further a compelling interest, such action is within constitutional constraints if it satisfies the "narrow tailoring" test this Court has set out in previous cases.

IV

Because our decision today alters the playing field in some important respects, we think it best to remand the case to the lower courts for further consideration in light of the principles we have announced. The Court of Appeals, following *Metro Broadcasting* and *Fullilove*, analyzed the case in terms of intermediate scrutiny. It upheld the challenged statutes and regulations because it found them to be "narrowly tailored to achieve [their] *significant governmental purpose* of providing subcontracting opportunities for small disadvantaged business enterprises" (emphasis added). The Court of Appeals did not decide the question whether the interests served by the use of subcontractor compensation clauses are properly described as "compelling." It also did not address the question of narrow tailoring in terms of our strict scrutiny cases, by asking, for example, whether there was "any consideration of the use of race-neutral means to increase minority business participation" in government contracting or whether the program was appropriately limited such that it "will not last longer than the discriminatory effects it is designed to eliminate."

Moreover, unresolved questions remain concerning the details of the complex regulatory regimes implicated by the use of subcontractor compensation clauses. For example, the SBA's 8(a) program requires an individualized inquiry into the economic disadvantage of every participant, whereas the DOT's regulations do not require certifying authorities to make such individualized inquiries. And the regulations seem unclear as to whether 8(d) subcontractors must make individualized showings, or instead whether the race-based presumption applies both to social *and* economic disadvantage.... We also note an apparent discrepancy between the definitions of which socially disadvantaged individuals qualify as economically disadvantaged for the 8(a) and 8(d) programs; the former requires a showing that such individuals' ability to compete has been impaired "as compared to others in the same or similar line of business *who are not socially disadvantaged*" (emphasis added), while the latter requires that showing only "as compared to others in the same or similar line of business." The question whether any of the ways in which the Government uses subcontractor compensation clauses can survive strict scrutiny, and any relevance distinctions such as these may have to that question, should be addressed in the first instance by the lower courts.

Accordingly, the judgment of the Court of Appeals is vacated, and the case is remanded for further proceedings consistent with this opinion.

It is so ordered.

JUSTICE SCALIA, concurring in part and concurring in the judgment.

I join the opinion of the Court, except Part III-C, and except insofar as it may be inconsistent with the following: In my view, government can never have a "compelling interest" in discriminating on the basis of race in order to "make up" for past racial discrimination in the opposite direction. Individuals who have been wronged by unlawful racial discrimination should be made whole; but under our Constitution there can be no such thing as either a creditor or a debtor race.... To pursue the concept of racial entitlement—even for the most admirable and benign of purposes—is to reinforce and preserve for future mischief the way of thinking that produced race slavery, race privilege and race hatred. In the eyes of government, we are just one race here. It is American.

It is unlikely, if not impossible, that the challenged program would survive under this understanding of strict scrutiny, but I am content to leave that to be decided on remand.

JUSTICE THOMAS, concurring in part and concurring in the judgment.

I agree with the majority's conclusion that strict scrutiny applies to all government classifications based on race. I write separately, however, to express my disagreement with the premise underlying JUSTICE STEVENS' and JUSTICE GINSBURG's dissents: that there is a racial paternalism exception to the principle of equal protection. I believe that there is a "moral [and] constitutional equivalence" (STEVENS, J., dissenting) between laws designed to subjugate a race and those that distribute benefits on the basis of race in order to foster some current notion of equality. Government cannot make us equal; it can only recognize, respect, and protect us as equal before the law.

That these programs may have been motivated, in part, by good intentions cannot provide refuge from the principle that under our Constitution, the government may not make distinctions on the basis of race. As far as the Constitution is concerned, it is irrelevant whether a government's racial classifications are drawn by those who wish to oppress a race or by those who have a sincere desire to help those thought to be disadvantaged. There can be no doubt that the paternalism that appears to lie at the heart of this program is at war with the principle of inherent equality that underlies and infuses our Constitution....

...[T]here can be no doubt that racial paternalism and its unintended consequences can be as poisonous and pernicious as any other form of discrimination. So-called "benign" discrimination teaches many that because of chronic and apparently immutable handicaps, minorities cannot compete with them without their patronizing indulgence. Inevitably, such programs engender attitudes of superiority or, alternatively, provoke resentment among those who believe that they have been wronged by the government's use of race. These programs stamp minorities with a badge of inferiority and may cause them to develop dependencies or to adopt an attitude that they are "entitled" to preferences....

In my mind, government-sponsored racial discrimination based on benign prejudice is just as noxious as discrimination inspired by malicious prejudice. In each instance, it is racial discrimination, plain and simple.

JUSTICE STEVENS, with whom JUSTICE GINSBURG joins, dissenting.

Instead of deciding this case in accordance with controlling precedent, the Court today delivers a disconcerting lecture about the evils of governmental racial classifications. For its text the Court has selected three propositions, represented by the bywords "skepticism," "consistency," and "congruence." I shall comment on each of these propositions, then add a few words about *stare decisis*, and finally explain why I believe this Court has a duty to affirm the judgment of the Court of Appeals.

I

The Court's concept of skepticism is, at least in principle, a good statement of law and of common sense. Undoubtedly, a court should be wary of a governmental decision that relies upon a racial classification. "Because racial characteristics so seldom provide a relevant basis for disparate treatment, and because classifications based on race are potentially so harmful to the entire body politic," a reviewing court must satisfy itself that the reasons for any such classification are "clearly identified and unquestionably legitimate." *Fullilove* v. *Klutznick* (1980) (STEVENS, J., dissenting). This principle is explicit in Chief Justice Burger's opinion, in Justice Powell's concurrence, and in my dissent in *Fullilove.* I welcome its renewed endorsement by the Court today. But, as the opinions in *Fullilove* demonstrate, substantial agreement on the standard to be applied in deciding difficult cases does not necessarily lead to agreement on how those cases actually should or will be resolved. In my judgment, because uniform standards are often anything but uniform, we should evaluate the Court's comments on "consistency," "congruence," and *stare decisis* with the same type of skepticism that the Court advocates for the underlying issue.

II

The Court's concept of "consistency" assumes that there is no significant difference between a decision by the majority to impose a special burden on the members of a minority race and a decision by the majority to provide a benefit to certain members of that minority notwithstanding its incidental burden on some members of the majority. In my opinion that assumption is untenable. There is no moral or constitutional equivalence between a policy that is designed to perpetuate a caste system and one that seeks to eradicate racial subordination. Invidious discrimination is an engine of oppression, subjugating a disfavored group to enhance or maintain the power of the majority. Remedial race-based preferences reflect the opposite impulse: a desire to foster equality in society. No sensible conception of the Government's constitutional obligation to "govern impartially" should ignore this distinction....

The consistency that the Court espouses would disregard the difference between a "No Trespassing" sign and a welcome mat. It would treat a Dixiecrat Senator's decision to vote against Thurgood Marshall's confirmation in order to keep African Americans off the Supreme Court as on a par with President Johnson's evaluation of his nominee's race as a positive factor. It would equate a law that made black citizens ineligible for military service with a program aimed at recruiting black soldiers. An attempt by the majority to exclude members of a minority race from a regulated market is fundamentally different from a subsidy that enables a relatively small group of newcomers to enter that market. An interest in "consistency" does not justify treating differences as though they were similarities.

The Court's explanation for treating dissimilar race-based decisions as though they were equally objectionable is a supposed inability to differentiate between "invidious" and "benign" discrimination. But the term "affirmative action" is common and well understood. Its presence in everyday parlance shows that people understand the difference between good intentions and bad. As with any legal concept, some cases may be difficult to classify, but our equal protection jurisprudence has identified a critical difference between state action that imposes burdens on a disfavored few and state action that benefits the few "in spite of" its adverse effects on the many....

Moreover, the Court may find that its new "consistency" approach to race-based classifications is difficult to square with its insistence upon rigidly separate categories for discrimination against different classes of individuals. For example, as the law currently stands, the Court will apply "intermediate scrutiny" to cases of invidious gender discrimination and "strict scrutiny" to cases of invidious race discrimination, while applying the same standard for benign classifications as for invidious ones. If this remains the law, then today's lecture about "consistency" will produce the anomalous result that the Government can more easily enact affirmative-action programs to remedy discrimination against women than it can enact affirmative-action programs to remedy discrimination against African Americans — even though the primary purpose of the Equal Protection Clause was to end discrimination against the former slaves....

As a matter of constitutional and democratic principle, a decision by representatives of the majority to discriminate against the members of a minority race is fundamentally different from those same representatives' decision to impose incidental costs on the majority of their constituents in order to provide a benefit to a disadvantaged minority. Indeed, as I have previously argued, the former is virtually always repugnant to the principles of a free and democratic society, whereas the latter is, in some circumstances, entirely consistent with the ideal of equality. By insisting on a doctrinaire notion of "consistency" in the standard applicable to all race-based governmental actions, the Court obscures this essential dichotomy.

III

The Court's concept of "congruence" assumes that there is no significant difference between a decision by the Congress of the United States to adopt an affirmative-action program and such a decision by a State or a municipality. In my opinion that assumption is untenable. It ignores important practical and legal differences between federal and state or local decisionmakers.

These differences have been identified repeatedly and consistently both in opinions of the Court and in separate opinions authored by members of today's majority. Thus, in *Metro Broadcasting, Inc.* v. *FCC* (1990), in which we upheld a federal program designed to foster racial diversity in broadcasting, we identified the special "institutional competence" of our National Legislature. "It is of overriding significance in these cases," we were careful to emphasize, "that the FCC's minority ownership programs have been specifically approved — indeed, mandated — by Congress."...

The majority in *Metro Broadcasting* and the plurality in *Fullilove* were not alone in relying upon a critical distinction between federal and state programs. In his separate opinion in *Richmond* v. *J. A. Croson Co.* (1989), JUSTICE SCALIA discussed the basis for this distinction. He observed that "it is one thing to permit racially based conduct by the Federal Government — whose legislative powers concerning matters of race were explicitly enhanced by the Fourteenth Amendment — and quite another to permit it by the precise entities against whose conduct in matters of race that Amendment was specifically directed....

In her plurality opinion in *Croson,* JUSTICE O'CONNOR also emphasized the importance of this distinction when she responded to the City's argument that *Fullilove* was controlling....

An additional reason for giving greater deference to the National Legislature than to a local law-making body is that federal affirmative-action programs represent the will of our entire Nation's elected representatives, whereas a state or local program may have an impact on nonresident entities who played no part in the decision to enact it. Thus, in the state or local context, individuals who were unable to vote for the local representatives who enacted a race-conscious program may nonetheless feel the effects of that program....

Our opinion in *Metro Broadcasting* relied on several constitutional provisions to justify the greater deference we owe to Congress when it acts with respect to private individuals. In the programs challenged in this case, Congress has acted both with respect to private individuals and, as in *Fullilove*, with respect to the States themselves.... One of the "provisions of this article" that Congress is thus empowered to enforce reads: "No State shall make or enforce any law which shall abridge the privileges or immunities of citizens of the United States; nor shall any State deprive any person of life, liberty, or property, without due process of law; nor deny to any person within its jurisdiction the equal protection of the laws." U.S. Const., Amdt. 14, §1. The Fourteenth Amendment directly empowers Congress at the same time it expressly limits the States. This is no accident. It represents our Nation's consensus, achieved after hard experience throughout our sorry history of race relations, that the Federal Government must be the primary defender of racial minorities against the States, some of which may be inclined to oppress such minorities. A rule of "congruence" that ignores a purposeful "incongruity" so fundamental to our system of government is unacceptable.

In my judgment, the Court's novel doctrine of "congruence" is seriously misguided. Congressional deliberations about a matter as important as affirmative action should be accorded far greater deference than those of a State or municipality.

IV

The Court's concept of *stare decisis* treats some of the language we have used in explaining our decisions as though it were more important than our actual holdings. In my opinion that treatment is incorrect....

In the Court's view, our decision in *Metro Broadcasting* was inconsistent with the rule announced in *Richmond* v. *J. A. Croson Co.* (1989). But two decisive distinctions separate those two cases. First, *Metro Broadcasting* involved a federal program, whereas *Croson* involved a city ordinance. *Metro Broadcasting* thus drew primary support from *Fullilove*, which predated *Croson* and which *Croson* distinguished on the grounds of the federal-state dichotomy that the majority today discredits. Although members of today's majority trumpeted the importance of that distinction in *Croson*, they now reject it in the name of "congruence." It is therefore quite wrong for the Court to suggest today that overruling *Metro Broadcasting* merely restores the *status quo ante*, for the law at the time of that decision was entirely open to the result the Court reached. *Today's* decision is an unjustified departure from settled law.

Second, *Metro Broadcasting's* holding rested on more than its application of "intermediate scrutiny." Indeed, I have always believed that, labels notwithstanding, the FCC program we upheld in that case would have satisfied any of our various standards in affirmative-action cases—including the one the majority fashions today. What truly distinguishes *Metro Broadcasting* from our other affirmative-action precedents is the distinctive goal of the federal program in that case. Instead of merely seeking to remedy past discrimination, the FCC program was intended to achieve future benefits in the form of broadcast diversity. Reliance on race as a legitimate means of achieving diversity was first endorsed by Justice Powell in *Regents of Univ. of California* v. *Bakke* (1978). Later, in *Wygant*

v. *Jackson Board of Ed.* (1986), I also argued that race is not always irrelevant to governmental decisionmaking (STEVENS, J., dissenting); in response, JUSTICE O'CONNOR correctly noted that, although the School Board had relied on an interest in providing black teachers to serve as role models for black students, that interest "should not be confused with the very different goal of promoting racial diversity among the faculty." She then added that, because the school board had not relied on an interest in diversity, it was not "necessary to discuss the magnitude of that interest or its applicability in this case."

Thus, prior to *Metro Broadcasting*, the interest in diversity had been mentioned in a few opinions, but it is perfectly clear that the Court had not yet decided whether that interest had sufficient magnitude to justify a racial classification. *Metro Broadcasting*, of course, answered that question in the affirmative. The majority today overrules *Metro Broadcasting* only insofar as it is "inconsistent with [the] holding" that strict scrutiny applies to "benign" racial classifications promulgated by the Federal Government. The proposition that fostering diversity may provide a sufficient interest to justify such a program is not inconsistent with the Court's holding today—indeed, the question is not remotely presented in this case—and I do not take the Court's opinion to diminish that aspect of our decision in *Metro Broadcasting*....

V

The Court's holding in *Fullilove* surely governs the result in this case. The Public Works Employment Act of 1977, which this Court upheld in *Fullilove*, is different in several critical respects from the portions of the Small Business Act (SBA) and the Surface Transportation and Uniform Relocation Assistance Act of 1987 (STURAA) challenged in this case. Each of those differences makes the current program designed to provide assistance to disadvantaged business enterprises (DBE's) significantly less objectionable than the 1977 categorical grant of $400 million in exchange for a 10% set-aside in public contracts to "a class of investors defined solely by racial characteristics." In no meaningful respect is the current scheme more objectionable than the 1977 Act. Thus, if the 1977 Act was constitutional, then so must be the SBA and STURAA. Indeed, even if my dissenting views in *Fullilove* had prevailed, this program would be valid.

Unlike the 1977 Act, the present statutory scheme does not make race the sole criterion of eligibility for participation in the program. Race does give rise to a rebuttable presumption of social disadvantage which, at least under STURAA, gives rise to a second rebuttable presumption of economic disadvantage. But a small business may qualify as a DBE, by showing that it is both socially and economically disadvantaged, even if it receives neither of these presumptions. Thus, the current preference is more inclusive than the 1977 Act because it does not make race a necessary qualification.

More importantly, race is not a sufficient qualification. Whereas a millionaire with a long history of financial successes, who was a member of numerous social clubs and trade associations, would have qualified for a preference under the 1977 Act merely because he was an Asian American or an African American, neither the SBA nor STURAA creates any such anomaly. The DBE program excludes members of minority races who are not, in fact, socially or economically disadvantaged. The presumption of social disadvantage reflects the unfortunate fact that irrational racial prejudice—along with its lingering effects—still survives. The presumption of economic disadvantage embodies a recognition that success in the private sector of the economy is often attributable, in part, to social skills and relationships. Unlike the 1977 set-asides, the current preference is designed to overcome the social and economic disadvantages that are often associated with racial characteristics. If, in a particular case, these disadvantages are not present, the presumptions can be rebutted. The program is thus designed to allow race to play a part in the decisional process only when there is a meaningful basis for assuming its relevance. In this connection, I think it is particularly significant that the current program targets the negotiation of subcontracts between private firms. The 1977 Act applied entirely to the award of public contracts.... In this case, in contrast, the program seeks to overcome barriers of prejudice between private parties—specifically, between general contractors and subcontractors. The SBA and STURAA embody Congress' recognition that such barriers may actually handicap minority firms seeking business as subcontractors from established leaders in the industry that have a history of doing business with their golfing partners. Indeed, minority subcontractors may face more obstacles than direct, intentional racial prejudice: they may face particular barriers simply because they are more likely to be new in the business and less likely to know others in the business. Given such difficulties, Congress could reasonably find that a minority subcontractor is less likely to receive favors from the entrenched businesspersons who award subcontracts only to people with whom—or with whose friends—they have an existing relationship. This program, then, if in part a remedy for past discrimination, is most importantly a forward-looking response to practical problems faced by minority subcontractors.

The current program contains another forward-looking component that the 1977 set-asides did not share. Section 8(a) of the SBA provides for periodic review of the status of DBE's, and DBE status can be challenged by a competitor at any time under any of the routes to certification. Such review prevents ineligible firms from taking part in the program solely because of their minority ownership, even when those firms were once disadvantaged but have since become successful. The emphasis on review also indicates the Administration's anticipation that after their presumed disadvantages have been overcome, firms will "graduate" into a status in which they will be able to compete for business, including prime contracts, on an equal basis....

Significantly, the current program, unlike the 1977 set-aside, does not establish any requirement—numerical or otherwise—that a general contractor must hire DBE subcontractors. The program we upheld in *Fullilove* required that 10% of the federal grant for every federally funded project be expended on minority business enterprises. In contrast, the current program contains no quota. Although it provides monetary incentives to general contractors to hire DBE subcontractors, it does not require them to hire DBE's, and they do not lose their contracts if they fail to do so. The importance of this incentive to general contractors (who always seek to offer the lowest bid) should not be underestimated; but the preference here is far less rigid, and thus more narrowly tailored, than the 1977 Act....

Finally, the record shows a dramatic contrast between the sparse deliberations that preceded the 1977 Act and the extensive hearings conducted in several Congresses before the current program was developed. However we might evaluate the benefits and costs—both fiscal and social—of this or any other affirmative-action program, our obligation to give deference to Congress' policy choices is much more demanding in this case than it was in *Fullilove.* If the 1977 program of race-based set-asides satisfied the strict scrutiny dictated by Justice Powell's vision of the Constitution—a vision the Court expressly endorses today—it must follow as night follows the day that the Court of Appeals' judgment upholding this more carefully crafted program should be affirmed....

JUSTICE SOUTER, with whom JUSTICE GINSBURG and JUSTICE BREYER join, dissenting.

As this case worked its way through the federal courts prior to the grant of certiorari that brought it here, petitioner Adarand Constructors, Inc. was understood to have raised only one significant claim: that before a federal agency may exceed the goals adopted by Congress in implementing a race-based remedial program, the Fifth and Fourteenth Amendments require the agency to make specific findings of discrimination, as under *Richmond* v. *J. A. Croson Co..* (1989), sufficient to justify surpassing the congressional objective....

Although the petition for certiorari added an antecedent question challenging the use, under the Fifth and Fourteenth Amendments, of any standard below strict scrutiny to judge the constitutionality of the statutes under which the respondents acted, I would not have entertained that question in this case. The statutory scheme must be treated as constitutional if *Fullilove* v. *Klutznick* (1980) is applied, and petitioners did not identify any of the factual premises on which *Fullilove* rested as having disappeared since that case was decided.

As the Court's opinion explains in detail, the scheme in question provides financial incentives to general contractors to hire subcontractors who have been certified as disadvantaged business enterprises on the basis of certain race-based presumptions. These statutes ... have previously been justified as providing remedies for the continuing effects of past discrimination, and the Government has so defended them in this case. Since petitioner has not claimed the obsolescence of any particular fact on which the *Fullilove* Court upheld the statute, no issue has come up to us that might be resolved in a way that would render *Fullilove* inapposite....

In these circumstances, I agree with JUSTICE STEVENS's conclusion that *stare decisis* compels the application of *Fullilove.* Although *Fullilove* did not reflect doctrinal consistency, its several opinions produced a result on shared grounds that petitioner does not attack: that discrimination in the construction industry had been subject to government acquiescence, with effects that remain and that may be addressed by some preferential treatment falling within the congressional power under §5 of the Fourteenth Amendment. Once *Fullilove* is applied, as JUSTICE STEVENS points out, it follows that the statutes in question here (which are substantially better tailored to the harm being remedied than the statute endorsed in *Fullilove*) pass muster under Fifth Amendment due process and Fourteenth Amendment equal protection.

The Court today, however, does not reach the application of *Fullilove* to the facts of this case.... Be that as it may, it seems fair to ask whether the statutes will meet a different fate from what *Fullilove* would have decreed. The answer is, quite probably not, though of course there will be some interpretive forks in the road before the significance of strict scrutiny for congressional remedial statutes becomes entirely clear....

JUSTICE GINSBURG, with whom JUSTICE BREYER joins, dissenting.

For the reasons stated by JUSTICE SOUTER, and in view of the attention the political branches are currently giving the matter of affirmative action, I see no compelling cause for the intervention the Court has made in this case. I further agree with JUSTICE STEVENS that, in this area, large deference is owed by the Judiciary to "Congress' institutional competence and constitutional authority to overcome historic racial subjugation." I write separately to underscore not the differences the several opinions in this case display, but the considerable field of agreement—the common understandings and concerns—revealed in opinions that together speak for a majority of the Court.

I

The statutes and regulations at issue, as the Court indicates, were adopted by the political branches in response to an "unfortunate reality": "[t]he unhappy persistence of both the practice and the lingering effects of racial discrimination against minority groups in this country." The United States suffers from those lingering effects because, for most of our Nation's history, the idea that "we are just one race," (SCALIA, J., concurring in part and concurring in judgment), was not embraced. For generations, our lawmakers and judges were unprepared to say that there is in this land no superior race, no race inferior to any other....

The divisions in this difficult case should not obscure the Court's recognition of the persistence of racial inequality and a majority's acknowledgement of Congress' authority to act affirmatively, not only to end discrimination, but also to counteract discrimination's lingering effects. Those effects, reflective of a system of racial caste only recently ended, are evident in our workplaces, markets, and neighborhoods. Job applicants with identical resumes, qualifications, and interview styles still experience different receptions, depending on their race. White and African-American consumers still encounter different deals. People of color looking for housing still face discriminatory treatment by landlords, real estate agents, and mortgage lenders. Minority entrepreneurs sometimes fail to gain contracts though they are the low bidders, and they are sometimes refused work even after winning contracts. Bias both conscious and unconscious, reflecting traditional and unexamined habits of thought, keeps up barriers that must come down if equal opportunity and nondiscrimination are ever genuinely to become this country's law and practice.

Given this history and its practical consequences, Congress surely can conclude that a carefully designed affirmative action program may help to realize, finally, the "equal protection of the laws" the Fourteenth Amendment has promised since 1868.

II

The lead opinion uses one term, "strict scrutiny," to describe the standard of judicial review for all governmental classifications by race. But that opinion's elaboration strongly suggests that the strict standard announced is indeed "fatal" for classifications burdening groups that have suffered discrimination in our society. That seems to me, and, I believe, to the Court, the enduring lesson one should draw from *Korematsu* v. *United States* (1944); for in that case, scrutiny the Court described as "most rigid" nonetheless yielded a pass for an odious, gravely injurious racial classification. A *Korematsu*-type classification, as I read the opinions in this case, will never again survive scrutiny: such a classification, history and precedent instruct, properly ranks as prohibited.

For a classification made to hasten the day when "we are just one race," however, the lead opinion has dispelled the notion that "strict scrutiny" is " 'fatal in fact.' " Properly, a majority of the Court calls for review that is searching, in order to ferret out classifications in reality malign, but masquerading as benign. The Court's once lax review of sex-based classifications demonstrates the need for such suspicion. [Citations omitted.] Today's decision thus usefully reiterates that the purpose of strict scrutiny "is precisely to distinguish legitimate from illegitimate uses of race in governmental decisionmaking," "to 'differentiate between' permissible and impermissible governmental use of race," to distinguish " 'between a "No Trespassing" sign and a welcome mat.' "

Close review also is in order for this further reason. As JUSTICE SOUTER points out, and as this very case shows, some members of the historically favored race can be hurt by catch-up mechanisms designed to cope with the lingering effects of entrenched racial subjugation. Court review can ensure that preferences are not so large as to trammel unduly upon the opportunities of others or interfere too harshly with legitimate expectations of persons in once-preferred groups.

* * *

While I would not disturb the programs challenged in this case, and would leave their improvement to the political branches, I see today's decision as one that allows our precedent to evolve, still to be informed by and responsive to changing conditions.

No. 93-1823

Missouri, et al., Petitioners v. Kalima Jenkins, et al.

On writ of certiorari to the United States Court of Appeals for the Eighth Circuit

[June 12, 1995]

CHIEF JUSTICE REHNQUIST delivered the opinion of the Court.

As this school desegregation litigation enters its 18th year, we are called upon again to review the decisions of the lower courts. In this case, the State of Missouri has challenged the District Court's order of salary increases for virtually all instructional and noninstructional staff within the Kansas City, Missouri, School District (KCMSD) and the District Court's order requiring the State to continue to fund remedial "quality education" programs because student achievement levels were still "at or below national norms at many grade levels."

I

A general overview of this litigation is necessary for proper resolution of the issues upon which we granted certiorari. This case has been before the same United States District Judge since 1977. In that year, the KCMSD, the school board, and the children of two school board members brought suit against the State and other defendants. Plaintiffs alleged that the State, the surrounding suburban school districts (SSD's), and various federal agencies had caused and perpetuated a system of racial segregation in the schools of the Kansas City metropolitan area. The District Court realigned the KCMSD as a nominal defendant and certified as a class, present and future KCMSD students. The KCMSD brought a cross-claim against the State for its failure to eliminate the vestiges of its prior dual school system.

After a trial that lasted 7½ months, the District Court dismissed the case against the federal defendants and the SSD's, but determined that the State and the KCMSD were liable for an intradistrict violation, *i.e.*, they had operated a segregated school system within the KCMSD. *Jenkins* v. *Missouri* (WD Mo. 1984). The District Court determined that prior to 1954 "Missouri mandated segregated schools for black and white children." Furthermore, the KCMSD and the State had failed in their affirmative obligations to eliminate the vestiges of the State's dual school system within the KCMSD.

In June 1985, the District Court issued its first remedial order and established as its goal the "elimination of all vestiges of state imposed segregation." The District Court determined that "[s]egregation ha[d] caused a system wide reduction in student achievement in the schools of the KCMSD." The District Court made no particularized findings regarding the extent that student achievement had been reduced or what portion of that reduction was attributable to segregation. The District Court also identified 25 schools within the KCMSD that had enrollments of 90% or more black students.

The District Court, pursuant to plans submitted by the KCMSD and the State, ordered a wide range of quality education programs for all students attending the KCMSD. First, the District Court ordered that the KCMSD be restored to an AAA classification, the highest classification awarded by the State

Board of Education. Second, it ordered that the number of students per class be reduced so that the student-to-teacher ratio was below the level required for AAA standing. The District Court justified its reduction in class size as "an essential part of any plan to remedy the vestiges of segregation in the KCMSD...."

The KCMSD was awarded an AAA rating in the 1987-1988 school year, and there is no dispute that since that time it has " 'maintained and greatly exceeded AAA requirements.' " The total cost for these quality education programs has exceeded $220 million.

The District Court also set out to desegregate the KCMSD but believed that "[t]o accomplish desegregation within the boundary lines of a school district whose enrollment remains 68.3% black is a difficult task." Because it had found no interdistrict violation, the District Court could not order mandatory interdistrict redistribution of students between the KCMSD and the surrounding SSD's. [Citing *Milliken* v. *Bradley* (1974) *(Milliken I)*.] The District Court refused to order additional mandatory student reassignments because they would "increase the instability of the KCMSD and reduce the potential for desegregation." Relying on favorable precedent from the Eighth Circuit, the District Court determined that "[a]chievement of AAA status, improvement of the quality of education being offered at the KCMSD schools, magnet schools, as well as other components of this desegregation plan can serve to maintain and hopefully attract non-minority student enrollment."

In November 1986, the District Court approved a comprehensive magnet school and capital improvements plan and held the State and the KCMSD jointly and severally liable for its funding. Under the District Court's plan, every senior high school, every middle school, and one-half of the elementary schools were converted into magnet schools. The District Court adopted the magnet-school program to "provide a greater educational opportunity to *all* KCMSD students," and because it believed "that the proposed magnet plan [was] so attractive that it would draw non-minority students from the private schools who have abandoned or avoided the KCMSD, and draw in additional non-minority students from the suburbs."... Since its inception, the magnet school program has operated at a cost, including magnet transportation, in excess of $448 million. In April 1993, the District Court considered, but ultimately rejected, the plaintiffs' and the KCMSD's proposal seeking approval of a long-range magnet renewal program that included a 10-year budget of well over $500 million, funded by the State and the KCMSD on a joint-and-several basis.

In June 1985, the District Court ordered substantial capital improvements to combat the deterioration of the KCMSD's facilities. In formulating its capital-improvements plan, the District Court dismissed as "irrelevant" the "State's argument that the present condition of the facilities [was] not traceable to unlawful segregation." Instead, the District Court focused on its responsibility to "remed[y] the vestiges of segregation" and to "implemen[t] a desegregation plan which w[ould] maintain and attract non-minority members." The initial phase of the capital improvements plan cost $37 million. The District Court also required the KCMSD to present further capital improvements proposals "in order to bring its facilities to a point comparable with the facilities in neighboring suburban school districts." In November 1986, the District Court approved further capital improvements in order to remove the vestiges of racial segregation and "to ... attract non-minority students back to the KCMSD."

In September 1987, the District Court adopted, for the most part, KCMSD's long-range capital improvements plan at a cost in excess of $187 million. The plan called for the renovation of approximately 55 schools, the closure of 18 facilities, and the construction of 17 new schools.... As of 1990, the District Court had ordered $260 million in capital improvements. Since then, the total cost of capital improvements ordered has soared to over $540 million.

As part of its desegregation plan, the District Court has ordered salary assistance to the KCMSD. In 1987, the District Court initially ordered salary assistance only for teachers within the KCMSD. Since that time, however, the District Court has ordered salary assistance to all but three of the approximately 5,000 KCMSD employees. The total cost of this component of the desegregation remedy since 1987 is over $200 million.

The District Court's desegregation plan has been described as the most ambitious and expensive remedial program in the history of school desegregation. The annual cost per pupil at the KCMSD far exceeds that of the neighboring SSD's or of any school district in Missouri. Nevertheless, the KCMSD, which has pursued a "friendly adversary" relationship with the plaintiffs, has continued to propose ever more expensive programs. As a result, the desegregation costs have escalated and now are approaching an annual cost of $200 million. These massive expenditures have financed

> "high schools in which every classroom will have air conditioning, an alarm system, and 15 microcomputers; a 2,000-square-foot planetarium; green houses and vivariums; a 25-acre farm with an air-conditioned meeting room for 104 people; a Model United Nations wired for language translation; broadcast capable radio and television studios with an editing and animation lab; a temperature controlled art gallery; movie editing and screening rooms; a 3,500-square-foot dust-free diesel mechanics room; 1,875-square-foot elementary school animal rooms for use in a zoo project; swimming pools; and numerous other facilities."
> [Citing *Missouri* v. *Jenkins* (1990) (*Jenkins II*) (KENNEDY, J., concurring in part and concurring in judgment).]

Not surprisingly, the cost of this remedial plan has "far exceeded KCMSD's budget, or for that matter, its authority to tax." The State, through the operation of joint-and-several liability, has borne the brunt of these costs....

II

With this background, we turn to the present controversy. First, the State has challenged the District Court's requirement that it fund salary increases for KCMSD instructional and noninstructional staff. The State claimed that funding for salaries was beyond the scope of the District Court's remedial authority. Second, the State has challenged the District Court's order requiring it to continue to fund the remedial quality education programs for the 1992–1993 school year. The State contended that under *Freeman* v. *Pitts* (1992), it had achieved partial unitary status with respect to the quality education programs already in place. As a result, the State argued that the District Court should have relieved it of responsibility for funding those programs.

The District Court rejected the State's arguments. It first determined that the salary increases were warranted because "high quality personnel are necessary not only to implement specialized desegregation programs intended to 'improve educational opportunities and reduce racial isolation' ... but also to 'ensure that there is no diminution in the quality of its regular academic program.'" Its "ruling [was] grounded in remedying the vestiges of segregation by improving the desegregative attractiveness of the KCMSD." The District Court did not address the State's *Freeman* arguments; nevertheless, it ordered the State to continue to fund the quality education programs for the 1992–1993 school year.

The Court of Appeals for the Eighth Circuit affirmed (1993). It rejected the State's argument that the salary increases did not directly address and relate to the State's constitutional violation and that "low teachers salaries d[id] not flow from any earlier constitutional violations by the State." In doing so, it observed that "[i]n addition to compensating the victims, the remedy in this case was also designed to reverse white flight by offering superior educational opportunities."

The Court of Appeals concluded that the District Court implicitly had rejected the State's *Freeman* arguments in spite of the fact that it had failed "to articulate ... even a conclusory rejection" of them....

Apparently, the Court of Appeals extrapolated from the findings regarding the magnet school program and later orders and imported those findings wholesale to reject the State's request for a determination of partial unitary status as to the quality education programs. It found significant the District Court's determination that although "there had been a trend of improvement in academic achievement, ... the school district was far from reaching its maximum potential because KCMSD is still at or below national norms at many grade levels."...

The Court of Appeals denied rehearing en banc, with five judges dissenting. The dissent first examined the salary increases ordered by the District Court and characterized "the current effort by the KCMSD and the American Federation of Teachers ... aided by the plaintiffs, to bypass the collective bargaining process" as "uncalled for" and "probably not an exercise reasonably related to the constitutional violations found by the court." The dissent also "agree[d] with the [S]tate that logic d[id] not directly relate the pay of parking lot attendants, trash haulers and food handlers ... to any facet or phase of the desegregation plan or to the constitutional violations."

Second, the dissent believed that in evaluating whether the KCMSD had achieved partial unitary status in its quality education programs, the District Court and the panel had

> "misrea[d] *Freeman* and create[d] a hurdle to the withdrawal of judicial intervention from public education that has no support in the law. The district court has, with the approbation of the panel, imbedded a student achievement goal measured by annual standardized tests into its test of whether the KCMSD has built a high-quality educational system sufficient to remedy past discrimination. The Constitution requires no such standard."

The dissent noted that "KCMSD students have in place a system that offers more educational opportunity than anywhere in America," but that the District Court was "'not satisfied that the District has reached anywhere close to its *maximum potential* because the District is still at or below national norms at many grade levels'" (emphasis added). The dissent concluded that this case "as it now proceeds, involves an exercise in pedagogical sociology, not constitutional adjudication."

Because of the importance of the issues, we granted certiorari to consider the following: (1) whether the District Court exceeded its constitutional authority when it granted salary increases to virtually all instructional and noninstructional employees of the KCMSD, and (2) whether the District Court properly relied upon the fact that student achievement test scores had failed to rise to some unspecified level when it declined to find that the State had achieved partial unitary status as to the quality education programs (1994).

III

Respondents argue that the State may no longer challenge the District Court's remedy, and in any event, the propriety of the remedy is not before the Court. We disagree on both counts. In *Jenkins II*, we granted certiorari to review the manner in which the District Court had funded this desegregation remedy. Because we had denied certiorari on the State's challenge to review the scope of the remedial order, we resisted the State's efforts to challenge the scope of the remedy. Thus, we neither "approved" nor "disapproved" the Court of Appeals' conclusion that the District Court's remedy was proper.

Here, however, the State has challenged the District Court's approval of across-the-board salary increases for instructional and noninstructional employees as an action beyond its remedial authority. An analysis of the permissible scope of the District Court's remedial authority is necessary for a proper determination of whether the order of salary increases is beyond the District Court's remedial authority, and thus, it is an issue subsidiary to our ultimate inquiry. Given that the District Court's basis for its salary order was grounded in "improving the desegregative attractiveness of the KCMSD," we must consider the propriety of that reliance in order to resolve properly the State's challenge to that order. We conclude that a challenge to the scope of the District Court's remedy is fairly included in the question presented....

Almost 25 years ago, in *Swann v. Charlotte-Mecklenburg Bd. of Ed.* (1971), we dealt with the authority of a district court to fashion remedies for a school district that had been segregated in law in violation of the Equal Protection Clause of the Fourteenth Amendment. Although recognizing the discretion that must necessarily adhere in a district court in fashioning a remedy, we also recognized the limits on such remedial power:

> "[E]limination of racial discrimination in public schools is a large task and one that should not be retarded by efforts to achieve broader purposes lying beyond the jurisdiction of the school authorities. One vehicle can carry only a limited amount of baggage. It would not serve the important objective of *Brown I* to seek to use school desegregation cases for purposes beyond their scope, although desegregation of schools ultimately will have impact on other forms of discrimination."

Three years later, in *Milliken I*, we held that a District Court had exceeded its authority in fashioning interdistrict relief where the surrounding school districts had not themselves been guilty of any constitutional violation. We said that a desegregation remedy "is necessarily designed, as all remedies are, to restore the victims of discriminatory conduct to the position they would have occupied in the absence of such conduct." "[W]ithout an interdistrict violation and interdistrict effect, there is no constitutional wrong calling for an interdistrict remedy." We also rejected "[t]he suggestion ... that schools which have a majority of Negro students are not 'desegregated,' whatever the makeup of the school district's population and however neutrally the district lines have been drawn and administered."...

Three years later, in *Milliken v. Bradley* (1977) *(Milliken II),* we articulated a three-part framework derived from our prior cases to guide district courts in the exercise of their remedial authority.

> "In the first place, like other equitable remedies, the nature of the desegregation remedy is to be determined by the nature and scope of the constitutional violation. The remedy must therefore be related to 'the condition alleged to offend the Constitution... .' Second, the decree must indeed be remedial in nature, that is, it must be designed as nearly as possible 'to restore the victims of discriminatory conduct to the position they would have occupied in the absence of such conduct.' Third, the federal courts in devising a remedy must take into account the interests of state and local authorities in managing their own affairs, consistent with the Constitution."

We added that the "principle that the nature and scope of the remedy are to be determined by the violation means simply that federal-court decrees must directly address and relate to the constitutional violation itself." In applying these principles, we have identified "student assignments, ... 'faculty, staff, transportation, extracurricular activities and facilities,' " as the most important indicia of a racially segregated school system.

Because "federal supervision of local school systems was intended as a temporary measure to remedy past discrimination," we also have considered the showing that must be made by a school district operating under a desegregation order for complete or partial relief from that order. In *Freeman,* we stated that

> "[a]mong the factors which must inform the sound discretion of the court in ordering partial withdrawal are the following: [1] whether there has been full and satisfactory compliance with the decree in those aspects of the system where supervision is to be withdrawn; [2] whether retention of judicial control is necessary or practicable to achieve compliance with the decree in other facets of the school system; and [3] whether the school district has demonstrated, to the public and to the parents and students of the once disfavored race, its good-faith commitment to the whole of the courts' decree and to those provisions of the law and the Constitution that were the predicate for judicial intervention in the first instance."

The ultimate inquiry is " 'whether the [constitutional violator] ha[s] complied in good faith with the desegregation decree since it was entered, and whether the vestiges of past discrimination have been eliminated to the extent practicable.' "

Proper analysis of the District Court's orders challenged here, then, must rest upon their serving as proper means to the end of restoring the victims of discriminatory conduct to the position they would have occupied in the absence of that conduct and their eventual restoration of "state and local authorities to the control of a school system that is operating in compliance with the Constitution." We turn to that analysis.

The State argues that the order approving salary increases is beyond the District Court's authority because it was crafted to serve an "interdistrict goal," in spite of the fact that the constitutional violation in this case is "intradistrict" in nature....

Here, the District Court has found, and the Court of Appeals has affirmed, that this case involved no interdistrict constitutional violation that would support interdistrict relief.... Thus, the proper response by the District Court should have been to eliminate to the extent practicable the vestiges of prior *de jure* segregation within the KCMSD: a system-wide reduction in student achievement and the existence of 25 racially identifiable schools with a population of over 90% black students.

The District Court and Court of Appeals, however, have felt that because the KCMSD's enrollment remained 68.3% black, a purely *intra*district remedy would be insufficient. But, as noted in *Milliken I*, we have rejected the suggestion "that schools which have a majority of Negro students are not 'desegregated' whatever the racial makeup of the school district's population and however neutrally the district lines have been drawn and administered."...

Instead of seeking to remove the racial identity of the various schools within the KCMSD, the District Court has set out on a program to create a school district that was equal to or superior to the surrounding SSD's. Its remedy has focused on "desegregative attractiveness," coupled with "suburban comparability." Examination of the District Court's reliance on "desegregative attractiveness" and "suburban comparability" is instructive for our ultimate resolution of the salary-order issue.

The purpose of desegregative attractiveness has been not only to remedy the system-wide reduction in student achievement, but also to attract nonminority students not presently enrolled in the KCMSD. This remedy has included an elaborate program of capital improvements, course enrichment, and extracurricular enhancement not simply in the formerly identifiable black schools, but in schools throughout the district. The District Court's remedial orders have converted every senior high school, every middle school, and one-half of the elementary schools in the KCMSD into "magnet" schools. The District Court's remedial order has all but made the KCMSD itself into a magnet district.

We previously have approved of intradistrict desegregation remedies involving magnet schools. Magnet schools have the advantage of encouraging voluntary movement of students within a school district in a pattern that aids desegregation on a voluntary basis, without requiring extensive busing and redrawing of district boundary lines. As a component in an intradistrict remedy, magnet schools also are attractive because they promote desegregation while limiting the withdrawal of white student enrollment that may result from mandatory student reassignment.

The District Court's remedial plan in this case, however, is not designed solely to redistribute the students within the KCMSD in order to eliminate racially identifiable schools within the KCMSD. Instead, its purpose is to attract nonminority students from outside the KCMSD schools. But this *inter*district goal is beyond the scope of the *intra*district violation identified by the District Court. In effect, the District Court has devised a remedy to accomplish indirectly what it admittedly lacks the remedial authority to mandate directly: the interdistrict transfer of students....

Respondents argue that the District Court's reliance upon desegregative attractiveness is justified in light of the District Court's statement that segregation has "led to white flight from the KCMSD to suburban districts." The lower courts' "findings" as to "white flight" are both inconsistent internally, and inconsistent with the typical supposition, bolstered here by the record evidence, that "white flight" may result from desegregation, not *de jure* segregation....

The District Court's pursuit of "desegregative attractiveness" cannot be reconciled with our cases placing limitations on a district court's remedial authority. It is certainly theoretically possible that the greater the expenditure per pupil within the KCMSD, the more likely it is that some unknowable number of nonminority students not presently attending schools in the KCMSD will choose to enroll in those schools. Under this reasoning, however, every increased expenditure, whether it be for teachers, noninstructional employees, books, or buildings, will make the KCMSD in some way more attractive, and thereby perhaps induce nonminority students to enroll in its schools. But this rationale is not susceptible to any objective limitation.... This case provides numerous examples demonstrating the limitless authority of the District Court operating under this rationale....

Nor are there limits to the duration of the District Court's involvement. The expenditures per pupil in the KCMSD currently far exceed those in the neighboring SSD's. [Citing estimate of $9,412 per-pupil costs within KCMSD, excluding capital costs, compared to a range of $2,854 to $5,956 for SSDs.] Sixteen years after this litigation began, the District Court recognized that the KCMSD has yet to offer a viable method of financing the "wonderful school system being built."... Each additional program ordered by the District Court—and financed by the State—to increase the "desegregative attractiveness" of the school district makes the KCMSD more and more dependent on additional funding from the State; in turn, the greater the KCMSD's dependence on state funding, the greater its reliance on continued supervision by the District Court. But our cases recognize that local autonomy of school districts is a vital national tradition, and that a district court must strive to restore state and local authorities to the control of a school system operating in compliance with the Constitution.

The District Court's pursuit of the goal of "desegregative attractiveness" results in so many imponderables and is so far removed from the task of eliminating the racial identifiability of the schools within the KCMSD that we believe it is beyond the admittedly broad discretion of the District Court. In this posture, we conclude that the District Court's order of salary increases ... is simply too far removed from an acceptable implementation of a permissible means to remedy previous legally mandated segregation.

Similar considerations lead us to conclude that the District Court's order requiring the State to continue to fund the quality education programs because student achievement levels were still "at or below national norms at many grade levels" cannot be sustained. The State does not seek from this Court a declaration of partial unitary status with respect to the quality education programs. It challenges the requirement of indefinite funding of a quality education program until national norms are met, based on the assumption that while a mandate for significant educational improvement, both in teaching and in facilities, may have been justified originally, its indefinite extension is not.

Our review in this respect is needlessly complicated because the District Court made no findings in its order approving continued funding of the quality education programs. Although the Court of Appeals later recognized that a determination of partial unitary status requires "careful factfinding and detailed articulation of findings," it declined to remand to the District Court. Instead it attempted to assemble an adequate record from the District Court's statements from the bench and subsequent orders. In one such order relied upon by the Court of Appeals, the District Court stated that the KCMSD had not reached anywhere close to its "maximum potential because the District is still at or below national norms at many grade levels."

But this clearly is not the appropriate test to be applied in deciding whether a previously segregated district has achieved partially unitary status. The basic task of the District Court is to decide whether the reduction in achievement by minority students attributable to prior *de jure* segregation has been remedied to the extent practicable. Under our precedents, the State and the KCMSD are "entitled to a rather precise statement of [their] obligations under a desegregation decree." Although the District Court has determined that "[s]egregation has caused a system wide reduction in achievement in the schools of the KCMSD," it never has identified the incremental effect that segregation has had on minority student achievement or the specific goals of the quality education programs.

In reconsidering this order, the District Court should apply our three-part test from *Freeman* v. *Pitts*. The District Court should consider that the State's role with respect to the quality education programs has been limited to the funding, not the implementation, of those programs. As all the parties agree that improved achievement on test scores is not necessarily required for the State to achieve partial unitary status as to the quality education programs, the District Court should sharply limit, if not dispense with, its reliance on this factor. Just as demographic changes independent of *de jure* segregation will affect the racial composition of student assignments, so too will numerous external factors beyond the control of the KCMSD and the State affect minority student achievement. So long as these external factors are not the result of segregation, they do not figure in the remedial calculus. Insistence upon academic goals unrelated to the effects of legal segregation unwarrantably postpones the day when the KCMSD will be able to operate on its own.

The District Court also should consider that many goals of its quality education plan already have been attained: the KCMSD now is equipped with "facilities and opportunities not available anywhere else in the country." KCMSD schools received an AAA rating eight years ago, and the present remedial programs have been in place for seven years. It may be that in education, just as it may be in economics, a "rising tide lifts all boats," but the remedial quality education program should be tailored to remedy the injuries suffered by the victims of prior *de jure* segregation. Minority students in kindergarten through grade 7 in the KCMSD always have attended AAA-rated schools; minority students in the KCMSD that previously attended schools rated below AAA have since received remedial education programs for a period of up to seven years.

On remand, the District Court must bear in mind that its end purpose is not only "to remedy the violation" to the extent practicable, but also "to restore state and local authorities to the control of a school system that is operating in compliance with the Constitution."

The judgment of the Court of Appeals is reversed.

It is so ordered.

JUSTICE O'CONNOR, concurring....

This case, like other school desegregation litigation, is concerned with "the elimination of the discrimination inherent in the dual school systems, not with myriad factors of human existence which can cause discrimination in a multitude of ways on racial, religious, or ethnic grounds." Those myriad factors are not readily corrected by judicial intervention, but are best addressed by the representative branches....

In this case, it may be the "myriad factors of human existence" that have prompted the white exodus from KCMSD, and the District Court cannot justify its transgression of the above constitutional principles simply by invoking desegregative attractiveness. The Court today discusses desegregative attractiveness only insofar as it supports the salary increase order under review and properly refrains from addressing the propriety of all the remedies that the District Court has ordered, revised, and extended in the 18–year history of this case. These remedies may also be improper to the extent that they serve the same goals of desegregative attractiveness and suburban comparability that we hold today to be impermissible, and, conversely, the District Court may be able to justify some remedies without reliance on these goals. But these are questions that the Court rightly leaves to be answered on remand. For now, it is enough to affirm the principle that "the nature of the desegregation remedy is to be determined by the nature and scope of the constitutional violation." *Milliken II.*

For these reasons, I join the opinion of the Court.

JUSTICE THOMAS, concurring.

It never ceases to amaze me that the courts are so willing to assume that anything that is predominantly black must be inferior. Instead of focusing on remedying the harm done to those black schoolchildren injured by segregation, the District Court here sought to convert the Kansas City, Missouri, School District (KCMSD) into a "magnet district" that would reverse the "white flight" caused by *de*segregation. In this respect, I join the Court's decision concerning the two remedial issues presented for review. I write separately, however, to add a few thoughts with respect to the overall course of this litigation. In order to evaluate the scope of the remedy, we must understand the scope of the constitutional violation and the nature of the remedial powers of the federal courts.

Two threads in our jurisprudence have produced this unfortunate situation, in which a District Court has taken it upon itself to experiment with the education of the KCMSD's black youth. First, the court has read our cases to support the theory that black students suffer an unspecified psychological harm from segregation that retards their mental and educational development. This approach not only relies upon questionable social science research rather than constitutional principle, but it also rests on an assumption of black inferiority. Second, we have permitted the federal courts to exercise virtually unlimited equitable powers to remedy this alleged constitutional violation. The exercise of this authority has trampled upon principles of federalism and the separation of powers and has freed courts to pursue other agendas unrelated to the narrow purpose of precisely remedying a constitutional harm.

I

A

The mere fact that a school is black does not mean that it is the product of a constitutional violation.... Instead, in order to find unconstitutional segregation, we require that plaintiffs "prove all of the essential elements of *de jure* segregation—that is, stated simply, a current condition of segregation resulting from *intentional state action directed specifically* to the [allegedly segregated] schools." *Keyes* v. *School Dist. No. 1, Denver* (1973) (emphasis added). "[T]he differentiating factor between *de jure* segregation and so-called *de facto* segregation ... is *purpose* or *intent* to segregate." *[Keyes]* (emphasis in original).

In the present case, the District Court inferred a continuing constitutional violation from two primary facts: the existence of *de jure* segregation in the KCMSD prior to 1954, and the existence of *de facto* segregation today.... For the District Court, it followed that the KCMSD had not dismantled the dual system entirely....

Without more, the District Court's findings could not have supported a finding of liability against the state. It should by now be clear that the existence of one-race schools is not by itself an indication that the State is practicing segregation. [Citations omitted.] The continuing "racial isolation" of schools after *de jure* segregation has ended may well reflect voluntary housing choices or other private decisions. Here, for instance, the demography of the entire KCMSD has changed considerably since 1954. Though blacks accounted for only 18.9% of KCMSD's enrollment in 1954, by 1983–1984 the school district was 67.7% black. That certain schools are overwhelmingly black in a district that is now more than two-thirds black is hardly a sure sign of intentional state action.

In search of intentional state action, the District Court linked the State and the dual school system of 1984 in two ways. First, the Court found that "[i]n the past" the State had placed its "imprimatur on racial discrimination."... But the District Court itself acknowledged that the State's alleged encouragement of private discrimination was a fairly tenuous basis for finding liability. The District Court therefore rested the State's liability on the simple fact that the State had intentionally created the dual school system before 1954, and had failed to fulfill "its affirmative duty of disestablishing a dual school system subsequent to 1954." According to the District Court, the schools whose student bodies were more than 90% black constituted "vestiges" of the prior *de jure* segregation, which the State and the KCMSD had an obligation to eliminate. Later, in the course of issuing its first "remedial" order, the District Court added that a "system wide reduction in student achievement in the schools of ... KCMSD" was also a vestige of the prior *de jure* segregation. In a subsequent order, the District Court indicated that post-1954 "white flight" was another vestige of the pre-1954 segregated system.

In order for a "vestige" to supply the ground for an exercise of remedial authority, it must be clearly traceable to the dual school system.... District Courts must not confuse the consequences of *de jure* segregation with the results of larger social forces or of private decisions.... As state-enforced segregation recedes farther into the past, it is more likely that "these kinds of continuous and massive demographic shifts" will be the real source of racial imbalance or of poor educational performance in a school district....

When a district court holds the State liable for discrimination almost 30 years after the last official state action, it must do more than show that there are schools with high black populations or low test scores. Here, the district judge did not make clear how the high black enrollments in certain schools were fairly traceable to the State of Missouri's actions. I do not doubt that Missouri maintained the despicable system of segregation until 1954. But I question the District Court's conclusion that because the State had enforced segregation until 1954, its actions, or lack thereof, proximately caused the "racial isolation" of the predominantly black schools in 1984....

B

Without a basis in any real finding of intentional government action, the District Court's imposition of liability upon the State of Missouri improperly rests upon a theory that racial imbalances are unconstitutional.... In effect, the court found that racial imbalances constituted an ongoing constitutional violation that continued to inflict harm on black students. This position appears to rest upon the idea that any school that is black is inferior, and that blacks cannot succeed without the benefit of the company of whites.

The District Court's willingness to adopt such stereotypes stemmed from a misreading of our earliest school desegregation case. In *Brown* v. *Board of Education* (1954) *(Brown I)*, the Court noted several psychological and sociological studies purporting to show that *de jure* segregation harmed black students by generating "a feeling of inferiority" in them. Seizing upon this passage in *Brown I*, the District Court asserted that "forced segregation ruins attitudes and is inherently unequal." The District Court suggested that this inequality continues in full force even after the end of *de jure* segregation. [Excerpt from opinion omitted.]

Thus, the District Court seemed to believe that black students in the KCMSD would continue to receive an "inferior education" despite the end of *de jure* segregation, as long as *de facto* segregation persisted....

It is clear that the District Court misunderstood the meaning of *Brown I. Brown I* did not say that "racially isolated" schools were inherently inferior; the harm that it identified was tied purely to *de jure* segregation, not *de facto* segregation. Indeed, *Brown I* itself did not need to rely upon any psychological or social-science research in order to announce the simple, yet fundamental truth that the Government cannot discriminate among its citizens on the basis of race....

Segregation was not unconstitutional because it might have caused psychological feelings of inferiority. Public school systems that separated blacks and provided them with superior educational resources—making blacks "feel" superior to whites sent to lesser schools—would violate the Fourteenth Amendment, whether or not the white students felt stigmatized, just as do school systems in which the positions of the races are reversed. Psychological injury or benefit is irrelevant to the question whether state actors have engaged in intentional discrimination—the critical inquiry for ascertaining violations of the Equal Protection Clause. The judiciary is fully competent to make independent determinations concerning the existence of state action without the unnecessary and misleading assistance of the social sciences.

Regardless of the relative quality of the schools, segregation violated the Constitution because the State classified students based on their race. Of course, segregation additionally harmed black students by relegating them to schools with substandard facilities and resources. But neutral policies, such as local school assignments, do not offend the Constitution when individual private choices concerning work or residence produce schools with high black populations. The Constitution does not prevent individuals from choosing to live together, to work together, or to send their children to school together, so long as the State does not interfere with their choices on the basis of race.

Given that desegregation has not produced the predicted leaps forward in black educational achievement, there is no reason to think that black students cannot learn as well when surrounded by members of their own race as when they are in an integrated environment. Indeed, it may very well be that what has been true for historically black colleges is true for black middle and high schools. Despite their origins in "the shameful history of state-enforced segregation," these institutions can be " 'both a source of pride to blacks who have attended them and a source of hope to black families who want the benefits of … learning for their children.' " [*United States* v.] *Fordice* (THOMAS, J., concurring). Because of their "distinctive histories and traditions," black schools can function as the center and symbol of black communities, and provide examples of independent black leadership, success, and achievement.

Thus, even if the District Court had been on firmer ground in identifying a link between the KCMSD's pre-1954 *de jure* segregation and the present "racial isolation" of some of the district's schools, mere *de facto* segregation (unaccompanied by discriminatory inequalities in educational resources) does not constitute a continuing harm after the end of *de jure* segregation. "Racial isolation" itself is not a harm; only state-enforced segregation is. After all, if separation itself is a harm, and if integration therefore is the only way that blacks can receive a proper education, then there must be something inferior about blacks. Under this theory, segregation injures blacks because blacks, when left on their own, cannot achieve. To my way of thinking, that conclusion is the result of a jurisprudence based upon a theory of black inferiority.

This misconception has drawn the courts away from the important goal in desegregation. The point of the Equal Protection Clause is not to enforce strict race-mixing, but to ensure that blacks and whites are treated equally by the State without regard to their skin color. The lower courts should not be swayed by the easy answers of social science, nor should they accept the findings, and the assumptions, of sociology and psychology at the price of constitutional principle....

JUSTICE SOUTER, with whom JUSTICE STEVENS, JUSTICE GINSBURG, and JUSTICE BREYER join, dissenting.

The Court's process of orderly adjudication has broken down in this case. The Court disposes of challenges to only two of the District Court's many discrete remedial orders by declaring that the District Court erroneously provided an interdistrict remedy for an intradistrict violation. In doing so, it resolves a foundational issue going to one element of the District Court's decree that we did not accept for review in this case, that we need not reach in order to answer the questions that we did accept for review, and that we specifically refused to consider when it was presented in a prior petition for certiorari.

Since, under these circumstances, the respondent school district and pupils naturally came to this Court without expecting that a fundamental premise of a portion of the District Court's remedial order would become the focus of the case, the essence of the Court's misjudgment in reviewing and repudiating that central premise lies in its failure to have warned the respondents of what was really at stake. This failure lulled the respondents into addressing the case without sufficient attention to the foundational issue, and their lack of attention has now infected the Court's decision....

I

In 1984, 30 years after our decision in *Brown* v. *Board of Education* (1954), the District Court found that the State of Missouri and the Kansas City, Missouri School District (KCMSD) had failed to reform the segregated scheme of public school education in the KCMSD, previously mandated by the State, which had required black and white children to be taught separately according to race. After *Brown*, neither the State nor the KCMSD moved to dismantle this system of separate education "root and branch," despite their affirmative obligation to do that under the Constitution. "Instead, the [KCMSD] chose to operate some completely segregated schools and some integrated ones," using devices like optional attendance zones and liberal transfer policies to "allo[w] attendance patterns to continue on a segregated basis." Consequently, on the 20th anniversary of *Brown* in 1974, 39 of the 77 schools in the KCMSD had student bodies that were more than 90 percent black, and 80 percent of all black schoolchildren in the KCMSD attended those schools. Ten years later, in the 1983–1984 school year, 24 schools remained racially isolated with more than 90 percent black enrollment. Because the State and the KCMSD intentionally created this segregated system of education, and subsequently failed to correct it, the District Court concluded that the State and the district had "defaulted in their obligation to uphold the Constitution."

Neither the State nor the KCMSD appealed this finding of liability, after which the District Court entered a series of remedial orders aimed at eliminating the vestiges of segregation. Since the District Court found that segregation had caused, among other things, "a system wide *reduction* in student achievement in the schools of the KCMSD," it ordered the adoption, starting in 1985, of a series of remedial programs to raise educational performance. As the Court recognizes, the District Court acted well within the bounds of its equitable discretion in doing so; in *Milliken* v. *Bradley* (1977) *(Milliken II)*, we held that a district court is authorized to remedy all conditions flowing directly from the constitutional violations committed by state or local officials, including the educational deficits that result from a segregated school system (programs aimed to correct those deficits are therefore frequently referred to as *Milliken II* programs). Nor was there any objection to the District Court's orders from the State and the KCMSD, who agreed that it was " 'appropriate to include a number of properly targeted educational programs in [the] desegregation plan.' "...

Between 1985 and 1987 the District Court also ordered the implementation of a magnet school concept and extensive capital improvements to the schools of the KCMSD. The District Court found that magnet schools would not only serve to remedy the deficiencies in student achievement in the KCMSD, but would also assist in desegregating the district by attracting white students back into the school system....

The District Court, finding that the physical facilities in the KCMSD had "literally rotted," similarly grounded its orders of capital improvements in the related remedial objects of improving student achievement and desegregating the KCMSD....

As a final element of its remedy, in 1987 the District Court ordered funding for increases in teachers' salaries as a step towards raising the level of student achievement.... Neither the State nor the KCMSD objected to increases in teachers' salaries as an element of the comprehensive remedy, or to this cost as an item in the desegregation budget.

In 1988, however, the State went to the Eighth Circuit with a broad challenge to the District Court's remedial concept of magnet schools and to its orders of capital improvements (though it did not appeal the salary order), arguing that the District Court had run afoul of *Milliken* v. *Bradley* (1974) *(Milliken I)*, by ordering an interdistrict remedy for an intradistrict violation. The Eighth Circuit rejected the State's position, and in 1989 the State petitioned for certiorari.

The State's petition presented two questions for review, one challenging the District Court's authority to order a property tax increase to fund its remedial program, the other going to the legitimacy of the magnet school concept at the very foundation of the Court's desegregation plan. [Quotation of question omitted.]

We accepted the taxation question, and decided that while the District Court could not impose the tax measure itself, it could require the district to tax property at a rate adequate to fund its share of the costs of the desegregation remedy. *Jenkins* v. *Missouri* (1990). If we had accepted the State's broader, foundational question going to the magnet school concept, we could also have made an informed decision on whether that element of the District Court's remedial scheme was within the limits of the Court's equitable discretion in response to the constitutional violation found. Each party would have briefed the question fully and would have identified in some detail those items in the record bearing on it. But none of these things happened. Instead of accepting the foundational question in 1989, we denied certiorari on it.

The State did not raise that question again when it returned to this Court with its 1994 petition for certiorari, which led to today's decision. Instead, the State presented, and we agreed to review, these two questions:

"1. Whether a remedial educational desegregation program providing greater educational opportunities to victims of past *de jure* segregation than provided anywhere else in the country nonetheless fails to satisfy the Fourteenth Amendment (thus precluding a finding of partial unitary status) solely because student achievement in the District, as measured by results on standardized test scores, has not risen to some unspecified level?

"2. Whether a federal court order granting salary increases to virtually every employee of a school district—including non-instructional personnel—as a part of a school desegregation remedy conflicts with applicable decisions of this court which require that remedial components must directly address and relate to the constitutional violation and be tailored to cure the condition that offends the Constitution?"

These questions focus on two discrete issues: the extent to which a district court may look at students' test scores in determining whether a school district has attained partial unitary status as to its *Milliken II* educational programs, and whether the particular salary increases ordered by the District Court constitute a permissible component of its remedy.

The State did not go beyond these discrete issues, and it framed no broader, foundational question about the validity of the District Court's magnet concept. The Court decides, however, that it can reach that question of its own initiative, and it sees no bar to this course in the provision of this Court's Rule 14.1 that "[o]nly the questions set forth in the petition, or fairly included therein, will be considered...." The broader issue, the Court claims, is "fairly included" in the State's salary question. But that claim does not survive scrutiny.

The standard under Rule 14.1 is quite simple: as the Court recognizes, we have held that an issue is fairly comprehended in a question presented when the issue must be resolved in order to answer the question. That should be the end of the matter here, since the State itself concedes that we can answer its salary and test-score questions without addressing the soundness of the magnet element of the District Court's underlying remedial scheme.... While the Court ignores that concession, it is patently correct. There is no reason why we cannot take the questions as they come to us; assuming the validity of the District Court's basic remedial concept, we can determine the significance of test scores and assess the salary orders in relation to that concept....

II

A

The test score question as it comes to us is one of word play, not substance. While the Court insists that the District Court's Order of June 17, 1992 (the only order relevant to the test score question on review here), "required the State to continue to fund the quality education programs because student achievement levels [in the KCMSD] were still 'at or below national norms at many grade levels...,' " that order contains no discussion at all of student achievement levels in the KCMSD in comparison to national norms, and in fact does not explicitly address the subject of partial unitary status. The reference to test scores "at or below national norms" comes from an entirely different and subsequent order of the District Court (dated Apr. 16, 1993) which is not under review. Its language presumably would not have been quoted to us, if the Court of Appeals's opinion affirming the District Court's June 17, 1992 order had not canvassed subsequent orders and mentioned the District Court's finding of fact that the "KCMSD is still at or below national norms at many grade levels" (CA8 1994), citing Order of Apr. 16, 1993. In any event, what is important here is that none of the District Court's or Court of Appeals's opinions or orders requires a certain level of test scores before unitary status can be found, or indicates that test scores are the only thing standing between the State and a finding of unitary status as to the KCMSD's *Milliken II* programs. Indeed, the opinion concurring in the denial of rehearing en banc below (not mentioned by the Court, although it is certainly more probative of the governing law in the Eighth Circuit than the dissenting opinion on which the Court does rely) expressly disavows any dispositive role for test scores. [Excerpt from opinion omitted.]

If, then, test scores do not explain why there was no finding of unitary status as to the *Milliken II* programs, one may ask what does explain it. The answer is quite straightforward. The Court of Appeals refused to order the District Court to enter a finding of partial unitary status as to the KCMSD's *Milliken II* programs (and apparently, the District Court did not speak to the issue itself) simply because the State did not attempt to make the showing required for that relief....

While the Court recognizes the three-part showing that the State must make under *Freeman* [v. *Pitts* (1992)] in order to get a finding of partial unitary status, it fails to acknowledge that the State did not even try to make a *Freeman* showing in the litigation leading up to the District Court's Order of June 17, 1992. The District Court's order was triggered not by a motion for partial unitary status filed by the State, but by a motion filed by the KCMSD for approval of its desegregation plan for the 1992–1993 school year. While the State's response to that motion suggested that the District Court should enter a finding of partial unitary status as to the district's *Milliken II* component of its decree, the State failed even to allege its compliance with two of the three prongs of the *Freeman* test....

Thus, it was the State's failure to meet or even to recognize its burden under *Freeman* that led the Court of Appeals to reject the suggestion that it make a finding of partial unitary status as to the district's *Milliken II* education programs....

Examining only the first *Freeman* prong, there can be no doubt that the Court of Appeals was correct. *Freeman* and [*Board of Ed. of Oklahoma City Public Schools* v.] *Dowell* [1991] make it entirely clear that the central focus of this prong of the unitary status enquiry is on effects: to the extent reasonably possible, a constitutional violator must remedy the ills caused by its actions before it can be freed of the court-ordered obligations it has brought upon itself. Under the logic of the State's arguments to the District Court, the moment the *Milliken II* programs were put in place, the State was at liberty to walk away from them, no matter how great the remaining consequences of segregation for educational quality or how great the potential for curing them if State funding continued.

Looking ahead, if indeed the State believes itself entitled to a finding of partial unitary status on the subject of educational programs, there is an orderly procedural course for it to follow. It may frame a proper motion for partial unitary status, and prepare to make a record sufficient to allow the District Court and the Court of Appeals to address the continued need for and efficacy of the *Milliken II* programs.

In the development of a proper unitary status record, test scores will undoubtedly play a role. It is true, as the Court recognizes, that all parties to this case agree that it would be error to require that the students in a school district attain the national average test score as a prerequisite to a finding of partial unitary status, if only because all sorts of causes independent of the vestiges of past school segregation might stand in the way of the goal. That said, test scores will clearly be relevant in determining whether the improvement programs have cured a deficiency in student achievement to the practicable extent....

B

The other question properly before us has to do with the propriety of the District Court's recent salary orders. While the Court suggests otherwise, the District Court did not ground its orders of salary increases solely on the goal of attracting students back to the KCMSD. From the start, the District Court has consistently treated salary increases as an important element in remedying the systemwide reduction in student achievement resulting from segregation in the KCMSD. As noted above, the Court does not question this remedial goal, which we expressly approved in *Milliken II*. The only issue, then, is whether the salary increases ordered by the District Court have been reasonably related to achieving that goal, keeping in mind the broad discretion enjoyed by the District Court in exercising its equitable powers.

The District Court first ordered KCMSD salary increases, limited to teachers, in 1987, basing its decision on the need to raise the level of student achievement.... The State raised no objection to the District Court's order, and said nothing about the issue of salary increases in its 1988 appeal to the Eighth Circuit.

When the District Court's 1987 order expired in 1990, all parties, including the State, agreed to a further order increasing salaries for both instructional and noninstructional personnel through the 1991–1992 school year. In 1992 the District Court merely ordered that salaries in the KCMSD be maintained at the same level for the following year, rejecting the State's argument that desegregation funding for salaries should be discontinued, and in 1993 the District Court ordered small salary increases for both instructional and non-instructional personnel through the end of the 1995–1996 school year.

It is the District Court's 1992 and 1993 orders that are before us, and it is difficult to see how the District Court abused its discretion in either instance. The District Court had evidence in front of it that adopting the State's position and discontinuing desegregation funding for salary levels would result in their abrupt drop to 1986–1987 levels, with the resulting disparity between teacher pay in the district and the nationwide level increasing to as much as 40–45 percent, and a mass exodus of competent employees likely taking place. Faced with this evidence, the District Court found that continued desegregation funding of salaries, and small increases in those salaries over time, were essential to the successful implementation of its remedial scheme, including the elevation of student achievement.... The Court of Appeals affirmed the District Court's orders on the basis of these findings, again taking special note of the importance of adequate salaries to the remedial goal of improving student achievement....

There is nothing exceptionable in the lower courts' findings about the relationship between salaries and the District Court's remedial objectives, and certainly nothing in the record suggests obvious error as to the amounts of the increases ordered. If it is tempting to question the place of salary increases for administrative and maintenance personnel in a desegregation order, the Court of Appeals addressed the temptation in specifically affirming the District Court's finding that such personnel are critical to the success of the desegregation effort, and did so in the circumstances of a district whose schools have been plagued by leaking roofs, defective lighting, and reeking lavatories. As for teachers' increases, the District Court and the Court of Appeals were beyond reproach in finding and affirming that in order to remedy the educational deficits flowing from segregation in the KCMSD, "those persons charged with implementing the [remedial] plan [must] be the most qualified persons reasonably attainable."

Indeed, the Court does not question the District Court's salary orders insofar as they relate to the objective of raising the level of student achievement in the KCMSD, but rather overlooks that basis for the orders altogether. The Court suggests that the District Court rested its approval of salary increases only on the object of drawing students into the district's schools, and rejects the increases for that reason. It seems clear, however, that the District Court and the Court of Appeals both viewed the salary orders as serving two complementary but distinct purposes, and to the extent that the District Court concludes on remand that its salary orders are justified by reference to the quality of education alone, nothing in the Court's opinion precludes those orders from remaining in effect....

JUSTICE GINSBURG, dissenting.

I join JUSTICE SOUTER's illuminating dissent and emphasize a consideration key to this controversy. The Court stresses that the present remedial programs have been in place for seven years. But compared to more than two centuries of firmly entrenched official discrimination, the experience with the desegregation remedies ordered by the District Court has been evanescent.

In 1724, Louis XV of France issued the Code Noir, the first slave code for the Colony of Louisiana, an area that included Missouri. When Missouri entered the Union in 1821, it entered as a slave State.

Before the Civil War, Missouri law prohibited the creation or maintenance of schools for educating blacks: "No person shall keep or teach any school for the instruction of negroes or mulattoes, in reading or writing, in this State." Act of February 16, 1847.

Beginning in 1865, Missouri passed a series of laws requiring separate public schools for blacks. The Missouri Constitution first permitted, then required, separate schools.

After this Court announced its decision in *Brown* v. *Board of Education* (1954), Missouri's Attorney General declared these provisions mandating segregated schools unenforceable. The statutes were repealed in 1957 and the constitutional provision was rescinded in 1976. Nonetheless, thirty years after *Brown*, the District Court found that "the inferior education indigenous of the state-compelled dual school system has lingering effects in the Kansas City, Missouri School District." The District Court concluded that "the State ... cannot defend its failure to affirmatively act to eliminate the structure and effects of its past dual system on the basis of restrictive state law." Just ten years ago, in June 1985, the District Court issued its first remedial order.

Today, the Court declares illegitimate the goal of attracting nonminority students to the Kansas City, Missouri, School District, and thus stops the District Court's efforts to integrate a school district that was, in the 1984/1985 school year, sorely in need and 68.3% black. Given the deep, inglorious history of segregation in Missouri, to curtail desegregation at this time and in this manner is an action at once too swift and too soon....

No. 94-590

Vernonia School District 47J, Petitioner v. Wayne Acton

on writ of certiorari to the United States Court of Appeals for the Ninth Circuit

[June 26, 1995]

JUSTICE SCALIA delivered the opinion of the Court.

The Student Athlete Drug Policy adopted by School District 47J in the town of Vernonia, Oregon, authorizes random urinalysis drug testing of students who participate in the District's school athletics programs. We granted certiorari to decide whether this violates the Fourth and Fourteenth Amendments to the United States Constitution.

I

A

Petitioner Vernonia School District 47J (District) operates one high school and three grade schools in the logging community of Vernonia, Oregon. As elsewhere in small-town America, school sports play a prominent role in the town's life, and student athletes are admired in their schools and in the community.

Drugs had not been a major problem in Vernonia schools. In the mid-to-late 1980's, however, teachers and administrators observed a sharp increase in drug use. Students began to speak out about their attraction to the drug culture, and to boast that there was nothing the school could do about it. Along with more drugs came more disciplinary problems. Between 1988 and 1989 the number of disciplinary referrals in Vernonia schools rose to more than twice the number reported in the early 1980's, and several students were suspended. Students became increasingly rude during class; outbursts of profane language became common.

Not only were student athletes included among the drug users but, as the District Court found, athletes were the leaders of the drug culture. This caused the District's administrators particular concern, since drug use increases the risk of sports-related injury. Expert testimony at the trial confirmed the deleterious effects of drugs on motivation, memory, judgment, reaction, coordination, and performance. The high school football and wrestling coach witnessed a severe sternum injury suffered by a wrestler, and various omissions of safety procedures and misexecutions by football players, all attributable in his belief to the effects of drug use.

Initially, the District responded to the drug problem by offering special classes, speakers, and presentations designed to deter drug use. It even brought in a specially trained dog to detect drugs, but the drug problem persisted....

At that point, District officials began considering a drug-testing program. They held a parent "input night" to discuss the proposed Student Athlete Drug Policy (Policy), and the parents in attendance gave their unanimous approval. The school board approved the Policy for implementation in the fall of 1989. Its expressed purpose is to prevent student athletes from using drugs, to protect their health and safety, and to provide drug users with assistance programs.

B

The Policy applies to all students participating in interscholastic athletics. Students wishing to play sports must sign a form consenting to the testing and must obtain the written consent of their parents. Athletes are tested at the beginning of the season for their sport. In addition, once each week of the season the names of the athletes are placed in a "pool" from which a student, with the supervision of two adults, blindly draws the names of 10% of the athletes for random testing. Those selected are notified and tested that same day, if possible.

The student to be tested completes a specimen control form which bears an assigned number. Prescription medications that the student is taking must be identified by providing a copy of the prescription or a doctor's authorization. The student then enters an empty locker room accompanied by an adult monitor of the same sex. Each boy selected produces a sample at a urinal, remaining fully clothed with his back to the monitor, who stands approximately 12 to 15 feet behind the student. Monitors may (though do not always) watch the student while he produces the sample, and they listen for normal sounds of urination. Girls produce samples in an enclosed bathroom stall, so that they can be heard but not observed. After the sample is produced, it is given to the monitor, who checks it for temperature and tampering and then transfers it to a vial.

The samples are sent to an independent laboratory, which routinely tests them for amphetamines, cocaine, and marijuana. Other drugs, such as LSD, may be screened at the request of the District, but the identity of a particular student does not determine which drugs will be tested. The laboratory's procedures are 99.94% accurate. The District follows strict procedures regarding the chain of custody and access to test results. The laboratory does not know the identity of the students whose samples it tests. It is authorized to mail written test reports only to the superintendent and to provide test results to District personnel by telephone only after the requesting official recites a code confirming his authority. Only the superintendent, principals, vice-principals, and athletic directors have access to test results, and the results are not kept for more than one year.

If a sample tests positive, a second test is administered as soon as possible to confirm the result. If the second test is negative, no further action is taken. If the second test is positive, the athlete's parents are notified, and the school principal convenes a meeting with the student and his parents, at which the student is given the option of (1) participating for six weeks in an assistance program that includes weekly urinalysis, or (2) suffering suspension from athletics for the remainder of the current season and the next athletic season. The student is then retested prior to the start of the next athletic season for which he or she is eligible. The Policy states that a second offense results in automatic imposition of option (2); a third offense in suspension for the remainder of the current season and the next two athletic seasons.

C

In the fall of 1991, respondent James Acton, then a seventh-grader, signed up to play football at one of the District's grade schools. He was denied participation, however, because he and his parents refused to sign the testing consent forms. The Actons filed suit, seeking declaratory and injunctive relief from enforcement of the Policy on the grounds that it violated the Fourth and Fourteenth Amendments to the United States Constitution and Article I, §9, of the Oregon Constitution. After a bench trial, the District Court entered an order denying the claims on the merits and dismissing the action. The United States Court of Appeals for the Ninth Circuit reversed, holding that Policy violated both the Fourth and Fourteenth Amendments and Article I, §9, of the Oregon Constitution. We granted certiorari (1994).

II

The Fourth Amendment to the United States Constitution provides that the Federal Government shall not violate "[t]he right of the people to be secure in their persons, houses, papers, and effects, against unreasonable searches and seizures...." We have held that the Fourteenth Amendment extends this constitutional guarantee to searches and seizures by state officers, including public school officials, *New Jersey* v. *T. L. O.* (1985). In *Skinner* v. *Railway Labor Executives' Assn.* (1989), we held that state-compelled collection and testing of urine, such as that required by the Student Athlete Drug Policy, constitutes a "search" subject to the demands of the Fourth Amendment. See also *Treasury Employees* v. *Von Raab* (1989).

As the text of the Fourth Amendment indicates, the ultimate measure of the constitutionality of a governmental search is "reasonableness." At least in a case such as this, where there was no clear practice, either approving or disapproving the type of search at issue, at the time the constitutional provision was enacted, whether a particular search meets the reasonableness standard "'is judged by balancing its intrusion on the individual's Fourth Amendment interests against its promotion of legitimate governmental interests.'" Where a search is undertaken by law enforcement officials to discover evidence of criminal wrongdoing, this Court has said that reasonableness generally requires the obtaining of a judicial warrant. Warrants cannot be issued, of course, without the showing of probable cause required by the Warrant Clause. But a warrant is not required to establish the reasonableness of *all* government searches; and when a warrant is not required (and the Warrant Clause therefore not applicable), probable cause is not invariably required either. A search unsupported by probable cause can be constitutional, we have said, "when special needs, beyond the normal need for law enforcement, make the warrant and probable cause requirement impracticable." *Griffin* v. *Wisconsin* (1987). We have found such "special needs" to exist in the public-school context.... The school search we approved in *T. L. O.*, while not based on probable cause, *was* based on individualized *suspicion* of wrongdoing. As we explicitly acknowledged, however, "'the Fourth Amendment imposes no irreducible requirement of such suspicion.'" We have upheld suspicionless searches and seizures to conduct drug testing of railroad personnel involved in train accidents, [*Skinner*], to conduct random drug testing of federal customs officers who carry arms or are involved in drug interdiction [*Von Raab*], and to maintain automobile checkpoints looking for illegal immigrants and contraband, *United States* v. *Martinez-Fuerte* [1976], and drunk drivers, *Michigan Dept. of State Police States* v. *Sitz* (1990).

III

The first factor to be considered is the nature of the privacy interest upon which the search here at issue intrudes. The Fourth Amendment does not protect all subjective expectations of privacy, but only those that society recognizes as "legitimate." What expectations are legitimate varies, of course, with context. ... In addition, the legitimacy of certain privacy expectations vis-à-vis the State may depend upon the individual's legal relationship with the State.... Central, in our view, to the present case is the fact that the subjects of the Policy are (1) children, who (2) have been committed to the temporary custody of the State as schoolmaster....

Fourth Amendment rights, no less than First and Fourteenth Amendment rights, are different in public schools than elsewhere; the "reasonableness" inquiry cannot disregard the schools' custodial and tutelary responsibility for children. For their own good and that of their classmates, public school children are routinely required to submit to various physical examinations, and to be vaccinated against various diseases.... Particularly with regard to medical examinations and procedures, therefore, "students within the school environment have a lesser expectation of privacy than members of the population generally." *T. L. O.* (Powell, J., concurring).

Legitimate privacy expectations are even less with regard to student athletes. School sports are not for the bashful. They require "suiting up" before each practice or event, and showering and changing afterwards. Public school locker rooms, the usual sites for these activities, are not notable for the privacy they afford. The locker rooms in Vernonia are typical: no individual dressing rooms are provided; shower heads are lined up along a wall, unseparated by any sort of partition or curtain; not even all the toilet stalls have doors. As the United States Court of Appeals for the Seventh Circuit has noted, there is "an element of 'communal undress' inherent in athletic participation," *Schaill by Kross v. Tippecanoe County School Corp.* (1988).

There is an additional respect in which school athletes have a reduced expectation of privacy. By choosing to "go out for the team," they voluntarily subject themselves to a degree of regulation even higher than that imposed on students generally. In Vernonia's public schools, they must submit to a preseason physical exam (James testified that his included the giving of a urine sample), they must acquire adequate insurance coverage or sign an insurance waiver, maintain a minimum grade point average, and comply with any "rules of conduct, dress, training hours and related matters as may be established for each sport by the head coach and athletic director with the principal's approval." Somewhat like adults who choose to participate in a "closely regulated industry," students who voluntarily participate in school athletics have reason to expect intrusions upon normal rights and privileges, including privacy.

IV

Having considered the scope of the legitimate expectation of privacy at issue here, we turn next to the character of the intrusion that is complained of. We recognized in *Skinner* that collecting the samples for urinalysis intrudes upon "an excretory function traditionally shielded by great privacy." We noted, however, that the degree of intrusion depends upon the manner in which production of the urine sample is monitored. Under the District's Policy, male students produce samples at a urinal along a wall. They remain fully clothed and are only observed from behind, if at all. Female students produce samples in an enclosed stall, with a female monitor standing outside listening only for sounds of tampering. These conditions are nearly identical to those typically encountered in public restrooms, which men, women, and especially school children use daily. Under such conditions, the privacy interests compromised by the process of obtaining the urine sample are in our view negligible.

The other privacy-invasive aspect of urinalysis is, of course, the information it discloses concerning the state of the subject's body, and the materials he has ingested. In this regard it is significant that the tests at issue here look only for drugs, and not for whether the student is, for example, epileptic, pregnant, or diabetic. Moreover, the drugs for which the samples are screened are standard, and do not vary according to the identity of the student. And finally, the results of the tests are disclosed only to a limited class of school personnel who have a need to know; and they are not turned over to law enforcement authorities or used for any internal disciplinary function....

V

Finally, we turn to consider the nature and immediacy of the governmental concern at issue here, and the efficacy of this means for meeting it. In both *Skinner* and *Von Raab*, we characterized the government interest motivating the search as "compelling." *Skinner* (interest in preventing railway accidents); *Von Raab* (interest in insuring fitness of customs officials to interdict drugs and handle firearms). Relying on these cases, the District Court held that because the District's program also called for drug testing in the absence of individualized suspicion, the District "must demonstrate a 'compelling need' for the program." The Court of Appeals appears to have agreed with this view. It is a mistake, however, to think that the phrase "compelling state interest," in the Fourth Amendment context, describes a fixed, minimum quantum of governmental concern, so that one can dispose of a case by answering in isolation the question: Is there a compelling state interest here? Rather, the phrase describes an interest which appears *important enough* to justify the particular search at hand, in light of other factors which show the search to be relatively intrusive upon a genuine expectation of privacy. Whether that relatively high degree of government concern is necessary in this case or not, we think it is met.

That the nature of the concern is important—indeed, perhaps compelling—can hardly be doubted. Deterring drug use by our Nation's school-children is at least as important as enhancing efficient enforcement of the Nation's laws against the importation of drugs ... or deterring drug use by engineers and trainmen.... School years are the time when the physical, psychological, and addictive effects of drugs are most severe.... And of course the effects of a drug-infested school are visited not just upon the users, but upon the entire student body and faculty, as the educational process is disrupted. In the present case, moreover, the necessity for the State to act is magnified by the fact that this evil is being visited not just upon individuals at large, but upon children for whom it has undertaken a special responsibility of care and direction. Finally, it must not be lost sight of that this program is directed more narrowly to drug use by school athletes, where the risk of immediate physical harm to the drug user or those with whom he is playing his sport is particularly high. Apart from psychological effects, which include impairment of judgment, slow reaction time, and a lessening of the perception of pain, the particular drugs screened by the District's Policy have been demonstrated to pose substantial physical risks to athletes....

As for the immediacy of the District's concerns: We are not inclined to question—indeed, we could not possibly find clearly erroneous—the District Court's conclusion that "a large segment of the student body, particularly those involved in interscholastic athletics, was in a state of rebellion," that "[d]isciplinary actions had reached 'epidemic proportions,'" and that "the rebellion was being fueled by alcohol and drug abuse as well as by the student's misperceptions about the drug culture." That is an immediate crisis of greater proportions than existed in *Skinner*, where we upheld the Government's drug testing program based on findings of drug use by railroad employees nationwide, without proof that a problem existed on the particular railroads whose employees were subject to the test. And of much greater proportions than existed in *Von Raab*, where there was no documented history of drug use by any customs officials.

As to the efficacy of this means for addressing the problem: It seems to us self-evident that a drug problem largely fueled by the "role model" effect of athletes' drug use, and of particular danger to athletes, is effectively addressed by making sure that athletes do not use drugs. Respondents argue that a "less intrusive means to the same end" was available, namely, "drug testing on suspicion of drug use." We have repeatedly refused to declare that only the "least intrusive" search practicable can be reasonable under the Fourth Amendment. Respondents' alternative entails substantial difficulties—if it is indeed practicable at all. It may be impracticable, for one thing, simply because the parents who are willing to accept random drug testing for athletes are not willing to accept accusatory drug testing for all students, which transforms the process into a badge of shame. Respondents' proposal brings the risk that teachers will impose testing arbitrarily upon troublesome but not drug-likely students. It generates the expense of defending lawsuits that charge such arbitrary imposition, or that simply demand greater process before accusatory drug testing is imposed. And not least of all, it adds to the ever-expanding diversionary duties of schoolteachers the new function of spotting and bringing to account drug abuse, a task for which they are ill prepared, and which is not readily compatible with their vocation.... In many respects, we think, testing based on "suspicion" of drug use would not be better, but worse.

VI

Taking into account all the factors we have considered above—the decreased expectation of privacy, the relative unobtrusiveness of the search, and the severity of the need met by the search—we conclude Vernonia's Policy is reasonable and hence constitutional.

We caution against the assumption that suspicionless drug testing will readily pass constitutional muster in other contexts. The most significant element in this case is the first we discussed: that the Policy was undertaken in furtherance of the government's responsibilities, under a public school system, as guardian and tutor of children entrusted to its care. Just as when the government conducts a search in its capacity as employer (a warrantless search of an absent employee's desk to obtain an urgently needed file, for example), the relevant question is whether that intrusion upon privacy is one that a reasonable employer might engage in; so also when the government acts as guardian and tutor the relevant question is whether the search is one that a reasonable guardian and tutor might undertake. Given the findings of need made by the District Court, we conclude that in the present case it is.

We may note that the primary guardians of Vernonia's schoolchildren appear to agree. The record shows no objection to this districtwide program by any parents other than the couple before us here—even though, as we have described, a public meeting was held to obtain parents' views. We find insufficient basis to contradict the judgment of Vernonia's parents, its school board, and the District Court, as to what was reasonably in the interest of these children under the circumstances.

* * *

The Ninth Circuit held that Vernonia's Policy not only violated the Fourth Amendment, but also, by reason of that violation, contravened Article I, § 9 of the Oregon Constitution. Our conclusion that the former holding was in error means that the latter holding rested on a flawed premise. We therefore vacate the judgment, and remand the case to the Court of Appeals for further proceedings consistent with this opinion.

It is so ordered.

JUSTICE GINSBURG, concurring.

The Court constantly observes that the School District's drug-testing policy applies only to students who voluntarily participate in interscholastic athletics. Correspondingly, the most severe sanction allowed under the District's policy is suspension from extracurricular athletic programs. I comprehend the Court's opinion as reserving the question whether the District, on no more than the showing made here, constitutionally could impose routine drug testing not only on those seeking to engage with others in team sports, but on all students required to attend school....

JUSTICE O'CONNOR, with whom JUSTICE STEVENS and JUSTICE SOUTER join, dissenting.

The population of our Nation's public schools, grades 7 through 12, numbers around 18 million. By the reasoning of today's decision, the millions of these students who participate in interscholastic sports, an overwhelming majority of whom have given school officials no reason whatsoever to suspect they use drugs at school, are open to an intrusive bodily search.

In justifying this result, the Court dispenses with a requirement of individualized suspicion on considered policy grounds. First, it explains that precisely because *every* student athlete is being tested, there is no concern that school officials might act arbitrarily in choosing who to test. Second, a broad-based search regime, the Court reasons, dilutes the accusatory nature of the search. In making these policy arguments, of course, the Court sidesteps powerful, countervailing privacy concerns. Blanket searches, because they can involve "thousands or millions" of searches, "pos[e] a greater threat to liberty" than do suspicion-based ones, which "affec[t] one person at a time," *Illinois* v. *Krull* (1987) (O'CONNOR, J., dissenting). Searches based on individualized suspicion also afford potential targets considerable control over whether they will, in fact, be searched because a person can avoid such a search by not acting in an objectively suspicious way. And given that the surest way to avoid acting suspiciously is to avoid the underlying wrongdoing, the costs of such a regime, one would think, are minimal.

But whether a blanket search is "better" than a regime based on individualized suspicion is not a debate in which we should engage. In my view, it is not open to judges or government officials to decide on policy grounds which is better and which is worse. For most of our constitutional history, mass, suspicionless searches have been generally considered *per se* unreasonable within the meaning of the Fourth Amendment. And we have allowed exceptions in recent years only where it has been clear that a suspicion-based regime would be ineffectual. Because that is not the case here, I dissent.

I

A

... [W]hat the Framers of the Fourth Amendment most strongly opposed ... were general searches—that is, searches by general warrant, by writ of assistance, by broad statute, or by any other similar authority. Although, ironically, such warrants, writs, and statutes typically required individualized suspicion,...

such requirements were subjective and unenforceable. Accordingly, these various forms of authority led in practice to "virtually unrestrained," and hence "general," searches....

... [T]he particular way the Framers chose to curb the abuses of general warrants—and by implication, *all* general searches—was not to impose a novel "evenhandedness" requirement; it was to retain the individualized suspicion requirement contained in the typical general warrant, but to make that requirement meaningful and enforceable, for instance, by raising the required level of individualized suspicion to objective probable cause....

True, not all searches around the time the Fourth Amendment was adopted required individualized suspicion—although most did. A search incident to arrest was an obvious example of one that did not, but even those searches shared the essential characteristics that distinguish suspicion-based searches from abusive general searches: they only "affec[t] one person at a time," and they are generally avoidable by refraining from wrongdoing. Protection of privacy, not evenhandedness, was then and is now the touchstone of the Fourth Amendment.

The view that mass, suspicionless searches, however evenhanded, are generally unreasonable remains inviolate in the criminal law enforcement context, see *Ybarra* v. *Illinois* (1979) (invalidating evenhanded, nonaccusatory patdown for weapons of all patrons in a tavern in which there was probable cause to think drug dealing was going on), at least where the search is more than minimally intrusive, see *Michigan Dept. of State Police* v. *Sitz* (1990) (upholding the brief and easily avoidable detention, for purposes of observing signs of intoxication, of all motorists approaching a roadblock). It is worth noting in this regard that state-compelled, state-monitored collection and testing of urine, while perhaps not the most intrusive of searches, see, *e.g., Bell* v. *Wolfish* (1979) (visual body cavity searches), is still "particularly destructive of privacy and offensive to personal dignity. *Treasury Employees* v. *Von Raab* (1989) (SCALIA, J., dissenting).... And certainly monitored urination combined with urine testing is more intrusive than some personal searches we have said trigger Fourth Amendment protections in the past....

Thus, it remains the law that the police cannot, say, subject to drug testing every person entering or leaving a certain drug-ridden neighborhood in order to find evidence of crime. And this is true even though it is hard to think of a more compelling government interest than the need to fight the scourge of drugs on our streets and in our neighborhoods. Nor could it be otherwise, for if being evenhanded were enough to justify evaluating a search regime under an open-ended balancing test, the Warrant Clause, which presupposes that there is *some* category of searches for which individualized suspicion is nonnegotiable, would be a dead letter.

Outside the criminal context, however, in response to the exigencies of modern life, our cases have upheld several evenhanded blanket searches, including some that are more than minimally intrusive, after balancing the invasion of privacy against the government's strong need. Most of these cases, of course, are distinguishable insofar as they involved searches either not of a personally intrusive nature, such as searches of closely regulated businesses ... or arising in unique contexts such as prisons.... This certainly explains why JUSTICE

SCALIA, in his dissent in our recent *Von Raab* decision, found it significant that "[u]ntil today this Court had upheld a bodily search separate from arrest and without individualized suspicion of wrong-doing only with respect to prison inmates, relying upon the uniquely dangerous nature of that environment."

In any event, in many of the cases that can be distinguished on the grounds suggested above and, more important, in *all* of the cases that cannot, see, *e.g.*, *Skinner* (blanket drug testing scheme); *Von Raab* (same); cf. *Camara* v. *Municipal Court of San Francisco* (1967) (area-wide searches of private residences), we upheld the suspicionless search only after first recognizing the Fourth Amendment's longstanding preference for a suspicion-based search regime, and then pointing to sound reasons why such a regime would likely be ineffectual under the unusual circumstances presented....

Moreover, an individualized suspicion requirement was often impractical in these cases because they involved situations in which even one undetected instance of wrongdoing could have injurious consequences for a great number of people. See, *e.g.*, *Camara* (even one safety code violation can cause "fires and epidemics [that] ravage large urban areas"); *Skinner* (even one drug- or alcohol-impaired train operator can lead to the "disastrous consequences" of a train wreck, such as "great human loss"); *Von Raab* (even one customs official caught up in drugs can, by virtue of impairment, susceptibility to bribes, or indifference, result in the noninterdiction of a "sizable drug shipmen[t]," which eventually injures the lives of thousands, or to a breach of "national security")....

B

The instant case stands in marked contrast. One searches today's majority opinion in vain for recognition that history and precedent establish that individualized suspicion is "usually required" under the Fourth Amendment (regardless of whether a warrant and probable cause are also required) and that, in the area of intrusive personal searches, the only recognized exception is for situations in which a suspicion-based scheme would be likely ineffectual. Far from acknowledging anything special about individualized suspicion, the Court treats a suspicion-based regime as if it were just any run-of-the-mill, less intrusive alternative — that is, an alternative that officials may bypass if the lesser intrusion, in their reasonable estimation, is outweighed by policy concerns unrelated to practicability.

As an initial matter, I have serious doubts whether the Court is right that the District reasonably found that the lesser intrusion of a suspicion-based testing program outweighed its genuine concerns for the adversarial nature of such a program, and for its abuses. For one thing, there are significant safeguards against abuses. The fear that a suspicion-based regime will lead to the testing of "troublesome but not drug-likely" students, for example, ignores that the required level of suspicion in the school context is objectively *reasonable* suspicion.... Moreover, any distress arising from what turns out to be a false accusation can be minimized by keeping the entire process confidential.

For another thing, the District's concern for the adversarial nature of a suspicion-based regime (which appears to extend even to those who are *rightly* accused) seems to ignore the fact that such a regime would not exist in a vacuum. Schools already have adversarial, disciplinary schemes that require teachers and administrators in many areas besides drug use to investigate student wrongdoing (often by means of accusatory searches); to make determinations about whether the wrongdoing occurred; and to impose punishment. To such a scheme, suspicion-based drug testing would be only a minor addition....

In addition to overstating its concerns with a suspicion-based program, the District seems to have *understated* the extent to which such a program is less intrusive of students' privacy. By invading the privacy of a few students rather than many (nationwide, of thousands rather than millions), and by giving potential search targets substantial control over whether they will, in fact, be searched, a suspicion-based scheme is *significantly* less intrusive.

In any event, whether the Court is right that the District reasonably weighed the lesser intrusion of a suspicion-based scheme against its policy concerns is beside the point. As stated, a suspicion-based search regime is not just any less intrusive alternative; the individualized suspicion requirement has a legal pedigree as old as the Fourth Amendment itself, and it may not be easily cast aside in the name of policy concerns. It may only be forsaken, our cases in the personal search context have established, if a suspicion-based regime would likely be ineffectual.

But having misconstrued the fundamental role of the individualized suspicion requirement in Fourth Amendment analysis, the Court never seriously engages the practicality of such a requirement in the instant case. And that failure is crucial because nowhere is it less clear that an individualized suspicion requirement would be ineffectual than in the school context. In most schools, the entire pool of potential search targets—students—is under constant supervision by teachers and administrators and coaches, be it in classrooms, hallways, or locker rooms.

The record here indicates that the Vernonia schools are no exception. The great irony of this case is that most (though not all) of the evidence the District introduced to justify its suspicionless drug-testing program consisted of first- or second-hand stories of particular, identifiable students acting in ways that plainly gave rise to reasonable suspicion of in-school drug use—and thus that would have justified a drug-related search under our *T. L. O.* decision.... Small groups of students, for example, were observed by a teacher "passing joints back and forth" across the street at a restaurant before school and during school hours. Another group was caught skipping school and using drugs at one of the students' houses. Several students actually *admitted* their drug use to school officials (some of them being caught with marijuana pipes). One student presented himself to his teacher as "clearly obviously inebriated" and had to be sent home. Still another was observed dancing and singing at the top of his voice in the back of the classroom; when the teacher asked what was going on, he replied, "Well, I'm just high on life." To take a final example, on a certain road trip, the school wrestling coach smelled marijuana smoke in a hotel room occupied by four wrestlers, an observation that (after some questioning) would probably have given him reasonable suspicion to test one or all of them....

In light of all this evidence of drug use by particular students, there is a substantial basis for concluding that a vigorous regime of suspicion-based testing (for which the District appears already to have rules in place) would have gone a long way toward solving Vernonia's school drug problem while preserving the Fourth Amendment rights of James Acton and others like him. And were there any doubt about such a conclusion, it is removed by indications in the record that suspicion-based testing could have been supplemented by an equally vigorous campaign to have Vernonia's parents encourage their children to submit to the District's *voluntary* drug testing program. In these circumstances, the Fourth Amendment dictates that a mass, suspicionless search regime is categorically unreasonable.

I recognize that a suspicion-based scheme, even where reasonably effective in controlling in-school drug use, may not be *as* effective as a mass, suspicionless testing regime. In one sense, that is obviously true — just as it is obviously true that suspicion-based law enforcement is not as effective as mass, suspicionless enforcement might be. "But there is nothing new in the realization" that Fourth Amendment protections come with a price. Indeed, the price we pay is higher in the criminal context, given that police do not closely observe the entire class of potential search targets (all citizens in the area) and must ordinarily adhere to the rigid requirements of a warrant and probable cause.

The principal counterargument to all this, central to the Court's opinion, is that the Fourth Amendment is more lenient with respect to school searches. That is no doubt correct, for, as the Court explains, schools have traditionally had special guardian-like responsibilities for children that necessitate a degree of constitutional leeway. This principle explains the considerable Fourth Amendment leeway we gave school officials in *T. L. O.* In that case, we held that children at school do not enjoy two of the Fourth Amendment's traditional categorical protections against unreasonable searches and seizures: the warrant requirement and the probable cause requirement....

The instant case, however, asks whether the Fourth Amendment is even more lenient than that, *i.e.*, whether it is *so* lenient that students may be deprived of the Fourth Amendment's only remaining, and most basic, categorical protection: its strong preference for an individualized suspicion requirement, with its accompanying antipathy toward personally intrusive, blanket searches of mostly innocent people....

For the contrary position, the Court relies on cases such as *T. L. O.*, *Ingraham* v. *Wright* (1977), and *Goss* v. *Lopez* (1975). But I find the Court's reliance on these cases ironic. If anything, they affirm that schools have substantial constitutional leeway in carrying out their traditional mission of responding to *particularized* wrongdoing. See *T. L. O.* (leeway in investigating particularized wrongdoing); *Ingraham* (leeway in punishing particularized wrongdoing); *Goss* (leeway in choosing procedures by which particularized wrongdoing is punished).

By contrast, intrusive, blanket searches of school children, most of whom are innocent, for evidence of serious wrongdoing are not part of any traditional school function of which I am aware. Indeed, many schools, like many parents, prefer to trust their children unless given reason to do otherwise. As James Acton's father said on the witness stand, "[suspicionless testing] sends a message to children that are trying to be responsible citizens ... that they have to prove that they're innocent..., and I think that kind of sets a bad tone for citizenship."

I find unpersuasive the Court's reliance on the widespread practice of physical examinations and vaccinations, which are both blanket searches of a sort. Of course, for these practices to have *any* Fourth Amendment significance, the Court has to assume that these physical exams and vaccinations are typically "required" to a similar extent that urine testing and collection is required in the instant case, *i.e.*, that they are required regardless of parental objection and that some meaningful sanction attaches to the failure to submit. In any event, without forming any particular view of such searches, it is worth noting that a suspicion requirement for vaccinations is not merely impractical; it is nonsensical, for vaccinations are not searches *for anything in particular* and so there is nothing about which to be suspicious.... As for physical examinations, the practicability of a suspicion requirement is highly doubtful because the conditions for which these physical exams ordinarily search, such as latent heart conditions, do not manifest themselves in observable behavior the way school drug use does.

It might also be noted that physical exams (and of course vaccinations) are not searches for conditions that reflect wrongdoing on the part of the student, and so are *wholly* nonaccusatory and have no consequences that can be regarded as punitive. These facts may explain the absence of Fourth Amendment challenges to such searches. By contrast, although I agree with the Court that the accusatory nature of the District's test program is *diluted* by making it a blanket one, any testing program that searches for conditions plainly reflecting serious wrongdoing can never be made wholly nonaccusatory from the student's perspective, the motives for the program notwithstanding; and for the same reason, the substantial consequences that can flow from a positive test, such as suspension from sports, are invariably—and quite reasonably—understood as punishment. The best proof that the District's testing program is to some extent accusatory can be found in James Acton's own explanation on the witness stand as to why he did not want to submit to drug testing: "Because I feel that they have no reason to think I was taking drugs." It is hard to think of a manner of explanation that resonates more intensely in our Fourth Amendment tradition than this.

[II omitted]

III

It cannot be too often stated that the greatest threats to our constitutional freedoms come in times of crisis. But we must also stay mindful that not all government responses to such times are hysterical overreactions; some crises are quite real, and when they are, they serve precisely as the compelling state interest that we have said may justify a measured intrusion on constitutional rights. The only way for judges to mediate these conflicting impulses is to do what they should do anyway: stay close to the record in each case that appears before them, and make their judgments based on that alone. Having reviewed the record here, I cannot avoid the conclusion that the District's suspicionless policy of testing all student-athletes sweeps too broadly, and too imprecisely, to be reasonable under the Fourth Amendment.

□ □ □

No. 94–329

Ronald W. Rosenberger, et al., Petitioners v. Rector and Visitors of the University of Virginia et al.

On writ of certiorari to the United States Court of Appeals for the Fourth Circuit

[June 29, 1995]

JUSTICE KENNEDY delivered the opinion of the Court.

The University of Virginia, an instrumentality of the Commonwealth for which it is named and thus bound by the First and Fourteenth Amendments, authorizes the payment of outside contractors for the printing costs of a variety of student publications. It withheld any authorization for payments on behalf of petitioners for the sole reason that their student paper "primarily promotes or manifests a particular belie[f] in or about a deity or an ultimate reality." That the paper did promote or manifest views within the defined exclusion seems plain enough. The challenge is to the University's regulation and its denial of authorization, the case raising issues under the Speech and Establishment Clauses of the First Amendment.

I

The public corporation we refer to as the "University" is denominated by state law as "the Rector and Visitors of the University of Virginia," and it is responsible for governing the school. Founded by Thomas Jefferson in 1819, and ranked by him, together with the authorship of the Declaration of Independence and of the Virginia Act for Religious Freedom, as one of his proudest achievements, the University is among the Nation's oldest and most respected seats of higher learning. It has more than 11,000 undergraduate students, and 6,000 graduate and professional students. An understanding of the case requires a somewhat detailed description of the program the University created to support extracurricular student activities on its campus.

Before a student group is eligible to submit bills from its outside contractors for payment by the fund described below, it must become a "Contracted Independent Organization" (CIO). CIO status is available to any group the majority of whose members are students, whose managing officers are fulltime students, and that complies with certain procedural requirements. A CIO must file its constitution with the University; must pledge not to discriminate in its membership; and must include in dealings with third parties and in all written materials a disclaimer, stating that the CIO is independent of the University and that the University is not responsible for the CIO....

All CIOs may exist and operate at the University, but some are also entitled to apply for funds from the Student Activities Fund (SAF). Established and governed by University Guidelines, the purpose of the SAF is to support a broad range of extracurricular student activities that are related to the educational purpose of the University....The SAF receives its money from a mandatory fee of $14 per semester assessed to each full-time student. The Student Council, elected by the students, has the initial authority to disburse the funds, but its actions are subject to review by a faculty body chaired by a designee of the Vice President for Student Affairs.

Some, but not all, CIOs may submit disbursement requests to the SAF. The Guidelines recognize 11 categories of student groups that may seek payment to third-party contractors because they "are related to the educational purpose of the University of Virginia." One of these is "student news, information, opinion, entertainment, or academic communications media groups." The Guidelines also specify, however, that the costs of certain activities of CIOs that are otherwise eligible for funding will not be reimbursed by the SAF. The student activities which are excluded from SAF support [include] religious activities.... A religious activity ... is defined as any activity that "primarily promotes or manifests a particular belie[f] in or about a deity or an ultimate reality."

... If an organization seeks SAF support, it must submit its bills to the Student Council, which pays the organization's creditors upon determining that the expenses are appropriate. No direct payments are made to the student groups....

Petitioners' organization, Wide Awake Productions (WAP), qualified as a CIO. Formed by petitioner Ronald Rosenberger and other undergraduates in 1990, WAP was established "[t]o publish a magazine of philosophical and religious expression," "[t]o facilitate discussion which fosters an atmosphere of sensitivity to and tolerance of Christian viewpoints," and "[t]o provide a unifying focus for Christians of multicultural backgrounds." WAP publishes Wide Awake: A Christian Perspective at the University of Virginia. The paper's Christian viewpoint was evident from the first issue, in which its editors wrote that the journal "offers a Christian perspective on both personal and community issues, especially those relevant to college students at the University of Virginia." The editors committed the paper to a two-fold mission: "to challenge Christians to live, in word and deed, according to the faith they proclaim and to encourage students to consider what a personal relationship with Jesus Christ means." The first issue had articles about racism, crisis pregnancy, stress, prayer, C. S. Lewis' ideas about evil and free will, and reviews of religious music. In the next two issues, Wide Awake featured stories about homosexuality, Christian missionary work, and eating disorders, as well as music reviews and interviews with University professors. Each page of Wide Awake, and the end of each article or review, is marked by a cross. The advertisements carried in Wide Awake also reveal the Christian perspective of the journal. For the most part, the advertisers are churches, centers for Christian study, or Christian bookstores. By June 1992, WAP had distributed about 5,000 copies of Wide Awake to University students, free of charge.

WAP had acquired CIO status soon after it was organized. This is an important consideration in this case, for had it been a "religious organization," WAP would not have been accorded CIO status. As defined by the Guidelines, a "religious organization" is "an organization whose purpose is to practice a devotion to an acknowledged ultimate reality or deity." At no stage in this controversy has the University contended that WAP is such an organization.

A few months after being given CIO status, WAP requested the SAF to pay its printer $5,862 for the costs of printing its newspaper. The Appropriations Committee of the Student Council denied WAP's request on the ground that Wide Awake was a "religious activity" within the meaning of the Guidelines, *i.e.,* that the newspaper "promote[d] or manifest[ed] a particular belie[f] in or about a deity or an ultimate reality." It made its determination after examining the first issue. WAP appealed the denial to the full Student Council, contending that WAP met all the applicable Guidelines and that denial of SAF support on the basis of the magazine's religious perspective violated the Constitution. The appeal was denied without further comment, and WAP appealed to the next level, the Student Activities Committee. In a letter signed by the Dean of Students, the committee sustained the denial of funding.

Having no further recourse within the University structure, WAP, Wide Awake, and three of its editors and members filed suit in the United States District Court for the Western District of Virginia, challenging the SAF's action as violative of 42 U. S. C. §1983. They alleged that refusal to authorize payment of the printing costs of the publication, solely on the basis of its religious editorial viewpoint, violated their rights to freedom of speech and press, to the free exercise of religion, and to equal protection of the law.

They relied also upon Article I of the Virginia Constitution and the Virginia Act for Religious Freedom, but did not pursue those theories on appeal. The suit sought damages for the costs of printing the paper, injunctive and declaratory relief, and attorney's fees.

On cross-motions for summary judgment, the District Court ruled for the University, holding that denial of SAF support was not an impermissible content or viewpoint discrimination against petitioners' speech, and that the University's Establishment Clause concern over its "religious activities" was a sufficient justification for denying payment to third-party contractors. The court did not issue a definitive ruling on whether reimbursement, had it been made here, would or would not have violated the Establishment Clause. (WD Va. 1992).

The United States Court of Appeals for the Fourth Circuit, in disagreement with the District Court, held that the Guidelines did discriminate on the basis of content. It ruled that, while the State need not underwrite speech, there was a presumptive violation of the Speech Clause when viewpoint discrimination was invoked to deny third-party payment otherwise available to CIOs. (1994). The Court of Appeals affirmed the judgment of the District Court nonetheless, concluding that the discrimination by the University was justified by the "compelling interest in maintaining strict separation of church and state."

II

It is axiomatic that the government may not regulate speech based on its substantive content or the message it conveys. Other principles follow from this precept. In the realm of private speech or expression, government regulation may not favor one speaker over another. Discrimination against speech because of its message is presumed to be unconstitutional. These rules informed our determination that the government offends the First Amendment when it imposes financial burdens on certain speakers based on the content of their expression. When the government targets not subject matter but particular views taken by speakers on a subject, the violation of the First Amendment is all the more blatant. Viewpoint discrimination is thus an egregious form of content discrimination. The government must abstain from regulating speech when the specific motivating ideology or the opinion or perspective of the speaker is the rationale for the restriction.

These principles provide the framework forbidding the State from exercising viewpoint discrimination, even when the limited public forum is one of its own creation. In a case involving a school district's provision of school facilities for private uses, we declared that "[t]here is no question that the District, like the private owner of property, may legally preserve the property under its control for the use to which it is dedicated." *Lamb's Chapel* v. *Center Moriches Union Free School Dist.* (1993). The necessities of confining a forum to the limited and legitimate purposes for which it was created may justify the State in reserving it for certain groups or for the discussion of certain topics. Once it has opened a limited forum, however, the State must respect the lawful boundaries it has itself set.... Thus, in determining whether the State is acting to preserve the limits of the forum it has created so that the exclusion of a class of speech is legitimate, we have observed a distinction between, on the one hand, content discrimination, which may be permissible if it preserves the purposes of that limited forum, and, on the other hand, viewpoint discrimination, which is presumed impermissible when directed against speech otherwise within the forum's limitations.

The SAF is a forum more in a metaphysical than in a spatial or geographic sense, but the same principles are applicable.... The most recent and most apposite case is our decision in *Lamb's Chapel.* There, a school district had opened school facilities for use after school hours by community groups for a wide variety of social, civic, and recreational purposes. The district, however, had enacted a formal policy against opening facilities to groups for religious purposes. Invoking its policy, the district rejected a request from a group desiring to show a film series addressing various child-rearing questions from a "Christian perspective." There was no indication in the record in *Lamb's Chapel* that the request to use the school facilities was "denied for any reason other than the fact that the presentation would have been from a religious perspective." Our conclusion was unanimous: "[I]t discriminates on the basis of viewpoint to permit school property to be used for the presentation of all views about family issues and child-rearing except those dealing with the subject matter from a religious standpoint."

The University does acknowledge ... that "ideologically driven attempts to suppress a particular point of view are presumptively unconstitutional in funding, as in other contexts," but insists that this case does not present that issue because the Guidelines draw lines based on content, not viewpoint. As we have noted, discrimination against one set of views or ideas is but a subset or particular instance of the more general phenomenon of content discrimination. And, it must be acknowledged, the distinction is not a precise one. It is, in a sense, something of an understatement to speak of religious thought and discussion as just a viewpoint, as distinct from a comprehensive body of thought. The nature of our origins and destiny and their dependence upon the existence of a divine being have been subjects of philosophic inquiry throughout human history. We conclude, nonetheless, that here, as in *Lamb's Chapel*, viewpoint discrimination is the proper way to interpret the University's objections to Wide Awake. By the very terms of the SAF prohibition, the University does not exclude religion as a subject matter but selects for disfavored treatment those student journalistic efforts with religious editorial viewpoints. Religion may be a vast area of inquiry, but it also provides, as it did here, a specific premise, a perspective, a standpoint from which a variety of subjects may be discussed and considered. The prohibited perspective, not the general subject matter, resulted in the refusal to make third-party payments, for the subjects discussed were otherwise within the approved category of publications.

The dissent's assertion that no viewpoint discrimination occurs because the Guidelines discriminate against an entire class of viewpoints reflects an insupportable assumption that all debate is bipolar and that anti-religious speech is the only response to religious speech. Our understanding of the complex and multifaceted nature of public discourse has not embraced such a contrived description of the marketplace of ideas. If the topic of debate is, for example, racism, then exclusion of several views on that problem is just as offensive to the First Amendment as exclusion of only one. It is as objectionable to exclude both a theistic and an atheistic perspective on the debate as it is to exclude one, the other, or yet another political, economic, or social viewpoint. The dissent's declaration that debate is not skewed so long as multiple voices are silenced is simply wrong; the debate is skewed in multiple ways.

The University's WAP's request for third-party payments in the present case is based upon viewpoint discrimination not unlike the discrimination the school district relied upon in *Lamb's Chapel* and that we found invalid....

The University tries to escape the consequences of our holding in *Lamb's Chapel* by urging that this case involves the provision of funds rather than access to facilities. The University begins with the unremarkable proposition that the State must have substantial discretion in determining how to allocate scarce resources to accomplish its educational mission. Citing our decisions in *Rust* v. *Sullivan* (1991), *Regan* v. *Taxation with Representation of Wash.* (1983), and *Widmar* v. *Vincent* (1981), the University argues that content-based funding decisions are both inevitable and lawful....

To this end the University relies on our assurance in *Widmar* v. *Vincent.* There, in the course of striking down a public university's exclusion of religious groups from use of school facilities made available to all other student groups, we stated: "Nor do we question the right of the University to make academic judgments as to how best to allocate scarce resources." The quoted language in *Widmar* was but a proper recognition of the principle that when the State is the speaker, it may make content-based choices....

It does not follow, however, and we did not suggest in *Widmar*, that viewpoint-based restrictions are proper when the University does not itself speak or subsidize transmittal of a message it favors but instead expends funds to encourage a diversity of views from private speakers. A holding that the University may not discriminate based on the viewpoint of private persons whose speech it facilitates does not restrict the University's own speech, which is controlled by different principles....

The distinction between the University's own favored message and the private speech of students is evident in the case before us. The University itself has taken steps to ensure the distinction in the agreement each CIO must sign. The University declares that the student groups eligible for SAF support are not the

University's agents, are not subject to its control, and are not its responsibility. Having offered to pay the third-party contractors on behalf of private speakers who convey their own messages, the University may not silence the expression of selected viewpoints.

The University urges that, from a constitutional standpoint, funding of speech differs from provision of access to facilities because money is scarce and physical facilities are not. Beyond the fact that in any given case this proposition might not be true as an empirical matter, the underlying premise that the University could discriminate based on viewpoint if demand for space exceeded its availability is wrong as well. The government cannot justify viewpoint discrimination among private speakers on the economic fact of scarcity. Had the meeting rooms in *Lamb's Chapel* been scarce, had the demand been greater than the supply, our decision would have been no different. It would have been incumbent on the State, of course, to ration or allocate the scarce resources on some acceptable neutral principle; but nothing in our decision indicated that scarcity would give the State the right to exercise viewpoint discrimination that is otherwise impermissible.

Vital First Amendment speech principles are at stake here. The first danger to liberty lies in granting the State the power to examine publications to determine whether or not they are based on some ultimate idea and if so for the State to classify them. The second, and corollary, danger is to speech from the chilling of individual thought and expression. That danger is especially real in the University setting, where the State acts against a background and tradition of thought and experiment that is at the center of our intellectual and philosophic tradition....

The Guideline invoked by the University to deny third-party contractor payments on behalf of WAP effects a sweeping restriction on student thought and student inquiry in the context of University sponsored publications. The prohibition on funding on behalf of publications that "primarily promot[e] or manifes[t] a particular belie[f] in or about a deity or an ultimate reality," in its ordinary and commonsense meaning, has a vast potential reach.... Were the prohibition applied with much vigor at all, it would bar funding of essays by hypothetical student contributors named Plato, Spinoza, and Descartes. And if the regulation covers, as the University says it does, those student journalistic efforts which primarily manifest or promote a belief that there is no deity and no ultimate reality, then undergraduates named Karl Marx, Bertrand Russell, and Jean-Paul Sartre would likewise have some of their major essays excluded from student publications. If any manifestation of beliefs in first principles disqualifies the writing, as seems to be the case, it is indeed difficult to name renowned thinkers whose writings would be accepted, save perhaps for articles disclaiming all connection to their ultimate philosophy. Plato could contrive perhaps to submit an acceptable essay on making pasta or peanut butter cookies, provided he did not point out their (necessary) imperfections.

Based on the principles we have discussed, we hold that the regulation invoked to deny SAF support, both in its terms and in its application to these petitioners, is a denial of their right of free speech guaranteed by the First Amendment. It remains to be considered whether the violation following from the University's action is excused by the necessity of complying with the Constitution's prohibition against state establishment of religion. We turn to that question.

III

... A central lesson of our decisions is that a significant factor in upholding governmental programs in the face of Establishment Clause attack is their neutrality towards religion.... We have held that the guarantee of neutrality is respected, not offended, when the government, following neutral criteria and evenhanded policies, extends benefits to recipients whose ideologies and viewpoints, including religious ones, are broad and diverse....

The governmental program here is neutral toward religion. There is no suggestion that the University created it to advance religion or adopted some ingenious device with the purpose of aiding a religious cause. The object of the SAF is to open a forum for speech and to support various student enterprises, including the publication of newspapers, in recognition of the diversity and creativity of student life. The University's SAF Guidelines have a separate classification for, and do not make third-party payments on behalf of, "religious organizations," which are those "whose purpose is to practice a devotion to an acknowledged ultimate reality or deity." The category of support here is for "student news, information, opinion, entertainment, or academic communications media groups," of which Wide Awake was 1 of 15 in the 1990 school year. WAP did not seek a subsidy because of its Christian editorial viewpoint; it sought funding as a student journal, which it was.

The neutrality of the program distinguishes the student fees from a tax levied for the direct support of a church or group of churches. A tax of that sort, of course, would run contrary to Establishment Clause concerns dating from the earliest days of the Republic. The apprehensions of our predecessors involved the levying of taxes upon the public for the sole and exclusive purpose of establishing and supporting specific sects. The exaction here, by contrast, is a student activity fee designed to reflect the reality that student life in its many dimensions includes the necessity of wide-ranging speech and inquiry and that student expression is an integral part of the University's educational mission. The fee is mandatory, and we do not have before us the question whether an objecting student has the First Amendment right to deiand a pro rata return to the extent the fee is expended for speech to which he or she does not subscribe. We must treat it, then, as an exaction upon the students. But the $14 paid each semester by the students is not a general tax designed to raise revenue for the University.... The SAF cannot be used for unlimited purposes, much less the illegitimate purpose of supporting one religion. Much like the arrangement in *Widmar*, the money goes to a special fund from which any group of students with CIO status can draw for purposes consistent with the University's educational mission; and to the extent the student is interested in speech, withdrawal is permitted to cover the whole spectrum of speech, whether it manifests a religious view, an antireligious view, or neither. Our decision, then, cannot be read as addressing an expenditure from a general tax fund. Here, the disbursements from the fund go to private contractors for the cost of printing that which is protected under the Speech Clause of the First Amendment. This is a far cry from a general public assessment designed and effected to provide financial support for a church.

Government neutrality is apparent in the State's overall scheme in a further meaningful respect. The program respects the critical difference "between *government* speech endorsing religion, which the Establishment Clause forbids, and *private* speech endorsing religion, which the Free Speech and Free Exercise Clauses protect." In this case, "the government has not willfully fostered or encouraged" any mistaken impression that the student newspapers speak for the University. The University has taken pains to disassociate itself from the private speech involved in this case. The Court of Appeals' apparent concern that Wide Awake's religious orientation would be attributed to the University is not a plausible fear, and there is no real likelihood that the speech in question is being either endorsed or coerced by the State....

It does not violate the Establishment Clause for a public university to grant access to its facilities on a religion-neutral basis to a wide spectrum of student groups, including groups which use meeting rooms for sectarian activities, accompanied by some devotional exercises. See *Widmar, [Board of Ed. of Westside Community Schools (Dist. 66) v.] Mergens* (1990). This is so even where the upkeep, maintenance, and repair of the facilities attributed to those uses is paid from a student activities fund to which students are required to contribute.... If the expenditure of governmental funds is prohibited whenever those funds pay for a service that is, pursuant to a religion-neutral program, used by a group for sectarian purposes, then *Widmar, Mergens* and *Lamb's Chapel* would have to be overruled. Given our holdings in these cases, it follows that a public university may maintain its own computer facility and give student groups access to that facility, including the use of the printers, on a religion neutral, say first-come first-served, basis. If a religious student organization obtained access on that religion-neutral basis and used a computer to compose or a printer or copy machine to print speech with a religious content or viewpoint, the State's action in providing the group with access would no more violate the Establishment Clause than would giving those groups access to an assembly hall. There is no difference in logic or principle, and no difference of constitutional significance, between a school using its funds to operate a facility to which students have access, and a school paying a third-party contractor to operate the facility on its behalf. The latter occurs here. The University provides printing services to a broad spectrum of student newspapers qualified as CIOs by reason of their officers and membership. Any benefit to religion is incidental to the government's provision of secular services for secular purposes on a religion-neutral basis. Printing is a routine, secular, and recurring attribute of student life.

By paying outside printers, the University in fact attains a further degree of separation from the student publication, for it avoids the duties of supervision, escapes the costs of upkeep, repair, and replacement attributable to student use, and has a clear record of costs. As a result, and as in *Widmar*, the University can charge the SAF, and not the taxpayers as a whole, for the discrete activity in question. It would be formalistic for us to say that the University must forfeit these advantages and provide the services itself in order to comply with the Establishment Clause. It is, of course, true that if the State pays a church's bills it is subsidizing it, and we must guard against this abuse. That is not a danger here, based on the considerations we have advanced and for the additional reason that the student publication is not a religious institution, at least in the usual sense of that term as used in our case law, and it is not a religious organization as used in the University's own regulations. It is instead a publication involved in a pure forum for the expression of ideas, ideas that would be both incomplete and chilled were the Constitution to be interpreted to require that state officials and courts scan the publication to ferret out views that principally manifest a belief in a divine being.

Were the dissent's view to become law, it would require the University, in order to avoid a constitutional violation, to scrutinize the content of student speech, lest the expression in question—speech otherwise protected by the Constitution—contain too great a religious content. The dissent, in fact, anticipates such censorship as "crucial" in distinguishing between "works characterized by the evangelism of Wide Awake and writing that merely happens to express views that a given religion might approve." That eventuality raises the specter of governmental censorship, to ensure that all student writings and publications meet some baseline standard of secular orthodoxy. To impose that standard on student speech at a university is to imperil the very sources of free speech and expression. As we recognized in *Widmar,* official censorship would be far more inconsistent with the Establishment Clause's dictates than would governmental provision of secular printing services on a religion-blind basis....

* * *

To obey the Establishment Clause, it was not necessary for the University to deny eligibility to student publications because of their viewpoint. The neutrality commanded of the State by the separate Clauses of the First Amendment was compromised by the University's course of action. The viewpoint discrimination inherent in the University's regulation required public officials to scan and interpret student publications to discern their underlying philosophic assumptions respecting religious theory and belief. That course of action was a denial of the right of free speech and would risk fostering a pervasive bias or hostility to religion, which could undermine the very neutrality the Establishment Clause requires. There is no Establishment Clause violation in the University's honoring its duties under the Free Speech Clause.

The judgment of the Court of Appeals must be, and is, reversed.

It is so ordered.

JUSTICE O'CONNOR, concurring.
... This case lies at the intersection of the principle of government neutrality and the prohibition on state funding of religious activities. It is clear that the University has established a generally applicable program to encourage the free exchange of ideas by its students, an expressive marketplace that includes some 15 student publications with predictably divergent viewpoints. It is equally clear that petitioners' viewpoint is religious and that publication of Wide Awake is a religious activity, under both the University's regulation and a fair reading of our precedents. Not to finance Wide Awake, according to petitioners, violates the principle of neutrality by sending a message of hostility toward religion. To finance Wide Awake, argues the University, violates the prohibition on direct state funding of religious activities.

When two bedrock principles so conflict, understandably neither can provide the definitive answer. Reliance on categorical platitudes is unavailing. Resolution instead depends on the hard task of judging—sifting through the details and determining whether the challenged program offends the Establishment Clause. Such judgment requires courts to draw lines, sometimes quite fine, based on the particular facts of each case....

So it is in this case. The nature of the dispute does not admit of categorical answers, nor should any be inferred from the Court's decision today. Instead, certain considerations specific to the program at issue lead me to conclude that by providing the same assistance to Wide Awake that it does to other publications, the University would not be endorsing the magazine's religious perspective.

First, the student organizations, at the University's insistence, remain strictly independent of the University....

Second, financial assistance is distributed in a manner that ensures its use only for permissible purposes....

Third, assistance is provided to the religious publication in a context that makes improbable any perception of government endorsement of the religious message....

Finally, although the question is not presented here, I note the possibility that the student fee is susceptible to a Free Speech Clause challenge by an objecting student that she should not be compelled to pay for speech with which she disagrees. There currently exists a split in the lower courts as to whether such a challenge would be successful.... While the Court does not resolve the question here, the existence of such an opt-out possibility not available to citizens generally provides a potential basis for distinguishing proceeds of the student fees in this case from proceeds of the general assessments in support of religion that lie at the core of the prohibition against religious funding, and from government funds generally....

Subject to these comments, I join the opinion of the Court.

JUSTICE THOMAS, concurring.

I agree with the Court's opinion and join it in full, but I write separately to express my disagreement with the historical analysis put forward by the dissent. Although the dissent starts down the right path in consulting the original meaning of the Establishment Clause, its misleading application of history yields a principle that is inconsistent with our Nation's long tradition of allowing religious adherents to participate on equal terms in neutral government programs.

Even assuming that the Virginia debate on the so-called "Assessment Controversy" was indicative of the principles embodied in the Establishment Clause, this incident hardly compels the dissent's conclusion that government must actively discriminate against religion. The dissent's historical discussion glosses over the fundamental characteristic of the Virginia assessment bill that sparked the controversy: The assessment was to be imposed for the support of clergy in the performance of their function of teaching religion....

James Madison's Memorial and Remonstrance Against Religious Assessments must be understood in this context. Contrary to the dissent's suggestion, Madison's objection to the assessment bill did not rest on the premise that religious entities may never participate on equal terms in neutral government programs. Nor did Madison embrace the argument that forms the linchpin of the dissent: that monetary subsidies are constitutionally different from other neutral benefits programs. Instead, Madison's comments are more consistent with the neutrality principle that the dissent inexplicably discards. According to Madison, the Virginia assessment was flawed because it "violate[d] that equality which ought to be the basis of every law." The assessment violated the "equality" principle not because it allowed religious groups to participate in a generally available government program, but because the bill singled out religious entities for special benefits....

Legal commentators have disagreed about the historical lesson to take from the Assessment Controversy. For some, the experience in Virginia is consistent with the view that the Framers saw the Establishment Clause simply as a prohibition on governmental preferences for some religious faiths over others.... Other commentators have rejected this view, concluding that the Establishment Clause forbids not only government preferences for some religious sects over others, but also government preferences for religion over irreligion....

I find much to commend the former view. Madison's focus on the preferential nature of the assessment was not restricted to the fourth paragraph of the Remonstrance discussed above. The funding provided by the Virginia assessment was to be extended only to Christian sects, and the Remonstrance seized on this defect. ...

But resolution of this debate is not necessary to decide this case. Under any understanding of the Assessment Controversy, the history cited by the dissent cannot support the conclusion that the Establishment Clause "categorically condemn[s] state programs directly aiding religious activity" when that aid is part of a neutral program available to a wide array of beneficiaries. Even if Madison believed that the principle of nonestablishment of religion precluded government financial support for religion *per se* (in the sense of government benefits specifically targeting religion), there is no indication that at the time of the framing he took the dissent's extreme view that the government must discriminate against religious adherents by excluding them from more generally available financial subsidies....

JUSTICE SOUTER, with whom JUSTICE STEVENS, JUSTICE GINSBURG, and JUSTICE BREYER join, dissenting.

The Court today, for the first time, approves direct funding of core religious activities by an arm of the State. It does so, however, only after erroneous treatment of some familiar principles of law implementing the First Amendment's Establishment and Speech Clauses, and by viewing the very funds in question beyond the reach of the Establishment Clause's funding restrictions as such. Because there is no warrant for distinguishing among public funding sources for purposes of applying the First Amendment's prohibition of religious establishment, I would hold that the University's refusal to support petitioners' religious activities is compelled by the Establishment Clause. I would therefore affirm.

I

The central question in this case is whether a grant from the Student Activities Fund to pay Wide Awake's printing expenses would violate the Establishment Clause. Although the Court does not dwell on the details of Wide Awake's message, it recognizes something sufficiently religious in the publication to demand Establishment Clause scrutiny. Although the Court places great stress on the eligibility of secular as well as religious activities for grants from the Student Activities Fund, it recognizes that such evenhanded availability is not by itself enough to satisfy constitutional requirements for any aid scheme that results in a benefit to religion. Something more is necessary to justify any religious aid. Some members of the Court, at least, may think the funding permissible on a view that it is indirect, since the money goes to Wide Awake's printer, not through Wide Awake's own checking account. The Court's principal reliance, however, is on an argument that providing religion with economically valuable services is permissible on the theory that services are economically indistinguishable from religious access to governmental speech forums, which sometimes is permissible. But this reasoning would commit the Court to approving direct religious aid beyond anything justifiable for the sake of access to speaking forums. The Court implicitly recognizes this in its further attempt to circumvent the clear bar to direct governmental aid to religion. Different members of the Court seek to avoid this bar in different ways. The opinion of the Court makes the novel assumption that only direct aid financed with tax revenue is barred, and draws the erroneous conclusion that the involuntary Student Activities Fee is not a tax. I do not read JUSTICE O'CONNOR's opinion as sharing that assumption; she places this Student Activities Fund in a category of student funding enterprises from which religious activities in public universities may benefit, so long as there is no consequent endorsement of religion. The resulting decision is in unmistakable tension with the accepted law that the Court continues to avow.

A

The Court's difficulties will be all the more clear after a closer look at Wide Awake than the majority opinion affords. The character of the magazine is candidly disclosed on the opening page of the first issue, where the editor-in-chief announces Wide Awake's mission in a letter to the readership signed, "Love in Christ": it is "to challenge Christians to live, in word and deed, according to the faith they proclaim and to encourage students to consider what a personal relationship with Jesus Christ means." The masthead of every issue bears St. Paul's exhortation, that "[t]he hour has come for you to awake from your slumber, because our salvation is nearer now than when we first believed. Romans 13:11." [Other citations from publication omitted.]

This writing is no merely descriptive examination of religious doctrine or even of ideal Christian practice in confronting life's social and personal problems. Nor is it merely the expression of editorial opinion that incidentally coincides with Christian ethics and reflects a Christian view of human obligation. It is straightforward exhortation to enter into a relationship with God as revealed in Jesus Christ, and to satisfy a series of moral obligations derived from the teachings of Jesus Christ. These are not the words of "student news, information, opinion, entertainment, or academic communicatio[n]..." (in the language of the University's funding criterion), but the words of "challenge [to] Christians to live, in word and deed, according to the faith they proclaim and ... to consider what a personal relationship with Jesus Christ means" (in the language of Wide Awake's founder). The subject is not the discourse of the scholar's study or the seminar room, but of the evangelist's mission station and the pulpit. It is nothing other than the preaching of the word, which (along with the sacraments) is what most branches of Christianity offer those called to the religious life.

Using public funds for the direct subsidization of preaching the word is categorically forbidden under the Establishment Clause, and if the Clause was meant to accomplish nothing else, it was meant to bar this use of public money. Evidence on the subject antedates even the Bill of Rights itself, as may be seen in the writings of Madison, whose authority on questions about the meaning of the Establishment Clause is well settled. Four years before the First Congress proposed the First Amendment, Madison gave his opinion on the legitimacy of using public funds for religious purposes, in the Memorial and Remonstrance Against Religious Assessments, which played the central role in ensuring the defeat of the Virginia tax assessment bill in 1786 and framed the debate upon which the Religion Clauses stand:

> "Who does not see that ... the same authority which can force a citizen to contribute three pence only of his property for the support of any one establishment, may force him to conform to any other establishment in all cases whatsoever?"

Madison wrote against a background in which nearly every Colony had exacted a tax for church support, the practice having become "so commonplace as to shock the freedom-loving colonials into a feeling of abhorrence." Madison's Remonstrance captured the colonists' "conviction that individual religious liberty could be achieved best under a government which was stripped of all power to tax, to support, or otherwise to assist any or all religions, or to interfere with the beliefs of any religious individual or group." Their sentiments as expressed by Madison in Virginia, led not only to the defeat of Virginia's tax assessment bill, but also directly to passage of the Virginia Bill for Establishing Religious Freedom, written by Thomas Jefferson. That bill's preamble declared that "to compel a man to furnish contributions of money for the propagation of opinions which he disbelieves, is sinful and tyrannical," and its text provided "[t]hat no man shall be compelled to frequent or support any religious worship, place, or ministry whatsoever...."

The principle against direct funding with public money is patently violated by the contested use of today's student activity fee. Like today's taxes generally, the fee is Madison's threepence. The University exercises the power of the State to compel a student to pay it, and the use of any part of it for the direct support of religious activity thus strikes at what we have repeatedly held to be the heart of the prohibition on establishment. [Citation of cases omitted.]

The Court, accordingly, has never before upheld direct state funding of the sort of proselytizing published in Wide Awake and, in fact, has categorically condemned state programs directly aiding religious activity. [Citation of cases omitted.]

Even when the Court has upheld aid to an institution performing both secular and sectarian functions, it has always made a searching enquiry to ensure that the institution kept the secular activities separate from its sectarian ones, with any direct aid flowing only to the former and never the latter. [Citation of cases omitted.]

Reasonable minds may differ over whether the Court reached the correct result in each of these cases, but their common principle has never been questioned or repudiated. "Although Establishment Clause jurisprudence is characterized by few absolutes, the Clause does absolutely prohibit government-financed ... indoctrination into the beliefs of a particular religious faith." *[Board of Ed. of Central] School Dist. [No. 1]* v. *Ball* [(1968)].

B

Why does the Court not apply this clear law to these clear facts and conclude, as I do, that the funding scheme here is a clear constitutional violation? The answer must be in part that the Court fails to confront the evidence set out in the preceding section. Throughout its opinion, the Court refers uninformatively to Wide Awake's "Christian viewpoint," or its "religious perspective," and in distinguishing funding of Wide Awake from the funding of a church, the Court maintains that "[Wide Awake] is not a religious institution, at least in the usual sense." The Court does not quote the magazine's adoption of Saint Paul's exhortation to awaken to the nearness of salvation, or any of its articles enjoining readers to accept Jesus Christ, or the religious verses, or the religious textual analyses, or the suggested prayers. And so it is easy for the Court to lose sight of what the University students and the Court of Appeals found so obvious, and to blanch the patently and frankly evangelistic character of the magazine by unrevealing allusions to religious points of view.

Nevertheless, even without the encumbrance of detail from Wide Awake's actual pages, the Court finds something sufficiently religious about the magazine to require examination under the Establishment Clause, and one may therefore ask why the unequivocal prohibition on direct funding does not lead the Court to conclude that funding would be unconstitutional. The answer is that the Court focuses on a subsidiary body of law, which it correctly states but ultimately misapplies. That subsidiary body of law accounts for the Court's substantial attention to the fact that the University's funding scheme is "neutral," in the formal sense that it makes funds available on an evenhanded basis to secular and sectarian applicants alike. While this is indeed true and relevant under our cases, it does not alone satisfy the requirements of the Establishment Clause, as the Court recognizes when it says that evenhandedness is only a "significant factor" in certain Establishment Clause analysis, not a dispositive one.... This recognition reflects the Court's appreciation of two general rules: that whenever affirmative government aid ultimately benefits religion, the Establishment Clause requires some justification beyond evenhandedness on the government's part; and that direct public funding of core sectarian activities, even if accomplished pursuant to an evenhanded program, would be entirely inconsistent with the Establishment Clause and would strike at the very heart of the Clause's protection....

In order to understand how the Court thus begins with sound rules but ends with an unsound result, it is necessary to explore those rules in greater detail than the Court does. As the foregoing quotations from the Court's opinion indicate, the relationship between the prohibition on direct aid and the requirement of evenhandedness when affirmative government aid does result in some benefit to religion reflects the relationship between basic rule and marginal criterion. At the heart of the Establishment Clause stands the prohibition against direct public funding, but that prohibition does not answer the questions that occur at the margins of the Clause's application. Is any government activity that provides any incidental benefit to religion likewise unconstitutional? Would it be wrong to put out fires in burning churches, wrong to pay the bus fares of students on the way to parochial schools, wrong to allow a grantee of special education funds to spend them at a religious college? These are the questions that call for drawing lines, and it is in drawing them that evenhandedness becomes important. However the Court may in the past have phrased its line-drawing test, the question whether such benefits are provided on an evenhanded basis has been relevant, for the question addresses one aspect of the issue whether a law is truly neutral with respect to religion (that is, whether the law either "advance[s] [or] inhibit[s] religion"). In *Widmar* v. *Vincent* (1981), for example, we noted that "[t]he provision of benefits to [a] broad … spectrum of [religious and nonreligious] groups is an important index of secular effect." In the doubtful cases (those not involving direct public funding), where there is initially room for argument about a law's effect, evenhandedness serves to weed out those laws that impermissibly advance religion by channelling aid to it exclusively. Evenhandedness is therefore a prerequisite to further enquiry into the constitutionality of a doubtful law, but evenhandedness goes no further. It does not guarantee success under Establishment Clause scrutiny.

Three cases permitting indirect aid to religion, *Mueller* v. *Allen* (1983), *Witters* v. *Washington Dept. of Services for Blind* (1986), and *Zobrest* v. *Catalina Foothills School Dist.* (1993), are among the latest of those to illustrate this relevance of evenhandedness when advancement is not so obvious as to be patently unconstitutional. Each case involved a program in which benefits given to individuals on a religion-neutral basis ultimately were used by the individuals, in one way or another, to support religious institutions. In each, the fact that aid was distributed generally and on a neutral basis was a necessary condition for upholding the program at issue. But the significance of evenhandedness stopped there. We did not, in any of these cases, hold that satisfying the condition was sufficient, or dispositive. Even more importantly, we never held that evenhandedness might be sufficient to render direct aid to religion constitutional. Quite the contrary. Critical to our decisions in these cases was the fact that the aid was indirect; it reached religious institutions "only as a result of the genuinely independent and private choices of aid recipients." In noting and relying on this particular feature of each of the programs at issue, we in fact reaffirmed the core prohibition on direct funding of religious activities....

Evenhandedness as one element of a permissibly attenuated benefit is, of course, a far cry from evenhandedness as a sufficient condition of constitutionality for direct financial support of religious proselytization, and our cases have unsurprisingly repudiated any such attempt to cut the Establishment Clause down to a mere prohibition against unequal direct aid....

C

Since conformity with the marginal or limiting principle of evenhandedness is insufficient of itself to demonstrate the constitutionality of providing a government benefit that reaches religion, the Court must identify some further element in the funding scheme that does demonstrate its permissibility. For one reason or another, the Court's chosen element appears to be the fact that under the University's Guidelines funds are sent to the printer chosen by Wide Awake, rather than to Wide Awake itself.

1

If the Court's suggestion is that this feature of the funding program brings this case into line with *Witters, Mueller,* and *Zobrest* , the Court has misread those cases, which turned on the fact that the choice to benefit religion was made by a nonreligious third party standing between the government and a religious institution. Here there is no third party standing between the government and the ultimate religious beneficiary to break the circuit by its independent discretion to put state money to religious use. The printer, of course, has no option to take the money and use it to print a secular journal instead of Wide Awake. It only gets the money because of its contract to print a message of religious evangelism at the direction of Wide Awake, and it will receive payment only for doing precisely that. The formalism of distinguishing between payment to Wide Awake so it can pay an approved bill and payment of the approved bill itself cannot be the basis of a decision of Constitutional law. If this indeed were a critical distinction, the Constitution would permit a State to pay all the bills of any religious institution; in fact, despite the Court's purported adherence to the no-direct-funding principle, the State could simply hand out credit cards to religious institutions and honor the monthly statements (so long as someone could devise an evenhanded umbrella to cover the whole scheme). *Witters* and the other cases cannot be distinguished out of existence this way.

2

It is more probable, however, that the Court's reference to the printer goes to a different attempt to justify the payment. On this purported justification, the payment to the printer is significant only as the last step in an argument resting on the assumption that a public university may give a religious group the use of any of its equipment or facilities so long as secular groups are likewise eligible. The Court starts with the cases of *Widmar* v. *Vincent* (1981), *Board of Ed. of Westside Community Schools* v. *Mergens* (1990), and *Lamb's Chapel* v. *Center Moriches Union Free School Dist.* (1993) in which religious groups were held to be entitled to access for speaking in government buildings open generally for that purpose. The Court reasons that the availability of a forum has economic value (the government built and maintained the building, while the speakers saved the rent for a hall); and that economically there is no difference between the University's provision of the value of the room and the value, say, of the University's printing equipment; and that therefore the University must be able to provide the use of the latter. Since it may do that, the argument goes, it would be unduly formalistic to draw the line at paying for an outside printer, who simply does what the magazine's publishers could have done with the University's own printing equipment.

The argument is as unsound as it is simple, and the first of its troubles emerges from an examination of the cases relied upon to support it. The common factual thread running through *Widmar, Mergens,* and *Lamb's Chapel* is that a governmental institution created a limited forum for the use of students in a school or college, or for the public at large, but sought to exclude speakers with religious messages. In each case the restriction was struck down either as an impermissible attempt to regulate the content of speech in an open forum (as in *Widmar* and *Mergens*) or to suppress a particular religious viewpoint (as in *Lamb's Chapel*). In each case, to be sure, the religious speaker's use of the room passed muster as an incident of a plan to facilitate speech generally for a secular purpose, entailing neither secular entanglement with religion nor risk that the religious speech would be taken to be the speech of the government or that the government's endorsement of a religious message would be inferred. But each case drew ultimately on unexceptionable Speech Clause doctrine treating the evangelist, the Salvation Army, the millennialist or the Hare Krishna like any other speaker in a public forum. It was the preservation of free speech on the model of the street corner that supplied the justification going beyond the requirement of evenhandedness.

The Court's claim of support from these forum-access cases is ruled out by the very scope of their holdings. While they do indeed allow a limited benefit to religious speakers, they rest on the recognition that all speakers are entitled to use the street corner (even though the State paves the roads and provides police protection to everyone on the street) and on the analogy between the public street corner and open classroom space.... There is no traditional street corner printing provided by the government on equal terms to all comers, and the forum cases cannot be lifted to a higher plane of generalization without admitting that new economic benefits are being extended directly to religion in clear violation of the principle barring direct aid....

3

It must, indeed, be a recognition of just this point that leads the Court to take a third tack, not in coming up with yet a third attempt at justification within the rules of existing case law, but in recasting the scope of the Establishment Clause in ways that make further affirmative justification unnecessary. JUSTICE O'CONNOR makes a comprehensive analysis of the manner in which the activity fee is assessed and distributed. She concludes that the funding differs so sharply from religious funding out of governmental treasuries generally that it falls outside the Establishment Clause's purview in the absence of a message of religious endorsement (which she finds not to be present). The opinion of the Court concludes more expansively that the activity fee is not a tax, and then proceeds to find the aid permissible on the legal assumption that the bar against direct aid applies only to aid derived from tax revenue. I have already indicated why it is fanciful to treat the fee as anything but a tax, and will not repeat the point again. The novelty of the assumption that the direct aid bar only extends to aid derived from taxation, however, requires some response.

Although it was a taxation scheme that moved Madison to write in the first instance, the Court has never held that government resources obtained without taxation could be used for direct religious support, and our cases on direct government aid have frequently spoken in terms in no way limited to tax revenues....

Allowing non-tax funds to be spent on religion would, in fact, fly in the face of clear principle. Leaving entirely aside the question whether public non-tax revenues could ever be used to finance religion without violating the endorsement test, any such use of them would ignore one of the dual objectives of the Establishment Clause, which was meant not only to protect individuals and their republics from the destructive consequences of mixing government and religion, but to protect religion from a corrupting dependence on support from the Government.... Since the corrupting effect of government support does not turn on whether the Government's own money comes from taxation or gift or the sale of public lands, the Establishment Clause could hardly relax its vigilance simply because tax revenue was not implicated. Accordingly, in the absence of a forthright disavowal, one can only assume that the Court does not mean to eliminate one half of the Establishment Clause's justification.

D

Nothing in the Court's opinion would lead me to end this enquiry into the application of the Establishment Clause any differently from the way I began it. The Court is ordering an instrumentality of the State to support religious evangelism with direct funding. This is a flat violation of the Establishment Clause....

□ □ □

Nos. 94-631, 94-797, and 94-929

Zell Miller, et al., Appellants v. Davida Johnson et al.

Lucious Abrams, Jr., et al., Appellants v. Davida Johnson et al.

United States, Appellant v. Davida Johnson et al.

On appeals from the United States District Court
for the Southern District of Georgia

[June 29, 1995]

JUSTICE KENNEDY delivered the opinion of the Court.

The constitutionality of Georgia's congressional redistricting plan is at issue here. In *Shaw* v. *Reno* (1993), we held that a plaintiff states a claim under the Equal Protection Clause by alleging that a state redistricting plan, on its face, has no rational explanation save as an effort to separate voters on the basis of race. The question we now decide is whether Georgia's new Eleventh District gives rise to a valid equal protection claim under the principles announced in *Shaw*, and, if so, whether it can be sustained nonetheless as narrowly tailored to serve a compelling governmental interest.

I

A

The Equal Protection Clause of the Fourteenth Amendment provides that no State shall "deny to any person within its jurisdiction the equal protection of the laws." U.S. Const., Amdt. 14, §1. Its central mandate is racial neutrality in governmental decisionmaking.... Laws classifying citizens on the basis of race cannot be upheld unless they are narrowly tailored to achieving a compelling state interest.

In *Shaw* v. *Reno,* we recognized that these equal protection principles govern a State's drawing of congressional districts, though, as our cautious approach there discloses, application of these principles to electoral districting is a most delicate task. Our analysis began from the premise that "[l]aws that explicitly distinguish between individuals on racial grounds fall within the core of [the Equal Protection Clause's] prohibition." This prohibition extends not just to explicit racial classifications, but also to laws neutral on their face but " 'unexplainable on grounds other than race.' " Applying this basic Equal Protection analysis in the voting rights context, we held that "redistricting legislation that is so bizarre on its face that it is 'unexplainable on grounds other than race,'... demands the same close scrutiny that we give other state laws that classify citizens by race."

This case requires us to apply the principles articulated in *Shaw* to the most recent congressional redistricting plan enacted by the State of Georgia.

B

In 1965, the Attorney General designated Georgia a covered jurisdiction under §4(b) of the Voting Rights Act, 42 U.S.C. §1973b(b) (Act). In consequence, §5 of the Act requires Georgia to obtain either administrative preclearance by the Attorney General or approval by the United States District Court for the District of Columbia of any change in a "standard, practice, or procedure with respect to voting" made after November 1, 1964. The preclearance mechanism applies to congressional redistricting plans and requires that the proposed change "not have the purpose and will not have the effect of denying or abridging the right to vote on account of race or color."...

Between 1980 and 1990, one of Georgia's 10 congressional districts was a majority-black district, that is, a majority of the district's voters were black. The 1990 Decennial Census indicated that Georgia's population of 6,478,216 persons, 27% of whom are black, entitled it to an additional eleventh congressional seat, prompting Georgia's General Assembly to redraw the State's congressional districts. Both the House and the Senate adopted redistricting guidelines which, among other things, required single-member districts of equal population, contiguous geography, nondilution of minority voting strength, fidelity to precinct lines where possible, and compliance with §§2 and 5 of the Act. Only after these requirements were met did the guidelines permit drafters to consider other ends, such as maintaining the integrity of political subdivisions, preserving the core of existing districts, and avoiding contests between incumbents.

A special session opened in August 1991, and the General Assembly sub-mitted a congressional redistricting plan to the Attorney General for preclear-ance on October 1, 1991. The legislature's plan contained two majority-minor-ity districts, the Fifth and Eleventh, and an additional district, the Second, in which blacks comprised just over 35% of the voting age population. Despite the plan's increase in the number of majority-black districts from one to two and the absence of any evidence of an intent to discriminate against minority vot-ers, the Department of Justice refused preclearance on January 21, 1992. The Department's objection letter noted a concern that Georgia had created only two majority-minority districts, and that the proposed plan did not "recognize" certain minority populations by placing them in a majority-black district.

The General Assembly returned to the drawing board. A new plan was enacted and submitted for preclearance. This second attempt assigned the black population in Central Georgia's Baldwin County to the Eleventh District and increased the black populations in the Eleventh, Fifth and Second Dis-tricts. The Justice Department refused preclearance again, relying on alterna-tive plans proposing three majority-minority districts. One of the alternative schemes relied on by the Department was the so-called "max-black" plan, draft-ed by the American Civil Liberties Union (ACLU) for the General Assembly's black caucus. The key to the ACLU's plan was the "Macon/Savannah trade." The dense black population in the Macon region would be transferred from the Eleventh District to the Second, converting the Second into a majority-black district, and the Eleventh District's loss in black population would be off-set by extending the Eleventh to include the black populations in Savannah. Pointing to the General Assembly's refusal to enact the Macon/Savannah swap into law, the Justice Department concluded that Georgia had "failed to explain adequately" its failure to create a third majority-minority district. The State did not seek a declaratory judgment from the District Court for the District of Columbia.

Twice spurned, the General Assembly set out to create three majority-minority districts to gain preclearance. Using the ACLU's "max-black" plan as its benchmark, the General Assembly enacted a plan that

> "bore all the signs of [the Justice Department's] involvement: The black population of Meriwether County was gouged out of the Third District and attached to the Second District by the narrowest of land bridges; Effingham and Chatham Counties were split to make way for the Savan-nah extension, which itself split the City of Savannah; and the plan as a whole split 26 counties, 23 more than the existing congressional dis-tricts." [Quoting District Court opinion.]

The new plan also enacted the Macon/Savannah swap necessary to create a third majority-black district. The Eleventh District lost the black population of Macon, but picked up Savannah, thereby connecting the black neighborhoods of metropolitan Atlanta and the poor black populace of coastal Chatham Coun-ty, though 260 miles apart in distance and worlds apart in culture. In short, the social, political and economic makeup of the Eleventh District tells a tale of dis-parity, not community.... Georgia's plan included three majority-black districts, though, and received Justice Department preclearance on April 2, 1992.

Elections were held under the new congressional redistricting plan on November 4, 1992, and black candidates were elected to Congress from all three majority-black districts. On January 13, 1994, appellees, five white voters from the Eleventh District, filed this action against various state officials (*Miller* Appellants) in the United States District Court for the Southern District of Georgia. As residents of the challenged Eleventh District, all appellees had standing. Their suit alleged that Georgia's Eleventh District was a racial gerry-mander and so a violation of the Equal Protection Clause as interpreted in *Shaw* v. *Reno.* A three-judge court was convened pursuant to 28 U.S.C. §2284, and the United States and a number of Georgia residents intervened in support of the defendant-state officials.

A majority of the District Court panel agreed that the Eleventh District was invalid under *Shaw,* with one judge dissenting. (SD Ga. 1994). After sharp criticism of the Justice Department for its use of partisan advocates in its deal-ings with state officials and for its close cooperation with the ACLU's vigorous advocacy of minority district maximization, the majority turned to a careful interpretation of our opinion in *Shaw.* It read *Shaw* to require strict scrutiny whenever race is the "overriding, predominant force" in the redistricting process. Citing much evidence of the legislature's purpose and intent in cre-ating the final plan, as well as the irregular shape of the District (in particular several appendages drawn for the obvious purpose of putting black popula-tions into the District), the court found that race was the overriding and pre-dominant force in the districting determination. The court proceeded to apply strict scrutiny. Though rejecting proportional representation as a com-pelling interest, it was willing to assume that compliance with the Voting Rights Act would be a compelling interest. As to the latter, however, the court found that the Act did not require three majority-black districts, and that Georgia's plan for that reason was not narrowly tailored to the goal of complying with the Act.

Appellants filed notices of appeal and requested a stay of the District Court's judgment, which we granted pending the filing and disposition of the appeals in this case (1994). We later noted probable jurisdiction (1995).

II

A

Finding that the "evidence of the General Assembly's intent to racially ger-rymander the Eleventh District is overwhelming, and practically stipulated by the parties involved," the District Court held that race was the predominant, overriding factor in drawing the Eleventh District. Appellants do not take issue with the court's factual finding of this racial motivation. Rather, they contend that evidence of a legislature's deliberate classification of voters on the basis of race cannot alone suffice to state a claim under *Shaw.* They argue that, regard-less of the legislature's purposes, a plaintiff must demonstrate that a district's shape is so bizarre that it is unexplainable other than on the basis of race, and that appellees failed to make that showing here. Appellants' conception of the constitutional violation misapprehends our holding in *Shaw* and the Equal Pro-tection precedent upon which *Shaw* relied.

Shaw recognized a claim "analytically distinct" from a vote dilution claim. Whereas a vote dilution claim alleges that the State has enacted a particular voting scheme as a purposeful device "to minimize or cancel out the voting potential of racial or ethnic minorities," an action disadvantaging voters of a particular race, the essence of the equal protection claim recognized in *Shaw* is that the State has used race as a basis for separating voters into districts. Just as the State may not, absent extraordinary justification, segregate citizens on the basis of race in its public parks, buses, golf courses, beaches, and schools, so did we recognize in *Shaw* that it may not separate its citizens into different voting districts on the basis of race.... When the State assigns voters on the basis of race, it engages in the offensive and demeaning assumption that voters of a particular race, because of their race, "think alike, share the same political interests, and will prefer the same candidates at the polls." Race-based assignments "embody stereotypes that treat individuals as the product of their race, evaluating their thoughts and efforts—their very worth as citizens—according to a criterion barred to the Government by history and the Constitution."... They also cause society serious harm. As we concluded in *Shaw*:

> "Racial classifications with respect to voting carry particular dangers. Racial gerrymandering, even for remedial purposes, may balkanize us into competing racial factions; it threatens to carry us further from the goal of a political system in which race no longer matters—a goal that the Fourteenth and Fifteenth Amendments embody, and to which the Nation continues to aspire. It is for these reasons that race-based districting by our state legislatures demands close judicial scrutiny."

Our observation in *Shaw* of the consequences of racial stereotyping was not meant to suggest that a district must be bizarre on its face before there is a constitutional violation. Nor was our conclusion in *Shaw* that in certain instances a district's appearance (or, to be more precise, its appearance in combination with certain demographic evidence) can give rise to an equal protection claim, a holding that bizarreness was a threshold showing, as appellants believe it to be. Our circumspect approach and narrow holding in *Shaw* did not erect an artificial rule barring accepted equal protection analysis in other redistricting cases. Shape is relevant not because bizarreness is a necessary element of the constitutional wrong or a threshold requirement of proof, but because it may be persuasive circumstantial evidence that race for its own sake, and not other districting principles, was the legislature's dominant and controlling rationale in drawing its district lines. The logical implication, as courts applying *Shaw* have recognized, is that parties may rely on evidence other than bizarreness to establish race-based districting.

Our reasoning in *Shaw* compels this conclusion. We recognized in *Shaw* that, outside the districting context, statutes are subject to strict scrutiny under the Equal Protection Clause not just when they contain express racial classifications, but also when, though race neutral on their face, they are motivated by a racial purpose or object....

Shaw applied these same principles to redistricting. "In some exceptional cases, a reapportionment plan may be so highly irregular that, on its face, it rationally cannot be understood as anything other than an effort to 'segregat[e]

... voters on the basis of race." In other cases, where the district is not so bizarre on its face that it discloses a racial design, the proof will be more "difficul[t]." Although it was not necessary in *Shaw* to consider further the proof required in these more difficult cases, the logical import of our reasoning is that evidence other than a district's bizarre shape can be used to support the claim.

Appellants and some of their *amici* argue that the Equal Protection Clause's general proscription on race-based decisionmaking does not obtain in the districting context because redistricting by definition involves racial considerations. Underlying their argument are the very stereotypical assumptions the Equal Protection Clause forbids. It is true that redistricting in most cases will implicate a political calculus in which various interests compete for recognition, but it does not follow from this that individuals of the same race share a single political interest. The view that they do is "based on the demeaning notion that members of the defined racial groups ascribe to certain 'minority views' that must be different from those of other citizens," *Metro Broadcasting* (KENNEDY, J., dissenting), the precise use of race as a proxy the Constitution prohibits. Nor can the argument that districting cases are excepted from standard equal protection precepts be resuscitated by *United Jewish Organizations of Williamsburgh, Inc.* v. *Carey* (1977), where the Court addressed a claim that New York violated the Constitution by splitting a Hasidic Jewish community in order to include additional majority-minority districts. As we explained in *Shaw*, a majority of the Justices in *UJO* construed the complaint as stating a vote dilution claim, so their analysis does not apply to a claim that the State has separated voters on the basis of race. To the extent any of the opinions in that "highly fractured decision" can be interpreted as suggesting that a State's assignment of voters on the basis of race would be subject to anything but our strictest scrutiny, those views ought not be deemed controlling.

In sum, we make clear that parties alleging that a State has assigned voters on the basis of race are neither confined in their proof to evidence regarding the district's geometry and makeup nor required to make a threshold showing of bizarreness. Today's case requires us further to consider the requirements of the proof necessary to sustain this equal protection challenge.

B

Federal court review of districting legislation represents a serious intrusion on the most vital of local functions. It is well settled that "reapportionment is primarily the duty and responsibility of the State." Electoral districting is a most difficult subject for legislatures, and so the States must have discretion to exercise the political judgment necessary to balance competing interests. Although race-based decisionmaking is inherently suspect, until a claimant makes a showing sufficient to support that allegation the good faith of a state legislature must be presumed. The courts, in assessing the sufficiency of a challenge to a districting plan, must be sensitive to the complex interplay of forces that enter a legislature's redistricting calculus. Redistricting legislatures will, for example, almost always be aware of racial demographics; but it does not follow that race predominates in the redistricting process.... The distinction between being aware of racial considerations and being motivated by them may be difficult to make. This evidentiary difficulty, together with the sensitive nature of redistricting and the presumption of good faith that must be accorded legislative enactments, requires courts to exercise extraordinary caution in adjudicating claims that a state has drawn district lines on the basis of race. The plaintiff's burden is to show, either through circumstantial evidence of a district's shape and demographics or more direct evidence going to legislative purpose, that race was the predominant factor motivating the legislature's decision to place a significant number of voters within or without a particular district. To make this showing, a plaintiff must prove that the legislature subordinated traditional race-neutral districting principles, including but not limited to compactness, contiguity, respect for political subdivisions or communities defined by actual shared interests, to racial considerations. Where these or other race-neutral considerations are the basis for redistricting legislation, and are not subordinated to race, a state can "defeat a claim that a district has been gerrymandered on racial lines." These principles inform the plaintiff's burden of proof at trial. Of course, courts must also recognize these principles, and the intrusive potential of judicial intervention into the legislative realm, when assessing under the Federal Rules of Civil Procedure the adequacy of a plaintiff's showing at the various stages of litigation and determining whether to permit discovery or trial to proceed.

In our view, the District Court applied the correct analysis, and its finding that race was the predominant factor motivating the drawing of the Eleventh District was not clearly erroneous. The court found it was "exceedingly obvious" from the shape of the Eleventh District, together with the relevant racial demographics, that the drawing of narrow land bridges to incorporate within the District outlying appendages containing nearly 80% of the district's total black population was a deliberate attempt to bring black populations into the district. Although by comparison with other districts the geometric shape of the Eleventh District may not seem bizarre on its face, when its shape is considered in conjunction with its racial and population densities, the story of racial gerrymandering seen by the District Court becomes much clearer. Although this evidence is quite compelling, we need not determine whether it was, standing alone, sufficient to establish a *Shaw* claim that the Eleventh District is unexplainable other than by race. The District Court had before it considerable additional evidence showing that the General Assembly was motivated by a predominant, overriding desire to assign black populations to the Eleventh District and thereby permit the creation of a third majority-black district in the Second.

The court found that "it became obvious," both from the Justice Department's objection letters and the three preclearance rounds in general, "that [the Justice Department] would accept nothing less than abject surrender to its maximization agenda."... It further found that the General Assembly acquiesced and as a consequence was driven by its overriding desire to comply with the Department's maximization demands. The court supported its conclusion not just with the testimony of Linda Meggers, the operator of "Herschel," Georgia's reapportionment computer, and "probably the most knowledgeable person available on the subject of Georgian redistricting," but also with the State's own concessions. The State admitted that it " 'would not have added those portions of Effingham and Chatham Counties that are now in the [far southeastern extension of the] present Eleventh Congressional District but for the need to include additional black population in that district to offset the loss of black population caused by the shift of predominantly black portions of Bibb County in the Second Congressional District which occurred in response to the Department of Justice's March 20th, 1992, objection letter.' " It conceded further that "[t]o the extent that precincts in the Eleventh Congressional District are split, a substantial reason for their being split was the objective of increasing the black population of that district." And in its brief to this Court, the State concedes that "[i]t is undisputed that Georgia's eleventh is the product of a desire by the General Assembly to create a majority black district." Hence the trial court had little difficulty concluding that the Justice Department "spent months demanding purely race-based revisions to Georgia's redistricting plans, and that Georgia spent months attempting to comply." On this record, we fail to see how the District Court could have reached any conclusion other than that race was the predominant factor in drawing Georgia's Eleventh District; and in any event we conclude the court's finding is not clearly erroneous....

In light of its well-supported finding, the District Court was justified in rejecting the various alternative explanations offered for the District. Although a legislature's compliance with "traditional districting principles such as compactness, contiguity, and respect for political subdivisions" may well suffice to refute a claim of racial gerrymandering, appellants cannot make such a refutation where, as here, those factors were subordinated to racial objectives. Georgia's Attorney General objected to the Justice Department's demand for three majority-black districts on the ground that to do so the State would have to "violate all reasonable standards of compactness and contiguity." This statement from a state official is powerful evidence that the legislature subordinated traditional districting principles to race when it ultimately enacted a plan creating three majority-black districts, and justified the District Court's finding that "every [objective districting] factor that could realistically be subordinated to racial tinkering in fact suffered that fate."...

Nor can the State's districting legislation be rescued by mere recitation of purported communities of interest. The evidence was compelling "that there are no tangible 'communities of interest' spanning the hundreds of miles of the Eleventh District." A comprehensive report demonstrated the fractured political, social, and economic interests within the Eleventh District's black population. It is apparent that it was not alleged shared interests but rather the object of maximizing the District's black population and obtaining Justice Department approval that in fact explained the General Assembly's actions. A State is free to recognize communities that have a particular racial makeup, provided its action is directed toward some common thread of relevant interests.... But where the State assumes from a group of voters' race that they "think alike, share the same political interests, and will prefer the same candidates at the polls," it engages in racial stereotyping at odds with equal protection mandates....

Race was, as the District Court found, the predominant, overriding factor explaining the General Assembly's decision to attach to the Eleventh District various appendages containing dense majority-black populations. As a result, Georgia's congressional redistricting plan cannot be upheld unless it satisfies strict scrutiny, our most rigorous and exacting standard of constitutional review.

III

To satisfy strict scrutiny, the State must demonstrate that its districting legislation is narrowly tailored to achieve a compelling interest. There is a "significant state interest in eradicating the effects of past racial discrimination." [Citing *Shaw.*] The State does not argue, however, that it created the Eleventh District to remedy past discrimination, and with good reason: there is little doubt that the State's true interest in designing the Eleventh District was creating a third majority-black district to satisfy the Justice Department's preclearance demands.... Whether or not in some cases compliance with the Voting Rights Act, standing alone, can provide a compelling interest independent of any interest in remedying past discrimination, it cannot do so here. As we suggested in *Shaw*, compliance with federal antidiscrimination laws cannot justify race-based districting where the challenged district was not reasonably necessary under a constitutional reading and application of those laws. The congressional plan challenged here was not required by the Voting Rights Act under a correct reading of the statute.

The Justice Department refused to preclear both of Georgia's first two submitted redistricting plans. The District Court found that the Justice Department had adopted a "black-maximization" policy under §5, and that it was clear from its objection letters that the Department would not grant preclearance until the State made the "Macon/Savannah trade" and created a third majority-black district. It is, therefore, safe to say that the congressional plan enacted in the end was required in order to obtain preclearance. It does not follow, however, that the plan was required by the substantive provisions of the Voting Rights Act.

We do not accept the contention that the State has a compelling interest in complying with whatever preclearance mandates the Justice Department issues. When a state governmental entity seeks to justify race-based remedies to cure the effects of past discrimination, we do not accept the government's mere assertion that the remedial action is required. Rather, we insist on a strong basis in evidence of the harm being remedied.... Our presumptive skepticism of all racial classifications prohibits us as well from accepting on its face the Justice Department's conclusion that racial districting is necessary under the Voting Rights Act. Where a State relies on the Department's determination that race-based districting is necessary to comply with the Voting Rights Act, the judiciary retains an independent obligation in adjudicating consequent equal protection challenges to ensure that the State's actions are narrowly tailored to achieve a compelling interest....

For the same reasons, we think it inappropriate for a court engaged in constitutional scrutiny to accord deference to the Justice Department's interpretation of the Act. Although we have deferred to the Department's interpretation in certain statutory cases, we have rejected agency interpretations to which we would otherwise defer where they raise serious constitutional questions. When the Justice Department's interpretation of the Act compels race-based districting, it by definition raises a serious constitutional question,... and should not receive deference.

Georgia's drawing of the Eleventh District was not required under the Act because there was no reasonable basis to believe that Georgia's earlier enacted plans violated §5. Wherever a plan is "ameliorative," a term we have used to describe plans increasing the number of majority-minority districts, it "cannot violate §5 unless the new apportionment itself so discriminates on the basis of race or color as to violate the Constitution." Georgia's first and second proposed plans increased the number of majority-black districts from 1 out of 10 (10%) to 2 out of 11 (18.18%). These plans were "ameliorative" and could not have violated §5's non-retrogression principle. Acknowledging as much, the United States now relies on the fact that the Justice Department may object to a state proposal either on the ground that it has a prohibited purpose or a prohibited effect. The Government justifies its preclearance objections on the ground that the submitted plans violated §5's purpose element. The key to the Government's position ... is and always has been that Georgia failed to proffer a nondiscriminatory purpose for its refusal in the first two submissions to take the steps necessary to create a third majority-minority district.

The Government's position is insupportable.... Although it is true we have held that the State has the burden to prove a nondiscriminatory purpose under §5, Georgia's Attorney General provided a detailed explanation for the State's initial decision not to enact the max-black plan. The District Court accepted this explanation and found an absence of any discriminatory intent. The State's policy of adhering to other districting principles instead of creating as many majority-minority districts as possible does not support an inference that the plan "so discriminates on the basis of race or color as to violate the Constitution," and thus cannot provide any basis under §5 for the Justice Department's objection.

Instead of grounding its objections on evidence of a discriminatory purpose, it would appear the Government was driven by its policy of maximizing majority-black districts. Although the Government now disavows having had that policy, and seems to concede its impropriety, the District Court's well-documented factual finding was that the Department did adopt a maximization policy and followed it in objecting to Georgia's first two plans.... In utilizing §5 to require States to create majority-minority districts wherever possible, the Department of Justice expanded its authority under the statute beyond what Congress intended and we have upheld.

IV

The Voting Rights Act, and its grant of authority to the federal courts to uncover official efforts to abridge minorities' right to vote, has been of vital importance in eradicating invidious discrimination from the electoral process and enhancing the legitimacy of our political institutions. Only if our political system and our society cleanse themselves of that discrimination will all members of the polity share an equal opportunity to gain public office regardless of race. As a Nation we share both the obligation and the aspiration of working toward this end. The end is neither assured nor well served, however, by carving electorates into racial blocs. "If our society is to continue to progress as a multiracial democracy, it must recognize that the automatic invocation of race stereotypes retards that progress and causes continued hurt and injury." *Edmonson* v. *Leesville Concrete Co.* (1991). It takes a shortsighted and unauthorized view of the Voting Rights Act to invoke that statute, which has played a decisive role in redressing some of our worst forms of discrimination, to demand the very racial stereotyping the Fourteenth Amendment forbids.

* * *

The judgment of the District Court is affirmed, and the case is remanded for further proceedings consistent with this decision.

It is so ordered.

JUSTICE O'CONNOR, concurring.

I understand the threshold standard the Court adopts—"that the legislature subordinated traditional race-neutral districting principles ... to racial considerations"—to be a demanding one. To invoke strict scrutiny, a plaintiff must show that the State has relied on race in substantial disregard of customary and traditional districting practices. Those practices provide a crucial frame of reference and therefore constitute a significant governing principle in cases of this kind. The standard would be no different if a legislature had drawn the boundaries to favor some other ethnic group; certainly the standard does not treat efforts to create majority-minority districts *less* favorably than similar efforts on behalf of other groups. Indeed, the driving force behind the adoption of the Fourteenth Amendment was the desire to end legal discrimination against blacks.

Application of the Court's standard does not throw into doubt the vast majority of the Nation's 435 congressional districts, where presumably the States have drawn the boundaries in accordance with their customary districting principles. That is so even though race may well have been considered in the redistricting process. But application of the Court's standard helps achieve *Shaw's* basic objective of making extreme instances of gerrymandering subject to meaningful judicial review. I therefore join the Court's opinion.

JUSTICE STEVENS, dissenting.

JUSTICE GINSBURG has explained why the District Court's opinion on the merits was erroneous and why this Court's law-changing decision will breed unproductive litigation. I join her excellent opinion without reservation. I add these comments because I believe the respondents in these cases, like the respondents in *United States* v. *Hays* [1995], have not suffered any legally cognizable injury.

In *Shaw* v. *Reno* (1993), the Court crafted a new cause of action with two novel, troubling features. First, the Court misapplied the term "gerrymander," previously used to describe grotesque line-drawing by a dominant group to maintain or enhance its political power at a minority's expense, to condemn the efforts of a majority (whites) to share its power with a minority (African Americans). Second, the Court dispensed with its previous insistence in vote dilution cases on a showing of injury to an identifiable group of voters, but it failed to explain adequately what showing a plaintiff must make to establish standing to litigate the newly minted *Shaw* claim. Neither in *Shaw* itself nor in the cases decided today has the Court coherently articulated what injury this cause of action is designed to redress. Because respondents have alleged no legally cognizable injury, they lack standing, and these cases should be dismissed....

JUSTICE GINSBURG, with whom JUSTICES STEVENS and BREYER join, and with whom JUSTICE SOUTER joins except as to Part III-B, dissenting.

Legislative districting is highly political business. This Court has generally respected the competence of state legislatures to attend to the task. When race is the issue, however, we have recognized the need for judicial intervention to prevent dilution of minority voting strength. Generations of rank discrimination against African-Americans, as citizens and voters, account for that surveillance.

Two Terms ago, in *Shaw* v. *Reno* (1993), this Court took up a claim "analytically distinct" from a vote dilution claim. *Shaw* authorized judicial intervention in "extremely irregular" apportionments, in which the legislature cast aside traditional districting practices to consider race alone—in the *Shaw* case, to create a district in North Carolina in which African-Americans would compose a majority of the voters.

Today the Court expands the judicial role, announcing that federal courts are to undertake searching review of any district with contours "predominantly motivated" by race: "strict scrutiny" will be triggered not only when traditional districting practices are abandoned, but also when those practices are "subordinated to"—given less weight than—race. Applying this new "race-as-predominant-factor" standard, the Court invalidates Georgia's districting plan even though Georgia's Eleventh District, the focus of today's dispute, bears the imprint of familiar districting practices. Because I do not endorse the Court's new standard and would not upset Georgia's plan, I dissent.

I

At the outset, it may be useful to note points on which the Court does not divide. First, we agree that federalism and the slim judicial competence to draw district lines weigh heavily against judicial intervention in apportionment decisions; as a rule, the task should remain within the domain of state legislatures.... Second, for most of our Nation's history, the franchise has not been enjoyed equally by black citizens and white voters. To redress past wrongs and to avert any recurrence of exclusion of blacks from political processes, federal courts now respond to Equal Protection Clause and Voting Rights Act complaints of state action that dilutes minority voting strength. Third, to meet statutory requirements, state legislatures must sometimes consider race as a factor highly relevant to the drawing of district lines.... Finally, state legislatures may recognize communities that have a particular racial or ethnic makeup, even in the absence of any compulsion to do so, in order to account for interests common to or shared by the persons grouped together....

Therefore, the fact that the Georgia General Assembly took account of race in drawing district lines—a fact not in dispute—does not render the State's plan invalid. To offend the Equal Protection Clause, all agree, the legislature had to do more than consider race. How much more, is the issue that divides the Court today.

A

... District lines are drawn to accommodate a myriad of factors—geographic, economic, historical, and political—and state legislatures, as arenas of compromise and electoral accountability, are best positioned to mediate competing claims; courts, with a mandate to adjudicate, are ill equipped for the task.

B

Federal courts have ventured into the political thicket of apportionment when necessary to secure to members of racial minorities equal voting rights — rights denied in many States, including Georgia, until not long ago.

The Fifteenth Amendment, ratified in 1870, declares that the right to vote "shall not be denied ... by any State on account of race." That declaration, for generations, was often honored in the breach; it was greeted by a near century of "unremitting and ingenious defiance" in several States, including Georgia. After a brief interlude of black suffrage enforced by federal troops but accompanied by rampant violence against blacks, Georgia held a constitutional convention in 1877. Its purpose, according to the convention's leader, was to " 'fix it so that the people shall rule and the Negro shall never be heard from.'" In pursuit of this objective, Georgia enacted a cumulative poll tax, requiring voters to show they had paid past as well as current poll taxes; one historian described this tax as the "most effective bar to Negro suffrage ever devised."

In 1890, the Georgia General Assembly authorized "white primaries"; keeping blacks out of the Democratic primary effectively excluded them from Georgia's political life, for victory in the Democratic primary was tantamount to election. Early in this century, Georgia Governor Hoke Smith persuaded the legislature to pass the "Disenfranchisement Act of 1908"; true to its title, this measure added various property, "good character," and literacy requirements that, as administered, served to keep blacks from voting. The result, as one commentator observed 25 years later, was an " 'almost absolute exclusion of the Negro voice in state and federal elections.' "

Faced with a political situation scarcely open to self-correction — disenfranchised blacks had no electoral influence, hence no muscle to lobby the legislature for change — the Court intervened. It invalidated white primaries, see *Smith* v. *Allwright* (1944), and other burdens on minority voting. See, *e.g.*, *Schnell* v. *Davis* (1949) *(per curiam)* (discriminatory application of voting tests); *Lane* v. *Wilson* (1939) (procedural hurdles); *Guinn* v. *United States* (1915) (grandfather clauses).

It was against this backdrop that the Court, construing the Equal Protection Clause, undertook to ensure that apportionment plans do not dilute minority voting strength. By enacting the Voting Rights Act of 1965, Congress heightened federal judicial involvement in apportionment, and also fashioned a role for the Attorney General. Section 2 creates a federal right of action to challenge vote dilution. Section 5 requires States with a history of discrimination to preclear any changes in voting practices with either a federal court (a three-judge United States District Court for the District of Columbia) or the Attorney General.

These Court decisions and congressional directions significantly reduced voting discrimination against minorities. In the 1972 election, Georgia gained its first black Member of Congress since Reconstruction, and the 1981 apportionment created the State's first majority-minority district. This voting district, however, was not gained easily. Georgia created it only after the United States

District Court for the District of Columbia refused to preclear a predecessor apportionment plan that included no such district—an omission due in part to the influence of Joe Mack Wilson, then Chairman of the Georgia House Reapportionment Committee. As Wilson put it only 14 years ago, " 'I don't want to draw nigger districts.' " *Busbee* v. *Smith* (DC 1982).

II

A

Before *Shaw* v. *Reno* (1993), this Court invoked the Equal Protection Clause to justify intervention in the quintessentially political task of legislative districting in two circumstances: to enforce the one-person-one-vote requirement and to prevent dilution of a minority group's voting strength.

In *Shaw*, the Court recognized a third basis for an equal protection challenge to a State's apportionment plan. The Court wrote cautiously, emphasizing that judicial intervention is exceptional: "Strict [judicial] scrutiny" is in order, the Court declared, if a district is "so extremely irregular on its face that it rationally can be viewed only as an effort to segregate the races for purposes of voting."...

The problem in *Shaw* was not the plan architects' consideration of race as relevant in redistricting. Rather, in the Court's estimation, it was the virtual exclusion of other factors from the calculus. Traditional districting practices were cast aside, the Court concluded, with race alone steering placement of district lines.

B

The record before us does not show that race similarly overwhelmed traditional districting practices in Georgia. Although the Georgia General Assembly prominently considered race in shaping the Eleventh District, race did not crowd out all other factors....

In contrast to the snake-like North Carolina district inspected in *Shaw*, Georgia's Eleventh District is hardly "bizarre," "extremely irregular," or "irrational on its face." Instead, the Eleventh District's design reflects significant consideration of "traditional districting factors (such as keeping political subdivisions intact) and the usual political process of compromise and trades for a variety of nonracial reasons."... The District covers a core area in central and eastern Georgia, and its total land area of 6,780 square miles is about average for the State. The border of the Eleventh District runs 1,184 miles, in line with Georgia's Second District, which has a 1,243-mile border, and the State's Eighth District, with a border running 1,155 miles.

Nor does the Eleventh District disrespect the boundaries of political subdivisions. Of the 22 counties in the District, 14 are intact and 8 are divided. That puts the Eleventh District at about the state average in divided counties. By contrast, of the Sixth District's 5 counties, none are intact, and of the Fourth District's 4 counties, just 1 is intact. Seventy-one percent of the Eleventh District's boundaries track the borders of political subdivisions. Of the State's 11 districts, 5 score worse than the Eleventh District on this criterion, and 5 score better. Eighty-three percent of the Eleventh District's geographic area is composed of intact counties, above average for the State's congressional districts. And notably, the Eleventh District's boundaries largely follow precinct lines.

Evidence at trial similarly shows that considerations other than race went into determining the Eleventh District's boundaries. For a "political reason"— to accommodate the request of an incumbent State Senator regarding the placement of the precinct in which his son lived— the DeKalb County portion of the Eleventh District was drawn to include a particular (largely white) precinct. The corridor through Effingham County was substantially narrowed at the request of a (white) State Representative. In Chatham County, the District was trimmed to exclude a heavily black community in Garden City because a State Representative wanted to keep the city intact inside the neighboring First District. The Savannah extension was configured by "the narrowest means possible" to avoid splitting the city of Port Wentworth.

Georgia's Eleventh District, in sum, is not an outlier district shaped without reference to familiar districting techniques. Tellingly, the District that the Court's decision today unsettles is not among those on a statistically calculated list of the 28 most bizarre districts in the United States, a study prepared in the wake of our decision in *Shaw*.

C

The Court suggests that it was not Georgia's legislature, but the U.S. Department of Justice, that effectively drew the lines, and that Department officers did so with nothing but race in mind. Yet the "Max-Black" plan advanced by the Attorney General was not the plan passed by the Georgia General Assembly....

And although the Attorney General refused preclearance to the first two plans approved by Georgia's legislature, the State was not thereby disarmed; Georgia could have demanded relief from the Department's objections by instituting a civil action in the United States District Court for the District of Columbia, with ultimate review in this Court. Instead of pursuing that avenue, the State chose to adopt the plan here in controversy— a plan the State forcefully defends before us. We should respect Georgia's choice by taking its position on brief as genuine.

D

Along with attention to size, shape, and political subdivisions, the Court recognizes as an appropriate districting principle, "respect for ... communities defined by actual shared interests." The Court finds no community here, however, because a report in the record showed "fractured political, social, and economic interests within the Eleventh District's black population."

But ethnicity itself can tie people together, as volumes of social science literature have documented— even people with divergent economic interests. For this reason, ethnicity is a significant force in political life....

To accommodate the reality of ethnic bonds, legislatures have long drawn voting districts along ethnic lines. Our Nation's cities are full of districts identified by their ethnic character—Chinese, Irish, Italian, Jewish, Polish, Russian, for example.... The creation of ethnic districts reflecting felt identity is not ordinarily viewed as offensive or demeaning to those included in the delineation.

III

To separate permissible and impermissible use of race in legislative apportionment, the Court orders strict scrutiny for districting plans "predominantly motivated" by race. No longer can a State avoid judicial oversight by giving— as in this case—genuine and measurable consideration to traditional districting practices. Instead, a federal case can be mounted whenever plaintiffs plausibly allege that other factors carried less weight than race. This invitation to litigate against the State seems to me neither necessary nor proper.

A

The Court derives its test from diverse opinions on the relevance of race in contexts distinctly unlike apportionment. The controlling idea, the Court says, is " 'the simple command [at the heart of the Constitution's guarantee of equal protection] that the Government must treat citizens as individuals, not as simply components of a racial, religious, sexual or national class.'"...

In adopting districting plans, however, States do not treat people as individuals. Apportionment schemes, by their very nature, assemble people in groups....

That ethnicity defines some of these groups is a political reality. Until now, no constitutional infirmity has been seen in districting Irish or Italian voters together, for example, so long as the delineation does not abandon familiar apportionment practices. If Chinese-Americans and Russian-Americans may seek and secure group recognition in the delineation of voting districts, then African-Americans should not be dissimilarly treated....

B

Under the Court's approach, judicial review of the same intensity, *i.e.*, strict scrutiny, is in order once it is determined that an apportionment is predominantly motivated by race. It matters not at all, in this new regime, whether the apportionment dilutes or enhances minority voting strength....

Special circumstances justify vigilant judicial inspection to protect minority voters—circumstances that do not apply to majority voters. A history of exclusion from state politics left racial minorities without clout to extract provisions for fair representation in the lawmaking forum. The equal protection rights of minority voters thus could have remained unrealized absent the Judiciary's close surveillance.... The majority, by definition, encounters no such blockage. White voters in Georgia do not lack means to exert strong pressure on their state legislators. The force of their numbers is itself a powerful determiner of what the legislature will do that does not coincide with perceived majority interests.

State legislatures like Georgia's today operate under federal constraints imposed by the Voting Rights Act—constraints justified by history and designed by Congress to make once-subordinated people free and equal citizens. But these federal constraints do not leave majority voters in need of extraordinary judicial solicitude. The Attorney General, who administers the Voting Rights Act's preclearance requirements, is herself a political actor. She has a duty to enforce the law Congress passed, and she is no doubt aware of the political cost of venturing too far to the detriment of majority voters. Majority voters, furthermore, can press the State to seek judicial review if the Attorney General refuses to preclear a plan that the voters favor. Finally, the Act is itself a political measure, subject to modification in the political process.

C

The Court's disposition renders redistricting perilous work for state legislatures. Statutory mandates and political realities may require States to consider race when drawing district lines. But today's decision is a counterforce; it opens the way for federal litigation if "traditional ... districting principles" arguably were accorded less weight than race. Genuine attention to traditional districting practices and avoidance of bizarre configurations seemed, under *Shaw*, to provide a safe harbor.... In view of today's decision, that is no longer the case.

Only after litigation—under either the Voting Rights Act, the Court's new *Miller* standard, or both—will States now be assured that plans conscious of race are safe. Federal judges in large numbers may be drawn into the fray. This enlargement of the judicial role is unwarranted. The reapportionment plan that resulted from Georgia's political process merited this Court's approbation, not its condemnation. Accordingly, I dissent.

□ □ □

No. 94-780

Capitol Square Review and Advisory Board, et al., Petitioners v. Vincent J. Pinette, Donnie A. Carr and Knights of the Ku Klux Klan

On writ of certiorari to the United States Court of Appeals for the Sixth Circuit

[June 29, 1995]

JUSTICE SCALIA announced the judgment of the Court and delivered the opinion of the Court with respect to Parts I, II, and III, and an opinion with respect to Part IV, in which the CHIEF JUSTICE, JUSTICE KENNEDY and JUSTICE THOMAS join.

The Establishment Clause of the First Amendment, made binding upon the States through the Fourteenth Amendment, provides that government "shall make no law respecting an establishment of religion." The question in this case is whether a State violates the Establishment Clause when, pursuant to a religiously neutral state policy, it permits a private party to display an unattended religious symbol in a traditional public forum located next to its seat of government.

I

Capitol Square is a 10-acre, state-owned plaza surrounding the Statehouse in Columbus, Ohio. For over a century the square has been used for public speeches, gatherings, and festivals advocating and celebrating a variety of causes, both secular and religious. Ohio Admin. Code Ann. §128-4-02(A) (1994) makes the square available "for use by the public ... for free discussion of public questions, or for activities of a broad public purpose," and Ohio Rev. Code Ann. §105.41 (1994) gives the Capitol Square Review and Advisory Board responsibility for regulating public access. To use the square, a group must simply fill out an official application form and meet several criteria, which concern primarily safety, sanitation, and non-interference with other uses of the square, and which are neutral as to the speech content of the proposed event.

It has been the Board's policy "to allow a broad range of speakers and other gatherings of people to conduct events on the Capitol Square." Such diverse groups as homosexual rights organizations, the Ku Klux Klan and the United Way have held rallies. The Board has also permitted a variety of unattended displays on Capitol Square: a State-sponsored lighted tree during the Christmas season, a privately-sponsored menorah during Chanukah, a display showing the progress of a United Way fundraising campaign, and booths and exhibits during an arts festival. Although there was some dispute in this litigation regarding the frequency of unattended displays, the District Court found, with ample justification, that there was no policy against them.

In November 1993, after reversing an initial decision to ban unattended holiday displays from the square during December 1993, the Board authorized the State to put up its annual Christmas tree. On November 29, 1993, the Board granted a rabbi's application to erect a menorah. That same day, the Board received an application from respondent Donnie Carr, an officer of the Ohio Ku Klux Klan, to place a cross on the square from December 8, 1993, to December 24, 1993. The Board denied that application on December 3, informing the Klan by letter that the decision to deny "was made upon the advice of counsel, in a good faith attempt to comply with the Ohio and United States Constitutions, as they have been interpreted in relevant decisions by the Federal and State Courts."

Two weeks later, having been unsuccessful in its effort to obtain administrative relief from the Board's decision, the Ohio Klan, through its leader Vincent Pinette, filed the present suit in the United States District Court for the Southern District of Ohio, seeking an injunction requiring the Board to issue the requested permit. The Board defended on the ground that the permit would violate the Establishment Clause. The District Court determined that Capitol Square was a traditional public forum open to all without any policy against free-standing displays; that the Klan's cross was entirely private expression entitled to full First Amendment protection; and that the Board had failed to show that the display of the cross could reasonably be construed as endorsement of Christianity by the State. The District Court issued the injunction and, after the Board's application for an emergency stay was denied (1993) (STEVENS, J., in chambers), the Board permitted the Klan to erect its cross. The Board then received, and granted, several additional applications to erect crosses on Capitol Square during December 1993 and January 1994.

On appeal by the Board, the United States Court of Appeals for the Sixth Circuit affirmed the District Court's judgment (1994). That decision agrees with a ruling by the Eleventh Circuit, *Chabad-Lubavitch v. Miller* (1993), but disagrees with decisions of the Second and Fourth Circuits, *Chabad-Lubavitch v.*

Burlington (CA2 1991), cert. denied (1992), *Kaplan* v. *Burlington* (CA2 1989), cert. denied (1990), *Smith* v. *County of Albemarle* (CA4), cert. denied (1990). We granted certiorari (1995).

II

First, a preliminary matter: Respondents contend that we should treat this as a case in which freedom of speech (the Klan's right to present the message of the cross display) was denied because of the State's disagreement with that message's political content, rather than because of the State's desire to distance itself from sectarian religion. They suggest in their merits brief and in their oral argument that Ohio's genuine reason for disallowing the display was disapproval of the political views of the Ku Klux Klan. Whatever the fact may be, the case was not presented and decided that way. The record facts before us and the opinions below address only the Establishment Clause issue; that is the question upon which we granted certiorari; and that is the sole question before us to decide.

Respondents' religious display in Capitol Square was private expression. Our precedent establishes that private religious speech, far from being a First Amendment orphan, is as fully protected under the Free Speech Clause as secular private expression. *Lamb's Chapel* v. *Center Moriches Union Free School Dist.* (1993); *Board of Ed. of Westside Community Schools (Dist. 66)* v. *Mergens* (1990); *Widmar* v. *Vincent* (1981); *Heffron* v. *International Soc. for Krishna Consciousness, Inc.* (1981). Indeed, in Anglo-American history, at least, government suppression of speech has so commonly been directed precisely at religious speech that a free-speech clause without religion would be *Hamlet* without the prince. Accordingly, we have not excluded from free-speech protections religious proselytizing, *Heffron*, or even acts of worship, *Widmar*. Petitioners do not dispute that respondents, in displaying their cross, were engaging in constitutionally protected expression. They do contend that the constitutional protection does not extend to the length of permitting that expression to be made on Capitol Square.

It is undeniable, of course, that speech which is constitutionally protected against state suppression is not thereby accorded a guaranteed forum on all property owned by the State. The right to use government property for one's private expression depends upon whether the property has by law or tradition been given the status of a public forum, or rather has been reserved for specific official uses. If the former, a State's right to limit protected expressive activity is sharply circumscribed: it may impose reasonable, content-neutral time, place and manner restrictions (a ban on all unattended displays, which did not exist here, might be one such), but it may regulate expressive *content* only if such a restriction is necessary, and narrowly drawn, to serve a compelling state interest. These strict standards apply here, since the District Court and the Court of Appeals found that Capitol Square was a traditional public forum.

Petitioners do not claim that their denial of respondents' application was based upon a content-neutral time, place, or manner restriction. To the contrary, they concede—indeed it is the essence of their case—that the Board rejected the display precisely because its content was religious. Petitioners advance a single justification for closing Capitol Square to respondents' cross: the State's interest in avoiding official endorsement of Christianity, as required by the Establishment Clause.

III

There is no doubt that compliance with the Establishment Clause is a state interest sufficiently compelling to justify content-based restrictions on speech. Whether that interest is implicated here, however, is a different question. And we do not write on a blank slate in answering it. We have twice previously addressed the combination of private religious expression, a forum available for public use, content-based regulation, and a State's interest in complying with the Establishment Clause. Both times, we have struck down the restriction on religious content.

In *Lamb's Chapel*, a school district allowed private groups to use school facilities during off-hours for a variety of civic, social and recreational purposes, excluding, however, religious purposes. We held that even if school property during off-hours was not a public forum, the school district violated an applicant's free-speech rights by denying it use of the facilities solely because of the religious viewpoint of the program it wished to present. We rejected the district's compelling-state-interest Establishment Clause defense (the same made here) because the school property was open to a wide variety of uses, the district was not directly sponsoring the religious group's activity, and "any benefit to religion or to the Church would have been no more than incidental." The *Lamb's Chapel* reasoning applies *a fortiori* here, where the property at issue is not a school but a full-fledged public forum.

Lamb's Chapel followed naturally from our decision in *Widmar*, in which we examined a public university's exclusion of student religious groups from facilities available to other student groups. There also we addressed official discrimination against groups who wished to use a "generally open forum" for religious speech. And there also the State claimed that its compelling interest in complying with the Establishment Clause justified the content-based restriction. We rejected the defense because the forum created by the State was open to a broad spectrum of groups and would provide only incidental benefit to religion. We stated categorically that "an open forum in a public university does not confer any imprimatur of state approval on religious sects or practices."

Quite obviously, the factors that we considered determinative in *Lamb's Chapel* and *Widmar* exist here as well. The State did not sponsor respondents' expression, the expression was made on government property that had been opened to the public for speech, and permission was requested through the same application process and on the same terms required of other private groups.

IV

Petitioners argue that one feature of the present case distinguishes it from *Lamb's Chapel* and *Widmar:* the forum's proximity to the seat of government, which, they contend, may produce the perception that the cross bears the State's approval. They urge us to apply the so-called "endorsement test," see, e.g., *Allegheny County* v. *American Civil Liberties Union, Greater Pittsburgh Chapter* (1989); *Lynch v. Donnelly* (1984), and to find that, because an observer might mistake private expression for officially endorsed religious expression, the State's content-based restriction is constitutional.

We must note, to begin with, that it is not really an "endorsement test" of any sort, much less the "endorsement test" which appears in our more recent Establishment Clause jurisprudence, that petitioners urge upon us. "Endorsement" connotes an expression or demonstration of approval or support. Our cases have accordingly equated "endorsement" with "promotion" or "favoritism." We find it peculiar to say that government "promotes" or "favors" a religious display by giving it the same access to a public forum that all other displays enjoy. And as a matter of Establishment Clause jurisprudence, we have consistently held that it is no violation for government to enact neutral policies that happen to benefit religion. See, *e.g., Bowen* v. *Kendrick* (1988); *Witters* v. *Washington Dept. of Services for Blind* (1986); *Mueller* v. *Allen* (1983); *McGowan* v. *Maryland* (1961). Where we have tested for endorsement of religion, the subject of the test was either expression *by the government itself* [*Lynch*], or else government action alleged to *discriminate in favor* of private religious expression or activity, *Board of Ed. of Kiryas Joel Village School Dist.* v. *Grumet* (1994); *Allegheny County.* The test petitioners propose, which would attribute to a neutrally behaving government *private* religious expression, has no antecedent in our jurisprudence, and would better be called a "transferred endorsement" test.

Petitioners rely heavily on *Allegheny County* and *Lynch,* but each is easily distinguished. In *Allegheny County* we held that the display of a privately-sponsored crèche on the "Grand Staircase" of the Allegheny County Courthouse violated the Establishment Clause. That staircase was not, however, open to all on an equal basis, so the County was *favoring* sectarian religious expression.... We expressly distinguished that site from the kind of public forum at issue here, and made clear that if the staircase were available to all on the same terms, "the presence of the crèche in that location for over six weeks would then *not* serve to associate the government with the crèche" (emphasis added). In *Lynch* we held that a city's display of a crèche did not violate the Establishment Clause because, in context, the display did not endorse religion. The opinion does assume, as petitioners contend, that the *government's* use of religious symbols is unconstitutional if it effectively endorses sectarian religious belief. But the case neither holds nor even remotely assumes that the government's neutral treatment of *private* religious expression can be unconstitutional.

Petitioners argue that absence of perceived endorsement was material in *Lamb's Chapel* and *Widmar.* We did state in *Lamb's Chapel* that there was "no realistic danger that the community would think that the District was endorsing religion or any particular creed." But that conclusion was not the result of empirical investigation; it followed directly, we thought, from the fact that the forum was open and the religious activity privately sponsored. It is significant that we referred only to what would be thought by "the community"—not by outsiders or individual members of the community uninformed about the school's practice. Surely some of the latter, hearing of religious ceremonies on school premises, and not knowing of the premises' availability and use for all sorts of other private activities, *might* leap to the erroneous conclusion of state endorsement. But, we in effect said, given an open forum and private sponsorship, erroneous conclusions do not count. So also in *Widmar.* Once we determined that the benefit to religious groups from the public forum was incidental and shared by other groups, we categorically rejected the State's Establishment Clause defense.

What distinguishes *Allegheny County* and the dictum in *Lynch* from *Widmar* and *Lamb's Chapel* is the difference between government speech and private speech. "[T]here is a crucial difference between *government* speech endorsing religion, which the Establishment Clause forbids, and *private* speech endorsing religion, which the Free Speech and Free Exercise Clauses protect." *Mergens* (O'CONNOR, J., concurring). Petitioners assert, in effect, that that distinction disappears when the private speech is conducted too close to the symbols of government. But that, of course, must be merely a subpart of a more general principle: that the distinction disappears whenever private speech can be mistaken for government speech. That proposition cannot be accepted, at least where, as here, the government has not fostered or encouraged the mistake.

Of course, giving sectarian religious speech preferential access to a forum close to the seat of government (or anywhere else for that matter) would violate the Establishment Clause (as well as the Free Speech Clause, since it would involve content discrimination). And one can conceive of a case in which a governmental entity manipulates its administration of a public forum close to the seat of government (or within a government building) in such a manner that only certain religious groups take advantage of it, creating an impression of endorsement *that is in fact accurate.* But those situations, which involve governmental *favoritism,* do not exist here. Capitol Square is a genuinely public forum, is known to be a public forum, and has been widely used as a public forum for many, many years. Private religious speech cannot be subject to veto by those who see favoritism where there is none.

The contrary view, most strongly espoused by JUSTICE STEVENS, but endorsed by JUSTICE SOUTER and JUSTICE O'CONNOR as well, exiles private religious speech to a realm of less-protected expression heretofore inhabited only by sexually explicit displays and commercial speech. *Young* v. *American Mini Theatres, Inc.* (1976); *Central Hudson Gas & Electric Corp.* v. *Public Serv. Comm'n of N. Y.* (1980). It will be a sad day when this Court casts piety in with pornography, and finds the First Amendment more hospitable to private expletives than to private prayers. This would be merely bizarre were religious speech simply *as* protected by the Constitution as other forms of private speech; but it is outright perverse when one considers that private religious expression receives *preferential* treatment under the Free Exercise Clause. It is no answer to say that the Establishment Clause tempers religious speech. By its terms that Clause applies only to the words and acts of *government.* It was never meant, and has never been read by this Court, to serve as an impediment to purely *private* religious speech connected to the State only through its occurrence in a public forum.

Since petitioners' "transferred endorsement" principle cannot possibly be restricted to squares in front of state capitols, the Establishment Clause regime that it would usher in is most unappealing. To require (and permit) access by a religious group in *Lamb's Chapel,* it was sufficient that the group's activity was not in fact government sponsored, that the event was open to the public, and that the benefit of the facilities was shared by various organizations. Petitioners' rule would require school districts adopting similar policies in the future to guess whether some undetermined critical mass of the community might nonetheless perceive the district to be advocating a religious viewpoint. Similarly, state universities would be forced to reassess our statement that "an open forum in a public university does not confer any imprimatur of state approval on religious sects or practices." [*Widmar*]. Whether it does would henceforth depend upon immediate appearances. Policy makers would find themselves in a vise between the Establishment Clause on one side and the Free Speech and Free Exercise Clauses on the other. Every proposed act of private, religious expression in a public forum would force officials to weigh a host of imponderables. How close to government is too close? What kind of building, and in what context, symbolizes state authority? If the State guessed wrong in one direction, it would be guilty of an Establishment Clause violation; if in the other, it would be liable for suppressing free exercise or free speech (a risk not run when the State restrains only its *own* expression).

The "transferred endorsement" test would also disrupt the settled principle that policies providing incidental benefits to religion do not contravene the Establishment Clause. That principle is the basis for the constitutionality of a broad range of laws, not merely those that implicate free-speech issues.... It has radical implications for our public policy to suggest that neutral laws are invalid whenever hypothetical observers may—*even reasonably*—confuse an incidental benefit to religion with state endorsement.

If Ohio is concerned about misperceptions, nothing prevents it from requiring all private displays in the Square to be identified as such. That would be a content-neutral "manner" restriction which is assuredly constitutional. But the State may not, on the claim of misperception of official endorsement, ban all private religious speech from the public square, or discriminate against it by requiring religious speech alone to disclaim public sponsorship.

* * *

Religious expression cannot violate the Establishment Clause where it (1) is purely private and (2) occurs in a traditional or designated public forum, publicly announced and open to all on equal terms. Those conditions are satisfied here, and therefore the State may not bar respondents' cross from Capitol Square.

The judgment of the Court of Appeals is

affirmed.

JUSTICE THOMAS, concurring.

I join the Court's conclusion that petitioner's exclusion of the Ku Klux Klan's cross cannot be justified on Establishment Clause grounds. But the fact that the legal issue before us involves the Establishment Clause should not lead anyone to think that a cross erected by the Ku Klux Klan is a purely religious symbol. The erection of such a cross is a political act, not a Christian one....

Although the Klan might have sought to convey a message with some religious component, I think that the Klan had a primarily nonreligious purpose in erecting the cross. The Klan simply has appropriated one of the most sacred of religious symbols as a symbol of hate. In my mind, this suggests that this case may not have truly involved the Establishment Clause, although I agree with the

Court's disposition because of the manner in which the case has come before us. In the end, there may be much less here than meets the eye.

JUSTICE O'CONNOR, with whom JUSTICE SOUTER and JUSTICE BREYER join, concurring in part and concurring in the judgment.

I join Parts I, II, and III of the Court's opinion and concur in the judgment. Despite the messages of bigotry and racism that may be conveyed along with religious connotations by the display of a Ku Klux Klan cross, at bottom this case must be understood as it has been presented to us — as a case about private religious expression and whether the State's relationship to it violates the Establishment Clause. In my view, "the endorsement test asks the right question about governmental practices challenged on Establishment Clause grounds, including challenged practices involving the display of religious symbols," *Allegheny County* v. *American Civil Liberties Union, Greater Pittsburgh Chapter* (1989) (O'CONNOR, J., concurring in part and concurring in judgment), even where a neutral state policy toward private religious speech in a public forum is at issue. Accordingly, I see no necessity to carve out, as the plurality opinion would today, an exception to the endorsement test for the public forum context.

For the reasons given by JUSTICE SOUTER, whose opinion I also join, I conclude on the facts of this case that there is "no realistic danger that the community would think that the [State] was endorsing religion or any particular creed," *Lamb's Chapel* v. *Center Moriches Union Free School Dist.* (1993), by granting respondents a permit to erect their temporary cross on Capitol Square. I write separately, however, to emphasize that, because it seeks to identify those situations in which government makes " 'adherence to a religion relevant ... to a person's standing in the political community,' " *Allegheny* (quoting *Lynch* v. *Donnelly* (1984) (O'CONNOR, J., concurring), the endorsement test necessarily focuses upon the perception of a reasonable, informed observer.

I

... The plurality today takes an exceedingly narrow view of the Establishment Clause that is out of step both with the Court's prior cases and with well-established notions of what the Constitution requires. The Clause is more than a negative prohibition against certain narrowly defined forms of government favoritism; it also imposes affirmative obligations that may require a State, in some situations, to take steps to avoid being perceived as supporting or endorsing a private religious message. That is, the Establishment Clause forbids a State from hiding behind the application of formally neutral criteria and remaining studiously oblivious to the effects of its actions. Governmental intent cannot control, and not all state policies are permissible under the Religion Clauses simply because they are neutral in form.

Where the government's operation of a public forum has the effect of endorsing religion, even if the governmental actor neither intends nor actively encourages that result, the Establishment Clause is violated. This is so not because of " 'transferred endorsement' " or mistaken attribution of private speech to the State, but because the State's own actions (operating the forum in a particular manner and permitting the religious expression to take place therein), and their relationship to the private speech at issue, *actually convey* a message of endorsement. At some point, for example, a private religious group may so dominate a public forum that a formal policy of equal access is transformed into a demonstration of approval.... Other circumstances may produce the same effect—whether because of the fortuity of geography, the nature of the particular public space, or the character of the religious speech at issue, among others. Our Establishment Clause jurisprudence should remain flexible enough to handle such situations when they arise....

JUSTICE SOUTER, with whom JUSTICE O'CONNOR and JUSTICE BREYER join, concurring in part and concurring in the judgment.

I concur in Parts I, II, and III of the Court's opinion. I also want to note specifically my agreement with the Court's suggestion that the State of Ohio could ban all unattended private displays in Capitol Square if it so desired. The fact that the Capitol lawn has been the site of public protests and gatherings, and is the location of any number of the government's own unattended displays, such as statues, does not disable the State from closing the square to all privately owned, unattended structures....

Otherwise, however, I limit my concurrence to the judgment. Although I agree in the end that, in the circumstances of this case, petitioners erred in denying the Klan's application for a permit to erect a cross on Capitol Square, my analysis of the Establishment Clause issue differs from JUSTICE SCALIA'S, and I vote to affirm in large part because of the possibility of affixing a sign to the cross adequately disclaiming any government sponsorship or endorsement of it.

The plurality's opinion declines to apply the endorsement test to the Board's action, in favor of a *per se* rule: religious expression cannot violate the Establishment Clause where it (1) is private and (2) occurs in a public forum, even if a reasonable observer would see the expression as indicating state endorsement. This *per se* rule would be an exception to the endorsement test, not previously recognized and out of square with our precedents....

JUSTICE STEVENS, dissenting.

The Establishment Clause should be construed to create a strong presumption against the installation of unattended religious symbols on public property. Although the State of Ohio has allowed Capitol Square, the area around the seat of its government, to be used as a public forum, and although it has occasionally allowed private groups to erect other sectarian displays there, neither fact provides a sufficient basis for rebutting that presumption. On the contrary, the sequence of sectarian displays disclosed by the record in this case illustrates the importance of rebuilding the "wall of separation between church and State" that Jefferson envisioned.

I

At issue in this case is an unadorned Latin cross, which the Ku Klux Klan placed, and left unattended, on the lawn in front of the Ohio State Capitol. The Court decides this case on the assumption that the cross was a religious symbol. I agree with that assumption notwithstanding the hybrid character of this particular object. The record indicates that the "Grand Titan of the Knights of the

Ku Klux Klan for the Realm of Ohio" applied for a permit to place a cross in front of the State Capitol because "the Jews" were placing a "symbol for the Jewish belief" in the Square. Some observers, unaware of who had sponsored the cross, or unfamiliar with the history of the Klan and its reaction to the menorah, might interpret the Klan's cross as an inspirational symbol of the crucifixion and resurrection of Jesus Christ. More knowledgeable observers might regard it, given the context, as an anti-semitic symbol of bigotry and disrespect for a particular religious sect. Under the first interpretation, the cross is plainly a religious symbol. Under the second, an icon of intolerance expressing an anti-clerical message should also be treated as a religious symbol because the Establishment Clause must prohibit official sponsorship of irreligious as well as religious messages. This principle is no less binding if the anti-religious message is also a bigoted message....

Thus, while this unattended, freestanding wooden cross was unquestionably a religious symbol, observers may well have received completely different messages from that symbol. Some might have perceived it as a message of love, others as a message of hate, still others as a message of exclusion—a Statehouse sign calling powerfully to mind their outsider status. In any event, it was a message that the State of Ohio may not communicate to its citizens without violating the Establishment Clause.

II

The plurality does not disagree with the proposition that the State may not espouse a religious message. It concludes, however, that the State has not sent such a message; it has merely allowed others to do so on its property. Thus, the State has provided an "incidental benefit" to religion by allowing private parties access to a traditional public forum. In my judgment, neither precedent nor respect for the values protected by the Establishment Clause justifies that conclusion.

The Establishment Clause, "at the very least, prohibits government from appearing to take a position on questions of religious belief or from 'making adherence to a religion relevant in any way to a person's standing in the political community.'" *County of Allegheny* v. *American Civil Liberties Union, Greater Pittsburgh Chapter* (1989), quoting *Lynch* v. *Donnelly* (1984) (O'CONNOR, J., concurring). At least when religious symbols are involved, the question of whether the state is "appearing to take a position" is best judged from the standpoint of a "reasonable observer." It is especially important to take account of the perspective of a reasonable observer who may not share the particular religious belief it expresses. A paramount purpose of the Establishment Clause is to protect such a person from being made to feel like an outsider in matters of faith, and a stranger in the political community. If a reasonable person could perceive a government endorsement of religion from a private display, then the State may not allow its property to be used as a forum for that display. No less stringent rule can adequately protect non-adherents from a well-grounded perception that their sovereign supports a faith to which they do not subscribe.

In determining whether the State's maintenance of the Klan's cross in front of the Statehouse conveyed a forbidden message of endorsement, we should be mindful of the power of a symbol standing alone and unexplained.

Even on private property, signs and symbols are generally understood to express the owner's views. The location of the sign is a significant component of the message it conveys....

Like other speakers, a person who places a sign on her own property has the autonomy to choose the content of her own message. Thus, the location of a stationary, unattended sign generally is both a component of its message and an implicit endorsement of that message by the party with the power to decide whether it may be conveyed from that location.

So it is with signs and symbols left to speak for themselves on public property. The very fact that a sign is installed on public property implies official recognition and reinforcement of its message. That implication is especially strong when the sign stands in front of the seat of the government itself. The "reasonable observer" of any symbol placed unattended in front of any capitol in the world will normally assume that the sovereign—which is not only the owner of that parcel of real estate but also the lawgiver for the surrounding territory—has sponsored and facilitated its message.

That the State may have granted a variety of groups permission to engage in uncensored expressive activities in front of the capitol building does not, in my opinion, qualify or contradict the normal inference of endorsement that the reasonable observer would draw from the unattended, freestanding sign or symbol. Indeed, parades and demonstrations at or near the seat of government are often exercises of the right of the people to petition their government for a redress of grievances—exercises in which the government is the recipient of the message rather than the messenger. Even when a demonstration or parade is not directed against government policy, but merely has made use of a particularly visible forum in order to reach as wide an audience as possible, there usually can be no mistake about the identity of the messengers as persons other than the State. But when a statue or some other free-standing, silent, unattended, immoveable structure—regardless of its particular message—appears on the lawn of the Capitol building, the reasonable observer must identify the State either as the messenger, or, at the very least, as one who has endorsed the message. Contrast, in this light, the image of the cross standing alone and unattended and the image the observer would take away were a hooded Klansman holding, or standing next to, the very same cross.

This Court has never held that a private party has a right to place an unattended object in a public forum. Today the Court correctly recognizes that a State may impose a ban on all private unattended displays in such a forum. This is true despite the fact that our cases have condemned a number of laws that foreclose an entire medium of expression, even in places where free speech is otherwise allowed....

Because structures on government property—and, in particular, in front of buildings plainly identified with the state—imply state approval of their message, the Government must have considerable leeway, outside of the religious arena, to choose what kinds of displays it will allow and what kinds it will not. Although the First Amendment requires the Government to allow leafletting or demonstrating outside its buildings, the state has greater power to exclude unattended symbols when they convey a type of message with which the state does not wish to be identified. I think it obvious, for example, that Ohio could prohibit certain categories of signs or symbols in Capitol Square — erotic exhibits, commercial advertising, and perhaps campaign posters as well — without violating the Free Speech Clause....

The State's general power to restrict the types of unattended displays does not alone suffice to decide this case, because Ohio did not profess to be exercising any such authority. Instead, the Capitol Square Review Board denied a permit for the cross because it believed the Establishment Clause required as much, and we cannot know whether the Board would have denied the permit on other grounds. Accordingly, we must evaluate the State's rationale on its own terms. But in this case, the endorsement inquiry under the Establishment Clause follows from the State's power to exclude unattended private displays from public property. Just as the Constitution recognizes the State's interest in preventing its property from being used as a conduit for ideas it does not wish to give the appearance of ratifying, the Establishment Clause prohibits government from allowing, and thus endorsing, unattended displays that take a position on a religious issue. If the State allows such stationary displays in front of its seat of government, viewers will reasonably assume that it approves of them. As the picture appended to this opinion demonstrates [omitted], a reasonable observer would likely infer endorsement from the location of the cross erected by the Klan in this case. Even if the disclaimer at the foot of the cross (which stated that the cross was placed there by a private organization) were legible, that inference would remain, because a property owner's decision to allow a third party to place a sign on her property conveys the same message of endorsement as if she had erected it herself.

When the message is religious in character, it is a message the state can neither send nor reinforce without violating the Establishment Clause. Accordingly, I would hold that the Constitution generally forbids the placement of a symbol of a religious character in, on, or before a seat of government....

JUSTICE GINSBURG, dissenting.

We confront here, as JUSTICES O'CONNOR and SOUTER point out, a large Latin cross that stood alone and unattended in close proximity to Ohio's Statehouse. Near the stationary cross were the government's flags and the government's statues. No human speaker was present to disassociate the religious symbol from the State. No other private display was in sight. No plainly visible sign informed the public that the cross belonged to the Klan and that Ohio's government did not endorse the display's message.

If the aim of the Establishment Clause is genuinely to uncouple government from church, a State may not permit, and a court may not order, a display of this character.... JUSTICE SOUTER, in the final paragraphs of his opinion, suggests two arrangements that might have distanced the State from "the principal symbol of Christianity around the world"[:] a sufficiently large and clear disclaimer[;] or an area reserved for unattended displays carrying no endorsement from the State, a space plainly and permanently so marked. Neither arrangement is even arguably present in this case. The District Court's order did not mandate a disclaimer.... And the disclaimer the Klan appended to the foot of the cross was unsturdy: it did not identify the Klan as sponsor; it failed to state unequivocally that Ohio did not endorse the display's message; and it was not shown to be legible from a distance. The relief ordered by the District Court thus violated the Establishment Clause.

Whether a court order allowing display of a cross, but demanding a sturdier disclaimer, could withstand Establishment Clause analysis is a question more difficult than the one this case poses. I would reserve that question for another day and case. But I would not let the prospect of what might have been permissible control today's decision on the constitutionality of the display the District Court's order in fact authorized.

□ □ □

No. 94-859

Bruce Babbitt, Secretary of the Interior, et al., Petitioners v. Sweet Home Chapter of Communities for a Great Oregon et al.

On writ of certiorari to the United States Court of Appeals for the District of Columbia Circuit

[June 29, 1995]

JUSTICE STEVENS delivered the opinion of the Court.

The Endangered Species Act of 1973, 16 U.S.C. §1531 (ESA or Act), contains a variety of protections designed to save from extinction species that the Secretary of the Interior designates as endangered or threatened. Section 9 of the Act makes it unlawful for any person to "take" any endangered or threatened species. The Secretary has promulgated a regulation that defines the statute's prohibition on takings to include "significant habitat modification or degradation where it actually kills or injures wildlife." This case presents the question whether the Secretary exceeded his authority under the Act by promulgating that regulation.

I

Section 9(a)(1) of the Endangered Species Act provides the following protection for endangered species:

"Except as provided in sections 1535(g)(2) and 1539 of this title, with respect to any endangered species of fish or wildlife listed pursuant to section 1533 of this title it is unlawful for any person subject to the jurisdiction of the United States to—

.   .   .   .   .

"(B) take any such species within the United States or the territorial sea of the United States[.]" 16 U.S.C. §1538(a)(1).

Section 3(19) of the Act defines the statutory term "take":

"The term 'take' means to harass, harm, pursue, hunt, shoot, wound, kill, trap, capture, or collect, or to attempt to engage in any such conduct." 16 U.S.C. §1532(19).

The Act does not further define the terms it uses to define "take." The Interior Department regulations that implement the statute, however, define the statutory term "harm":

"*Harm* in the definition of 'take' in the Act means an act which actually kills or injures wildlife. Such act may include significant habitat modification or degradation where it actually kills or injures wildlife by significantly impairing essential behavioral patterns, including breeding, feeding, or sheltering." 50 CFR §17.3 (1994).

This regulation has been in place since 1975.

A limitation on the §9 "take" prohibition appears in §10(a)(1)(B) of the Act, which Congress added by amendment in 1982. That section authorizes the Secretary to grant a permit for any taking otherwise prohibited by §9(a)(1)(B) "if such taking is incidental to, and not the purpose of, the carrying out of an otherwise lawful activity." 16 U.S.C. §1539(a)(1)(B).

In addition to the prohibition on takings, the Act provides several other protections for endangered species. Section 4, 16 U.S.C. §1533, commands the Secretary to identify species of fish or wildlife that are in danger of extinction and to publish from time to time lists of all species he determines to be endangered or threatened. Section 5, 16 U.S.C. §1534, authorizes the Secretary, in cooperation with the States, see 16 U.S.C. §1535, to acquire land to aid in preserving such species. Section 7 requires federal agencies to ensure that none of their activities, including the granting of licenses and permits, will jeopardize the continued existence of endangered species "or result in the destruction or adverse modification of habitat of such species which is determined by the Secretary ... to be critical." 16 U.S.C. §1536(a)(2).

Respondents in this action are small landowners, logging companies, and families dependent on the forest products industries in the Pacific Northwest and in the Southeast, and organizations that represent their interests. They brought this declaratory judgment action against petitioners, the Secretary of the Interior and the Director of the Fish and Wildlife Service, in the United States District Court for the District of Columbia to challenge the statutory validity of the Secretary's regulation defining "harm," particularly the inclusion of habitat modification and degradation in the definition. Respondents challenged the regulation on its face. Their complaint alleged that application of the "harm" regulation to the red-cockaded woodpecker, an endangered species, and the northern spotted owl, a threatened species, had injured them economically.

Respondents advanced three arguments to support their submission that Congress did not intend the word "take" in §9 to include habitat modification, as the Secretary's "harm" regulation provides. First, they correctly noted that language in the Senate's original version of the ESA would have defined "take" to include "destruction, modification, or curtailment of [the] habitat or range" of fish or wildlife, but the Senate deleted that language from the bill before enacting it. Second, respondents argued that Congress intended the Act's express authorization for the Federal Government to buy private land in order to prevent habitat degradation in §5 to be the exclusive check against habitat modification on private property. Third, because the Senate added the term "harm" to the definition of "take" in a floor amendment without debate, respondents argued that the court should not interpret the term so expansively as to include habitat modification.

The District Court considered and rejected each of respondents' arguments, finding "that Congress intended an expansive interpretation of the word 'take,' an interpretation that encompasses habitat modification." (1992)....

A divided panel of the Court of Appeals initially affirmed the judgment of the District Court. After granting a petition for rehearing, however, the panel reversed (1994). Although acknowledging that "[t]he potential breadth of the word 'harm' is indisputable," the majority concluded that the immediate statutory context in which "harm" appeared counseled against a broad reading; like the other words in the definition of "take," the word "harm" should be read as applying only to "the perpetrator's direct application of force against the animal taken....The forbidden acts fit, in ordinary language, the basic model 'A hit B.'" The majority based its reasoning on a canon of statutory construction called *noscitur a sociis*, which holds that a word is known by the company it keeps....

Chief Judge Mikva, who had announced the panel's original decision, dissented. In his view, a proper application of *Chevron* [*U.S.A. Inc.* v. *Natural Resources Defense Council* (1984)] indicated that the Secretary had reasonably defined "harm," because respondents had failed to show that Congress unambiguously manifested its intent to exclude habitat modification from the ambit of "take." Chief Judge Mikva found the majority's reliance on *noscitur a sociis* inappropriate in light of the statutory language and unnecessary in light of the strong support in the legislative history for the Secretary's interpretation....

The Court of Appeals' decision created a square conflict with a 1988 decision of the Ninth Circuit that had upheld the Secretary's definition of "harm."... We granted certiorari to resolve the conflict. (1995). Our consideration of the text and structure of the Act, its legislative history, and the significance of the 1982 amendment persuades us that the Court of Appeals' judgment should be reversed.

II

Because this case was decided on motions for summary judgment, we may appropriately make certain factual assumptions in order to frame the legal issue. First, we assume respondents have no desire to harm either the red-cockaded woodpecker or the spotted owl; they merely wish to continue logging activities that would be entirely proper if not prohibited by the ESA. On the other hand, we must assume *arguendo* that those activities will have the effect, even though unintended, of detrimentally changing the natural habitat of both listed species and that, as a consequence, members of those species will be killed or injured. Under respondents' view of the law, the Secretary's only means of forestalling that grave result—even when the actor knows it is certain to occur—is to use his §5 authority to purchase the lands on which the survival of the species depends. The Secretary, on the other hand, submits that the §9 prohibition on takings, which Congress defined to include "harm," places on respondents a duty to avoid harm that habitat alteration will cause the birds unless respondents first obtain a permit pursuant to §10.

The text of the Act provides three reasons for concluding that the Secretary's interpretation is reasonable. First, an ordinary understanding of the word "harm" supports it. The dictionary definition of the verb form of "harm" is "to cause hurt or damage to: injure." In the context of the ESA, that definition naturally encompasses habitat modification that results in actual injury or death to members of an endangered or threatened species. Respondents argue that the Secretary should have limited the purview of "harm" to direct applications of force against protected species, but the dictionary definition does not include the word "directly" or suggest in any way that only direct or willful action that leads to injury constitutes "harm." Moreover, unless the statutory term "harm" encompasses indirect as well as direct injuries, the word has no meaning that does not duplicate the meaning of other words that §3 uses to define "take." A reluctance to treat statutory terms as surplusage supports the reasonableness of the Secretary's interpretation.

Second, the broad purpose of the ESA supports the Secretary's decision to extend protection against activities that cause the precise harms Congress enacted the statute to avoid. In *TVA* v. *Hill* (1978), we described the Act as "the most comprehensive legislation for the preservation of endangered species ever enacted by any nation." Whereas predecessor statutes enacted in 1966 and 1969 had not contained any sweeping prohibition against the taking of endangered species except on federal lands, the 1973 Act applied to all land in the United States and to the Nation's territorial seas. As stated in §2 of the Act, among its central purposes is "to provide a means whereby the ecosystems upon which endangered species and threatened species depend may be conserved...."

In *Hill*, we construed §7 as precluding the completion of the Tellico Dam because of its predicted impact on the survival of the snail darter. Both our holding and the language in our opinion stressed the importance of the statutory policy. "The plain intent of Congress in enacting this statute," we recognized, "was to halt and reverse the trend toward species extinction, whatever the cost. This is reflected not only in the stated policies of the Act, but in literally every section of the statute." Although the §9 "take" prohibition was not at issue in *Hill*, we took note of that prohibition, placing particular emphasis on the Secretary's inclusion of habitat modification in his definition of "harm." In light of that provision for habitat protection, we could "not understand how TVA intends to operate Tellico Dam without 'harming' the snail darter." Congress' intent to provide comprehensive protection for endangered and threatened species supports the permissibility of the Secretary's "harm" regulation.

Respondents advance strong arguments that activities that cause minimal or unforeseeable harm will not violate the Act as construed in the "harm" regulation. Respondents, however, present a facial challenge to the regulation. Thus, they ask us to invalidate the Secretary's understanding of "harm" in every circumstance, even when an actor knows that an activity, such as draining a pond, would actually result in the extinction of a listed species by destroying its habitat. Given Congress' clear expression of the ESA's broad purpose to protect endangered and threatened wildlife, the Secretary's definition of "harm" is reasonable.

Third, the fact that Congress in 1982 authorized the Secretary to issue permits for takings that §9(a)(1)(B) would otherwise prohibit, "if such taking is incidental to, and not the purpose of, the carrying out of an otherwise lawful activity," strongly suggests that Congress understood §9(a)(1)(B) to prohibit indirect as well as deliberate takings. The permit process requires the applicant to prepare a "conservation plan" that specifies how he intends to "minimize and mitigate" the "impact" of his activity on endangered and threatened species, making clear that Congress had in mind foreseeable rather than merely accidental effects on listed species. No one could seriously request an "incidental" take permit to avert §9 liability for direct, deliberate action against a member of an endangered or threatened species, but respondents would read "harm" so narrowly that the permit procedure would have little more than that absurd purpose.... Congress' addition of the §10 permit provision supports the Secretary's conclusion that activities not intended to harm an endangered species, such as habitat modification, may constitute unlawful takings under the ESA unless the Secretary permits them.

The Court of Appeals made three errors in asserting that "harm" must refer to a direct application of force because the words around it do. First, the court's premise was flawed. Several of the words that accompany "harm" in the §3 definition of "take," especially "harass," "pursue," "wound," and "kill," refer to action or effects that do not require direct applications of force. Second, to the extent the court read a requirement of intent or purpose into the words used to define "take," it ignored §9's express provision that a "knowing" action is enough to violate the Act. Third, the court employed *noscitur a sociis* to give "harm" essentially the same function as other words in the definition, thereby denying it independent meaning. The canon, to the contrary, counsels that a word "gathers meaning from the words around it." The statutory context of "harm" suggests that Congress meant that term to serve a particular function in the ESA, consistent with but distinct from the functions of the other verbs used to define "take." The Secretary's interpretation of "harm" to include indirectly injuring endangered animals through habitat modification permissibly interprets "harm" to have "a character of its own not to be submerged by its association."

Nor does the Act's inclusion of the §5 land acquisition authority and the §7 directive to federal agencies to avoid destruction or adverse modification of critical habitat alter our conclusion. Respondents' argument that the Government lacks any incentive to purchase land under §5 when it can simply prohibit takings under §9 ignores the practical considerations that attend enforcement of the ESA. Purchasing habitat lands may well cost the Government less in many circumstances than pursuing civil or criminal penalties. In addition, the §5 procedure allows for protection of habitat before the seller's activity has harmed any endangered animal, whereas the Government cannot enforce the §9 prohibition until an animal has actually been killed or injured. The Secretary may also find the §5 authority useful for preventing modification of land that is not yet but may in the future become habitat for an endangered or threatened species. The §7 directive applies only to the Federal Government, whereas the §9 prohibition applies to "any person." Section 7 imposes a broad,

affirmative duty to avoid adverse habitat modifications that §9 does not repli-
cate, and §7 does not limit its admonition to habitat modification that "actually kills or injures wildlife." Conversely, §7 contains limitations that §9 does not,
applying only to actions "likely to jeopardize the continued existence of any
endangered species or threatened species" and to modifications of habitat that
have been designated "critical" pursuant to §4. Any overlap that §5 or §7 may
have with §9 in particular cases is unexceptional and simply reflects the broad
purpose of the Act set out in §2 and acknowledged in *TVA* v. *Hill.*

We need not decide whether the statutory definition of "take" compels the
Secretary's interpretation of "harm," because our conclusions that Congress
did not unambiguously manifest its intent to adopt respondents' view and that
the Secretary's interpretation is reasonable suffice to decide this case. The latitude the ESA gives the Secretary in enforcing the statute, together with the
degree of regulatory expertise necessary to its enforcement, establishes that we
owe some degree of deference to the Secretary's reasonable interpretation.

III

Our conclusion that the Secretary's definition of "harm" rests on a permissible construction of the ESA gains further support from the legislative history
of the statute. The Committee Reports accompanying the bills that became the
ESA do not specifically discuss the meaning of "harm," but they make clear that
Congress intended "take" to apply broadly to cover indirect as well as purposeful actions. The Senate Report stressed that " '[t]ake' is defined ... in the broadest possible manner to include every conceivable way in which a person can
'take' or attempt to 'take' any fish or wildlife." The House Report stated that "the
broadest possible terms" were used to define restrictions on takings. The House
Report underscored the breadth of the "take" definition by noting that it included "harassment, whether intentional or not." The Report explained that the definition "would allow, for example, the Secretary to regulate or prohibit the activities of birdwatchers where the effect of those activities might disturb the birds
and make it difficult for them to hatch or raise their young." These comments,
ignored in the dissent's welcome but selective foray into legislative history, support the Secretary's interpretation that the term "take" in §9 reached far more
than the deliberate actions of hunters and trappers.

Two endangered species bills, S. 1592 and S. 1983, were introduced in the
Senate and referred to the Commerce Committee. Neither bill included the
word "harm" in its definition of "take," although the definitions otherwise closely resembled the one that appeared in the bill as ultimately enacted. Senator
Tunney, the floor manager of the bill in the Senate, subsequently introduced a
floor amendment that added "harm" to the definition, noting that this and
accompanying amendments would "help to achieve the purposes of the bill."
Respondents argue that the lack of debate about the amendment that added
"harm" counsels in favor of a narrow interpretation. We disagree. An obviously
broad word that the Senate went out of its way to add to an important statutory
definition is precisely the sort of provision that deserves a respectful reading.

The definition of "take" that originally appeared in S. 1983 differed from
the definition as ultimately enacted in one other significant respect: It included "the destruction, modification, or curtailment of [the] habitat or range" of

fish and wildlife. Respondents make much of the fact that the Commerce Committee removed this phrase from the "take" definition before S. 1983 went to the floor. We do not find that fact especially significant. The legislative materials contain no indication why the habitat protection provision was deleted. That provision differed greatly from the regulation at issue today. Most notably, the habitat protection in S. 1983 would have applied far more broadly than the regulation does because it made adverse habitat modification a categorical violation of the "take" prohibition, unbounded by the regulation's limitation to habitat modifications that actually kill or injure wildlife. The S. 1983 language also failed to qualify "modification" with the regulation's limiting adjective "significant." We do not believe the Senate's unelaborated disavowal of the provision in S. 1983 undermines the reasonableness of the more moderate habitat protection in the Secretary's "harm" regulation.

The history of the 1982 amendment that gave the Secretary authority to grant permits for "incidental" takings provides further support for his reading of the Act. The House Report expressly states that "[b]y use of the word 'incidental' the Committee intends to cover situations in which it is known that a taking will occur if the other activity is engaged in but such taking is incidental to, and not the purpose of, the activity." This reference to the foreseeability of incidental takings undermines respondents' argument that the 1982 amendment covered only accidental killings of endangered and threatened animals that might occur in the course of hunting or trapping other animals. Indeed, Congress had habitat modification directly in mind: both the Senate Report and the House Conference Report identified as the model for the permit process a cooperative state-federal response to a case in California where a development project threatened incidental harm to a species of endangered butterfly by modification of its habitat. Thus, Congress in 1982 focused squarely on the aspect of the "harm" regulation at issue in this litigation. Congress' implementation of a permit program is consistent with the Secretary's interpretation of the term "harm."

IV

When it enacted the ESA, Congress delegated broad administrative and interpretive power to the Secretary. The task of defining and listing endangered and threatened species requires an expertise and attention to detail that exceeds the normal province of Congress. Fashioning appropriate standards for issuing permits under §10 for takings that would otherwise violate §9 necessarily requires the exercise of broad discretion. The proper interpretation of a term such as "harm" involves a complex policy choice. When Congress has entrusted the Secretary with broad discretion, we are especially reluctant to substitute our views of wise policy for his. In this case, that reluctance accords with our conclusion, based on the text, structure, and legislative history of the ESA, that the Secretary reasonably construed the intent of Congress when he defined "harm" to include "significant habitat modification or degradation that actually kills or injures wildlife."

In the elaboration and enforcement of the ESA, the Secretary and all persons who must comply with the law will confront difficult questions of proximity and degree; for, as all recognize, the Act encompasses a vast range of economic and social enterprises and endeavors. These questions must be addressed in the usual course of the law, through case-by-case resolution and adjudication.

The judgment of the Court of Appeals is reversed.

It is so ordered.

JUSTICE O'CONNOR, concurring.

My agreement with the Court is founded on two understandings. First, the challenged regulation is limited to significant habitat modification that causes actual, as opposed to hypothetical or speculative, death or injury to identifiable protected animals. Second, even setting aside difficult questions of scienter, the regulation's application is limited by ordinary principles of proximate causation, which introduce notions of foreseeability. These limitations, in my view, call into question *Palila* v. *Hawaii Dept. of Land and Natural Resources* (CA9 1988) *(Palila II)*, and with it, many of the applications derided by the dissent. Because there is no need to strike a regulation on a facial challenge out of concern that it is susceptible of erroneous application, however, and because there are many habitat-related circumstances in which the regulation might validly apply, I join the opinion of the Court....

JUSTICE SCALIA, with whom THE CHIEF JUSTICE and JUSTICE THOMAS join, dissenting.

I think it unmistakably clear that the legislation at issue here (1) forbade the hunting and killing of endangered animals, and (2) provided federal lands and federal funds *for the acquisition of private lands*, to preserve the habitat of endangered animals. The Court's holding that the hunting and killing prohibition incidentally preserves habitat on private lands imposes unfairness to the point of financial ruin—not just upon the rich, but upon the simplest farmer who finds his land conscripted to national zoological use. I respectfully dissent.

I

The Endangered Species Act of 1973, 16 U.S.C. §1531 *et seq.*, provides that "it is unlawful for any person subject to the jurisdiction of the United States to take any [protected] species within the United States." §1538(a)(1)(B). The term "take" is defined as "to harass, *harm*, pursue, hunt, shoot, wound, kill, trap, capture, or collect, or to attempt to engage in any such conduct." §1532(19) (emphasis added). The challenged regulation defines "harm" thus:

> "'Harm' in the definition of "take" in the Act means an act which actually kills or injures wildlife. Such act may include significant habitat modification or degradation where it actually kills or injures wildlife by significantly impairing essential behavioral patterns, including breeding, feeding or sheltering." 50 CFR 17.3 (1994)....

The regulation has three features which do not comport with the statute. First, it interprets the statute to prohibit habitat modification that is no more than the cause-in-fact of death or injury to wildlife. Any "significant habitat modification" that in fact produces that result by "impairing essential behavioral patterns" is made unlawful, regardless of whether that result is intended or even foreseeable, and no matter how long the chain of causality between modification and injury. See, *e.g.*, *Palila* v. *Hawaii Dept. of Land and Natural Resources (Palila II)* (CA9 1988) (sheep grazing constituted "taking" of palila birds, since although sheep do not destroy full-grown mamane trees, they do destroy mamane seedlings, which will not grow to full-grown trees, on which the palila feeds and nests)....

Second, the regulation does not require an "act": the Secretary's officially stated position is that an *omission* will do....

The third and most important unlawful feature of the regulation is that it encompasses injury inflicted, not only upon individual animals, but upon populations of the protected species. "Injury" in the regulation includes "significantly impairing essential behavioral patterns, including *breeding*" (1994) (emphasis added). Impairment of breeding does not "injure" living creatures; it prevents them from propagating, thus "injuring" a *population* of animals which would otherwise have maintained or increased its numbers....

None of these three features of the regulation can be found in the statutory provisions supposed to authorize it. The term "harm" in §1532(19) has no legal force of its own. An indictment or civil complaint that charged the defendant with "harming" an animal protected under the Act would be dismissed as defective, for the only operative term in the statute is to "take." If "take" were not elsewhere defined in the Act, none could dispute what it means, for the term is as old as the law itself. To "take," when applied to wild animals, means to reduce those animals, by killing or capturing, to human control.... And that meaning fits neatly with the rest of §1538(a)(1), which makes it unlawful not only to take protected species, but also to import or export them (§1538(a)(1)(A)); to possess, sell, deliver, carry, transport, or ship any taken species (§1538(a)(1)(D)); and to transport, sell, or offer to sell them in interstate or foreign commerce (§1538(a)(1)(E), (F))....

The Act's definition of "take" does expand the word slightly (and not unusually), so as to make clear that it includes not just a completed taking, but the process of taking, and all of the acts that are customarily identified with or accompany that process ("to harass, harm, pursue, hunt, shoot, wound, kill, trap, capture, or collect"); and so as to include attempts. The tempting fallacy—which the Court commits with abandon—is to assume that *once defined*, "take" loses any significance, and it is only the definition that matters....

That is what has occurred here. The verb "harm" has a range of meaning: "to cause injury" at its broadest, "to do hurt or damage" in a narrower and more direct sense.... To define "harm" as an act or omission that, however remotely, "actually kills or injures" a population of wildlife through habitat modification, is to choose a meaning that makes nonsense of the word that "harm" defines— requiring us to accept that a farmer who tills his field and causes erosion that makes silt run into a nearby river which depletes oxygen and thereby "impairs [the] breeding" of protected fish, has "taken" or "attempted to take" the fish....

Here the evidence shows the opposite. "Harm" is merely one of 10 prohibitory words in §1532(19), and the other 9 fit the ordinary meaning of "take" perfectly. To "harass, pursue, hunt, shoot, wound, kill, trap, capture, or collect" are all affirmative acts ... which are directed immediately and intentionally against a particular animal—not acts or omissions that indirectly and accidentally cause injury to a population of animals. The Court points out that several of the words ("harass," "pursue," "wound," and "kill") "refer to actions or effects that do not require direct *applications of force.*" That is true enough, but force is not the point. Even "taking" activities in the narrowest sense, activities traditionally engaged in by hunters and trappers, do not all consist of direct applications of force; pursuit and harassment are part of the business of "taking" the prey even before it has been touched. What the nine other words in §1532(19) have in common—and share with the narrower meaning of "harm" described above, but not with the Secretary's ruthless dilation of the word—is the sense of affirmative conduct intentionally directed against a particular animal or animals....

The penalty provisions of the Act counsel this interpretation as well. Any person who "knowingly" violates §1538(a)(1)(B) is subject to criminal penalties under §1540(b)(1) and civil penalties under §1540(a)(1); moreover, under the latter section, any person "who otherwise violates" the taking prohibition (*i.e.,* violates it *un*knowingly) may be assessed a civil penalty of $500 for each violation, with the stricture that "[e]ach such violation shall be a separate offense." This last provision should be clear warning that the regulation is in error, for when combined with the regulation it produces a result that no legislature could reasonably be thought to have intended: A large number of routine private activities—farming, for example, ranching, roadbuilding, construction and logging—are subjected to strict-liability penalties when they fortuitously injure protected wildlife, no matter how remote the chain of causation and no matter how difficult to foresee (or to disprove) the "injury" may be (*e.g.,* an "impairment" of breeding). The Court says that "[the strict-liability provision] is potentially sweeping, but it would be so with or without the Secretary's 'harm' regulation." That is not correct. Without the regulation, the routine "habitat modifying" activities that people conduct to make a daily living would not carry exposure to strict penalties; only acts directed at animals, like those described by the other words in §1532(19), would risk liability....

II

The Court makes four other arguments. First, "the broad purpose of the [Act] supports the Secretary's decision to extend protection against activities that cause the precise harms Congress enacted the statute to avoid.... Deduction from the "broad purpose" of a statute begs the question if it is used to decide by what *means* (and hence to what *length*) Congress pursued that purpose; to get the right answer to that question there is no substitute for the hard job (or in this case, the quite simple one) of reading the whole text. "The Act must do everything necessary to achieve its broad purpose" is the slogan of the enthusiast, not the analytical tool of the arbiter.

Second, the Court maintains that the legislative history of the 1973 Act supports the Secretary's definition. Even if legislative history were a legitimate and reliable tool of interpretation (which I shall assume in order to rebut the Court claim); and even if it could appropriately be resorted to when the enacted text is as clear as this, here it shows quite the opposite of what the Court says. I shall not pause to discuss the Court's reliance on such statements in the Committee Reports as " '[t]ake' is defined ... in the broadest possible manner to include every conceivable way in which a person can 'take' or attempt to 'take' any fish or wildlife." This sort of empty flourish— to the effect that "this statute means what it means all the way"— counts for little even when enacted into the law itself.

Much of the Court's discussion of legislative history is devoted to two items: first, the Senate floor manager's introduction of an amendment that added the word "harm" to the definition of "take," with the observation that (along with other amendments) it would "help to achieve the purposes of the bill"; second, the relevant Committee's removal from the definition of a provision stating that "take" includes "the destruction, modification or curtailment of [the] habitat or range" of fish and wildlife. The Court inflates the first and belittles the second, even though the second is on its face far more pertinent. But this elaborate inference from various pre-enactment actions and inactions is quite unnecessary, since we have *direct* evidence of what those who brought the legislation to the floor thought it meant— evidence as solid as any ever to be found in legislative history, but which the Court banishes to a footnote.

Both the Senate and House floor managers of the bill explained it in terms which leave no doubt that the problem of habitat destruction on private lands was to be solved principally by the land acquisition program of §1534, while §1538 solved a different problem altogether— the problem of takings. Senator Tunney stated:

> *"Through [the] land acquisition provisions, we will be able to conserve habitats necessary to protect fish and wildlife from further destruction...."* [Emphasis added.]

The House floor manager, Representative Sullivan, put the same thought in this way:

> "[T]he principal threat to animals stems from destruction of their habitat. ... *[The bill] will meet this problem by providing funds for acquisition of critical habitat....* " [Emphasis added.]

Third, the Court seeks support from a provision which was added to the Act in 1982, the year after the Secretary promulgated the current regulation. The provision states:

> "[T]he Secretary may permit, under such terms and conditions as he shall prescribe—

.   .   .   .   .

> "any taking otherwise prohibited by section 1538(a)(1)(B) ... if such taking is incidental to, and not the purpose of, the carrying out of an otherwise lawful activity." 16 U.S.C. §1539(a)(1)(B)."

This provision does not, of course, implicate our doctrine that reenactment of a statutory provision ratifies an extant judicial or administrative interpretation, for neither the taking prohibition in §1538(a)(1)(B) nor the definition in §1532(19) was reenacted. The Court claims, however, that the provision "strongly suggests that Congress understood [§1538(a)(1)(B)] to prohibit indirect as well as deliberate takings." That would be a valid inference if habitat modification were the only substantial "otherwise lawful activity" that might incidentally and nonpurposefully cause a prohibited "taking." Of course it is not. This provision applies to the many otherwise lawful takings that incidentally take a protected species—as when fishing for unprotected salmon also takes an endangered species of salmon....

Fourth and lastly, the Court seeks to avoid the evident shortcomings of the regulation on the ground that the respondents are challenging it on its face rather than as applied. The Court seems to say that *even if* the regulation dispenses with the foreseeability of harm that it acknowledges the statute to require, that does not matter because this is a facial challenge: so long as habitat modification that *would* foreseeably cause harm is prohibited by the statute, the regulation must be sustained. Presumably it would apply the same reasoning to all the other defects of the regulation: the regulation's failure to require injury to particular animals survives the present challenge, because at least *some* environmental modifications kill particular animals. This evisceration of the facial challenge is unprecedented. It is one thing to say that a facial challenge to a regulation that omits statutory element *x* must be rejected if there is any set of facts on which the statute *does not require x*. It is something quite different—and unlike any doctrine of "facial challenge" I have ever encountered—to say that the challenge must be rejected if the regulation could be applied to a state of facts in which element *x happens to be present*. On this analysis, the only regulation susceptible to facial attack is one that *not only* is invalid in all its applications, but also does not sweep up *any* person who *could have been* held liable under a proper application of the statute. That is not the law....

[III omitted]

* * *

The Endangered Species Act is a carefully considered piece of legislation that forbids all persons to hunt or harm endangered animals, but places upon the public at large, rather than upon fortuitously accountable individual landowners, the cost of preserving the habitat of endangered species. There is neither textual support for, nor even evidence of congressional consideration of, the radically different disposition contained in the regulation that the Court sustains. For these reasons, I respectfully dissent.

□ □ □

5 | *Preview of the 1995–1996 Term*

Colorado in the 1990s seemed to offer a hospitable political climate for homosexuals. The state had issued an executive order in 1990 banning discrimination on the basis of sexual orientation in state hiring. Three cities—Aspen, Boulder, and Denver—also had passed local gay rights ordinances covering employment, housing, and public accommodations. Other cities were considering similar measures, and the legislature was also being urged to pass a statewide law on the issue.

The gay rights measures added to Colorado's liberal, cosmopolitan image, but they provoked opposition among political and religious conservatives. A new group calling itself Colorado Family Values organized to fight the proposals. The organization failed in a 1991 referendum to repeal the Denver ordinance. Chastened, it then adopted a more ambitious goal: a statewide initiative that would amend Colorado's constitution to prohibit any state or local measure to grant homosexuals legal protection against discrimination.

"We decided that instead of trying to fight this issue with brushfires or trying to deal with the legislature, we would try to write a Colorado constitutional amendment that would be the final word throughout the state," recalled Kevin Tebedo, executive director of the group.

Most political observers expected Colorado voters to reject the initiative, which was listed as Amendment 2 on the 1992 ballot. But supporters, campaigning on the slogan "Equal Rights—Not Special Rights," won approval of the measure by more than 100,000 votes, a 7 percentage point margin.

The amendment has never gone into effect, though. A trial court judge and the state's supreme court have both ruled that the measure violates the rights of homosexuals to "equal protection under the laws" as guaranteed by the Fourteenth Amendment to the U.S. Constitution. Now, the issue is before the U.S. Supreme Court, in a politically charged, legally intricate case that tops the justices' calendar for the 1995–1996 term. (*Romer v. Evans*)

The Court had agreed to carry over some forty cases into the new term as it began its summer recess at the end of June. For the third year in a row, however, the Court announced its decision to review additional cases in the last week of September, before the formal opening of the new term. The justices agreed to review twelve more cases on September 27 and set expedited briefing schedules to permit the disputes to be argued in January. Traditionally, the justices gathered for their first conference in late

September, but did not announce orders until the formal opening of the new term on the first Monday in October.

The new cases included an important challenge by a number of cities to the federal government's refusal to adjust 1990 census results because of an acknowledged undercount of African-American and Hispanic residents of large cities. The cities, including New York, Los Angeles, and Chicago, among others, contend that the Bush administration's decision in 1991 not to revise the census figures unfairly disadvantaged them in terms of congressional apportionment and allocation of federal funds. The federal appeals court in New York agreed that the Census Bureau had not done enough to ensure an accurate head count. In urging the Court to review the ruling, the Clinton administration said the refusal to adjust the figures was within a range of "constitutionally permissible options." (*United States v. City of New York; Wisconsin v. New York City; Oklahoma v. New York City*)

The Court also agreed to hear an important intellectual property case testing whether federal copyright law provides protection for computer software. Lotus Development Corp. had filed a copyright infringement suit against another computer software company, Borland International, Inc., for allegedly imitating Lotus's popular spreadsheet program. But the federal appeals court in Boston ruled that the program was a "method of operation" that is exempt from copyright protection. (*Lotus Development Corp. v. Borland International, Inc.*)

With the additional cases, the Court was set to begin the new term with a total of fifty-two cases, slightly higher than the figure of forty-eight cases from the previous year but substantially lower than in the recent past. The Court began the 1990–1991 term, for example, with seventy cases.

The relatively low number of cases set for the new term did not, however, lack for interest. In the Colorado case, the justices would deal with gay rights for the first time since 1986, when the Court upheld state antisodomy statutes by a 5–4 vote. Two other familiar and emotional topics were also returning to the Court's calendar: racial redistricting and punitive damages.

In the racial redistricting cases, the Court agreed to hear challenges to remap plans in North Carolina and Texas aimed at electing minorities to the U.S. House of Representatives. The decision to hear the cases came hours after the Court had closed the 1994–1995 term with a 5–4 ruling limiting the room to consider race in drawing district lines.

Conservative groups cheered the Court's decision to continue scrutinizing racial line-drawing, while civil rights forces braced for another setback on the issue. But the action to hear both cases puzzled some observers, since the lower federal courts had struck down the minority districts in Texas but upheld the North Carolina plan. "The Court is saying that we have to review [all] of these," said Pamela Karlan, a voting rights expert at the University of Virginia Law School. "And there are another dozen of these winding their way through the courts."

On punitive damages, the Court was to return to an issue that it had examined half a dozen times since 1980, with mostly inconclusive results. Business interests had repeatedly urged the Court to impose constitutional limits on juries and courts in imposing penalties against defendants in tort suits. The justices refused to set fixed guidelines for punitive damages. But the Court did rule in 1994 that states must provide some form of review of jury awards for punitive damages. *(See* Supreme Court Yearbook, 1993–1994, *pp. 42–43.)*

Business groups were pleased that the justices decided to revisit the issue in an Alabama case, where an automobile owner was awarded $2 million in punitive damages for a damaged paint job on his new car. "This case has facts very favorable to business," said Robin Conrad, director of litigation for the U.S. Chamber of Commerce. But some tort reform supporters cautioned against expecting a broad ruling. "It appears that the Supreme Court will continue to take a minimalist approach toward the use of the Constitution to achieve civil justice reform," remarked Paul Capuccio, a conservative lawyer with the Washington office of Kirkland & Ellis, a major corporate law firm.

In a second case testing the rules for civil litigation, the justices also agreed to decide whether a state court settlement of securities litigation can bar plaintiffs from pursuing a related federal court suit. The case involves fraud claims brought by investors after the $6.6 billion acquisition of MCA, Inc., the California-based entertainment company, by the Japanese company Matsushita Electric Industrial Co.

The Court had two important First Amendment cases on its calendar as the term began. In one, the justices were to decide a high-stakes regulatory fight between telephone companies and cable operators over access to the growing market for entertainment and information in the home. The telephone companies have won court rulings to overturn a federal law that prevents them from offering cable services. The government and the cable industry both urge the Court to reinstate the law or allow the Federal Communications Commission (FCC) to allow exceptions to the ban under yet-to-be written regulatory guidelines. The second First Amendment case presented a new challenge to laws regulating commercial speech — specifically, a Rhode Island law prohibiting the advertising of liquor prices. Two liquor stores in Rhode Island and Massachusetts claimed the law violates the First Amendment. They were joined in their plea by an array of publishing companies and advertising groups, trade associations for the alcoholic beverage industries, and the American Civil Liberties Union.

In criminal law, the Court again took up the growing use of criminal forfeiture by local, state, and federal law enforcement. The justices in recent years had moved to restrain the government's power to seize money and property tied to criminal activities. The two new cases gave the Court the opportunity to set new procedural limits.

In one case, the justices were to decide whether the Constitution guarantees an owner the right to contest government seizure of property by showing she did not know the property was being used for an improper purpose. In the second, the Court was to rule on a federal drug defendant's argument that the judge in his case should not have allowed the government to confiscate his money and property after he entered a guilty plea without first examining the factual basis for the forfeiture.

"No Protected Status"

In contrast to most of the other cases on the Court's calendar, the dispute over the Colorado anti–gay rights initiative posed a truly novel legal issue. None of the Court's prior cases offered a clear precedent to decide whether a state can ban the enactment of any law protecting an identified class of persons from discriminatory conduct by government, businesses, or private individuals.

On the ballot, Amendment 2 bore the title "No Protected Status Based on Homosexual, Lesbian, or Bisexual Orientation." Supporters said the measure would counter the efforts of "militant homosexuals" to get the government to endorse and promote homosexual behavior. "Any community that affirms homosexuality as morally and legally equal to heterosexuality is headed down the tubes," Tebedo says. "I didn't want to see my city or state turn into another New York or Seattle or San Francisco if there was anything I could do about it."

Opponents, however, maintained that the amendment barred homosexuals, lesbians, and bisexuals from equal participation in the political process. "The question here is whether a majority of voters can fence a minority group out of the political process," says Suzanne Goldberg, legal director of the New York–based Lambda Legal Defense and Educational Fund, which has helped direct the legal fight against the measure. "If Amendment 2 is upheld, all Americans are vulnerable to having their civil rights challenged or removed in the same way."

Supporters of the amendment conducted a low-visibility campaign, concentrated in churches and in conservative suburban and rural areas. A flyer distributed to most of the households in the state on the eve of the election warned that gay rights laws would force schools to hire gay teachers, require landlords to rent to homosexuals, and threaten ministers with "severe consequences" for opposing homosexuality.

Gay rights groups were generally confident of defeating the measure. In retrospect, Mary Celeste, one of the organizers of the opposition group Equal Protection Ordinance Coalition (EPOC), concedes that opponents failed to develop an effective response to the "No Special Rights" slogan and did too little to reach out to other constituencies, especially minority

Opponents of Colorado's anti-gay rights initiative celebrate outside the courtroom following a judge's ruling that blocked the measure, known as Amendment 2, from going into effect.

groups. On Election Night, gay rights supporters gathered expecting to celebrate victory. When the amendment passed, they staged an impromptu protest march to the Denver municipal building. Democratic governor Ray Romer, who opposed the amendment but did not actively campaign against it, joined the protesters.

Opponents began mapping a possible legal strategy against the amendment even before it passed. They filed their suit in state court in Denver a week after the election. The individual plaintiffs, all gay men or lesbians, included civil servants, a Denver police officer, a university professor, a Boulder minister, and the former chair of a Denver task force on gay and lesbian issues. The suit said that all of the plaintiffs had sought "through the political process" enactment of laws or regulations to prohibit discrimination on the basis of sexual orientation. The cities of Aspen, Boulder, and Denver also joined the suit. Richard Evans, a Denver city administrator, was listed as the first plaintiff. In an ironic twist, Governor Romer was named as defendant.

The legal team, headed by Jean Dubofsky, a former state supreme court justice, developed a variety of legal theories under both the federal and Colorado constitutions to challenge the amendment. The lawyers argued that the amendment violated freedom of speech under the First Amendment and local home rule provisions of the Colorado Constitution.

But in their initial request to block the amendment, they asked for a ruling only on one claim—that the amendment violates the Fourteenth Amendment's Equal Protection Clause by denying gay people the same rights other citizens have to use the political process.

The Supreme Court has enforced the Equal Protection Clause by requiring courts to give more rigorous review to laws that treat people differently according to race or gender. Racial classifications are subject to "strict scrutiny" and usually struck down; differential treatment based on gender is subject to "intermediate scrutiny" and can be upheld in some instances. But the Court has never held homosexuals to be a so-called "suspect class" entitled to this type of judicial protection. On that basis, the state attorney general's office asked the judge in Denver to dismiss the suit.

Judge Jeffrey Bayless held a four-day hearing on the amendment before issuing a preliminary injunction on January 15, 1993, blocking the measure from taking effect. Bayless said he wanted to preserve the status quo until the constitutional issues were resolved, but he also found that the plaintiffs had demonstrated a "reasonable probability of success."

The state appealed to the Colorado Supreme Court, which upheld the injunction. The 6–1 ruling accepted the plaintiffs' key argument that the amendment restricted the rights of homosexuals to participate in the political process. To uphold the amendment, the justices ruled, the state had to show that it served a "compelling interest." Gay rights groups said the ruling dealt a fatal blow to the amendment. But the state's Republican attorney general, Gale Norton, said the state would try to prove that the amendment helped protect "family values" and that enactment of gay rights laws could dilute the enforcement of other civil rights measures.

Bayless held a six-day trial on the case in October 1993 and two months later again ruled against the amendment. The state appealed, but the state supreme court upheld the decision on October 11, 1994, again by a 6–1 vote. "States have no compelling interest in amending their constitution in ways that violate fundamental Federal rights," Chief Justice Luis Rovira wrote. In his lone dissent, Justice William Erickson said the majority had "crafted a new fundamental right, never recognized by the U.S. Supreme Court."

In its petition asking the Court to review the ruling, the state depicted the decision as a broad threat to majority rule. "The Colorado Supreme Court's holding places into constitutional doubt any attempt by state or federal governments to preempt countervailing social policies favored by lesser political units," the state's lawyers said. The justices agreed to hear the dispute on February 21.

An outpouring of briefs on both sides followed. Conservative groups, including the American Center for Law and Justice, the Christian Legal Society, and Concerned Women for America, filed arguments in support of the amendment. At least seventeen briefs were filed in opposition. The opponents included gay rights organizations, racial and ethnic minority groups, labor unions, mental health organizations, liberal religious groups, and the American Bar Association and other bar groups in seventeen states.

The Clinton administration, however, disappointed opponents of the amendment by deciding not to join the case on their side. Solicitor General Drew S. Days reportedly circulated a memo urging the government to file a friend-of-the-court brief opposing the amendment, but Attorney General Janet Reno decided to stay out. "This was a matter in which we were not a party," Reno told a regular weekly news conference on June 8. "We were not asked by the Court to participate. There was no federal program or federal statute involved."

Reno said she made the decision herself and insisted that political factors did not play a part in the decision. But gay rights groups noted that President Clinton had been hurt politically at the start of his administration by advocating lifting the ban on homosexuals in the military. "They missed an opportunity to stand up for civil rights," Suzanne Goldberg told the *Washington Post* after Reno's announcement, "although they don't view it as an opportunity, I'm sure."

Advocates on both sides wrestled with the difficulty of framing the issue for the justices to decide. Opponents relied primarily on a line of cases since 1969, when the Court in *Hunter v. Erickson* struck down an Akron, Ohio, charter amendment requiring a referendum on any local fair housing law. In that decision, the justices said that imposing an additional requirement on legislation to benefit a particular group had the effect of "vote dilution"— reducing the value of their vote in comparison to the votes of other people.

Supporters of the amendment countered with a ruling two years later, *James v. Valtierra*, in which the Court refused to strike down a California constitutional amendment requiring that construction of low-income housing be subject to local referendum. They contended that the 1971 decision shows that the earlier ruling applies only to race cases and cannot be extended to cover legislation dealing with homosexuals. They also noted that the Court in 1986 upheld state antisodomy laws in a 5–4 decision, *Bowers v. Hardwick*, that rejected arguments the laws infringed on homosexuals' right of privacy and freedom of association.

Conservative experts predict the Court will uphold the Colorado amendment while steering clear of any broad ruling on gay rights. "I think that's going to be an easy case," says Douglas Kmiec, a Notre Dame law professor. "The Court is not going to accept [the Colorado Supreme Court's] novel proposition of [gays] being excluded from participation in the political process. They're not going to be anxious to create a new fundamental right."

Liberal experts acknowledge they face an uphill fight in persuading

Kevin Tebedo, executive director of Colorado for Family Values, tells reporters that the group will seek to overturn the Court ruling against Amendment 2.

the Court to invalidate the measure. "It's kind of an odd case," says the University of Virginia's Pamela Karlan, who coauthored a brief against the amendment. "It's falling under the doctrinal radar. Pretty much everybody who looks at it on the liberal side of things thinks there's something wrong with the initiative, but aren't quite sure what it is."

In Colorado, supporters and opponents of the amendment had similar assessments as the arguments in the case neared. Kevin Tebedo of Colorado for Family Values predicted the justices will uphold the measure. "We believe that the danger that the Court sees is the danger to the right of the people to make their own laws," Tebedo said.

But Jean Dubofsky, the lawyer for the opponents, cautiously predicted a ruling against the amendment. "Amendment 2 is so sweeping, I just don't think it has any place in our society to treat a group like that, no matter how unpopular," Dubofsky said. The Court "may not like the political participation theory," she added, "but it will find a theory to strike it down."

Following are some of the other major cases on the Supreme Court calendar as it began its 1995–1996 term:

Business Law

Securities law. The acquisition of a major U.S. entertainment company by a Japanese firm led to securities fraud suits that pose the issue whether a state court settlement can end federal court litigation over the same transactions.

Matsushita Electric Industrial Co. agreed to buy MCA, the parent company of Universal Studios and other entertainment concerns, for about $6.6 billion in 1990. The acquisition included a public tender offer valued at about $66 per share and a private stock swap with MCA's long-time chairman, Lew Wasserman, to allow him to avoid more than $100 million in income taxes on his gains from the deal.

Investors filed securities fraud suits in Delaware state court and in federal court in California claiming, among other things, that Wasserman was given preferential treatment in violation of a federal securities regulation requiring equal treatment of all investors in a tender offer. The Delaware litigation was settled in 1993, with about $2 million going to plaintiff shareholders. But investors won a ruling from the federal appeals court in California that allowed them to proceed to trial with their claims.

The appeals court rejected Matsushita's argument that the federal suit should be dismissed because the Delaware settlement covered all claims arising from the transaction. In urging the Court to review the case, Matsushita's attorneys argued that the decision "plays havoc" with state court judgments and settlements. The company also argued that the Court should bar individual suits to enforce the ban on discriminatory tender offers—Securities and Exchange Commission Rule 14d-10. The Business Roundtable, an organization of major U.S. corporations, filed a supporting brief.

Opposing Matsushita's plea, lawyers for the investors called the Delaware settlement a "sellout" that did not and could not resolve the far larger claims at issue in the federal court case. (*Matsushita Electric Industrial Co., Ltd. v. Epstein*)

Bankruptcy. The Court agreed to decide an important question for the banking industry: whether a bank can freeze the account of a depositor who has filed for bankruptcy protection after defaulting on a loan.

The case involves a Maryland man, David Strumpf, who filed a bankruptcy petition in January 1991. Strumpf owed Citizens Bank of Maryland about $2,500 on a personal loan and also maintained a checking account there. Although the bank did not participate in the bankruptcy proceeding, it put an "administrative hold" on Strumpf's account in October 1991.

Creditors generally must go through court proceedings to demand payment after an individual files for bankruptcy protection. A federal bankruptcy court held the bank in contempt of the "automatic stay" it had issued in the case and ordered the freeze lifted. Strumpf then withdrew his funds. The Fourth U.S. Circuit Court of Appeals upheld the contempt finding.

Citizens Bank urged the Court to review the decision, saying that it ignored the bank's rights and could raise the cost of making loans. The plea was joined by several banking groups, including the American Banking Association and Credit Union National Association, and by the country's largest bank, NationsBank.

In his brief, Strumpf argued that the bank froze his account "unilaterally and without prior notice" in violation of Bankruptcy Code provisions that prohibit any "set off" while an automatic stay is in effect.

In a separate filing, the federal government also urged the Court to hear the case. The government said it had an interest in collecting unpaid taxes in bankruptcy cases. It argued that a temporary administrative hold should not be deemed a set-off under the Bankruptcy Code. (*Citizens Bank of Maryland v. Strumpf*)

Criminal Law

Criminal forfeiture. Tina Bennis said she did not know her husband John was having sex with a prostitute in their family car while it was parked on a Detroit street on the evening of October 3, 1988. But after John's arrest, the Wayne County prosecutor's office refused to let her challenge their action to seize the car as a public nuisance.

In a 4–3 decision, the Michigan Supreme Court agreed that Tina Bennis had no standing to block the forfeiture under the state's nuisance abatement law. The justices said the state statute did not allow a property owner to block a forfeiture on grounds she did not know it was being used for an illegal purpose. They rejected arguments that the Constitution required the state to recognize the so-called innocent owner defense.

In urging the Court to review the case, Tina Bennis's attorney said the case presented an opportunity to ensure that "broad property confiscation statutes ... are not used to deprive innocent owners of their property." But Wayne County prosecutors disagreed. "... [I]nnocence ... does not excuse possible abatement of the offending property," they wrote. (*Bennis v. Michigan*)

In a second case, the justices agreed to decide whether the Federal Rules of Criminal Procedure require a judge to examine the factual basis for a forfeiture even if the defendant agrees to give up property as part of a guilty plea.

The defendant in the case, Joseph Libretti, pleaded guilty in federal court in Wyoming to drug trafficking and money laundering charges. As part of the plea, Libretti agreed to forfeit the property used in his drug operation and the proceeds from the enterprise. After sentencing, however, he argued that the judge had failed to establish a "factual basis" for the forfeiture.

The Federal Rules of Criminal Procedure do require a judge to determine the factual basis for a guilty plea. But the Tenth U.S. Circuit Court of Appeals rejected Libretti's argument that the rule required a similar examination of the basis for a forfeiture order. The National Association of Criminal Defense Lawyers backed Libretti's appeal to the Court, saying judicial review was needed to prevent "prosecutorial overreaching" and to protect the rights of third parties. (*Libretti v. United States*)

Firearms statute. The Court agreed to decide whether a defendant may be convicted under a federal law against using a firearm in a drug offense even if the weapon is out of reach or locked away at the time of the offense.

Two defendants convicted under the law in Washington, D.C., asked the Court to set aside the firearms counts. Roland Bailey had been charged in 1989 after police stopped him for a traffic violation and found bags of cocaine in the front of his car and a loaded handgun underneath a number of items in the trunk. Candisha Robinson was arrested in her apartment after selling a "rock" of crack cocaine to an undercover officer for $20. A later search uncovered an unloaded pistol stored in a locked footlocker near Robinson's bed.

Both defendants were convicted on the drug and firearms counts. Bailey received a sixty-month sentence on the firearm count on top of a fifty-one-month sentence for the cocaine charges. Robinson was sentenced to 157 months' imprisonment in total. Different panels of the U.S. Circuit Court of Appeals for the District of Columbia affirmed Robinson's conviction but reversed Bailey's conviction on the gun charge. The full appeals court then combined the cases and upheld both convictions in a 5–4 decision.

The appeals court said two factors should be used to determine whether a gun was "used" in a drug offense: its accessibility and its proximity to the drugs in question. In their appeal, the defendants argued the test went beyond the statute, enacted in the mid-1980s, and conflicted with rulings in other federal circuits. The government countered that Congress intended that the statute be interpreted broadly and that the appellate ruling coincided with decisions in other circuits. (*Bailey v. United States; Robinson v. United States*)

Habeas corpus. The Court took up two habeas corpus cases even while Congress was considering legislation that would sharply curtail state prisoners' ability to use the procedure to challenge convictions in federal court.

In the first case, an Alaska man convicted of murdering his wife asked federal courts to decide whether police had improperly interrogated him by failing to give him *Miranda* warnings. Alaska courts had ruled that the defendant, Carl Thompson, was not in custody during the questioning.

The Ninth U.S. Circuit Court of Appeals refused to consider the issue in Thompson's habeas corpus filing. It ruled that the custody issue was a factual question, and the state courts were entitled to a presumption of correctness.

Thompson, represented by a Court-appointed counsel after filing an initial petition on his own, argued the custody question was "essentially legal" and should be reviewable in federal court. But the Alaska attorney general's office countered that state courts were entitled to deference because of "principles of finality, federalism, and fairness." (*Thompson v. Keohane*)

In the second case, the Court was being asked to decide whether a state prisoner can be refused a hearing on a federal habeas corpus petition solely because of a six-year delay in filing it.

The case involves a Georgia death row inmate, Larry Lonchar, whose death sentence for three murder convictions was upheld by the state's supreme court in 1988. Lonchar refused to seek postconviction review in state or federal court and opposed efforts by his sister and brother to challenge the sentences. But on June 27, on the eve of his scheduled execution, Lonchar filed a federal habeas corpus petition.

A federal district court judge initially ordered a hearing, but the Eleventh U.S. Circuit Court of Appeals ordered the petition dismissed because of what it called Lonchar's "willful delay and manipulation of the judicial system." But Lonchar's attorney argued that the appellate decision was "the first time ever that a court has totally barred a man who is facing execution from ever litigating one federal habeas corpus petition." (*Lonchar v. Thomas*)

Prisoners' rights. A federal court judge in Arizona issued a sweeping order in 1993 requiring the state to provide prison inmates with improved access to legal materials. The ruling, based on a 1977 Supreme Court decision, directed prison officials to open prison law libraries at least fifty hours a week, hire trained librarians or paralegals, and allow inmates direct access to library stacks unless the state could document a security risk.

State officials challenged the ruling, but the Ninth U.S. Circuit Court of Appeals upheld the order. The state then asked the Court to review the decision. The Court blocked the order from taking effect in May 1994. One year later, it agreed to hear the case in the coming term.

In their petition, Arizona officials said the judge's order was "intrusive" and amounted to "micro-management of state prisons." But the inmates, represented by the National Prison Project of the American Civil Liberties Union, praised the decision as "a thoughtful and cautious approach" to remedying violations in inmates' constitutionally guaranteed access to courts. (*Lewis v. Casey*)

Elections

Racial redistricting. North Carolina's Twelfth Congressional District, a snakelike configuration winding through the state for more than 160 miles, achieved national notoriety in 1993 as the subject of the Court's first ruling against racial gerrymandering. Now the district map is back before the Court following a ruling by a three-judge federal district court in August 1994 upholding the unusual line-drawing.

In its first decision, the Court held that white voters can challenge "highly irregular" district lines drawn on the basis of race. But it returned the case to the three-judge panel to give the state a chance to demonstrate a "compelling" interest to justify the remapping plan. During a week-long trial, North Carolina officials argued that the Twelfth District, combining predominantly black areas in three widely separated cities, should be upheld because it helped overcome past racial discrimination and combined citizens with "shared economic, social, and cultural interests." The panel, in a split decision, agreed.

The white voters challenging the plan again asked the Court to strike it down, arguing that the state had used "post hoc rationalizations" to defend it. A group of Republican voters, represented by lawyers for the Republican National Committee, also intervened to oppose the plan. They said the lower court had failed to give "sufficient emphasis" to the configuration of the challenged district. But lawyers for the state countered that "the formation of districts based on communities of interest, instead of geographic compactness, provides for fair and effective representation of voters." (*Shaw v. Hunt; Pope v. Hunt*)

A second redistricting case, challenging three majority-minority districts in Texas, gives the justices the chance to decide whether protection of incumbent officeholders can help justify racial line-drawing. The redistricting plan drawn by the Texas legislature for the 1992 election included majority black districts in the Houston and Dallas areas and a majority Hispanic district in Houston. The districts took on some unusual shaping as legislators accommodated requests by incumbent white members of Congress, of both parties, to keep some of their strongholds in their adjoining districts.

A multiethnic group of voters, led by a Hispanic school teacher, Al Vera, challenged a total of twenty-four of the state's thirty districts as a product of illegal racial gerrymandering. State officials defended the plan, and the Clinton administration and separate groups of African-American and Latino voters intervened in the case to support it. After a five-day trial, the three-judge court unanimously rejected the lines for the three majority-minority districts in Houston and Dallas. It called the district lines "convoluted" and "tortuously drawn" and rejected what it termed the state's "talismanic" use of incumbent protection to defend the shapes.

Texas officials, the minority voters, and the Justice Department filed separate appeals urging the Court to reinstate the districting plan. All three appeals emphasized that the majority minority districts were drawn in part on the basis of what the state called "non-racial policy reasons." But the plaintiffs urged the Court to uphold the decision striking the plan. They argued the lines amounted to racial gerrymandering and were not justified on grounds of remedying past discrimination or protecting incumbent officeholders. (*Bush v. Vera; Lawson v. Vera; United States v. Vera*)

Party conventions. The Court agreed to decide whether the Republican Party of Virginia violated the federal Voting Rights Act by charging a $45 fee to participate in its 1992 senatorial nominating convention.

Three University of Virginia law students claimed that the fee was covered by the provision in the 1965 act requiring Virginia and other states to obtain "preclearance" from the Justice Department for any change in election procedure. They also said the fee violated another section of the law prohibiting poll taxes.

A three-judge federal court rejected the suit. The panel agreed with the Virginia GOP that the law does not apply to internal party rules and that private individuals do not have standing to bring suit under the poll tax provision. In urging the Court to hear the case, the students said the fee "threatens the sorts of discrimination and vote buying that motivated Congress to ban poll taxes and to require preclearance of new qualifications for participation." (*Morse v. Republican Party of Virginia*)

Federal Government

Agent Orange settlement. Chemical companies that manufactured the defoliant Agent Orange for use in the Vietnam War paid $180 million in 1987 to settle a class action suit by veterans. The veterans blamed a variety of serious health problems on a toxic byproduct contained in the defoliant dioxin.

Two of the companies—Hercules, Inc. and W. T. Thompson Co.— sued the government in 1990 for reimbursement. They argued that defense contractors are protected from liability for any adverse consequences resulting from manufacturing products to government specification. The Court of Federal Claims and the Court of Appeals for the Federal Circuit both rejected the suit, saying the companies had made a voluntary decision to settle the litigation.

The Thompson company, which later went out of business, and Hercules urged the Court to review the case. They argued the lower court rulings would discourage settlements and ultimately increase the cost of government contracting. But the government said the companies' stand would allow government contractors to create "indirect governmental liability" by allowing plaintiffs "to accomplish by suing the contractor what they could not accomplish by suing the government directly." (*Hercules, Inc. v. United States*)

First Amendment

Telecommunications. The country's local telephone companies want to bring the video revolution into the nation's living rooms, but they have been blocked by a federal law aimed at preventing unfair competition with local cable systems. The telephone companies say the law violates the First Amendment, and the Court may settle the issue in the coming term.

Telephone companies have been prohibited from providing cable services within their own service areas under a provision established by the Federal Communications Commission (FCC) in 1981 and enacted into law by Congress in 1984. The restriction was designed to prevent telephone companies from using revenues from their regulated phone service to finance a competitive, profit-making cable system.

Technological advances now enable phone companies to offer an array of video services over the same lines used to provide telephone service. They called for repealing the crossownership ban in order to permit greater competition, but Congress in 1992 refused. Bell Atlantic Corp., one of the seven regional phone companies created after the breakup of AT&T, then filed a constitutional challenge to the law in federal court in Virginia.

The government and the cable industry defended the law, but both the trial judge and the Fourth U.S. Circuit Court of Appeals ruled the measure unconstitutional. The courts held the law violated the First Amendment because the government had less restrictive ways of accomplishing its goals of promoting media diversity. Other telephone companies won similar rulings elsewhere in the country.

The government, along with the National Cable Television Association, again defended the constitutionality of the law in petitions asking the Court to review the Bell Atlantic decision. In an unusual twist, however, both urged the Court to postpone any ruling and send the case back to lower federal courts because of a policy change announced by the FCC in May. The commission said it would use a provision in the law to grant waivers to phone companies to offer video services in their areas subject to regulatory limits to be developed later.

Bell Atlantic derided the government's move as an "administrative shell game." It urged the Court to agree to hear the case in order to give the nation's telecommunications industry an "authoritative adjudication" on the issue. (*United States v. Chesapeake & Potomac Telephone, Inc.*; *National Cable Television Association v. Bell Atlantic Corp.*)

Commercial speech. The Court agreed to hear a First Amendment challenge by liquor stores in Rhode Island and Massachusetts to a Rhode Island law prohibiting price advertising for alcoholic beverages. The state defended the law by contending it prevented "abusive consumption" of alcoholic beverages.

A federal district court judge ruled the law unconstitutional, but the First U.S. Circuit Court of Appeals upheld it. The appeals court relied in part on the Twenty-First Amendment, which repealed Prohibition but included a broad provision authorizing state regulation of alcoholic beverages. The Court last considered the issue in 1982, when it dismissed a challenge to a similar law "for want of a substantial federal question." (*44 Liquormart, Inc. v. Rhode Island*)

Labor Law

Union organizers. To aid unionization efforts, unions sometimes try to get paid organizers hired by targeted companies so that they can solicit support for the union from within the workplace. Companies typically try to avoid hiring these paid organizers and sometimes fire them if they are hired.

In several cases, the National Labor Relations Board (NLRB) has ruled that the union organizers are "employees" for purposes of federal labor law and protected from discrimination or discharge on account of their union activity. Some federal appeals courts have agreed, but others have rejected the NLRB's interpretation and ruled companies are free to fire.

The Court agreed to resolve the issue in the new term in a dispute involving the International Brotherhood of Electrical Workers and a Wisconsin-based, nonunion electrical contractor, Town & Country Electric. The company in 1989 rejected applications from several union members for a job in Minnesota. It did hire one union member but later fired him, ostensibly because he engaged in union activities on company time.

The NLRB ruled the discharge was an unfair labor practice, but the Eighth U.S. Circuit Court of Appeals overturned the board's ruling. In asking the Court to review the case, the NLRB said the appeals court's ruling was "antithetical" to federal labor law's "core purpose" of protecting the right to organize. But the company, backed by the U.S. Chamber of Commerce, argued it had a right to fire the organizer because he had a primary obligation to the union instead of to the company. (*NLRB v. Town & Country Electric, Inc.*)

Pensions and benefits. The Court agreed to decide whether federal law permits current and retired employees to sue an employer on their own behalf for using dishonest means to cut off health insurance or other benefits. The dispute stems from a corporate reorganization by Varity Corporation, a manufacturer of farm and industrial machinery. The company, which is based in Buffalo, New York, set up a new unit, Massey Combines Corp., in Des Moines, Iowa, and persuaded employees of another unit, Massey-Ferguson, Inc., to transfer to the new concern. Massey Combines quickly failed, however, and cut off benefits to the transferred workers and retirees.

Some of the retirees filed suit under the federal Employee Retirement Income Security Act (ERISA). They claimed the company had breached its duty to protect the workers' interest—a so-called fiduciary duty. They won a jury verdict totaling $46 million (reduced later to less than $10 million and finally to $797,000) plus reinstatement to the retirement plan. But Varity contended that ERISA did not allow workers to bring such suits. (*Varity Corp. v. Howe*)

States

Indian gaming. Gambling has become a booming, $7 billion per year industry for Indian tribes. State governments have tried to limit the development, but Congress in 1988 passed a law protecting tribes' rights to operate gaming businesses if a state allows others to do so.

The law, the Indian Gaming Regulatory Act, includes a provision requiring a state to negotiate in good faith with the tribes on the terms for Indian gaming. Tribes are authorized to sue the state in federal court if it refuses. But the Eleventh U.S. Circuit Court of Appeals held that provision unconstitutional in August 1994. Ruling in a pair of cases brought by the Seminole Tribe against the state of Florida and the Porach Tribe against the state of Alabama, the appeals court said the provision violates the Eleventh Amendment, which generally protects states from being sued in federal court.

At the urging of the Clinton administration, the Court agreed in January to hear the Seminoles' appeal of the decision. In its brief, the administration argued that Congress can override the states' Eleventh Amendment immunity and that it intended to do so in the Indian gaming law. But Florida, backed by the National Governors' Association and other state and local government associations, urged the justices to uphold the appeals court ruling. (*Seminole Tribe of Florida v. Florida*)

Torts

Punitive damages. Ira Gore, an Alabama physician, thought he was buying a flawless luxury car when he paid $40,000 for a new BMW sedan in January 1990. But nine months later, he learned that the German automaker had repainted virtually the entire car, apparently because of acid rain damage, before shipping it to the United States for sale.

For BMW and other automakers, damage to original paint jobs is a recognized risk in moving cars from factory to dealer showrooms. But Gore, surprised and infuriated, sued BMW for fraud in failing to disclose the damage. An Alabama jury agreed and awarded him $4,000 to cover the car's reduced value and an eye-popping $4 million in punitive damages.

In January, the Court agreed to hear BMW's plea to throw out the award, which the Alabama Supreme Court had already reduced to $2 million. The automaker, backed by several business groups and conservative public interest organizations, urged the Court to use the case to establish new procedural requirements and substantive limits on punitive damage awards.

Procedurally, the company contended that the Alabama Supreme Court had "abdicated its responsibility to provide a remedy" for a constitutional violation by approving the $2 million award even after finding that the jury had considered improper evidence in its verdict. BMW also argued that the "grossly excessive" award violated the "substantive component" of the Fourteenth Amendment's Due Process Clause. It urged the Court to adopt some guidelines for punitive damage awards, such as limiting penalties to some "small multiple" of the actual or potential harm.

Gore's lawyers countered that the punitive damage award was proper in light of what it called BMW's "decade-long fleecing of consumers on a large scale." They noted in their brief to the Court that BMW had changed its policy on disclosing defects to car buyers five days following the jury verdict in the case. Trial lawyer groups and proplaintiff law professors filed half a dozen supporting briefs that argued, among other things, that the Court should leave tort reform to Congress, state legislatures, or state courts. (*BMW of North America, Inc. v. Gore*)

International air crashes. A suit stemming from the shooting down of Korean Air Lines flight 007 in 1983 gave the Court the opportunity to clarify the rules for damages in international air crashes.

The Court granted a petition by relatives of one of the victims of the crash seeking to relax the damage rules for "loss of society" or loss of companionship and an opposing petition by the airline aimed at limiting such damages. The plaintiffs, the victim's mother and sister, had won jury awards of $124,000 and $151,000 respectively, for mental injury, loss of society, and loss of support and inheritance.

The Second U.S. Circuit Court of Appeals threw out the awards, however. It ruled that the Warsaw Convention, the international treaty governing liability for air crashes, bars damages for loss of society unless the plaintiff was financially dependent on the victim and bars any damage for mental injury.

In urging the Court to review the decision, the plaintiffs called the limitation "a cruel and irrational rule of law." Attorneys for other plaintiffs in

Flight 007 cases filed a supporting brief, as did lawyers representing plaintiffs in the bombing of Pan American flight 183 over Scotland in 1988. Korean Air Lines filed an opposing petition. It argued that the crash was covered by a federal law governing deaths on the high seas that allowed no recovery for loss of society under any circumstances. (*Zicherman v. Korean Air Lines; Korean Air Lines v. Zicherman*)

Appendix

How the Court Works

The Constitution makes the Supreme Court the final arbiter in "cases" and "controversies" arising under the Constitution or the laws of the United States. As the interpreter of the law, the Court often is viewed as the least mutable and most tradition-bound of the three branches of the federal government. But the Court has undergone innumerable changes in its history, some of which have been mandated by law. Some of these changes are embodied in Court rules; others are informal adaptations to needs and circumstances.

The Schedule of the Term

Annual Terms

By law the Supreme Court begins its regular annual term on the first Monday in October, and the term lasts approximately nine months. This session is known as the October term. The summer recess, which is not determined by statute or Court rules, generally begins in late June or early July of the following year. This system—staying in continuous session throughout the year, with periodic recesses—makes it unnecessary to convene a special term to deal with matters arising in the summer.

The justices actually begin work before the official opening of the term. They hold their initial conference during the last week in September. When the justices formally convene on the first Monday in October, oral arguments begin.

Arguments and Conferences

At least four justices must request that a case be argued before it can be accepted. Arguments are heard on Monday, Tuesday, and Wednesday for seven two-week sessions, beginning in the first week in October and ending in mid-April. Recesses of two weeks or longer occur between the sessions of oral arguments so that justices can consider the cases and deal with other Court business.

The schedule for oral arguments is 10:00 a.m. to noon and 1 p.m. to 3 p.m. Because most cases receive one hour apiece for argument, the Court can hear up to twelve cases a week.

The Court holds conferences on the Friday just before the two-week oral argument periods and on Wednesday and Friday during the weeks when oral arguments are scheduled. The conferences are designed for consideration of cases already heard in oral argument.

Before each of the Friday conferences, the chief justice circulates a "discuss" list—a list of cases deemed important enough for discussion and a vote. Appeals are placed on the discuss list almost automatically, but as many as three-quarters of the petitions for certiorari are dismissed. No case is denied review during conference, however, without an initial examination by the justices and their law clerks. Any justice can have a case placed on the Court's conference agenda for review. Most of the cases scheduled for the discuss list also are denied review in the end but only after discussion by the justices during the conference.

Although the last oral arguments have been heard by mid-April each year, the conferences of the justices continue until the end of the term to consider cases remaining on the Court's agenda. All conferences are held in secret, with no legal assistants or other staff present. The attendance of six justices constitutes a quorum. Conferences begin with handshakes all around. In discussing a case, the chief justice speaks first, followed by each justice in order of seniority.

Decision Days

Opinions are released on Tuesdays and Wednesdays during the weeks that the Court is hearing oral arguments; during other weeks, they are released on Mondays. In addition to opinions, the Court also releases an "orders" list—the summary of the Court's action granting or denying review. The orders list is posted at the beginning of the Monday session. It is not announced orally but can be obtained from the clerk and the public information officer. When urgent or important matters arise, the Court's summary orders may be made available on a day other than Monday.

Unlike its orders, decisions of the Court are announced orally in open Court. The justice who wrote the opinion announces the Court's decision, and justices writing concurring or dissenting opinions may state their views as well. When more than one decision is to be rendered, the justices who wrote the opinion make their announcements in reverse order of seniority. Occasionally, all or a large portion of the opinion is read aloud. More often the author summarizes the opinion or simply announces the result and states that a written opinion has been filed.

Reviewing Cases

In determining whether to accept a case for review, the Court has considerable discretion, subject only to the restraints imposed by the

Visiting the Supreme Court

The Supreme Court building has six levels, two of which—the ground and main floors—are accessible to the public. The basement contains a parking garage, a printing press, and offices for security guards and maintenance personnel. On the ground floor are the John Marshall statue, the exhibition area, the public information office, and a cafeteria. The main corridor, known as the Great Hall, the courtroom, and justices' offices are on the main floor. The second floor contains dining rooms, the justices' reading room, and other offices; the third floor, the Court library; and the fourth floor, the gym and storage areas.

From October to mid-April, the Court hears oral arguments Monday through Wednesday for about two weeks a month. These sessions begin at 10 a.m. and continue until 3 p.m., with a one-hour recess starting at noon. They are open to the public on a first-come, first-served basis.

Visitors may inspect the Supreme Court chamber any time the Court is not in session. Historical exhibits and a free motion picture on how the Court works also are available throughout the year. The Supreme Court building is open from 9 a.m. to 4:30 p.m. Monday through Friday, except for legal holidays. When the Court is not in session, lectures are given in the courtroom every hour on the half hour between 9:30 a.m. and 3:30 p.m.

Constitution and Congress. Article III, section 2, of the Constitution provides that "In all Cases affecting Ambassadors, other public Ministers and Consuls, and those in which a State shall be Party, the supreme Court shall have original Jurisdiction. In all the other Cases ... the supreme Court shall have appellate Jurisdiction, both as to Law and Fact, with such Exceptions, and under such Regulations as the Congress shall make."

Original jurisdiction refers to the right of the Supreme Court to hear a case before any other court does. Appellate jurisdiction is the right to review the decision of a lower court. The vast majority of cases reaching the Supreme Court are appeals from rulings of the lower courts; generally only a handful of original jurisdiction cases are filed each term.

After enactment of the Judiciary Act of 1925, the Supreme Court gained broad discretion to decide for itself what cases it would hear. In 1988 Congress virtually eliminated the Court's mandatory jurisdiction, which obliged it to hear most appeals. Since then that discretion has been nearly unlimited.

Methods of Appeal

Cases come to the Supreme Court in several ways: through petitions for writs of certiorari, appeals, and requests for certification.

In petitioning for a writ of certiorari, a litigant who has lost a case in a lower court sets out the reasons why the Supreme Court should review the case. If a writ is granted, the Court requests a certified record of the case from the lower court.

The main difference between the certiorari and appeal routes is that the Court has complete discretion to grant a request for a writ of certiorari but is under more obligation to accept and decide a case that comes to it on appeal.

Most cases reach the Supreme Court by means of the writ of certiorari. In the relatively few cases to reach the Court by means of appeal, the appellant must file a jurisdictional statement explaining why the case qualifies for review and why the Court should grant it a hearing. Often the justices dispose of these cases by deciding them summarily, without oral argument or formal opinion.

Those whose petitions for certiorari have been granted must pay the Court's standard $300 fee for docketing the case. The U.S. government does not have to pay these fees, nor do persons too poor to afford them. The latter may file in forma pauperis (in the character or manner of a pauper) petitions. Another, seldom used, method of appeal is certification, the request by a lower court—usually a court of appeals—for a final answer to questions of law in a particular case. The Court, after examining the certificate, may order the case argued before it.

Process of Review

In the 1994–1995 term the Court was asked to review about 8,100 cases. All petitions are examined by the staff of the clerk of the Court; those found to be in reasonably proper form are placed on the docket and given a number. All cases, except those falling within the Court's original jurisdiction, are placed on a single docket, known simply as "the docket." Only in the numbering of the cases is a distinction made between prepaid and in forma pauperis cases on the docket. The first case filed in the 1995–1996 term, for example, would be designated 95–1. In forma pauperis cases contain the year and begin with the number 5001. The second in forma pauperis case filed in the 1995–1996 term would thus be number 95–5002.

Each justice, aided by law clerks, is responsible for reviewing all cases on the docket. In recent years a number of justices have used a "cert pool" system in this review. Their clerks work together to examine cases, writing a pool memo on several petitions. The memo then is given to the justices who determine if more research is needed. Other justices may prefer to review each petition themselves or have their clerks do it.

Petitions on the docket vary from elegantly printed and bound documents, of which multiple copies are submitted to the Court, to single sheets of prison stationery scribbled in pencil. The decisions to grant or deny review of cases are made in conferences, which are held in the conference room adjacent to the chief justice's chambers. Justices are summoned to the conference room by a buzzer, usually between 9:30 and 10:00 a.m. They shake hands with each other and take their appointed seats, and the chief justice then begins the discussion.

Discuss and Orders Lists

A few days before the conference convenes, the chief justice compiles the discuss list of cases deemed important enough for discussion and a vote. As many as three-quarters of the petitions for certiorari are denied a place on the list and thus rejected without further consideration. Any justice can have a case placed on the discuss list simply by requesting that it be placed there.

Only the justices attend conferences; no legal assistants or staff are present. The junior associate justice acts as doorkeeper and messenger, sending for reference material and receiving messages and data. Unlike with other parts of the federal government, few leaks have occurred about what transpires during the conferences.

At the start of the conference, the chief justice makes a brief statement outlining the facts of each case. Then each justice, beginning with the senior associate justice, comments on the case, usually indicating in the course of the comments how he or she intends to vote. A traditional but unwritten rule is that four affirmative votes puts a case on the schedule for oral argument.

Petitions for certiorari, appeals, and in forma pauperis motions that are approved for review or denied review during conference are placed on a certified orders list to be released the next Monday in open court.

Arguments

Once the Court announces it will hear a case, the clerk of the Court arranges the schedule for oral argument. Cases are argued roughly in the order in which they were granted review, subject to modification if more time is needed to acquire all the necessary documents. Cases generally are heard not sooner than three months after the Court has agreed to review

The Supreme Court's law library contains about 300,000 volumes and houses the most complete available set of the printed briefs, appendices, and records of Court cases.

them. Under special circumstances the date scheduled for oral argument can be advanced or postponed.

Well before oral argument takes place, the justices receive the briefs and records from counsel in the case. The measure of attention the brief receives—from a thorough and exhaustive study to a cursory glance— depends both on the nature of the case and the work habits of the justice.

As one of the two public functions of the Court, oral arguments are viewed by some as very important. Others dispute the significance of oral arguments, contending that by the time a case is heard most of the justices already have made up their minds.

Time Limits

The time allowed each side for oral argument is thirty minutes. Because the time allotted must accommodate any questions the justices may wish to ask, the actual time for presentation may be considerably shorter than thirty minutes. Under the current rules of the Court, one counsel only will be heard for each side, except by special permission.

An exception is made for an amicus curiae, a "friend of the court," a person who volunteers or is invited to take part in matters before a court but is not a party in the case. Counsel for an amicus curiae may participate in oral argument if the party supported by the amicus allows use of part of its argument time or the Court grants a motion permitting argument by this counsel. The motion must show, the rules state, that the amicus's argument "is thought to provide assistance to the Court not otherwise available." The Court is generally unreceptive to such motions.

Court rules provide advice to counsel presenting oral arguments before the Court: "Oral argument should emphasize and clarify the written arguments appearing in the briefs on the merits." That same rule warns— with italicized emphasis— that the Court "looks with disfavor on oral argument read from a prepared text." Most attorneys appearing before the Court use an outline or notes to make sure they cover the important points.

Circulating the Argument

The Supreme Court has tape-recorded oral arguments since 1955. In 1968 the Court, in addition to its own recording, began contracting with private firms to tape and transcribe all oral arguments. The contract stipulates that the transcript "shall include everything spoken in argument, by Court, counsel, or others, and nothing shall be omitted from the transcript unless the Chief Justice or Presiding Justice so directs." But "the names of Justices asking questions shall not be recorded or transcribed; questions shall be indicated by the letter 'Q.' "

The marshal of the Court keeps the tapes during the term, and their use usually is limited to the justices and their law clerks. At the end of the term, the tapes are sent to the National Archives. Persons wishing to listen to the tapes or buy a copy of a transcript can apply to the Archives for permission to do so.

Transcripts made by a private firm can be acquired more quickly. These transcripts usually are available a week after arguments are heard. Those who purchase the transcripts must agree that they will not be photographically reproduced. Transcripts usually run from forty to fifty pages for one hour of oral argument.

Proposals have been made to tape arguments for television and radio use or to permit live broadcast coverage of arguments. The Court has rejected these proposals.

Use of Briefs

The brief of the petitioner or appellant must be filed within forty-five days of the Court's announced decision to hear the case. Except for in forma pauperis cases, forty copies of the brief must be filed with the Court. For in forma pauperis proceedings, the Court requires only that documents be legible. The opposing brief from the respondent or appellee is to be filed within thirty days of receipt of the brief of the petitioner or appellant. Either party may appeal to the clerk for an extension of time in filing the brief.

Court Rule 24 sets forth the elements that a brief should contain. These are: the questions presented for review; a list of all parties to the proceeding; a table of contents and table of authorities; citations of the opinions and judgments delivered in the lower courts; "a concise statement of the grounds on which the jurisdiction of this Court is invoked"; constitutional provisions, treaties, statutes, ordinances, and regulations involved; "a concise statement of the case containing all that is material to the consideration of the questions presented"; a summary of argument; the argument, which exhibits "clearly the points of fact and of law being presented and citing the authorities and statutes relied upon"; and a conclusion "specifying with particularity the relief which the party seeks."

The form and organization of the brief are covered by rules 33 and 34. The rules limit the number of pages in various types of briefs. The rules also set out a color code for the covers of different kinds of briefs. Petitions are white; motions opposing them are orange. Petitioner's briefs on the merits are light blue, while those of respondents are red. Reply briefs are yellow; amicus curiae, green; and documents filed by the United States, gray.

Questioning

During oral argument the justices may interrupt with questions or remarks as often as they wish. Unless counsel has been granted special permission extending the thirty-minute limit, he or she can continue talking after the time has expired only to complete a sentence.

The frequency of questioning, as well as the manner in which questions are asked, depends on the style of the justices and their interest in a particular case. Of the current justices, all but Clarence Thomas participate, more or less actively, in questioning during oral arguments. Thomas was reported to have asked no questions whatsoever from the bench during the 1993–1994 term.

Questions from the justices may upset and unnerve counsel by interrupting a well-rehearsed argument and introducing an unexpected element. Nevertheless, questioning has several advantages. It serves to alert counsel about what aspects of the case need further elaboration or more information. For the Court, questions can bring out weak points in an argument—and sometimes strengthen it.

Conferences

Cases for which oral arguments have been heard are then dealt with in conference. During the Wednesday afternoon conference, the cases that were argued the previous Monday are discussed and decided. At the all-day Friday conference, the cases argued on the preceding Tuesday and

The Supreme Court's bench, angled at the ends, allows justices to see each other during oral arguments

Wednesday are discussed and decided. Justices also consider new motions, appeals, and petitions while in conference.

Conferences are conducted in complete secrecy. No secretaries, clerks, stenographers, or messengers are allowed into the room. This practice began many years ago when the justices became convinced that decisions were being disclosed prematurely.

The justices meet in an oak-paneled, book-lined conference room adjacent to the chief justice's suite. Nine chairs surround a large rectangular table, each chair bearing the nameplate of the justice who sits there. The chief justice sits at the east end of the table, and the senior associate justice at the west end. The other justices take their places in order of seniority. The junior justice is charged with sending for and receiving documents or other information the Court needs.

On entering the conference room the justices shake hands with each other, a symbol of harmony that began in the 1880s. The chief justice begins the conference by calling the first case to be decided and discussing it. When the chief justice is finished, the senior associate justice speaks, followed by the other justices in order of seniority.

The justices can speak for as long as they wish, but they practice restraint because of the amount of business to be completed. By custom each justice speaks without interruption. Other than these procedural arrangements, little is known about what transpires in conference.

Although discussions generally are said to be polite and orderly, occasionally they can be acrimonious. Likewise, consideration of the issues in a particular case may be full and probing, or perfunctory, leaving the real debate on the question until later when the written drafts of opinions are circulated up and down the Court's corridors between chambers.

Generally the discussion of the case clearly indicates how a justice plans to vote on it. A majority vote is needed to decide a case—five votes if all nine justices are participating.

Opinions

After the justices have voted on a case, the writing of the opinion or opinions begins. An opinion is a reasoned argument explaining the legal issues in the case and the precedents on which the opinion is based. Soon after a case is decided in conference, the task of writing the majority opinion is assigned. When in the majority, the chief justice designates the writer. When the chief justice is in the minority, the senior associate justice voting with the majority assigns the job of writing the majority opinion.

Any justice may write a separate opinion. If in agreement with the Court's decision but not with some of the reasoning in the majority opinion, the justice writes a concurring opinion giving his or her reasoning. If in disagreement with the majority, the justice writes a dissenting opinion or simply goes on record as a dissenter without an opinion. More than one justice can sign a concurring opinion or a dissenting opinion.

The amount of time between the vote on a case and the announcement of the decision varies from case to case. In simple cases where few points of law are at issue, the opinion sometimes can be written and cleared by the other justices in a week or less. In more complex cases, especially those with several dissenting or concurring opinions, the process can take six months or more. Some cases may have to be reargued or the initial decision reversed after the drafts of opinions have been circulated.

The assigning justice may consider the points made by majority justices during the conference discussion, the workload of the other justices, the need to avoid the more extreme opinions within the majority, and expertise in the particular area of law involved in a case.

The style of writing a Court opinion—majority, concurring, or dissenting—depends primarily on the individual justice. In some cases, the justice may prefer to write a restricted and limited opinion; in others, he or she may take a broader approach to the subject. The decision likely is to be influenced by the need to satisfy the other justices in the majority.

When a justice is satisfied that the written opinion is conclusive or "unanswerable," it goes into print. Draft opinions are circulated, revised, and printed on a computerized typesetting system. The circulation of the drafts—whether computer-to-computer or on paper—provokes further discussion in many cases. Often the suggestions and criticisms require the writer to juggle opposing views. To retain a majority, the author of the draft opinion frequently feels obliged to make major emendations to satisfy justices who are unhappy with the initial draft. Some opinions have to be rewritten several times.

One reason for the secrecy surrounding the circulation of drafts is that some of the justices who voted with the majority may find the majority draft opinion so unpersuasive—or one or more of the dissenting drafts so convincing—that they change their vote. If enough justices alter their votes, the majority may shift, so that a former dissent becomes the majority opinion. When a new majority emerges from this process, the task of writing, printing, and circulating a new majority draft begins all over again.

When the drafts of an opinion—including dissents and concurring views—have been written, circulated, discussed, and revised, if necessary, the final versions then are printed. Before the opinion is produced the reporter of decisions adds a "headnote" or syllabus summarizing the decision and a "lineup" showing how the justices voted.

Two hundred copies of the "bench opinion" are made. As the decision is announced in Court, the bench opinion is distributed to journalists and others in the public information office. Another copy, with any necessary corrections noted on it, is sent to the U.S. Government Printing Office, which prints 3,397 "slip" opinions, which are distributed to federal and state courts and agencies. The Court receives 400 of these, and they are available to the public free through the Public Information Office as long as supplies last. The Government Printing Office also prints the opinion for inclusion in *United States Reports,* the official record of Supreme Court opinions.

The Court also makes opinions available electronically, through its so-called Hermes system, to a number of large legal publishers, the Government Printing Office, and other information services. These organizations allow redistribution of the opinions to their own subscribers and users. Opinions are available on the Internet through Case Western Reserve University. The Hermes system was established as a pilot project in 1991 and expanded and made permanent in 1993.

The public announcement of opinions in Court probably is the Court's most dramatic function. It may also be the most expendable. Depending on who delivers the opinion and how, announcements can take a considerable amount of the Court's time. Opinions are given simultaneously to the public information officer for distribution. Nevertheless, those who are in the courtroom to hear the announcement of a ruling are participating in a very old tradition. The actual delivery may be tedious or exciting, depending on the nature of the case, the eloquence of the opinion, and the style of its oral delivery.

Brief Biographies

William Hubbs Rehnquist

Born: October 1, 1924, Milwaukee, Wisconsin.

Education: Stanford University, B.A., Phi Beta Kappa, and M.A., 1948; Harvard University, M.A., 1949; Stanford University Law School, LL.B., 1952.

Family: Married Natalie Cornell, 1953; died, 1991; two daughters, one son.

Career: Law clerk to Justice Robert H. Jackson, U.S. Supreme Court, 1952–1953; practiced law, 1953–1969; assistant U.S. attorney general, Office of Legal Counsel, 1969–1971.

Supreme Court Service: Nominated as associate justice of the U.S. Supreme Court by President Richard Nixon, October 21, 1971; confirmed, 68–26, December 10, 1971; nominated as chief justice of the United States by President Ronald Reagan, June 17, 1986; confirmed, 65–33, September 17, 1986.

President Reagan's appointment of William H. Rehnquist as chief justice in 1986 was a clear indication that the president was hoping to shift

the Court to the right. Since his early years as an associate justice in the 1970s, Rehnquist has been one of the Court's most conservative justices.

Rehnquist, the fourth associate justice to become chief, argues that the original intent of the Framers of the Constitution and the Bill of Rights is the proper standard for interpreting those documents today. He also takes a literal approach to individual rights. These beliefs have led him to dissent from the Court's rulings protecting a woman's privacy-based right to abortion, to argue that no constitutional barrier exists to school prayer, and to side with police and prosecutors on questions of criminal law. In 1991 he wrote the Court's decision upholding an administration ban on abortion counseling at publicly financed clinics and in 1992 vigorously dissented from the Court's affirmation of *Roe v. Wade,* the 1973 opinion that made abortion legal nationwide.

Born in Milwaukee, Wisconsin, October 1, 1924, Rehnquist attended Stanford University, where he earned both a B.A. and M.A. He received a second M.A. from Harvard before returning to Stanford for law school. His classmates there recalled him as an intelligent student with already well-entrenched conservative views.

After graduating from law school in 1952, Rehnquist came to Washington, D.C., to serve as a law clerk to Supreme Court justice Robert H. Jackson. There he wrote a memorandum that later would come back to haunt him during his Senate confirmation hearings. In the memo Rehnquist favored separate but equal schools for blacks and whites. Asked about those views by the Senate Judiciary Committee in 1971, Rehnquist repudiated them, declaring that they were Justice Jackson's—not his own, although Jackson was a moderate.

Following his clerkship, Rehnquist decided to practice law in the Southwest. He moved to Phoenix and immediately became immersed in Arizona Republican politics. From his earliest days in the state, he was associated with the party's conservative wing. A 1957 speech denouncing the liberalism of the Warren Court typified his views at the time.

During the 1964 presidential race, Rehnquist campaigned ardently for Barry Goldwater. It was then that Rehnquist met and worked with Richard G. Kleindienst, who later, as President Richard Nixon's deputy attorney general, would appoint Rehnquist to head the Justice Department's Office of Legal Counsel as an assistant attorney general. In 1971 Nixon nominated him to the Supreme Court.

Rehnquist drew opposition from liberals and civil rights organizations before winning confirmation and again before being approved as chief justice in 1986. The Senate voted to approve his nomination in December 1971 by a vote of 68–26 at the same time that another Nixon nominee, Lewis F. Powell, Jr., was winning nearly unanimous confirmation. In 1986 Rehnquist faced new accusations of having harassed voters as a Republican poll watcher in Phoenix in the 1950s and 1960s. He was also found to have accepted anti-Semitic restrictions in a property deed to a Vermont home. Despite the charges, the Senate approved his appointment 65–33. Liberal Democratic senators cast most of the no votes in both confirmations.

Despite his strong views, Rehnquist is popular among his colleagues and staff. When he was nominated for chief justice, Justice William J. Brennan, Jr., the leader of the court's liberal bloc, said Rehnquist would be "a splendid chief justice." After becoming chief justice, Rehnquist was credited with speeding up the court's conferences, in which the justices decide what cases to hear, vote on cases, and assign opinions.

Rehnquist was married to Natalie Cornell, who died in 1991. They had two daughters and a son. In 1994 news reports said that Rehnquist was dating Cynthia Holcomb Hall, a judge on the Ninth U.S. Circuit Court of Appeals.

John Paul Stevens

Born: April 20, 1920, Chicago, Illinois.

Education: University of Chicago, B.A., Phi Beta Kappa, 1941; Northwestern University School of Law, J.D., 1947.

Family: Married Elizabeth Jane Sheeren, 1942; three daughters, one son; divorced 1979; married Maryan Mulholland Simon, 1980.

Career: Law clerk to Justice Wiley B. Rutledge, U.S. Supreme Court, 1947–1948; practiced law, Chicago, 1949–1970; judge, U.S. Court of Appeals for the Seventh Circuit, 1970–1975.

Supreme Court Service: Nominated as associate justice of the U.S. Supreme Court by President Gerald R. Ford, November 28, 1975; confirmed, 98–0, December 17, 1975.

When President Gerald R. Ford nominated federal appeals court judge John Paul Stevens to the Supreme Court seat vacated by veteran liberal William O. Douglas in 1975, Court observers struggled to pin an ideological label on the new nominee. The consensus that finally emerged was that Stevens was neither a doctrinaire liberal nor conservative, but a judicial centrist. His subsequent opinions bear out this description, although in recent years he has leaned more toward the liberal side.

Stevens is a soft-spoken, mild-mannered man who occasionally sports a bow tie under his judicial robes. A member of a prominent Chicago family, he had a long record of excellence in scholarship, graduating Phi Beta Kappa from the University of Chicago in 1941. After a wartime stint in the navy, during which he earned the Bronze Star, he returned to Chicago to enter Northwestern University Law School, from which he graduated magna cum laude in 1947. From there Stevens left for Washington, where he served as a law clerk to Supreme Court justice Wiley B. Rutledge. He returned to Chicago to join the prominent law firm of Poppenhusen, Johnston, Thompson & Raymond, which specialized in antitrust law. Stevens developed a reputation as a preeminent antitrust lawyer, and after three years with Poppenhusen he left in 1952 to form his own firm, Rothschild, Stevens, Barry & Myers. He remained there, engaging in private practice and teaching part time at Northwestern and the University of Chicago law schools, until his appointment by President Richard Nixon in 1970 to the U.S. Court of Appeals for the Seventh Circuit.

Stevens developed a reputation as a political moderate during his undergraduate days at the University of Chicago, then an overwhelmingly liberal campus. Although he is a registered Republican, he has never been active in partisan politics. Nevertheless, Stevens served as Republican counsel in 1951 to the House Judiciary Subcommittee on the Study of Monopoly Power. He also served from 1953 to 1955, during the Eisenhower administration, as a member of the attorney general's committee to study antitrust laws.

Stevens has frequently dissented from the most conservative rulings of the Burger and Rehnquist courts. For example, he dissented from the Burger Court's 1986 decision upholding state antisodomy laws and the Rehnquist Court's 1989 decision permitting states to execute someone for committing a murder at the age of sixteen or seventeen. He has taken liberal positions on abortion rights, civil rights, and church-state issues. Among his most important opinions is a 1985 decision striking down an Alabama law that allowed a moment of silence for prayer or silent meditation at the beginning of each school day.

In 1942 Stevens married Elizabeth Jane Sheeren. They have four children. They were divorced in 1979. Stevens subsequently married Maryan Mulholland Simon, a longtime neighbor in Chicago.

Sandra Day O'Connor

Born: March 26, 1930, El Paso, Texas.

Education: Stanford University, B.A., 1950; Stanford University Law School, LL.B., 1952.

Family: Married John J. O'Connor III, 1952; three sons.

Career: Deputy county attorney, San Mateo, California, 1952–1953; assistant attorney general, Arizona, 1965–1969; Arizona state senator, 1969–1975; Arizona Senate majority leader, 1972–1975; judge, Maricopa County Superior Court, 1974–1979; judge, Arizona Court of Appeals, 1979–1981.

Supreme Court Service: Nominated as associate justice of the U.S. Supreme Court by President Ronald Reagan August 19, 1981; confirmed, 99–0, September 21, 1981.

Sandra Day O'Connor was the Court's first woman justice, and in 1992, after a decade on the Court, she emerged as a coalition builder in the Court's legal doctrine on abortion and other controversial issues.

Pioneering came naturally to O'Connor. Her grandfather left Kansas in 1880 to take up ranching in the desert land that eventually would become the state of Arizona. O'Connor, born in El Paso, Texas, where her mother's parents lived, was raised on the Lazy B Ranch, the 198,000-acre spread that her grandfather founded in southeastern Arizona near Duncan. She spent her school years in El Paso, living with her grandmother. She graduated from high school at age sixteen and then entered Stanford University.

Six years later, in 1952, Sandra Day had won degrees with great distinction, both from the university, in economics, and from Stanford Law School. At Stanford she met John J. O'Connor III, her future husband, and William H. Rehnquist, a future colleague on the Supreme Court. While in law school, Sandra Day was an editor of the *Stanford Law Review* and a member of Order of the Coif, both reflecting her academic leadership.

Despite her outstanding law school record, she found securing a job as an attorney difficult in 1952 when relatively few women were practicing law. She applied, among other places, to the firm in which William French Smith—first attorney general in the Reagan administration—was a partner, only to be offered a job as a secretary.

After she completed a short stint as deputy county attorney for San Mateo County (California) while her new husband completed law school at Stanford, the O'Connors moved with the U.S. Army to Frankfurt, Germany. There Sandra O'Connor worked as a civilian attorney for the army, while John O'Connor served his tour of duty. In 1957 they returned to Phoenix, where, during the next eight years, their three sons were born. O'Connor's life was a mix of parenthood, homemaking, volunteer work, and some "miscellaneous legal tasks" on the side.

In 1965 she resumed her legal career full time, taking a job as an assistant attorney general for Arizona. After four years in that post she was appointed to fill a vacancy in the state Senate, where she served on the judiciary committee. In 1970 she was elected to the same body and two years later was chosen its majority leader, the first woman in the nation to hold such a post. O'Connor was active in Republican Party politics, serving as co-chair of the Arizona Committee for the Re-election of the President in 1972.

In 1974 she was elected to the Superior Court for Maricopa County, where she served for five years. Then in 1979 Gov. Bruce Babbitt—acting, some said, to remove a potential rival for the governorship—appointed O'Connor to the Arizona Court of Appeals. It was from that seat that President Reagan chose her as his first nominee to the Supreme Court, succeeding Potter Stewart, who had retired. Reagan described her as "a person for all seasons."

By a vote of 99–0 the Senate confirmed O'Connor September 21, 1981, and she became the first woman associate justice of the U.S. Supreme Court.

O'Connor has helped push the Court in conservative directions in a number of areas, including criminal law and affirmative action. In 1989 she wrote the Court's opinion striking down a local minority contractor set-aside program. The same year she also wrote the Court's opinion permitting the death penalty for mentally retarded defendants. O'Connor has also been a strong voice for restricting state prisoners' ability to use federal habeas corpus to overturn criminal convictions or sentences.

Throughout the 1980s, O'Connor voted to uphold state laws regulating abortion procedures or restricting government funding of abortions. In 1992, however, she joined with two other Republican-appointed justices, Anthony M. Kennedy and David H. Souter, to form a majority for preserving a modified form of the Court's original abortion rights ruling, *Roe v. Wade.* In a jointly authored opinion the three justices said that *Roe*'s "essential holding"—guaranteeing a woman's right to an abortion during most of her pregnancy—should be reaffirmed. But the joint opinion also said that states could regulate abortion procedures as long as they did not impose "an undue burden" on a woman's choice—a test that O'Connor had advocated in previous opinions.

Antonin Scalia

Born: March 11, 1936, Trenton, New Jersey.

Education: Georgetown University, A.B., 1957; Harvard University Law School, LL.B., 1960.

Family: Married Maureen McCarthy, 1960; five sons, four daughters.

Career: Practiced law, Cleveland, 1960–1967; taught at the University of Virginia, 1967–1971; general counsel, White House Office of Telecommunications Policy, 1971–1972; chairman, Administrative Conference of the United States, 1972–1974; head, Justice Department Office of Legal Counsel, 1974–1977; taught at the University of Chicago Law School, 1977–1982; judge, U.S. Court of Appeals for the District of Columbia, 1982–1986.

Supreme Court Service: Nominated as associate justice of the U.S. Supreme Court by President Ronald Reagan June 17, 1986; confirmed, 98–0, September 17, 1986.

After Warren E. Burger retired from the Court and Ronald Reagan named William H. Rehnquist to succeed him as chief justice, the president's next move—appointing Antonin Scalia as associate justice—was not surprising. On issues dear to Reagan, Scalia clearly met the president's tests for conservatism. Scalia, whom Reagan had named to the U.S. Court of Appeals for the District of Columbia in 1982, became the first Supreme Court justice of Italian ancestry. A Roman Catholic, he opposes abortion. He also has expressed opposition to "affirmative action" preferences for minorities.

Deregulation, which Reagan pushed as president, was a subject of considerable interest to Scalia, a specialist in administrative law. From 1977 to 1982 he was editor of the magazine *Regulation,* published by the American Enterprise Institute for Public Policy Research.

In contrast to the hours of floor debate over Rehnquist's nomination as chief justice, only a few brief speeches were given in opposition to the equally conservative Scalia before he was confirmed, 98–0. He has since become the scourge of some members of Congress because of his suspicion of committee reports, floor speeches, and other artifacts of legislative history that courts traditionally rely on to interpret a statute.

Born in Trenton, New Jersey, March 11, 1936, Scalia grew up in Queens, New York. His father was a professor of Romance languages at Brooklyn College, and his mother was a schoolteacher. Scalia graduated from Georgetown University in 1957 and from Harvard Law School in 1960. He worked for six years for the firm of Jones, Day, Cockley & Reavis in Cleveland and then taught contract, commercial, and comparative law at the University of Virginia Law School.

Scalia served as general counsel of the White House Office of Telecommunications Policy from 1971 to 1972. He then headed the Administrative Conference of the United States, a group that advises the government on questions of administrative law and procedure. From 1974 through the Ford administration he headed the Justice Department's Office of Legal Counsel, a post Rehnquist had held three years earlier. Scalia then returned to academia, to teach at the University of Chicago Law School.

Scalia showed himself to be a hard worker, an aggressive interrogator, and an articulate advocate. On the appeals court he was impatient with what he saw as regulatory or judicial overreaching. In 1983 he dissented from a ruling requiring the Food and Drug Administration (FDA) to consider whether drugs used for lethal injections met FDA standards as safe and effective. The Supreme Court agreed, reversing the appeals court in 1985.

Scalia was thought to be the principal author of an unsigned decision in 1986 that declared major portions of the Gramm-Rudman-Hollings budget-balancing act unconstitutional. The Supreme Court upheld the decision later in the year.

On the Supreme Court Scalia quickly became a forceful voice for conservative positions. He joined in conservative decisions limiting procedural rights in criminal cases and in a series of rulings in 1989 limiting remedies in employment discrimination cases. He also strongly dissented from rulings upholding affirmative action and reaffirming abortion rights.

In many of his constitutional law opinions, Scalia argued for an "original intent" approach that limited rights to those intended when the Constitution was adopted. He also sharply challenged the use of legislative history in interpreting statutes. He argued that judges should look only to the words of the statute itself.

Anthony McLeod Kennedy

Born: July 23, 1936, Sacramento, California.

Education: Stanford University, A.B., Phi Beta Kappa, 1958; Harvard University Law School, LL.B., 1961.

Family: Married Mary Davis, 1963; two sons, one daughter.

Career: Practiced law, San Francisco, 1961–1963, Sacramento, 1963–1975; professor of constitutional law, McGeorge School of Law, University of the Pacific, 1965–1988; judge, U.S. Court of Appeals for the Ninth Circuit, 1975–1988.

Supreme Court Service: Nominated as associate justice of the U.S. Supreme Court by President Ronald Reagan November 11, 1987; confirmed, 97–0, February 3, 1988.

Quiet, scholarly Anthony M. Kennedy, President Reagan's third choice for his third appointment to the Supreme Court, made all the difference when the Court's conservative majority began coalescing in 1989.

Kennedy proved to be a crucial fifth vote for the Court's conservative wing in civil rights cases, a firm supporter of state authority over defendants' rights in criminal cases, and a strict constructionist in the mode of Chief Justice William H. Rehnquist in most cases. Kennedy's presence effectively ushered in a new era on the Court. Reagan's earlier  appointees, Sandra Day O'Connor and Antonin Scalia, had moved the Court somewhat to the right. But when Kennedy succeeded Lewis F. Powell, Jr., a moderate conservative and a critical swing vote, the balance of power shifted. On a range of issues where Powell often joined the Court's four liberals, Kennedy has gone the other way. Kennedy, however, broke with the hardline conservatives in 1992. He voted to disallow prayer at public school graduations and to uphold a woman's right to abortion.

Before Kennedy's nomination in November 1987, the Senate and the country had agonized through Reagan's two unsuccessful attempts to replace Powell, first with Robert H. Bork and then with Douglas H. Ginsburg. The Senate rejected Bork's nomination after contentious hearings, and Ginsburg withdrew his name amid controversy about his qualifications and admitted past use of marijuana.

A quiet sense of relief prevailed when Reagan finally selected a nominee who could be confirmed without another wrenching confrontation. Later, Republicans would note the irony in Kennedy's tipping the balance of the Court because anti-Bork Democrats had so willingly embraced him as a moderate.

Kennedy spent twelve years as a judge on the U.S. Court of Appeals for the Ninth Circuit. But unlike Bork, who wrote and spoke extensively for twenty years, Kennedy's record was confined mostly to his approximately five hundred judicial opinions. His views thus were based in large part on issues that were distilled at the trial level and further refined by legal and oral arguments. Furthermore, Kennedy sought to decide issues narrowly instead of using his opinions as a testing ground for constitutional theories. He continued this approach in the decisions he has written on the high Court.

Kennedy has taken conservative positions on most criminal law and civil rights issues. He also voted in 1989 to overturn the Court's original abortion rights ruling, *Roe v. Wade.* In 1992, however, he disappointed conservatives by joining with Justices Sandra Day O'Connor and David H. Souter in the pivotal opinion reaffirming *Roe v. Wade.* Kennedy has also taken liberal positions on some First Amendment issues. In his first full term on the Court, he helped form the 5–4 majority that overturned state laws against burning or desecrating the U.S. flag.

A native Californian, Kennedy attended Stanford University from 1954 to 1957 and the London School of Economics from 1957 to 1958. He received an A.B. from Stanford in 1958 and an LL.B. from Harvard Law School in 1961. Admitted to the California bar in 1962, he was in private law practice until 1975, when President Gerald R. Ford appointed him to the appeals court. From 1965 to 1988 he taught constitutional law at McGeorge School of Law, University of the Pacific. Confirmed by the Senate, 97–0, February 3, 1988, Kennedy was sworn in as an associate justice of the Supreme Court February 18.

He and his wife, the former Mary Davis, have three children.

David Hackett Souter

Born: September 17, 1939, Melrose, Massachusetts.

Education: Harvard College, B.A., 1961; Rhodes scholar, Oxford University, 1961–1963; Harvard University Law School, LL.B., 1966.

Family: Unmarried.

Career: Private law practice, Concord, New Hampshire, 1966–1968; assistant attorney general, New Hampshire, 1968–1971; deputy attorney general, New Hampshire, 1971–1976; attorney general, New Hampshire, 1976–1978; associate justice, New Hampshire Superior Court, 1978–1983; associate justice, New Hampshire Supreme Court, 1983–1990; judge, U.S. Court of Appeals for the First Circuit, 1990.

Supreme Court Service: Nominated as associate justice of the U.S. Supreme Court by President George Bush July 23, 1990; confirmed, 90–9, October 2, 1990.

At first the Senate did not know what to make of David H. Souter, a cerebral, button-down nominee who was President Bush's first appointment to the Court. Souter was little known outside of his home state of New Hampshire, where he had been attorney general, a trial judge, and a state supreme court justice.

Unlike Antonin Scalia and Anthony M. Kennedy, his immediate predecessors on the Court, Souter had virtually no scholarly writings to dissect and little federal court experience to scrutinize. Only three months earlier Bush had appointed him to the U.S. Court of Appeals for the First Circuit. Souter had yet to write a legal opinion on the appeals court.

During his confirmation hearings, the Harvard graduate and former Rhodes scholar demonstrated intellectual rigor and a masterly approach to constitutional law. His earlier work as state attorney general and New Hampshire Supreme Court justice had a conservative bent, but he came across as more moderate during the hearings.

Under persistent questioning from Democratic senators, Souter refused to say how he would vote on the issue of abortion rights. Abortion rights supporters feared he would provide a fifth vote for overturning the 1973 *Roe v. Wade* decision. Senators in both parties, however, said they were impressed with his legal knowledge. He was confirmed by the Senate 90–9; dissenting senators cited his refusal to take a stand on abortion.

On the bench Souter proved to be a tenacious questioner but reserved in his opinions. He generally voted with the Court's conservative majority in his first term. But in the 1991–1992 term he staked out a middle ground with Justices Sandra Day O'Connor and Kennedy in two crucial cases. In a closely watched abortion case Souter joined with the other two Republican-appointed justices in writing the main opinion reaffirming the "essential holding" of *Roe v. Wade.* The three also joined in forming a 5–4 majority to prohibit school-sponsored prayers at public high school graduation ceremonies.

In the Court's next two terms Souter moved markedly to the left, while Kennedy and O'Connor appeared to move back toward the right. Although Souter continued to vote most often with the Court's conservatives, he took liberal positions in a number of civil rights, church-state, and criminal law cases. On the final day of the Court's 1993–1994 term, Souter wrote the Court's opinions in two closely watched cases that reaffirmed racial line-drawing in legislative redistricting cases and struck down a New York law creating a special school district for an exclusively Jewish community.

Souter is known for his intensely private, ascetic life. He was born September 17, 1939, in Melrose, Massachusetts. An only child, he moved with his parents to Weare, New Hampshire, at age eleven. Except for college, he lived in Weare until 1990.

Graduating from Harvard College in 1961, Souter attended Oxford University on a Rhodes Scholarship from 1961 to 1963, then returned to Cambridge for Harvard Law School. Graduating in 1966, he worked for two years in a Concord law firm. In 1968 he became an assistant attorney general, rose to deputy attorney general in 1971, and in 1976 was appointed attorney general. Under conservative governor Meldrim Thomson, Jr., Attorney General Souter defended a number of controversial orders, including the lowering of state flags to half-staff on Good Friday to observe the death of Jesus. He prosecuted Jehovah's Witnesses who obscured the state motto "Live Free or Die" on their license plates.

Souter served as attorney general until 1978, when he was named to the state's trial court. Five years later Gov. John H. Sununu appointed Souter to the state Supreme Court. Sununu was Bush's chief of staff when Souter was named to the U.S. Supreme Court.

Souter, a bachelor, is a nature enthusiast and avid hiker.

Clarence Thomas

Born: June 23, 1948, Savannah, Georgia.

Education: Immaculate Conception Seminary, 1967–1968; Holy Cross College, B.A., 1971; Yale University Law School, J.D., 1974.

Family: Married Kathy Grace Ambush, 1971; one son; divorced 1984; married Virginia Lamp, 1987.

Career: Assistant attorney general, Missouri, 1974–1977; attorney, Monsanto Co., 1977–1979; legislative assistant to Sen. John C. Danforth, R-Mo., 1979–1981; assistant secretary of education for civil rights, 1981–1982; chairman, Equal Employment Opportunity Commission, 1982–1990; judge, U.S. Court of Appeals for the District of Columbia, 1990–1991.

Supreme Court Service: Nominated as associate justice of the U.S. Supreme Court by President George Bush July 1, 1991; confirmed, 52–48, October 15, 1991.

Clarence Thomas won a narrow confirmation to the Supreme Court in 1991 after surviving dramatic accusations of sexual harassment and went on to generate continuing controversy with outspoken conservative views as a justice.

The Senate's 52–48 vote on Thomas was the closest Supreme Court confirmation vote in more than a century. It followed a tumultuous nomination process that included close scrutiny of Thomas's judicial philosophy and sensational charges of sexual harassment brought by a former aide. Thomas denied the charges and accused the Senate Judiciary Committee of conducting a "high-tech lynching."

President George Bush nominated Thomas to succeed Thurgood Marshall, the Court's first black justice and a pioneer of the civil rights movement. Thomas came to prominence as a black conservative while serving as chairman of the Equal Employment Opportunity Commission during the Reagan administration. Bush appointed him to the U.S. Court of Appeals for the District of Columbia in 1990.

Thomas was only forty-three at the time of his nomination to the Court, and senators noted that he likely would be affecting the outcome of major constitutional rulings well into the twenty-first century. Democratic senators closely questioned him on a range of constitutional issues—in particular, abortion. Thomas declined to give his views on abortion, saying he had never discussed the issue.

The committee decided to close the hearing even though it had received an allegation from a University of Oklahoma law professor, Anita Hill, that Thomas had sexually harassed her while she worked for him at the U.S. Department of Education and the EEOC. When the accusation leaked out, the Judiciary Committee reopened the hearing to take testimony from Hill, Thomas, and other witnesses.

In the end most senators said they could not resolve the conflict between Hill's detailed allegations and Thomas's categorical denials. Instead, senators fell back on their previous positions based on Thomas's judicial philosophy or his determined character and rise from poverty in rural Georgia.

After joining the Court, Thomas became one of the Court's most conservative members. He closely aligned himself with fellow conservative Antonin Scalia, voting with Scalia about 90 percent of the time. In 1992, he voted as his opponents had warned to overturn the 1973 abortion rights ruling, *Roe v. Wade,* but the Court reaffirmed the decision by a 5–4 vote.

In later cases, Thomas wrote lengthy opinions sharply challenging existing legal doctrines. In 1994, for example, he called for scrapping precedents that allowed courts to order the creation of majority-black districts for legislative or congressional seats. In 1995, he authored opinions that called for restricting the basis for Congress to regulate interstate commerce and for re-examining federal courts' role in desegregating public schools.

Thomas graduated from Yale Law School in 1974 and became an assistant attorney general of Missouri and, three years later, a staff attorney for Monsanto Company. He worked for Sen. John C. Danforth, R-Mo., as a legislative assistant and served in the Department of Education as assistant secretary for civil rights for one year before being named chairman of the EEOC.

Thomas's wife, the former Virginia Lamp, is a lawyer who served as a legislative official with the U.S. Department of Labor during the Bush administration and since 1993 as a senior policy analyst with the House Republican Conference. They were married in 1987. He has a son from his first marriage, which ended in divorce in 1984.

Ruth Bader Ginsburg

Born: March 15, 1933, Brooklyn, New York.

Education: Cornell University, B.A., 1954; attended Harvard University Law School, 1956–1958; graduated Columbia Law School, J.D., 1959.

Family: Married Martin D. Ginsburg, 1954; one daughter, one son.

Career: Law clerk to U.S. District Court Judge Edmund L. Palmieri, 1959–1961; Columbia Law School Project on International Procedure, 1961–1963; professor, Rutgers University School of Law, 1963–1972; director, Women's Rights Project, American Civil Liberties Union, 1972–1980; professor, Columbia Law School, 1972–1980; judge, U.S. Court of Appeals for the District of Columbia, 1980–1993.

Supreme Court Service: Nominated as associate justice of the U.S. Supreme Court by President Bill Clinton, June 22, 1993; confirmed, 96–3, August 3, 1993.

Ruth Bader Ginsburg's path to the U.S. Supreme Court is a classic American story of overcoming obstacles and setbacks through intelligence, persistence, and quiet hard work. Her achievements as a student, law teacher, advocate, and judge came against a background of personal adversity and institutional discrimination against women. Ginsburg not only surmounted those hurdles for herself but also charted the legal strategy in the 1970s that helped broaden opportunities for women by establishing constitutional principles limiting sex discrimination in the law.

Born into a Jewish family of modest means in Brooklyn, Ruth Bader was greatly influenced by her mother, Celia, who imparted a love of learning and a determination to be independent. Celia Bader died of cancer on the eve of her daughter's high school graduation in 1948.

Ruth Bader attended Cornell University, where she graduated first in her class and met her future husband, Martin Ginsburg, who became a tax lawyer and later a professor at Georgetown University Law Center in Washington.

At Harvard Law School Ruth Bader Ginsburg made law review, cared for an infant daughter, and then helped her husband complete his studies after he was diagnosed with cancer. He recovered, graduated, and got a job in New York, and she transferred to Columbia for her final year of law school.

Although she was tied for first place in her class when she graduated, Ginsburg was unable to land a Supreme Court clerkship or job with a top New York law firm. Instead, she won a two-year clerkship with a federal district court judge. She then accepted a research position at Columbia that took her to Sweden, where she studied civil procedure and began to be stirred by feminist thought.

Ginsburg taught at Rutgers University Law School in New Jersey from 1963 to 1972. She also worked with the New Jersey affiliate of the American Civil Liberties Union (ACLU), where her caseload included several early sex discrimination complaints. In 1972 Ginsburg became the first woman to be named to a tenured position on the Columbia Law School faculty. As director of the national ACLU's newly established Women's Rights Project, she also handled the cases that over the course of several years led the Supreme Court to require heightened scrutiny of legal classifications based on sex. Ginsburg won five of the six cases she argued before the Court.

President Jimmy Carter named Ginsburg to the U.S. Court of Appeals for the District of Columbia in 1980. There she earned a reputation as a judicial moderate on a sharply divided court. Although she is prochoice, she stirred controversy among abortion rights groups by criticizing some aspects of the way the Supreme Court's landmark abortion case, *Roe v. Wade*, was decided.

When Justice Byron R. White announced plans for his retirement in March 1993, Ginsburg was among the large field of candidates President Bill Clinton considered for the vacancy. Clinton considered and passed over two other leading candidates for the position before deciding to interview Ginsburg. White House aides told reporters later that Clinton had been especially impressed with Ginsburg's life story. Reaction to the nomination was overwhelmingly positive. On Capitol Hill Ginsburg won the support of some pivotal Republican senators, including Minority Leader Robert Dole of Kansas.

In three days of confirmation hearings before the Senate Judiciary Committee, Ginsburg depicted herself as an advocate of judicial restraint, but she also said courts sometimes had a role to play in bringing about social change. On specific issues she strongly endorsed abortion rights, equal rights for women, and the constitutional right to privacy. But she declined to give her views on many other issues, including capital punishment. Some senators said that she had been less than forthcoming, but the committee voted unanimously to recommend her for confirmation.

The full Senate confirmed her four days later by a vote of 96–3. Three conservative Republicans cast the only negative votes. Ginsburg was sworn in August 10, 1993, as the court's second female justice—joining Justice Sandra Day O'Connor—and the first Jewish justice since 1969.

In her first weeks on the bench, Ginsburg startled observers and drew some criticism with her unusually active questioning. She eased up a bit as the term progressed but continued to be one of the Court's most active interrogators during oral arguments. Although as a junior justice she wrote no major opinions, her voting appeared to bear out predictions made after her confirmation hearings. She took liberal positions on women's rights, civil rights, church-state, and First Amendment issues, but she had a more mixed record in other areas, including criminal law. She voted to back death penalty appeals in five out of seven capital punishment cases and sided with liberals in most of the closely divided criminal law rulings. Overall, however, she voted to uphold convictions or sentences in most of the Court's criminal law decisions of the term.

Stephen Gerald Breyer

Born: August 15, 1938, San Francisco, California.

Education: Stanford University, A.B., Phi Beta Kappa, 1959; Oxford University, B.A. (Marshall scholar), 1961; Harvard Law School, LL.B., 1964.

Family: Married Joanna Hare, 1967; two daughters, one son.

Career: Law clerk to Justice Arthur J. Goldberg, U.S. Supreme Court, 1964–1965; assistant to assistant attorney general, antitrust, U.S. Justice Department, 1965–1967; professor, Harvard Law School, 1967–1981; assistant special prosecutor, Watergate Special Prosecution Force, 1973; special counsel, Senate Judiciary Committee, 1974–1975; chief counsel, Senate Judiciary Committee, 1979–1980; judge, U.S. Court of Appeals for the First Circuit, 1980–1994.

Supreme Court Service: Nominated as associate justice of the U.S. Supreme Court by President Bill Clinton May 17, 1994; confirmed, 87–9, July 29, 1994.

When President Bill Clinton introduced Stephen G. Breyer, his second Supreme Court nominee, at a White House ceremony on May 16, 1994, he described the federal appeals court judge as a "consensus-builder." The reaction to the nomination proved his point. Senators from both parties quickly endorsed Breyer. The only vocal dissents came from a few liberals and consumer advocates, who said Breyer was too probusiness.

Breyer, chosen to replace the retiring liberal justice Harry A. Blackmun, won a reputation as a centrist in fourteen years on the federal appeals court in Boston and two earlier stints as a staff member for the Senate Judiciary Committee. Breyer's work crossed ideological lines. He played a critical role in enacting airline deregulation in the 1970s and writing federal sentencing guidelines in the 1980s.

Born in 1938 to a politically active family in San Francisco, Breyer earned degrees from Stanford University and Harvard Law School. He clerked for Supreme Court Justice Arthur J. Goldberg and helped draft Goldberg's influential opinion in the 1965 case establishing the right of married couples to use contraceptives. Afterward he served two years in the Justice Department's antitrust division and then took a teaching position at Harvard Law School in 1967.

Breyer took leaves from Harvard to serve as an assistant prosecutor in the Watergate investigation in 1973, special counsel to the Judiciary Committee's Administrative Practices Subcommittee from 1974 to 1975, and the full committee's chief counsel from 1979 to 1980. He worked for Sen. Edward Kennedy, D-Mass., but also established good relationships with Republican committee members. His ties to senators paid off when President Jimmy Carter nominated him for the federal appeals court in

November 1980. Even though Ronald Reagan had been elected president, Republican senators allowed a vote on Breyer's nomination.

As a judge, Breyer was regarded as scholarly, judicious, and open-minded, with generally conservative views on economic issues and more liberal views on social questions. He wrote two books on regulatory reform that criticized economic regulations as anticompetitive and questioned priorities in some environmental and health rulemaking. He also served as a

member of the newly created United States Sentencing Commission from 1985 to 1989. Later he defended the commission's guidelines against criticism from judges and others who viewed them as overly restrictive.

President Clinton interviewed Breyer before his first Supreme Court appointment in 1993 but chose Ruth Bader Ginsburg instead. He picked Breyer in 1994 after Senate Majority Leader George Mitchell took himself out of consideration and problems developed with two other leading candidates.

In his confirmation hearings before the Senate Judiciary Committee, Breyer defused two potential controversies by saying that he accepted Supreme Court precedents upholding abortion rights and capital punishment. The only contentious issue in the confirmation process concerned Breyer's investment in the British insurance syndicate Lloyd's of London. Some senators said Breyer should have recused himself from several environmental pollution cases because of the investment. Breyer told the committee that the cases could not have affected his holdings but also promised to get out of Lloyd's as soon as possible. The panel went on to recommend the nomination unanimously.

One Republican senator, Indiana's Richard Lugar, raised the Lloyd's issue during debate, but Breyer was strongly supported by senators from both parties, including Kennedy and the Judiciary Committee's ranking Republican, Orrin Hatch of Utah. The Senate voted to confirm Breyer 87–9. Breyer disposed of his investment in Lloyd's shortly after taking office.

In his first term, Breyer compiled a moderately liberal record. He dissented from several conservative rulings on race and religion and wrote the dissenting opinion for the four liberal justices in a decision that struck down a federal law prohibiting the possession of firearms near schools. But he had a more conservative record on criminal law issues and joined the Court's opinion permitting random drug testing of high school athletes.

Breyer joined Ginsburg as the Court's second Jewish justice. The Court had two Jewish members only once before, in the 1930s when Louis Brandeis and Benjamin Cardozo served together for six years.

Glossary of Legal Terms

Accessory. In criminal law, a person not present at the commission of an offense who commands, advises, instigates, or conceals the offense.

Acquittal. A person is acquitted when a jury returns a verdict of not guilty. A person also may be acquitted when a judge determines that insufficient evidence exists to convict him or that a violation of due process precludes a fair trial.

Adjudicate. To determine finally by the exercise of judicial authority, to decide a case.

Affidavit. A voluntary written statement of facts or charges affirmed under oath.

A fortiori. With stronger force, with more reason.

Amicus curiae. Friend of the court; a person, not a party to litigation, who volunteers or is invited by the court to give his or her views on a case.

Appeal. A legal proceeding to ask a higher court to review or modify a lower court decision. In a civil case, either the plaintiff or the defendant can appeal an adverse ruling. In criminal cases a defendant can appeal a conviction, but the Double Jeopardy Clause prevents the government from appealing an acquittal. In Supreme Court practice an appeal is a case that falls within the Court's mandatory jurisdiction as opposed to a case that the Court agrees to review under the discretionary writ of certiorari. With the virtual elimination of the Court's mandatory jurisdiction in 1988, the Court now hears very few true appeals, but petitions for certiorari are often referred to imprecisely as appeals.

Appellant. The party who appeals a lower court decision to a higher court.

Appellee. One who has an interest in upholding the decision of a lower court and is compelled to respond when the case is appealed to a higher court by an appellant.

Arraignment. The formal process of charging a person with a crime, reading that person the charge, asking whether he or she pleads guilty or not guilty, and entering the plea.

Attainder, Bill of. A legislative act pronouncing a particular individual guilty of a crime without trial or conviction and imposing a sentence.

Bail. The security, usually money, given as assurance of a prisoner's due appearance at a designated time and place (as in court) to procure in the interim the prisoner's release from jail.

Bailiff. A minor officer of a court, usually serving as an usher or a messenger.

Brief. A document prepared by counsel to serve as the basis for an argument in court, setting out the facts of and the legal arguments in support of the case.

Burden of proof. The need or duty of affirmatively providing a fact or facts that are disputed.

Case law. The law as defined by previously decided cases, distinct from statutes and other sources of law.

Cause. A case, suit, litigation, or action, civil or criminal.

Certiorari, Writ of. A writ issued from the Supreme Court, at its discretion, to order a lower court to prepare the record of a case and send it to the Supreme Court for review.

Civil law. Body of law dealing with the private rights of individuals, as distinguished from criminal law.

Class action. A lawsuit brought by one person or group on behalf of all persons similarly situated.

Code. A collection of laws, arranged systematically.

Comity. Courtesy, respect; usually used in the legal sense to refer to the proper relationship between state and federal courts.

Common law. Collection of principles and rules of action, particularly from unwritten English law, that derive their authority from longstanding usage and custom or from courts recognizing and enforcing these customs. Sometimes used synonymously with case law.

Consent decree. A court-sanctioned agreement settling a legal dispute and entered into by the consent of the parties.

Contempt (civil and criminal). Civil contempt arises from a failure to follow a court order for the benefit of another party. Criminal contempt occurs when a person willfully exhibits disrespect for the court or obstructs the administration of justice.

Conviction. Final judgment or sentence that the defendant is guilty as charged.

Criminal law. The branch of law that deals with the enforcement of laws and the punishment of persons who, by breaking laws, commit crimes.

Declaratory judgment. A court pronouncement declaring a legal right or interpretation but not ordering a specific action.

De facto. In fact, in reality.

Defendant. In a civil action, the party denying or defending itself against charges brought by a plaintiff. In a criminal action, the person indicted for commission of an offense.

De jure. As a result of law or official action.

De novo. Anew; afresh; a second time.

Deposition. Oral testimony from a witness taken out of court in response to written or oral questions, committed to writing, and intended to be used in the preparation of a case.

Dicta. *See* Obiter dictum.

Dismissal. Order disposing of a case without a trial.

Docket. A calendar prepared by the clerks of the court listing the cases set to be tried.

Due process. Fair and regular procedure. The Fifth and Fourteenth amendments guarantee persons that they will not be deprived of life, liberty, or property by the government until fair and usual procedures have been followed.

Error, Writ of. A writ issued from an appeals court to a lower court requiring it to send to the appeals court the record of a case in which it has entered a final judgment and which the appeals court will review for error.

Ex parte. Only from, or on, one side. Application to a court for some ruling or action on behalf of only one party.

Ex post facto. After the fact; an ex post facto law makes an action a crime after it already has been committed, or otherwise changes the legal consequences of some past action.

Ex rel. Upon information from; the term is usually used to describe legal proceedings begun by an official in the name of the state but at the instigation of, and with information from, a private individual interested in the matter.

Grand jury. Group of twelve to twenty-three persons impanelled to hear, in private, evidence presented by the state against an individual or persons accused of a criminal act and to issue indictments when a majority of the jurors find probable cause to believe that the accused has committed a crime. Called a "grand" jury because it comprises a greater number of persons than a "petit" jury.

Grand jury report. A public report, often called "presentments," released by a grand jury after an investigation into activities of public officials that fall short of criminal actions.

Guilty. A word used by a defendant in entering a plea or by a jury in returning a verdict, indicating that the defendant is legally responsible as charged for a crime or other wrongdoing.

Habeas corpus. Literally, "you have the body"; a writ issued to inquire whether a person is lawfully imprisoned or detained. The writ demands that the persons holding the prisoner justify the detention or release the prisoner.

Immunity. A grant of exemption from prosecution in return for evidence or testimony.

In camera. In chambers. Refers to court hearings in private without spectators.

In forma pauperis. In the manner of a pauper, without liability for court costs.

In personam. Done or directed against a particular person.

In re. In the affair of, concerning. Frequent title of judicial proceedings in which there are no adversaries but instead where the matter itself — such as a bankrupt's estate — requires judicial action.

In rem. Done or directed against the thing, not the person.

Indictment. A formal written statement, based on evidence presented by the prosecutor, from a grand jury. Decided by a majority vote, an indictment charges one or more persons with specified offenses.

Information. A written set of accusations, similar to an indictment, but filed directly by a prosecutor.

Injunction. A court order prohibiting the person to whom it is directed from performing a particular act.

Interlocutory decree. A provisional decision of the court before completion of a legal action that temporarily settles an intervening matter.

Judgment. Official decision of a court based on the rights and claims of the parties to a case that was submitted for determination.

Jurisdiction. The power of a court to hear a case in question, which exists when the proper parties are present and when the point to be decided is within the issues authorized to be handled by the particular court.

Juries. *See* Grand jury; Petit jury.

Magistrate. A judicial officer having jurisdiction to try minor criminal cases and conduct preliminary examinations of persons charged with serious crimes.

Majority opinion. An opinion joined by a majority of the justices explaining the legal basis for the Court's decision and regarded as binding precedent for future cases.

Mandamus. "We command." An order issued from a superior court directing a lower court or other authority to perform a particular act.

Moot. Unsettled, undecided. A moot question also is one that no longer is material; a moot case is one that has become hypothetical.

Motion. Written or oral application to a court or a judge to obtain a rule or an order.

Nolo contendere. "I will not contest it." A plea entered by a defendant at the discretion of the judge with the same legal effect as a plea of guilty, but it may not be cited in other proceedings as an admission of guilt.

Obiter dictum. Statements by a judge or justice expressing an opinion and included with, but not essential to, an opinion resolving a case before the court. Dicta are not necessarily binding in future cases.

Parole. A conditional release from imprisonment under conditions that, if the prisoner abides by the law and other restrictions that may be imposed, the prisoner will not have to serve the remainder of the sentence.

Per curiam. "By the court." An unsigned opinion of the court, or an opinion written by the whole court.

Petit jury. A trial jury, originally a panel of twelve persons who tried to reach a unanimous verdict on questions of fact in criminal and civil proceedings. Since 1970 the Supreme Court has upheld the legality of state juries with fewer than twelve persons. Fewer persons serve on a "petit" jury than on a "grand" jury.

Petitioner. One who files a petition with a court seeking action or relief, including a plaintiff or an appellant. But a petitioner also is a person who files for other court action where charges are not necessarily made; for example, a party may petition the court for an order requiring another person or party to produce documents. The opposite party is called the respondent.

When a writ of certiorari is granted by the Supreme Court, the parties to the case are called petitioner and respondent in contrast to the appellant and appellee terms used in an appeal.

Plaintiff. A party who brings a civil action or sues to obtain a remedy for injury to his or her rights. The party against whom action is brought is termed the defendant.

Plea bargaining. Negotiations between a prosecutor and the defendant aimed at exchanging a plea of guilty from the defendant for concessions by the prosecutor, such as reduction of the charges or a request for leniency.

Pleas. *See* Guilty; Nolo contendere.

Plurality opinion. An opinion supported by the largest number of justices but less than a majority. A plurality opinion typically is not regarded as establishing a binding precedent for future cases.

Precedent. A judicial decision that may be used as a basis for ruling on subsequent similar cases.

Presentment. *See* Grand jury report.

Prima facie. At first sight; referring to a fact or other evidence presumably sufficient to establish a defense or a claim unless otherwise contradicted.

Probation. Process under which a person convicted of an offense, usually a first offense, receives a suspended sentence and is given freedom, usually under the guardianship of a probation officer.

Quash. To overthrow, annul, or vacate; as to quash a subpoena.

Recognizance. An obligation entered into before a court or magistrate requiring the performance of a specified act—usually to appear in court at a later date. It is an alternative to bail for pretrial release.

Remand. To send back. When a decision is remanded, it is sent back by a higher court to the court from which it came for further action.

Respondent. One who is compelled to answer the claims or questions posed in court by a petitioner. A defendant and an appellee may be called respondents, but the term also includes those parties who answer in court during actions where charges are not necessarily brought or where the Supreme Court has granted a writ of certiorari.

Seriatim. Separately, individually, one by one.

Stare decisis. "Let the decision stand." The principle of adherence to settled cases, the doctrine that principles of law established in earlier judicial decisions should be accepted as authoritative in similar subsequent cases.

Statute. A written law enacted by a legislature. A collection of statutes for a particular governmental division is called a code.

Stay. To halt or suspend further judicial proceedings.

Subpoena. An order to present oneself before a grand jury, court, or legislative hearing.

Subpoena duces tecum. An order to produce specified documents or papers.

Tort. An injury or wrong to the person or property of another.

Transactional immunity. Protects a witness from prosecution for any offense mentioned in or related to his or her testimony, regardless of independent evidence against the witness.

Use immunity. Protects a witness from the use of his or her testimony against the witness in prosecution.

Vacate. To make void, annul, or rescind.

Writ. A written court order commanding the designated recipient to perform or not perform specified acts.

United States Constitution

We the People of the United States, in Order to form a more perfect Union, establish Justice, insure domestic Tranquility, provide for the common defence, promote the general Welfare, and secure the Blessings of Liberty to ourselves and our Posterity, do ordain and establish this Constitution for the United States of America.

Article I

Section 1. All legislative Powers herein granted shall be vested in a Congress of the United States, which shall consist of a Senate and House of Representatives.

Section 2. The House of Representatives shall be composed of Members chosen every second Year by the People of the several States, and the Electors in each State shall have the Qualifications requisite for Electors of the most numerous Branch of the State Legislature.

No Person shall be a Representative who shall not have attained to the age of twenty five Years, and been seven Years a Citizen of the United States, and who shall not, when elected, be an Inhabitant of that State in which he shall be chosen.

[Representatives and direct Taxes shall be apportioned among the several States which may be included within this Union, according to their respective Numbers, which shall be determined by adding to the whole Number of free Persons, including those bound to Service for a Term of Years, and excluding Indians not taxed, three fifths of all other Persons.][1] The actual Enumeration shall be made within three Years after the first Meeting of the Congress of the United States, and within every subsequent Term of ten Years, in such Manner as they shall by Law direct. The Number of Representatives shall not exceed one for every thirty Thousand, but each State shall have at Least one Representative; and until such enumeration shall be made, the State of New Hampshire shall be entitled to chuse three, Massachusetts eight, Rhode-Island and Providence Plantations one, Connecticut five, New-York six, New Jersey four, Pennsylvania eight, Delaware one, Maryland six, Virginia ten, North Carolina five, South Carolina five, and Georgia three.

When vacancies happen in the Representation from any State, the Executive Authority thereof shall issue Writs of Election to fill such Vacancies.

The House of Representatives shall chuse their Speaker and other Officers; and shall have the sole Power of Impeachment.

Section 3. The Senate of the United States shall be composed of two Senators from each State, [chosen by the Legislature thereof,][2] for six Years; and each Senator shall have one Vote.

Immediately after they shall be assembled in Consequence of the first Election, they shall be divided as equally as may be into three Classes. The Seats of the Senators of the first Class shall be vacated at the Expiration of the second Year, of the second Class at the Expiration of the fourth Year, and of the third Class at the Expiration of the sixth Year, so that one third may be chosen every second Year; [and if Vacancies happen by Resignation, or otherwise, during the Recess of the Legislature of any State, the Executive thereof may make temporary Appointments until the next Meeting of the Legislature, which shall then fill such Vacancies.][3]

No Person shall be a Senator who shall not have attained to the Age of thirty Years, and been nine Years a Citizen of the United States, and who shall not, when elected, be an Inhabitant of that State for which he shall be chosen.

The Vice President of the United States shall be President of the Senate, but shall have no Vote, unless they be equally divided.

The Senate shall chuse their other Officers, and also a President pro tempore, in the Absence of the Vice President, or when he shall exercise the Office of President of the United States.

The Senate shall have the sole Power to try all Impeachments. When sitting for that Purpose, they shall be on Oath or Affirmation. When the President of the United States is tried, the Chief Justice shall preside: And no Person shall be convicted without the Concurrence of two thirds of the Members present.

Judgment in Cases of Impeachment shall not extend further than to removal from Office, and disqualification to hold and enjoy any Office of honor, Trust or Profit under the United States: but the Party convicted shall nevertheless be liable and subject to Indictment, Trial, Judgment and Punishment, according to Law.

Section 4. The Times, Places and Manner of holding Elections for Senators and Representatives, shall be prescribed in each State by the Legislature thereof; but the Congress may at any time by Law make or alter such Regulations, except as to the Places of chusing Senators.

The Congress shall assemble at least once in every Year, and such Meeting shall [be on the first Monday in December],[4] unless they shall by Law appoint a different Day.

Section 5. Each House shall be the Judge of the Elections, Returns and Qualifications of its own Members, and a Majority of each shall constitute a Quorum to do Business; but a smaller Number may adjourn from day to day, and may be authorized to compel the Attendance of absent Members, in such Manner, and under such Penalties as each House may provide.

Each House may determine the Rules of its Proceedings, punish its Members for disorderly Behaviour, and, with the Concurrence of two thirds, expel a Member.

Each House shall keep a Journal of its Proceedings, and from time to time publish the same, excepting such Parts as may in their Judgment require Secrecy; and the Yeas and Nays of the Members of either House on any question shall, at the Desire of one fifth of those Present, be entered on the Journal.

Neither House, during the Session of Congress, shall, without the Consent of the other, adjourn for more than three days, nor to any other Place than that in which the two Houses shall be sitting.

Section 6. The Senators and Representatives shall receive a Compensation for their Services, to be ascertained by Law, and paid out of the Treasury of the United States. They shall in all Cases, except Treason, Felony and Breach of the

Peace, be privileged from Arrest during their Attendance at the Session of their respective Houses, and in going to and returning from the same; and for any Speech or Debate in either House, they shall not be questioned in any other Place.

No Senator or Representative shall, during the Time for which he was elected, be appointed to any civil Office under the Authority of the United States, which shall have been created, or the Emoluments whereof shall have been encreased during such time; and no Person holding any Office under the United States, shall be a Member of either House during his Continuance in Office.

Section 7. All Bills for raising Revenue shall originate in the House of Representatives; but the Senate may propose or concur with Amendments as on other Bills.

Every Bill which shall have passed the House of Representatives and the Senate, shall, before it become a Law, be presented to the President of the United States; If he approve he shall sign it, but if not he shall return it, with his Objections to that House in which it shall have originated, who shall enter the Objections at large on their Journal, and proceed to reconsider it. If after such Reconsideration two thirds of that House shall agree to pass the Bill, it shall be sent, together with the Objections, to the other House, by which it shall likewise be reconsidered, and if approved by two thirds of that House, it shall become a Law. But in all such Cases the Votes of both Houses shall be determined by yeas and Nays, and the Names of the Persons voting for and against the Bill shall be entered on the Journal of each House respectively. If any Bill shall not be returned by the President within ten Days (Sundays excepted) after it shall have been presented to him, the Same shall be a Law, in like Manner as if he had signed it, unless the Congress by their Adjournment prevent its Return, in which Case it shall not be a Law.

Every Order, Resolution, or Vote to which the Concurrence of the Senate and House of Representatives may be necessary (except on a question of Adjournment) shall be presented to the President of the United States; and before the Same shall take Effect, shall be approved by him, or being disapproved by him, shall be repassed by two thirds of the Senate and House of Representatives, according to the Rules and Limitations prescribed in the Case of a Bill.

Section 8. The Congress shall have Power To lay and collect Taxes, Duties, Imposts and Excises, to pay the Debts and provide for the common Defence and general Welfare of the United States; but all Duties, Imposts and Excises shall be uniform throughout the United States;

To borrow Money on the credit of the United States;

To regulate Commerce with foreign Nations, and among the several States, and with the Indian Tribes;

To establish an uniform Rule of Naturalization, and uniform Laws on the subject of Bankruptcies throughout the United States;

To coin Money, regulate the Value thereof, and of foreign Coin, and fix the Standard of Weights and Measures;

To provide for the Punishment of counterfeiting the Securities and current Coin of the United States;

To establish Post Offices and post Roads;

To promote the Progress of Science and useful Arts, by securing for limited Times to Authors and Inventors the exclusive Right to their respective Writings and Discoveries;

To constitute Tribunals inferior to the supreme Court;

To define and punish Piracies and Felonies committed on the high Seas, and Offences against the Law of Nations;

To declare War, grant Letters of Marque and Reprisal, and make Rules concerning Captures on Land and Water;

To raise and support Armies, but no Appropriation of Money to that Use shall be for a longer Term than two Years;

To provide and maintain a Navy;

To make Rules for the Government and Regulation of the land and naval Forces;

To provide for calling forth the Militia to execute the Laws of the Union, suppress Insurrections and repel Invasions;

To provide for organizing, arming, and disciplining, the Militia, and for governing such Part of them as may be employed in the Service of the United States, reserving to the States respectively, the Appointment of the Officers, and the Authority of training the Militia according to the discipline prescribed by Congress;

To exercise exclusive Legislation in all Cases whatsoever, over such District (not exceeding ten Miles square) as may, by Cession of particular States, and the Acceptance of Congress, become the Seat of the Government of the United States, and to exercise like Authority over all Places purchased by the Consent of the Legislature of the State in which the Same shall be, for the Erection of Forts, Magazines, Arsenals, dock-Yards, and other needful Buildings; — And

To make all Laws which shall be necessary and proper for carrying into Execution the foregoing Powers, and all other Powers vested by this Constitution in the Government of the United States, or in any Department or Officer thereof.

Section 9. The Migration or Importation of such Persons as any of the States now existing shall think proper to admit, shall not be prohibited by the Congress prior to the Year one thousand eight hundred and eight, but a Tax or duty may be imposed on such Importation, not exceeding ten dollars for each Person.

The Privilege of the Writ of Habeas Corpus shall not be suspended, unless when in Cases of Rebellion or Invasion the public Safety may require it.

No Bill of Attainder or ex post facto Law shall be passed.

No Capitation, or other direct, Tax shall be laid, unless in Proportion to the Census or Enumeration herein before directed to be taken.[5]

No Tax or Duty shall be laid on Articles exported from any State.

No Preference shall be given by any Regulation of Commerce or Revenue to the Ports of one State over those of another; nor shall Vessels bound to, or from, one State, be obliged to enter, clear, or pay Duties in another.

No Money shall be drawn from the Treasury, but in Consequence of Appropriations made by Law; and a regular Statement and Account of the Receipts and Expenditures of all public Money shall be published from time to time.

No Title of Nobility shall be granted by the United States: And no Person holding any Office of Profit or Trust under them, shall, without the Consent of the

Congress, accept of any present, Emolument, Office, or Title, of any kind whatever, from any King, Prince, or foreign State.

Section 10. No State shall enter into any Treaty, Alliance, or Confederation; grant Letters of Marque and Reprisal; coin Money; emit Bills of Credit; make any Thing but gold and silver Coin a Tender in Payment of Debts; pass any Bill of Attainder, ex post facto Law, or Law impairing the Obligation of Contracts, or grant any Title of Nobility.

No State shall, without the Consent of the Congress, lay any Imposts or Duties on Imports or Exports, except what may be absolutely necessary for executing it's inspection Laws: and the net Produce of all Duties and Imposts, laid by any State on Imports or Exports, shall be for the Use of the Treasury of the United States; and all such Laws shall be subject to the Revision and Controul of the Congress.

No State shall, without the Consent of Congress, lay any Duty of Tonnage, keep Troops, or Ships of War in time of Peace, enter into any Agreement or Compact with another State, or with a foreign Power, or engage in War, unless actually invaded, or in such imminent Danger as will not admit of delay.

Article II

Section 1. The executive Power shall be vested in a President of the United States of America. He shall hold his Office during the Term of four Years, and, together with the Vice President, chosen for the same Term, be elected, as follows

Each State shall appoint, in such Manner as the Legislature thereof may direct, a Number of Electors, equal to the whole Number of Senators and Representatives to which the State may be entitled in the Congress: but no Senator or Representative, or Person holding an Office of Trust or Profit under the United States, shall be appointed an Elector.

[The Electors shall meet in their respective States, and vote by Ballot for two Persons, of whom one at least shall not be an Inhabitant of the same State with themselves. And they shall make a List of all the Persons voted for, and of the Number of Votes for each; which List they shall sign and certify, and transmit sealed to the Seat of the Government of the United States, directed to the President of the Senate. The President of the Senate shall, in the Presence of the Senate and House of Representatives, open all the Certificates, and the Votes shall then be counted. The Person having the greatest Number of Votes shall be the President, if such Number be a Majority of the whole Number of Electors appointed; and if there be more than one who have such Majority, and have an equal Number of Votes, then the House of Representatives shall immediately chuse by Ballot one of them for President; and if no Person have a Majority, then from the five highest on the list the said House shall in like Manner chuse the President. But in chusing the President, the Votes shall be taken by States, the Representation from each State having one Vote; A quorum for this Purpose shall consist of a Member or Members from two thirds of the States, and a Majority of all the States shall be necessary to a Choice. In every Case, after the Choice of the President, the Person having the greatest Number of Votes of the Electors shall be the Vice President. But if there should remain two or more who have equal Votes, the Senate shall chuse from them by Ballot the Vice President.][6]

The Congress may determine the Time of chusing the Electors, and the Day on which they shall give their Votes; which Day shall be the same throughout the United States.

No Person except a natural born Citizen, or a Citizen of the United States, at the time of the Adoption of this Constitution, shall be eligible to the Office of President; neither shall any Person be eligible to that Office who shall not have attained to the Age of thirty five Years, and been fourteen Years a Resident within the United States.

In Case of the Removal of the President from Office, or of his Death, Resignation, or Inability to discharge the Powers and Duties of the said Office,[7] the Same shall devolve on the Vice President, and the Congress may by Law provide for the Case of Removal, Death, Resignation or Inability, both of the President and Vice President, declaring what Officer shall then act as President, and such Officer shall act accordingly, until the Disability be removed, or a President shall be elected.

The President shall, at stated Times, receive for his Services, a Compensation, which shall neither be encreased nor diminished during the Period for which he shall have been elected, and he shall not receive within that Period any other Emolument from the United States, or any of them.

Before he enter on the Execution of his Office, he shall take the following Oath or Affirmation:—"I do solemnly swear (or affirm) that I will faithfully execute the Office of President of the United States, and will to the best of my Ability, preserve, protect and defend the Constitution of the United States."

Section 2. The President shall be Commander in Chief of the Army and Navy of the United States, and of the Militia of the several States, when called into the actual Service of the United States; he may require the Opinion, in writing, of the principal Officer in each of the executive Departments, upon any Subject relating to the Duties of their respective Offices, and he shall have Power to grant Reprieves and Pardons for Offences against the United States, except in Cases of Impeachment.

He shall have Power, by and with the Advice and Consent of the Senate, to make Treaties, provided two thirds of the Senators present concur; and he shall nominate, and by and with the Advice and Consent of the Senate, shall appoint Ambassadors, other public Ministers and Consuls, Judges of the supreme Court, and all other Officers of the United States, whose Appointments are not herein otherwise provided for, and which shall be established by Law: but the Congress may by Law vest the Appointment of such inferior Officers, as they think proper, in the President alone, in the Courts of Law, or in the Heads of Departments.

The President shall have Power to fill up all Vacancies that may happen during the Recess of the Senate, by granting Commissions which shall expire at the End of their next Session.

Section 3. He shall from time to time give to the Congress Information of the State of the Union, and recommend to their Consideration such Measures as he shall judge necessary and expedient; he may, on extraordinary Occasions, convene both Houses, or either of them, and in Case of Disagreement between them, with Respect to the Time of Adjournment, he may adjourn them to such Time as he shall think proper; he shall receive Ambassadors and other public Ministers; he shall take Care that the Laws be faithfully executed, and shall Commission all the Officers of the United States.

Section 4. The President, Vice President and all civil Officers of the United States, shall be removed from Office on Impeachment for, and Conviction of, Treason, Bribery, or other high Crimes and Misdemeanors.

Article III

Section 1. The judicial Power of the United States, shall be vested in one supreme Court, and in such inferior Courts as the Congress may from time to time ordain and establish. The Judges, both of the supreme and inferior Courts, shall hold their Offices during good Behaviour, and shall, at stated Times, receive for their Services, a Compensation, which shall not be diminished during their Continuance in Office.

Section 2. The judicial Power shall extend to all Cases, in Law and Equity, arising under this Constitution, the Laws of the United States, and Treaties made, or which shall be made, under their Authority; — to all Cases affecting Ambassadors, other public Ministers and Consuls; — to all Cases of admiralty and maritime Jurisdiction; — to Controversies to which the United States shall be a Party; — to Controversies between two or more States; — between a State and Citizens of another State;[8] — between Citizens of different States; — between Citizens of the same State claiming Lands under Grants of different States, and between a State, or the Citizens thereof, and foreign States, Citizens or Subjects.[8]

In all Cases affecting Ambassadors, other public Ministers and Consuls, and those in which a State shall be Party, the supreme Court shall have original Jurisdiction. In all the other Cases before mentioned, the supreme Court shall have appellate Jurisdiction, both as to Law and Fact, with such Exceptions, and under such Regulations as the Congress shall make.

The Trial of all Crimes, except in Cases of Impeachment, shall be by Jury; and such Trial shall be held in the State where the said Crimes shall have been committed; but when not committed within any State, the Trial shall be at such Place or Places as the Congress may by Law have directed.

Section 3. Treason against the United States, shall consist only in levying War against them, or in adhering to their Enemies, giving them Aid and Comfort. No Person shall be convicted of Treason unless on the Testimony of two Witnesses to the same overt Act, or on Confession in open Court.

The Congress shall have Power to declare the Punishment of Treason, but no Attainder of Treason shall work Corruption of Blood, or Forfeiture except during the Life of the Person attainted.

Article IV

Section 1. Full Faith and Credit shall be given in each State to the public Acts, Records, and judicial Proceedings of every other State. And the Congress may by general Laws prescribe the Manner in which such Acts, Records and Proceedings shall be proved, and the Effect thereof.

Section 2. The Citizens of each State shall be entitled to all Privileges and Immunities of Citizens in the several States.

A Person charged in any State with Treason, Felony, or other Crime, who shall flee from Justice, and be found in another State, shall on Demand of the executive Authority of the State from which he fled, be delivered up, to be removed to the State having Jurisdiction of the Crime.

[No Person held to Service or Labour in one State, under the Laws thereof, escaping into another, shall, in Consequence of any Law or Regulation therein, be discharged from such Service or Labour, but shall be delivered up on Claim of the Party to whom such Service or Labour may be due.][9]

Section 3. New States may be admitted by the Congress into this Union; but no new State shall be formed or erected within the Jurisdiction of any other State; nor any State be formed by the Junction of two or more States, or Parts of States, without the Consent of the Legislatures of the States concerned as well as of the Congress.

The Congress shall have Power to dispose of and make all needful Rules and Regulations respecting the Territory or other Property belonging to the United States; and nothing in this Constitution shall be so construed as to Prejudice any Claims of the United States, or of any particular State.

Section 4. The United States shall guarantee to every State in this Union a Republican Form of Government, and shall protect each of them against Invasion; and on Application of the Legislature, or of the Executive (when the Legislature cannot be convened) against domestic Violence.

Article V

The Congress, whenever two thirds of both Houses shall deem it necessary, shall propose Amendments to this Constitution, or, on the Application of the Legislatures of two thirds of the several States, shall call a Convention for proposing Amendments, which, in either Case, shall be valid to all Intents and Purposes, as Part of this Constitution, when ratified by the Legislatures of three fourths of the several States, or by Conventions in three fourths thereof, as the one or the other Mode of Ratification may be proposed by the Congress; Provided [that no Amendment which may be made prior to the Year One thousand eight hundred and eight shall in any Manner affect the first and fourth Clauses in the Ninth Section of the first Article; and][10] that no State, without its Consent, shall be deprived of its equal Suffrage in the Senate.

Article VI

All Debts contracted and Engagements entered into, before the Adoption of this Constitution, shall be as valid against the United States under this Constitution, as under the Confederation.

This Constitution, and the Laws of the United States which shall be made in Pursuance thereof; and all Treaties made, or which shall be made, under the Authority of the United States, shall be the supreme Law of the Land; and the Judges in every State shall be bound thereby, any Thing in the Constitution or Laws of any State to the Contrary notwithstanding.

The Senators and Representatives before mentioned, and the Members of the several State Legislatures, and all executive and judicial Officers, both of the United States and of the several States, shall be bound by Oath or Affirmation, to support this Constitution; but no religious Test shall ever be required as a Qualification to any Office or public Trust under the United States.

Article VII

The Ratification of the Conventions of nine States, shall be sufficient for the Establishment of this Constitution between the States so ratifying the Same.

Done in Convention by the Unanimous Consent of the States present the Seventeenth Day of September in the Year of our Lord one thousand seven hundred and Eighty seven and of the Independence of the United States of America the Twelfth. IN WITNESS whereof We have hereunto subscribed our Names,

George Washington,
President and
deputy from Virginia.

New Hampshire: John Langdon,
Nicholas Gilman.

Massachusetts: Nathaniel Gorham,
Rufus King.

Connecticut: William Samuel Johnson,
Roger Sherman.

New York: Alexander Hamilton.

New Jersey: William Livingston,
David Brearley,
William Paterson,
Jonathan Dayton.

Pennsylvania: Benjamin Franklin,
Thomas Mifflin,
Robert Morris,
George Clymer,
Thomas FitzSimons,
Jared Ingersoll,
James Wilson,
Gouverneur Morris.

Delaware:	George Read,
	Gunning Bedford Jr.,
	John Dickinson,
	Richard Bassett,
	Jacob Broom.
Maryland:	James McHenry,
	Daniel of St. Thomas Jenifer,
	Daniel Carroll.
Virginia:	John Blair,
	James Madison Jr.
North Carolina:	William Blount,
	Richard Dobbs Spaight,
	Hugh Williamson.
South Carolina:	John Rutledge,
	Charles Cotesworth Pinckney,
	Charles Pinckney,
	Pierce Butler.
Georgia:	William Few,
	Abraham Baldwin.

[The language of the original Constitution, not including the Amendments, was adopted by a convention of the states on September 17, 1787, and was subsequently ratified by the states on the following dates: Delaware, December 7, 1787; Pennsylvania, December 12, 1787; New Jersey, December 18, 1787; Georgia, January 2, 1788; Connecticut, January 9, 1788; Massachusetts, February 6, 1788; Maryland, April 28, 1788; South Carolina, May 23, 1788; New Hampshire, June 21, 1788.

Ratification was completed on June 21, 1788.

The Constitution subsequently was ratified by Virginia, June 25, 1788; New York, July 26, 1788; North Carolina, November 21, 1789; Rhode Island, May 29, 1790; and Vermont, January 10, 1791.]

Amendments

Amendment I

(First ten amendments ratified December 15, 1791.)

Congress shall make no law respecting an establishment of religion, or prohibiting the free exercise thereof; or abridging the freedom of speech, or of the press; or the right of the people peaceably to assemble, and to petition the Government for a redress of grievances.

Amendment II

A well regulated Militia, being necessary to the security of a free State, the right of the people to keep and bear Arms, shall not be infringed.

Amendment III

No Soldier shall, in time of peace be quartered in any house, without the consent of the Owner, nor in time of war, but in a manner to be prescribed by law.

Amendment IV

The right of the people to be secure in their persons, houses, papers, and effects, against unreasonable searches and seizures, shall not be violated, and no Warrants shall issue, but upon probable cause, supported by Oath or affirmation, and particularly describing the place to be searched, and the persons or things to be seized.

Amendment V

No person shall be held to answer for a capital, or otherwise infamous crime, unless on a presentment or indictment of a Grand Jury, except in cases arising in the land or naval forces, or in the Militia, when in actual service in time of War or public danger; nor shall any person be subject for the same offence to be twice put in jeopardy of life or limb; nor shall be compelled in any criminal case to be a witness against himself, nor be deprived of life, liberty, or property, without due process of law; nor shall private property be taken for public use, without just compensation.

Amendment VI

In all criminal prosecutions, the accused shall enjoy the right to a speedy and public trial, by an impartial jury of the State and district wherein the crime shall have been committed, which district shall have been previously ascertained by law, and to be informed of the nature and cause of the accusation; to be confronted with the witnesses against him; to have compulsory process for obtaining witnesses in his favor, and to have the Assistance of Counsel for his defence.

Amendment VII

In Suits at common law, where the value in controversy shall exceed twenty dollars, the right of trial by jury shall be preserved, and no fact tried by a jury, shall be otherwise re-examined in any Court of the United States, than according to the rules of the common law.

Amendment VIII

Excessive bail shall not be required, nor excessive fines imposed, nor cruel and unusual punishments inflicted.

Amendment IX

The enumeration in the Constitution, of certain rights, shall not be construed to deny or disparage others retained by the people.

Amendment X

The powers not delegated to the United States by the Constitution, nor pro-hibited by it to the States, are reserved to the States respectively, or to the people.

Amendment XI

(Ratified February 7, 1795)

The Judicial power of the United States shall not be construed to extend to any suit in law or equity, commenced or prosecuted against one of the United States by Citizens of another State, or by Citizens or Subjects of any Foreign State.

Amendment XII

(Ratified June 15, 1804)

The Electors shall meet in their respective states and vote by ballot for President and Vice-President, one of whom, at least, shall not be an inhabitant of the same state with themselves; they shall name in their ballots the person voted for as Presi-dent, and in distinct ballots the person voted for as Vice-President, and they shall make distinct lists of all persons voted for as President, and of all persons voted for as Vice-President, and of the number of votes for each, which lists they shall sign and certify, and transmit sealed to the seat of the government of the United States, direct-ed to the President of the Senate; — The President of the Senate shall, in the pres-ence of the Senate and House of Representatives, open all the certificates and the votes shall then be counted; — The person having the greatest number of votes for President, shall be the President, if such number be a majority of the whole number of Electors appointed; and if no person have such majority, then from the persons having the highest numbers not exceeding three on the list of those voted for as Pres-ident, the House of Representatives shall choose immediately, by ballot, the Presi-dent. But in choosing the President, the votes shall be taken by states, the represen-tation from each state having one vote; a quorum for this purpose shall consist of a member or members from two-thirds of the states, and a majority of all the states shall be necessary to a choice. [And if the House of Representatives shall not choose a President whenever the right of choice shall devolve upon them, before the fourth day of March next following, then the Vice-President shall act as President, as in the case of the death or other constitutional disability of the President. —][11] The person having the greatest number of votes as Vice-President, shall be the Vice-President, if such number be a majority of the whole number of Electors appointed, and if no person have a majority, then from the two highest numbers on the list, the Senate shall choose the Vice-President; a quorum for the purpose shall consist of two-thirds of the whole number of Senators, and a majority of the whole number shall be necessary to a choice. But no person constitutionally ineligible to the office of President shall be eligible to that of Vice-President of the United States.

Amendment XIII

(Ratified December 6, 1865)

Section 1. Neither slavery nor involuntary servitude, except as a punishment for crime whereof the party shall have been duly convicted, shall exist within the United States, or any place subject to their jurisdiction.

Section 2. Congress shall have power to enforce this article by appropriate legislation.

Amendment XIV

(Ratified July 9, 1868)

Section 1. All persons born or naturalized in the United States, and subject to the jurisdiction thereof, are citizens of the United States and of the State wherein they reside. No State shall make or enforce any law which shall abridge the privileges or immunities of citizens of the United States; nor shall any State deprive any person of life, liberty, or property, without due process of law; nor deny to any person within its jurisdiction the equal protection of the laws.

Section 2. Representatives shall be apportioned among the several States according to their respective numbers, counting the whole number of persons in each State, excluding Indians not taxed. But when the right to vote at any election for the choice of electors for President and Vice President of the United States, Representatives in Congress, the Executive and Judicial officers of a State, or the members of the Legislature thereof, is denied to any of the male inhabitants of such State, being twenty-one years of age,[12] and citizens of the United States, or in any way abridged, except for participation in rebellion, or other crime, the basis of representation therein shall be reduced in the proportion which the number of such male citizens shall bear to the whole number of male citizens twenty-one years of age in such State.

Section 3. No person shall be a Senator or Representative in Congress, or elector of President and Vice President, or hold any office, civil or military, under the United States, or under any State, who, having previously taken an oath, as a member of Congress, or as an officer of the United States, or as a member of any State legislature, or as an executive or judicial officer of any State, to support the Constitution of the United States, shall have engaged in insurrection or rebellion against the same, or given aid or comfort to the enemies thereof. But Congress may by a vote of two-thirds of each House, remove such disability.

Section 4. The validity of the public debt of the United States, authorized by law, including debts incurred for payment of pensions and bounties for services in suppressing insurrection or rebellion, shall not be questioned. But neither the United States nor any State shall assume or pay any debt or obligation incurred in aid of insurrection or rebellion against the United States, or any claim for the loss or emancipation of any slave; but all such debts, obligations and claims shall be held illegal and void.

Section 5. The Congress shall have power to enforce, by appropriate legislation, the provisions of this article.

Amendment XV

(Ratified February 3, 1870)

Section 1. The right of citizens of the United States to vote shall not be denied or abridged by the United States or by any State on account of race, color, or previous condition of servitude.

Section 2. The Congress shall have power to enforce this article by appropriate legislation.

Amendment XVI

(Ratified February 3, 1913)

The Congress shall have power to lay and collect taxes on incomes, from whatever source derived, without apportionment among the several States, and without regard to any census or enumeration.

Amendment XVII

(Ratified April 8, 1913)

The Senate of the United States shall be composed of two Senators from each State, elected by the people thereof, for six years; and each Senator shall have one vote. The electors in each State shall have the qualifications requisite for electors of the most numerous branch of the State legislatures.

When vacancies happen in the representation of any State in the Senate, the executive authority of such State shall issue writs of election to fill such vacancies: *Provided,* That the legislature of any State may empower the executive thereof to make temporary appointments until the people fill the vacancies by election as the legislature may direct.

This amendment shall not be so construed as to affect the election or term of any Senator chosen before it becomes valid as part of the Constitution.

Amendment XVIII

(Ratified January 16, 1919) [13]

Section 1. After one year from the ratification of this article the manufacture, sale, or transportation of intoxicating liquors within, the importation thereof into, or the exportation thereof from the United States and all territory subject to the jurisdiction thereof for beverage purposes is hereby prohibited.

Section 2. The Congress and the several States shall have concurrent power to enforce this article by appropriate legislation.

Section 3. This article shall be inoperative unless it shall have been ratified as an amendment to the Constitution by the legislatures of the several States, as provided in the Constitution, within seven years from the date of the submission hereof to the States by the Congress.

Amendment XIX

(Ratified August 18, 1920)

The right of citizens of the United States to vote shall not be denied or abridged by the United States or by any State on account of sex.

Congress shall have power to enforce this article by appropriate legislation.

Amendment XX

(Ratified January 23, 1933)

Section 1. The terms of the President and Vice President shall end at noon on the 20th day of January, and the terms of Senators and Representatives at noon on the 3d day of January, of the years in which such terms would have ended if this article had not been ratified; and the terms of their successors shall then begin.

Section 2. The Congress shall assemble at least once in every year, and such meeting shall begin at noon on the 3d day of January, unless they shall by law appoint a different day.

Section 3.[14] If, at the time fixed for the beginning of the term of the President, the President elect shall have died, the Vice President elect shall become President. If a President shall not have been chosen before the time fixed for the beginning of his term, or if the President elect shall have failed to qualify, then the Vice President elect shall act as President until a President shall have qualified; and the Congress may by law provide for the case wherein neither a President elect nor a Vice President elect shall have qualified, declaring who shall then act as President, or the manner in which one who is to act shall be selected, and such person shall act accordingly until a President or Vice President shall have qualified.

Section 4. The Congress may by law provide for the case of the death of any of the persons from whom the House of Representatives may choose a President whenever the right of choice shall have devolved upon them, and for the case of the death of any of the persons from whom the Senate may choose a Vice President whenever the right of choice shall have devolved upon them.

Section 5. Sections 1 and 2 shall take effect on the 15th day of October following the ratification of this article.

Section 6. This article shall be inoperative unless it shall have been ratified as an amendment to the Constitution by the legislatures of three-fourths of the several States within seven years from the date of its submission.

Amendment XXI

(Ratified December 5, 1933)

Section 1. The eighteenth article of amendment to the Constitution of the United States is hereby repealed.

Section 2. The transportation or importation into any State, Territory, or possession of the United States for delivery or use therein of intoxicating liquors, in violation of the laws thereof, is hereby prohibited.

Section 3. This article shall be inoperative unless it shall have been ratified as an amendment to the Constitution by conventions in the several States, as provided in the Constitution, within seven years from the date of the submission hereof to the States by the Congress.

Amendment XXII

(Ratified February 27, 1951)

Section 1. No person shall be elected to the office of the President more than twice, and no person who has held the office of President, or acted as President, for more than two years of a term to which some other person was elected President shall be elected to the office of the President more than once. But this Article shall not apply to any person holding the office of President when this Article was proposed by the Congress, and shall not prevent any person who may be holding the office of President, or acting as President, during the term within which this Article become operative from holding the office of President or acting as President during the remainder of such term.

Section 2. This article shall be inoperative unless it shall have been ratified as an amendment to the Constitution by the legislatures of three-fourths of the several States within seven years from the date of its submission to the States by the Congress.

Amendment XXIII

(Ratified March 29, 1961)

Section 1. The District constituting the seat of Government of the United States shall appoint in such manner as the Congress may direct:

A number of electors of President and Vice President equal to the whole number of Senators and Representatives in Congress to which the District would be entitled if it were a State, but in no event more than the least populous State; they shall be in addition to those appointed by the States, but they shall be considered, for the purposes of the election of President and Vice President, to be electors appointed by a State; and they shall meet in the District and perform such duties as provided by the twelfth article of amendment.

Section 2. The Congress shall have power to enforce this article by appropriate legislation.

Amendment XXIV

(Ratified January 23, 1964)

Section 1. The right of citizens of the United States to vote in any primary or other election for President or Vice President, for electors for President or Vice President, or for Senator or Representative in Congress, shall not be denied or abridged by the United States or any State by reason of failure to pay any poll tax or other tax.

Section 2. The Congress shall have power to enforce this article by appropriate legislation.

Amendment XXV

(Ratified February 10, 1967)

Section 1. In case of the removal of the President from office or of his death or resignation, the Vice President shall become President.

Section 2. Whenever there is a vacancy in the office of the Vice President, the President shall nominate a Vice President who shall take office upon confirmation by a majority vote of both Houses of Congress.

Section 3. Whenever the President transmits to the President pro tempore of the Senate and the Speaker of the House of Representatives his written declaration that he is unable to discharge the powers and duties of his office, and until he transmits to them a written declaration to the contrary, such powers and duties shall be discharged by the Vice President as Acting President.

Section 4. Whenever the Vice President and a majority of either the principal officers of the executive departments or of such other body as Congress may by law provide, transmit to the President pro tempore of the Senate and the Speaker of the House of Representatives their written declaration that the President is unable to discharge the powers and duties of his office, the Vice President shall immediately assume the powers and duties of the office as Acting President.

Thereafter, when the President transmits to the President pro tempore of the Senate and the Speaker of the House of Representatives his written declaration that no inability exists, he shall resume the powers and duties of his office unless the Vice President and a majority of either the principal officers of the executive department or of such other body as Congress may by law provide, transmit within four days to the President pro tempore of the Senate and the Speaker of the House of Representatives their written declaration that the President is unable to discharge the powers and duties of his office. Thereupon Congress shall decide the issue, assembling within forty-eight hours for that purpose if not in session. If the Congress, within twenty-one days after receipt of the latter written declaration, or, if Congress is not in session, within twenty-one days after Congress is required to assemble, determines by two-thirds vote of both Houses that the President is unable to discharge the powers and duties of his office, the Vice President shall continue to discharge the same as Acting President; otherwise, the President shall resume the powers and duties of his office.

Amendment XXVI

(Ratified July 1, 1971)

Section 1. The right of citizens of the United States, who are eighteen years of age or older, to vote shall not be denied or abridged by the United States or by any State on account of age.

Section 2. The Congress shall have power to enforce this article by appropriate legislation.

Amendment XXVII

(Ratified May 7, 1992)

No law varying the compensation for the services of the Senators and Representatives shall take effect, until an election of Representatives shall have intervened.

Notes

1. The part in brackets was changed by section 2 of the Fourteenth Amendment.
2. The part in brackets was changed by the first paragraph of the Seventeenth Amendment.
3. The part in brackets was changed by the second paragraph of the Seventeenth Amendment.
4. The part in brackets was changed by section 2 of the Twentieth Amendment.
5. The Sixteenth Amendment gave Congress the power to tax incomes.
6. The material in brackets has been superseded by the Twelfth Amendment.
7. This provision has been affected by the Twenty-fifth Amendment.
8. These clauses were affected by the Eleventh Amendment.
9. This paragraph has been superseded by the Thirteenth Amendment.
10. Obsolete.
11. The part in brackets has been superseded by section 3 of the Twentieth Amendment.
12. See the Nineteenth and Twenty-sixth Amendments.
13. This Amendment was repealed by section 1 of the Twenty-first Amendment.
14. See the Twenty-fifth Amendment.

Source: U.S. Congress, House, Committee on the Judiciary, *The Constitution of the United States of America, as Amended,* 100th Cong., 1st sess., 1987, H Doc 100–94.

Index